JANET GUTHRIE

A Life At Full Throttle

AT INDIANAPOLIS, 1976

JANET GUTHRIE

A Life At Full Throttle

by JANET GUTHRIE

www.sportclassicbooks.com

Published in the United States of America by Sport Media Publishing Inc., Wilmington, Delaware, and simultaneously in Canada.

For information about permission to reproduce selections from this book, please write to:
Permissions
Sport Media Publishing, Inc.,
21 Carlaw Ave.,
Toronto, Ontario, Canada, M4M 2R6
www.sportclassicbooks.com

Cover design: Paul Hodgson
Cover photo: Kevin Fitzgerald, The SPORT Collection

Back cover photo (left): www.greenfieldgallery.net
Back cover photo (right): Author's collection
Interior design: Paul Hodgson and Greg Oliver
This book is set in Swift.

ISBN: 1-894963-31-8

Library of Congress Cataloging-in-Publication Data

Guthrie, Janet, 1938-
Janet Guthrie : a life at full throttle / by Janet Guthrie
    p. cm.
Includes bibliographical references and index.
ISBN 1-894963-31-8 (hardcover : alk. paper)
1. Guthrie, Janet, 1938- 2. Automobile racing drivers—United States—Biography. I. Title.

GV1032.G87A3 2005
796.72'092–dc22

2004026599

Printed in Canada

*Dedicated to Rolla Vollstedt and
to the memory of Lynda Lacek Ferreri
and Ralph J. Farnham, Jr.*

Acknowledgements

My first version of this book was nearly twice as long. The worst part of cutting was letting go of the vital contributions by dozens of people over the years—people who lent a transmission, or offered long nights of labor in a freezing garage. You know who you are. Racing couldn't exist without you, nor would this book.

My heartfelt thanks go to Anne O'Brien, who guided me through the first cut; Jennifer Young, the second; and Candace Hogan and Le Anne Schreiber, the last and most difficult cut of all. Their wisdom and patience were invaluable.

It was a rare privilege to work with my agent, the legendary Sterling Lord. Thanks to Doris Kearns Goodwin for introducing us.

The enthusiasm of Wayne Parrish, Jim O'Leary, Greg Oliver and Wes Seeley of Sport Media Publishing has made the publication process a pleasure.

Without the support of my husband, this book might not be finished yet.

Contents

FOREWORD ix

PROLOGUE xiii

PART I

Indianapolis, May 1977 1

PART II

Growing Up 55

That First Fine Careless Rapture 71

Passionate Amateur 79

Whatever It Takes 87

Changing Perspectives 95

Turning Pro 109

The Chance of a Lifetime 126

The Heat Isn't In the Kitchen 146

Trial By Fire 158

Indianapolis, May 1976 178

NASCAR Winston Cup, Charlotte, May 1976 196

Big-Time Auto Racing 210

Settling In, Holding Our Own 221

Having Fun At Last 230

Top Rookie: The Daytona 500 and Richmond 235

Loaded for Bear 251

Seismic Changes 267

Onward and Upward in the Deep South 279

A Tale of Two Cities 289

NASCAR Flexes Its Muscle 302

Cliffhanger 314

Ducks in a Row 326

PART III

Indianapolis, May 1978 337

EPILOGUE 381

INDEX 384

BILLIE JEAN & JANET IN 1974

FOREWORD

by Billie Jean King

It is easy to admire Janet Guthrie. She is my kindred spirit, my sister in sport.

When you look at the origins of the women's movement, you know that Janet was one of the pioneers. She was a true trailblazer for women's sports. Before Janet, women were not even allowed in the pits at many racetracks, let alone rev an engine beside the likes of A. J. Foyt, Johnny Rutherford and Tom Sneva at the Indianapolis 500. Her pit crew would tell you that Janet's cars ran on the same fuel that powered the machines of her male competitors. But I always knew better—her daring flowed from her additives: determination and courage.

The 1960s and '70s were challenging years for women who couldn't relate to womanhood as depicted by the Harriet Nelsons and June Cleavers of TV fame. Although women's rights were finally being recognized by legislators and judges, the courts of public opinion were far less responsive—or kind. Milestone achievements such as Title IX and the Equal Rights Amendment in 1972, the Roe vs. Wade Supreme Court decision in 1973, and even the gender integration of Little League baseball in 1974, reflected an almost-overnight shift in social policy. But new laws didn't change old attitudes.

Janet and I first met in December 1974 on the set of the Women's Sports Superstars competition (pictured at left), a made-for-television format that was popular in those days and pitted stars from a variety of sports competing against each other in a variety of sports-themed events. Right off, I realized that beneath the quiet and unassuming public face of Janet Guthrie was a fiercely competitive, highly intelligent person. It's not every day you run into someone in professional sports who has a degree in physics. Looking back, it always amazes me that Janet was able to combine her intelligence and grit with her quick wit to make her mark in the loud-mouthed world of motorsports.

She and I faced similar challenges in those days. Sure, when I played Bobby Riggs in the "Battle of the Sexes" match I was nervous, mostly because there was a lot at stake. I believed that losing to Riggs would set back women's sports and women in general by fifty years and be a blow to the self-esteem of all women. We were at the height of the women's movement. Change was happening. Equality was coming. For me, playing Riggs was not about tennis or about money. It was about social change. It was about making people believe that women could chew gum and walk at the same time. It was about pushing the women's movement forward at a time when women made forty per cent less than men and few could hold credit cards.

The entire experience was quite illuminating and, a few years later, provided the window for me to watch—and admire—Janet's incursion into the male bastion of oval-track auto racing.

Janet Guthrie is a person of rock-solid belief in herself, in women, and in equality. When you combine those attributes with Janet's strength, confidence and determination you have the building blocks of success. Her racing career began in sports cars and she earned her stripes long before she tasted the thrill of the straightaway at the Indianapolis Motor Speedway. Once there, she endured scorn from fans, resentment from drivers, apathy from sponsors, and ridicule from the media. And yet she persevered.

Janet was forced to run a gauntlet that was more mean-spirited than anything I endured. Although his comments dripped with condescension, Bobby Riggs had an impishness about him that could take the edge off his remarks. He purposely said things to get a rise out of people. We became good friends. But when Richard Petty belittled Janet ("she's no lady"), his remarks reeked of malice; when an award-winning newspaper columnist suggested having Janet in the field at Indianapolis was like putting a drunk driver on the track, it read like spite, not spoof; when rival teams ignored racing etiquette and refused to lend auto parts to Janet, the motivation was pure malevolence; and when crackpot 'fans' wrote hateful, threatening letters to Janet, her peril seemed real.

I followed Janet's quest for the Indianapolis 500 crown and I could sympathize with her. Her success enabled other women to seize opportunities in a sport that, up to then, was run by men for men. After I beat Bobby Riggs, *The New York Times* opined that I had "convinced skeptics that a female athlete can survive pressure-filled situations and that men are as susceptible to nerves as women." But, unfortunately, *The Times* was wrong. The skeptics were still out in force when Janet arrived at Indianapolis. They harrumphed that women lacked the stamina to endure a 500-mile race, the strength to control a race car at 200 mph, and the steady nerves required to make the split-second decisions necessary to avoid catastrophe. Janet proved them all wrong, and her success was as much a testament to valor as ability.

The biggest difference between my challenge match with Bobby Riggs and Janet's historic races at Indianapolis and Daytona is the difference between hitting a ball into the net and hitting a concrete wall at 200 mph. Janet put everything on the line, including her life. She was fearless in her quest. And perhaps the most striking similarity between our dates with destiny is that, prior to lining up against men, we faced an unknown foe. When the match was finally over, it was a wonderful feeling. I'm sure Janet enjoyed that same feeling on the track the moment she realized she belonged among the legends of her sport.

Women of our generation have witnessed a great social transition. New doors have been opened in the arenas of business, politics, sport, and most other areas of human endeavor. Women now sit as CEOs of major corporations, fly in space, and sit in the U.S. Senate. Someday, a woman will be president. For the most part, the daughters of our generation have been taught that there is nothing that they cannot do. Men who saw me beat Bobby Riggs as boys routinely approach me to say they remember that match and now insist their daughters receive an equal opportunity. That is wonderful to hear. I call them the first generation of men of the women's movement. They are standard-bearers for equality and represent a huge phenomenon that has not received much attention.

It wasn't like that when Janet and I were little girls. I loved baseball and basketball as a child and vividly remember the moment when I realized girls didn't play in the Major Leagues or the NBA. For Janet, her first love was aviation. But she too learned at a young age that no commercial airline or branch of the military would accept a female pilot. Racing was her next choice.

None of this is to suggest that the gender gap has been eliminated. It hasn't. Many doors remain barred to women and, even though it has been more than thirty years since enactment of the Equal Rights Amendment, old attitudes often still prevail. Tracking the story of Annika Sorenstam's foray into men's professional golf in 2003 was like turning back the clock to 1973. Annika was told she had no business playing with men and, even if she did, she had no chance of success because—and here we go again—she lacked the strength, the stamina and the nerves to compete on the PGA Tour. In 1977,

Richard Petty said Janet belonged at home. In 2003, Vijay Singh said Annika should go play with the women. Progress? What progress?

Women's sport has come a long way, yet women still trail men when it comes to media exposure, salaries, prize money, sponsorships, endorsements, respect and opportunity. Fifty years after I realized I could never be a ballplayer, a big-league career seems no closer for little girls today. Title IX was intended to end inequality in college sport, but three decades later full compliance remains a dream. Yes, the playing fields are less uneven and women are taken more seriously, but there is still much work to do.

Brave women like Janet Guthrie made it more acceptable for women to be elite athletes. She dared—no, demanded—to compete at the highest level of her sport in an era when entry and acceptance were a much greater challenge. Her achievements deserve to be remembered and applauded. But the checkered flag has yet to be dropped on the race to end inequality. It is the job of this generation and those that follow to be vocal and active in order to ensure girls and women have equal opportunities to play and compete at all levels of sport.

I hope you enjoy this book and, like me, become truly appreciative of Janet Guthrie's contribution to our world.

— Billie Jean King, 2005

PROLOGUE

The Indianapolis 500 is more than a race, more than another rite of spring; it's a red-white-and-blue institution. For generations of race fans, the month of May has meant the gathering of forces for yet another running of the world's most famous race.

Until the present high-tech era, many of the cars officially entered at Indianapolis came from deceptively modest garages attached to modest homes—neatly maintained white frame dwellings with shade tree, lawn and dog such as appear in our folksiest TV commercials. Homes like this still make up much of the community of Speedway, Indiana, where the race track stands. From Portland, Oregon to Long Island, New York, their garages cradled the hopes of many a driver and owner: a chassis, an engine, machinery, tools and parts. Through thousands of hours of late-night labor and the intricate, hard-earned racing savvy of the owner and his friends and associates, these elements would coalesce in late April into a rolling, fire-breathing Indianapolis 500 race car. If the team and its driver had luck, talent, and ferocious desire, they would be among the thirty-three fastest qualifiers out of the eighty or ninety cars entered and thus would take the green flag on race day.

The Indianapolis 500 runs on dedication and obsession. Scores of men and women arrange their year's work so as to be at the Speedway in May—as unpaid gofers, as track guards, as emergency workers. The whole structure of the race is bound and cemented with the contributions of a vast range of volunteers. All month long, for example, volunteers bring little groups of the disabled to trackside, many in wheelchairs; some on respirators, unable even to breath on their own. Carefully and tenderly, the volunteers bring them to the fence at the trackside pits, to participate for a while in one of the most electric atmospheres on earth.

What is the Indianapolis 500, in more hard-boiled terms? It's the most heavily attended paid-admission one-day sporting event in the entire world. Four years' worth of Super Bowl spectators wouldn't equal one Indianapolis race-day crowd. The total purse was $10.25

million in 2004. Current estimates of the cost of a competitive, front-running effort at Indianapolis begin around $10 million on an annual basis, and go up. Auto racing is, in most years, the most heavily attended non-betting sport in the United States. It usually outdraws all forms of football and all forms of baseball.

The first Indianapolis 500-mile race was held in 1911. Queen Victoria, granddaughter of our own King George III, had been dead ten years. Most horsepower came on four feet. Except during World War I and World War II, the Indianapolis 500 has been held every year since.

The running of the 500 is as bound in tradition as the coronation of any British monarch. From the call of "Gentlemen, start your engines" to the victor's glass of milk, things are done a certain way because they have always been done that way. And some things were always anathema: the color green, peanut shells ... and women.

In 1977, I became the first woman to compete in the Indianapolis 500 (and also in the Daytona 500, the top event in stock car racing). My racing career had begun in 1963 in the Sports Car Club of America, where gender was not an issue, and I was bemused by the sensationalism that greeted my appearance at the famed Speedway. Women had been licensed to race in the SCCA since at least 1952; but until 1971, women were not even allowed in the press box at Indianapolis,[1] much less the garage area or the pits. A woman might be a reporter, a photographer, a timer/scorer, she might *own* the race car—but she couldn't get near it at any time for any reason. A woman on the track itself was unthinkable.

In *West to the Sunrise*,[2] pilot Grace Harris recounts how she officiated at a hot-air balloon meet at Indianapolis Motor Speedway in the 1960s and was forbidden to pass beyond the pit gates when time came to inspect the lift-off area. Her footsteps, it seemed, would profane the sacred turf.

All that began to change in 1971, in the wake of changes wrought by the women's movement. A woman reporter filed suit, and won access. Signs were hung every fifty feet on the chain-link fence surrounding the garage area. "By agreement with the Commission on Human Rights," the signs said, "Gasoline Alley is open to all otherwise qualified pass holders without reference to sex."

[1] An exception was made in 1956 for driver/journalist Denise McCluggage of the *New York Herald Tribune*, after Frank Blunk of *The New York Times* threatened to leave unless she was allowed into the press box.
[2] The Iowa State University Press, 1980

The women's movement was a cultural upheaval of major proportions, and many volumes have been written about its effects. Without the women's movement, women would never have had the opportunity to compete at the top levels of American motorsports. Those top levels, Indy-car racing and NASCAR stock car racing, had their roots in the "bull rings," the hundreds of quarter-mile and half-mile tracks that were patterned after—and often, had originally been—horse racing tracks, roughly oval in shape. Back then, the bull rings were where most Indy-car and stock car drivers cut their teeth. Incursions by women were vigorously resisted at most bull rings (except for occasional all-women "powder puff" events, mostly in the lesser categories of stock cars).

Bull ring promoters usually hid their exclusion of women behind "insurance reasons," and dug in their heels. In 1974, the promoter at Flemington, N. J., announced that of course women were welcome in the pits there—provided they presented a certificate issued on that same date by a hospital stating that the bearer had been examined by a doctor and was not pregnant. A new certificate was required each day. Some who came back from the hospital with a certificate were refused admission because the phrase "examined by a doctor" was missing.

This kind of resistance to women in sports was hardly unique. Who could forget the Boston Marathon of 1967, when officials sprang from the sidelines to attempt to rip the competitor's bib from Kathy Switzer, who had entered the race as "K. Switzer"? Protected by other runners, Switzer completed the race. As a result, she was suspended from the Amateur Athletic Union, which meant she could no longer compete in any running event. The grounds for her suspension were these: running with men, running more than a mile, and running without a chaperone!

Broader opportunities for women in sports were made possible by the passage of Title IX of the Education Amendments of 1972, banning sex discrimination in education. Before Title IX, women in American colleges and universities received *one percent* of total athletic budgets, and athletic scholarships for women were virtually nonexistent. The changes wrought by Title IX were revolutionary, as women took up sports by the hundreds of thousands. Between 1970 and 1980, in track and field for example, the men's world record for the 1,500 meter distance dropped by a second, while the women's record dropped by more than 25 seconds.

In 1973, millions of people watched Billie Jean King defeat Bobby

Riggs in tennis' famous Battle of the Sexes. It's hard to remember, now, how fraught with emotion and significance that moment was. Besides being a great tennis player, Billie Jean was one of the most forward-thinking women of our time. She was the guiding light behind the founding of the Women's Sports Foundation, the organization that established the Women's Sports Hall of Fame in 1980.

Relatively recent history, however, should not prevent us from looking back at what women have accomplished in the past. Even the Olympic games of antiquity had a corresponding contest for women. The meticulous Greek travel writer Pausanius, in the 2nd century AD, described the games of Hera, which were foot races at Olympia for unmarried women. He commented that the Heraean games had been founded "in ancient times." Kyniska of Sparta, the daughter and sister of Spartan kings, received the victory wreath for the Olympic chariot races in 396 and 392 BC. Historians say that the actual charioteer was a man (the wreath went to the owner), and that Kyniska was the Roger Penske of her time; but Spartan women were known to be great athletes.

Leaping ahead a couple of millennia, French women entered bicycle races at Bordeaux in 1869. In 1873, ten women swam a one-mile race in the Harlem River. In 1874, Mary Ewing Outerbridge introduced the game of tennis to the United States, importing the equipment from Bermuda. Annie Smith Peck climbed the Matterhorn in 1895. Before the turn of the century, women were also playing basketball, volleyball, lacrosse, field hockey, entering archery contests, ice skating, rowing, and more. It seems that our notion that women never did anything except tatting and crocheting until yesterday, or maybe the day before, has a few flaws.

In fact, women have always been eager to seek adventure, to tackle the difficult stuff. The first woman to make a solo flight in a hot-air balloon, Jeanne Labrosse, did so in 1798. Balloonist Madeleine Sophie Blanchard was Official Aeronaut of the Empire under Napoleon, making an ascension in honor of his marriage in 1810. She was so politically adept that after his defeat at Waterloo, she became Official Aeronaut of the Kingdom under the restored French monarchy. Elise Garnerin had made forty parachute jumps from her hot-air balloon by the time she retired in 1836. Raymonde de la Roche became the first licensed woman pilot of fixed-wing aircraft on March 8, 1910; and before that, she had been a racing driver.

The first woman racing driver that I know of, however, was

Mme. Laumaille, who finished fourth in the automobile race from Marseilles to Nice in 1898. Three years later, in 1901, Camille du Gast competed in the race from Paris to Berlin. In 1903, du Gast was running eighth in a field of 275 cars in the Great Race from Paris to Madrid when a leading driver crashed. Du Gast stopped, bandaged up the seriously injured man, waited until an ambulance came, and then resumed the race. In 1928, Elsa Junek led and nearly won the Targa Florio, a 335-mile race that lasted more than seven hours, against world-renowned drivers like Tazio Nuvolari and René Dreyfus. And so on and on.

But how many people even know that this history exists? When women lose their history, they lose the secure foundation for what they want to do next. A woman airline pilot said recently that when she was a child, "there were no role models, so being a pilot didn't enter my mind." There were thousands of role models, including America's Women Air Service Pilots of World War II, who flew all the hottest fighters and bombers, and the Russian women combat pilots of that time. She just didn't know about them. When the history of what women have accomplished in the past is ignored or trivialized, each new generation of achieving women must first re-invent the wheel. That's an obstacle not to be underestimated.

In this book, I have tried to put the reader inside a driver's mind, both on the track and off. I hope to convey, through my personal experiences, the passion and intensity of the sport of auto racing; to give an insider's view of its complexity and its demands, physical, emotional, and intellectual. And I hope that working women who still encounter unreasonable obstacles, whatever their field, will find encouragement in these pages.

PART I

INDY 500, 1977 ... I've just qualified for the Indianapolis 500 for the first time.
Front row, from left: teammate Dick Simon, crew chief Phil Casey, me. Second row: Jim Lindholm, team owner
Rolla Vollstedt, Joe Hoff (partly hidden), Carl Holtman, Al Kissler, Bob Sowle, Dick Oeffinger, Roy East, Phil Hedback.

INDIANAPOLIS, MAY 1977

You could live a whole lifetime at Indianapolis Motor Speedway in the single month of May.

On a mild spring afternoon at the western edge of the city, a swath of dove-grey pavement baked in the sun. The pavement covered a track laid out in the year 1909, two and a half miles long, fifty to sixty feet wide, shaped as a rounded rectangle. Within the track lay four hundred acres of park-like grass and trees. At its outer edge stood a white concrete wall, sturdy enough to withstand violent impacts. Close to the wall, on the pavement, a dozen of the fastest racing machines on earth shrieked down the straightaways and into the turns. They covered the length of a football field in less than a second.

It was Tuesday May 10, 1977. The fourth day of practice for the sixty-first annual running of the Indianapolis 500 was nearing its end, and I was in a fine fierce hurry to make the most of what time remained. My turbocharged green and white Lightning howled out of Turn 2, its naked wheels a foot away from the outer wall. My mind leaped ahead, toward the next turn.

I eased the steering wheel back toward center. The lateral scrubbing of tires on pavement, a sensory input more felt than heard, diminished. Tire scrub was a small but significant item in the dense thicket of engine and chassis sounds to which my ears were tuned. The tachometer needle crept upward.

I was hurtling north now, on the back straight, at something like 200 mph, with nothing to do but check the gauges and mirrors, wiggle my fingers inside the thick Nomex and leather gloves, and jam my throttle foot against the firewall, as if pushing harder would increase my speed. At the inside edge of the track, next to the huge infield swath of green, another race car crawled through its warmup lap.

The Turn 3 grandstands swept closer. At full speed in an Indianapolis 500 Championship car, that five-eighths-mile straight seemed to shrink to the length of a bowling alley. Could I go into the next turn just a little bit deeper before lifting my foot ever so slightly from the floor?

A crew member had held up our blackboard at my pits on the front straight. It had read 189 on each of the last two laps. That was my one-lap average speed from the previous lap. The number would rise only if I could make improvements in the turns. I steeled myself; went just a few feet deeper into Turn 3. On the short chute between the two north turns, I flicked a glance at the tachometer. Yes, this was faster. I carried the extra speed into Turn 4. But the Lightning was sending me a faint message, unlike anything I had felt before.

For the tiniest fraction of a second, in Turns 3 and 4, the grip of the tires seemed softer and stickier—as if they had suddenly turned to bubble gum.

The Lightning had long since become an extension of myself. I was melted into it, centrifugal force smearing me like putty against the torso support and headrest as the side loads rose in the turns. My nerve endings extended out to the contact patches where the tires gripped the pavement, like the fingertips and toes of a rock climber. This curious sensation of stickiness was entirely new. I filed it in the back of my head with the rest of the data from this set of laps.

Halfway down the front straight, Rolla Vollstedt watched intently. The owner of my team, Rolla was an old hand at this game. Standing next to him, inside the low white wall that separated the racing surface from pit road, a crewman held up the pit board. For the third time in a row, it read 189.

Damn.

I was doing my utmost to nail us a lap at 190 mph, or better. Two days earlier, I had posted a speed of 188.442 mph. That lap remained among the ten fastest laps by any driver so far this year, tied to the sixth digit with Danny Ongais. I had also set the fastest time of any driver on opening day of practice; but speeds would rise as the first week of practice went on.

This time I went even deeper into Turn 1 before easing a fraction off the gas. There was that wisp of a bubble-gum sensation again ... odd. Midway through Turn 2, the tires seemed suddenly even stickier than before. Then the car twitched.

Uh-oh.

The rear of the car whipped out a few inches. I moved to catch it, flicking the steering wheel to the right.

No good. It twitched the other way.

This isn't saveable.

In that fraction of a second, I understood that the new Lightning was an unforgiving car.

If I try to save it again, I'm going into the wall nose first. That was the most unhealthy way to meet the wall.

There was only one answer.

Turn left and lock up the brakes.

Brakes locked. A spin; the scream of tortured rubber. Clouds of tire smoke, flashes of green and white bodywork rotated through my line of sight. Like the rest of the practice session, the spin seemed to take place in slow motion. It felt like half an hour before the nose pointed down the back straight again. The wall was three or four feet away. I had burned off a lot of speed.

Release the brakes now and you'll roll ahead, home free.

But when the tires gripped, the car lurched right instead.

The Lightning nosed into the wall at an angle of about thirty degrees. It hit hard. Bouncing once, it scraped along the white-painted concrete to a stop.

Out! Out out out. In case of fire. Even though I had killed all the switches before it came to rest, there was still that possibility.

I slammed open the buckle release, wiggled from the seat-belt harness, past the steering wheel and other impediments, assessing the damage as I went. First, to myself: nothing major. Then, was there any fire? I could activate the onboard fire system with the pull of a pin, but that would mean a day's work for the crew, cleaning harsh chemicals from sensitive engine parts. Smoke curled from the back of the car, but there was no flame. By now my feet were under me, on the seat, and I stepped out onto the track. Crash trucks screeched to a halt.

I turned toward the crumpled front end, stuffed against the wall. How bad was it? My spirits sank at what I saw.

I had broken Rolla's new car.

The right front wheel was askew, the lower A arm of the right suspension twisted, the dive plane crunched. The tub didn't look bent, but looks could be deceiving.

People were surrounding me, grasping my arms, offering unwanted support. "I'm okay," I said. The fifth time I said it, they let go.

"You'll have to go to the hospital," someone was saying. That was the rule, as I knew, after a crash. A stretcher and gurney stood ominously at the Lightning's side. "Would you like to ride in the front?"

"Oh, yes, thank you very much." I had zero interest in providing a melodramatic photo opportunity.

As we rolled past our pit, I saw the blackboard propped against the wall.

It read 191.

The guys on my crew were staring intently at the ambulance, and I waved to them, though I couldn't manage a smile. I was dreadfully chagrined. Rolla Vollstedt had sunk a large portion of his 1977 sponsorship into a 1976 prototype Lightning chassis, and now I had done it some serious damage. Rolla was by no means a millionaire. In real life, he was an Oregon lumber merchant.

At the infield hospital, the same young doctor who conducted the regulation physical exam five days ago was waiting for the ambulance. His hands had been cool then, and trembled a little. No one, not even the medical staff, was used to the idea of a woman driver at the Speedway. Now, he and the nurses radiated alarm. When a car crashed here, the best efforts of a trauma team might be required.

It was time for an act. I bounced in the door, feigning good cheer. "I told you guys I didn't want to see you again!"

They laughed, checked my pulse, made me follow a moving finger with my eyes, took my blood pressure.

The doctor said, "I guess you're not too excited."

"What's the reading?"

"One fifteen over seventy."

"That's about what it usually is."

"Okay," he said, "you're released. Come on, I'll drive you over to the garage area."

I was grateful for his protection. On foot I would have to cope with reporters, spectators, track guards, other crews.

Halfway to the garages we encountered Rolla Vollstedt, striding toward the hospital. His lean form and vigorous pace might have been those of a man forty years his junior. We stopped. I opened the door.

"Hi, Boss."

Rolla peered at us, his blue eyes intent behind rimless bifocals.

"Come on," I said, "get in, we'll take you back."

"How are you?"

"I'm okay."

He swung in beside me.

"How's the car?" I asked.

"It's not back in the garage area yet."

At Rolla's garage, a crowd had formed. Rolla rushed me through it, pulled shut the doors, sat me down, pulled up a chair and sat himself facing me.

"Now," he said, "tell me, how *are* you?"

Rolla knew his racing drivers. Decades of experience had taught him that we would conceal any injury we could manage, in order not to be barred from the track.

"I'm *fine*," I protested. "Here, look, this is the most damage, big deal." A thin tracing of blood marked the edges of my thumbnails; the steering wheel spokes had whacked both thumbs when it whipped around as the right front wheel hit the wall.

Rolla's eyes searched mine, and some of his tension eased.

"I guess I found out where the edge is," I said. It was something I had complained about since first testing the Lightning less than a month before. I couldn't find the edge—the edge of adhesion, the point at which the car would no longer stick to the pavement in the turns, the speed that broke it loose. If you couldn't find the edge, couldn't feel in the seat of your pants and the pit of your stomach just where it was, then you didn't know how much faster you might be able to get through the turns. And if you tried to take a turn faster than what the car was capable of, you fell off the edge. The tires lost their grip and you were cut adrift; spun, usually. That was what had happened to me.

Now I knew. That wispy little flash of a bubble-gum stickiness was all the Lightning was going to tell you about the edge. Rolla's older car, the one I had driven in four Indy-car races the year before, was a pussycat compared to this.

A commotion outside marked the wrecker's arrival. The Lightning dangled by its roll bar from the hook. The guys on the crew winched it down onto its three good wheels and a dolly, then pushed it inside, getting their first look at the damage.

I moved to Rolla's ancient desk in the back of the garage and phoned home. If my folks down in Florida got news of the crash from someone else, they'd be scared to death. They worried enough anyway. My strange obsession with the sport had baffled my family for the past decade and a half, and Indianapolis represented risk at its peak. My father called it "playing footsie with the inevitable."

"I'm fine," I said. "I just scraped the wall, nothing serious." My mother's voice, soft and gentle, conveyed her suppressed alarm. We talked for a bit, until she sounded more at ease. Then I handed the phone to Walter, my youngest brother, who was with me in Indianapolis these two days.

I turned to Rolla. "The next thing we'd better do," I said, "is go see the press before they start spreading lurid stories."

"Are you sure you're up to it?" You could count on Rolla to be thoughtful and considerate.

"Yeah, sure."

A dozen reporters and a TV camera crew waited outside the garage doors. The rest of the crowd had dwindled to fifty or so. Some of the print reporters would probably want to suggest a "womanish" upset. No woman had ever competed in the Indianapolis 500, and the press loved melodrama. I would have been happier to see a few more cameras. Videotape was a bit harder to embellish.

"I just plain lost it," I said. "For a couple of twitches I thought I could catch it and save it, but when I saw that was impossible, I turned left and locked up the brakes. I'm fine, I'm just sorry I broke Rolla's new toy."

We talked with them until they had what they needed.

Back inside the garage, the car was up on sawhorses and the crew had torn into the damaged front end, surrounding it like surgeons at an operating table. They worked easily and fast, joking a little, their movements smooth and efficient.

Phil Casey, my new crew chief, stood a little apart. Just arrived from California that morning, he brought with him an excellent reputation. I had been told he was quiet, not the sort to take charge; but he moved with unassuming authority, and all our guys deferred to him. He had spent much of the day looking things over, studying various parts of the car, saying little. Now he was at the bench with some of the bent and broken pieces.

I put an arm around his shoulders. "You got here just in time, didn't you?" I said.

Phil laughed. "It's not too bad."

Surely this accident would prove to be just another setback in a week when we'd already seen and surmounted our fair share of them.

I settled into a corner with my notebook. I had started keeping notes three days before, on Saturday May 7, the first day of practice. That had been a different sort of day, a day that ended with my posting the fastest time of any driver on the track. Danny Ongais was nearly three miles an hour slower in a Cosworth-engined Parnelli,

Wally Dallenbach third in George Bignotti's Wildcat-Offy. It was an occasion for quiet glee, in the privacy of Vollstedt's garages.

"Well, Guthrie," Rolla had said, his blue eyes sparkling, "that ought to get their attention."

Indeed.

Just a year earlier, the preponderance of racing opinion stated firmly and passionately that no woman could possibly handle a 750-horsepower, 200-plus mph Indianapolis 500 Championship race car. Rolla Vollstedt, a respected team owner and long-time car builder in United States Auto Club racing, had flown in the face of sixty-five years of tradition when he announced his intention of bringing a woman driver to the Indianapolis 500.

The resulting heat was blistering. Established drivers complained loudly, publicly, and at length. "Women don't have the strength, women don't have the endurance, women don't have the emotional stability, women are going to endanger our lives." The records of women in European auto racing, stretching back to the nineteenth century, and those of American women sports car racers might as well not have existed, for all the roundy-round boys cared. My own thirteen years of experience on the road-racing circuits, my Two-Liter Prototype class win at the Sebring 12-Hour, my North Atlantic Road Racing Championship seemed to count for nothing in the world of oval-track racing. Tradition was all, and tradition said that women, peanuts and the color green were not allowed.

We hadn't made the field at Indianapolis in 1976. A series of mechanical problems kept me from even making a qualifying attempt in Rolla's car. We had, however, done well for ourselves at four other Indy-car races. I qualified as high as twelfth, and competed vigorously. By the end of the year, we thought we should have managed to lump the disbelievers with members of the Flat Earth Society.

Meanwhile, the tidal wave of headlines that followed our efforts opened up a second opportunity. I was offered a shot at top-level stock car racing: the NASCAR (National Association for Stock Car Auto Racing) Winston Cup series. This was another venue in which "woman driver" was thought to be an oxymoron. I wasn't sure whether I felt more like Walter Mitty or Clark Kent; but I threw myself into it, body, heart and soul.

Within six months, I finished as Top Rookie at the 1977 Daytona 500, NASCAR's premier event. In that 500-mile race I was running eighth with fifty miles to go, against the likes of Cale Yarborough, Benny Parsons, A. J. Foyt and David Pearson, when a mechanical problem dropped me to twelfth at the end.

In spite of all this, the air was still far from clear. At our sponsor's employee picnic the night before practice opened at Indianapolis, the night before I set the fastest time of the day, a woman had asked, "How do you train? I wondered because [driver] Johnny Parsons Jr. said on the radio last night that even if you make the field, you don't have the strength to finish a five-hundred mile race."

So it seemed the members of the Flat Earth Society still had company. I found it agreeable to imagine the effect that opening day's results might have on them.

When the froth in Rolla's garage calmed down and people went back to work, I had called home. "I have the honor to inform you that *your* daughter set fastest time of day on opening day of the sixty-first Indianapolis 500..."

Two months earlier, I had written for tickets to that evening's performance of the Indianapolis Symphony Orchestra. Andre Watts was to play a great voluptuous favorite of mine, Tchaikovsky's First Piano Concerto. Neither my brother nor the current man in my life was in town yet, so I invited one of the crew, Pete Gross, who was new to Rolla's team this year. He was platinum blond, quiet, and intelligent; in real life, he had his own automotive business. Pete leaped lightly over the transition from crewman to concert-goer, turning up in a well-cut wool suit. It was good to be with one of the team, someone who had been part of the day's intensity.

Four descending notes from the horns summoned the full orchestra to Tchaikovsky's opening theme. Watts underscored it with the piano's initial crashing chords. His fluid, long-fingered hands were as elegant and exquisite to watch as ballet. I settled back in my seat in a state of perfect bliss. Life could offer no more than a day such as this had been, that ended in such music.

One can't, I suppose, ask for two perfect days in a row. At Rolla's garage on the morning of the second day of practice, I found the Lightning in pieces. Rolla had ordered the right front hub disassembled in order to check on a faint wheel bearing noise I had reported.

The whine of other cars at speed drifted through the garage. Clucking impatiently, I watched while the hub was pulled apart. Finally, Pete had the bearing in his hands; raised his eyebrows, and gave it to me. As I rotated the inner and outer races, the thick grease clinging to my fingers, I was shocked.

A metallurgical failure or crack caused the bearing to gripe and stutter. My fingertips told me that sure enough, Rolla had made the right decision once again. Sometimes I thought he was psychic. Probably he had to be. He ran his team on what, for Indianapolis, was a shoestring budget.

It was late before I was back on the track; but when the six-o'clock gun ended practice for the day, only two drivers had posted a faster time than ours. Both were previous winners of the Indianapolis 500. Gordon Johncock was fastest at 192.596, Al Unser second at 189.235. We were tied exactly with Danny Ongais at 188.442.

Ongais, a former drag-racing champion, was an Indianapolis rookie like me—sort of. He was Al Unser's teammate on one of the top-ranking teams, and was funded by megamillionaire Ted Field of the Marshall Field department-store dynasty.

So far, our Lightning had been powered by an obsolete engine. Rolla's old pickup truck held our secret weapon, the engine that we intended to use for qualifying and for the race. It was a new-style Offenhauser that might put out as much as a hundred additional horsepower.

After those first two exhilarating practice days came a day of setbacks. Dick Simon peered over the shoulders of the crewmen, offering advice and assistance. He was the senior driver on Rolla's team, and his Indy-car experience was enormously helpful to me. The race car he was to drive this year, newly built in Vollstedt's Oregon shop, hadn't yet arrived at the Speedway. Many drivers in his situation might have been sulking in a corner, rather than helping their teammate.

On this day, however, all our variations in chassis and suspension setup gained us nothing, not a decimal more of speed, but my time from the day before remained among the top ten clocked to date.

Johnny Rutherford, three-time winner of the 500, turned the fastest lap of the day at 196.850 mph. I was at the fence near our pit signing autographs when he came up behind. Johnny was by far my favorite among the star drivers—good-looking, elegant, sophisticated yet warm. We had run against each other in two of the Winston Cup stock car races so far that year, and I had qualified faster both times. Johnny was a big enough guy not to get bent out of shape over it.

"That green machine is really flying," he said. "Congratulations!"

"It really feels good."

"Is it a good car?"

Close to his ear, so the pressing crowds couldn't hear it, I gave him a ribald answer. Johnny laughed all the way down pit row, leaving me amazed at myself. Those fast laps sure loosened up my prim and proper persona.

Dick Simon reported later that A. J. Foyt had been giving Johnny a hard time about my outqualifying him, in the middle of a big audience in the garage area. That kind of thing was the single most uncomfortable aspect of being a woman in a man's game, one I tried hard to defuse. The underlying principle, of course, was that a woman was such an inferior creature that defeat at her hands was shameful. Only when they understood that on the race track we were all equal would real progress be made.

Rolla was in the best of spirits; he had gotten additional sponsorship just that afternoon. The moment seemed propitious to discuss the crew chief on my NASCAR team, Jim Lindholm, who was begging me for a position on Rolla's crew. However, Jim wouldn't come without being paid. Many on Rolla's crew were volunteers.

"He's a good man," I told Rolla. "He's smart, thorough, and he works well with people. He has a lot of initiative, learns fast, and he's a darn good mechanic on taxicabs." NASCAR racing was thought to be a couple of pegs down from the mechanical sophistication of Championship racing cars; but in the end, Rolla acquiesced. Before the week was out, we would both be very glad that Lindholm was on hand.

The next morning was Tuesday May 10, the day of the crash. Early on, I retreated into my shell. I went into my head, thinking about going faster. I thought about melting into the car, not fighting it. I thought about letting myself be smeared onto the right-hand side of the cockpit in the turns, under the influence of some two and a half G's of lateral acceleration. I thought about feeling like part of the car, about having my nerve endings out at the tire contact patches. I thought about feeling joy in making it go. I sat in the quiet car, and soaked it up. My brother Walt was watching. I said to him, "Know what I feel like? The yolk and white of a Faberge egg." Live and delicate, snugly enclosed in an elaborate structure of gleaming, sparkling, intricate, expensive craftsmanship....

At one o'clock Tuesday, we were running. The car felt terrible. It was unstable entering the turns, then developed an awful push as I came back on the throttle in mid-turn, before neutralizing at the exit. The speed went down to 177. I pitted. They found and fixed a broken rear sway bar link.

Back out on the track, the speeds climbed right back to 187. Then the oil pressure dropped. I pitted again. They checked the spark plugs, and found one that was wet. They took the car back to the garage. It might mean an engine change.

"If I get close to one-ninety again," I said to Walt, "and they take it away from me again, I'm going to drop face down on the pavement, pound my hands and feet, and yell like a two-year-old!"

They brought it back.

Okay, time to do it; time to break that elusive mark.

The sun was low, the oil and water cool. After a single warm-up lap, I pitted for duct tape across the top of my helmet visor, to block the sun's declining rays.

Now. Stand on the gas.

On three successive laps they showed me 189. Then came the lap they couldn't show me, because I didn't come around again afterwards: the lap the official timers got at 191.083.

Late in the day, I drove Walt out to the airport to catch his plane home. At twenty-eight, he was the youngest of my four younger brothers and sisters—tall, blond, and possessed of a fine, sharp wit that generally lightened up any situation.

His humor hadn't been much in evidence since the crash.

As we turned out of the Speedway gates, he looked as serious as he ever got.

"Well," he said, "you're still squeaking."

I stole a sidelong glance. His distress was clear, and pained me. I loved him dearly.

"Those cars are a lot safer than they seem," I said reassuringly. "You never see the big fires any more, because fuel cells and dry-break fittings keep the fuel from spilling."

"Oh, good, so you're not going to be toast."

I laughed, as he had meant me to do.

We passed slowly through the little town of Speedway: green lawns laced with redbud, delicious drifting scents of home-cooked dinners, clumps of beautiful purple iris, lovely evening light. Life. I was still alive. The car radio was tuned to Indianapolis' classical music station. I didn't know what they were playing, but I wanted it never to end.

While we waited for his flight to be called, we walked to a window to watch the jets take off and land. Walt was an airline pilot, like my father. "It's amazing," he said, "you lap that track at an average speed faster than I lift off with two hundred people on board." His voice was somber, though the sentiment was light, touched with relief, and concern for what might lie ahead. "And I don't think I've ever seen anything quite like the teamwork," he went on. "There's no bullshit. The way everybody meshes, pulls together…"

He was right. Vollstedt's team was something special. The tone was set by its owner. Rolla loved the racing game beyond measure, and was passionately involved in every aspect of the sport. He could weld and run a lathe, though nowadays he mostly left that to his crew. He knew the theory of suspension design and every other aspect of the cars that bore his name. His network of contacts extended throughout the racing world. He could house his crew for next to nothing, often in the homes of friends. He sat on the USAC Board of Directors as the car owners' elected representative, helping set rules for the benefit of the sport. His mind seemed to run on ten tracks at once, missing nothing, and he looked after me as if I were a daughter. Fifty-nine years old and grey-haired at the time of this race, he was tireless in attending to the welfare of his team.

But then, throughout auto racing, people do impossible things—that's part of the compelling nature of the game. To the public, it seems that the driver is all; but the members of a team know better. Walter had quite rightly picked up on that.

When Walter's plane left, I went back to the track. Rolla was on the phone. When Rolla hung up, he sighed. "Replacement parts for the Lightning don't exist. Our prototype isn't like the production models. We're going to have to fabricate everything from scratch, except what we made extras of in Portland, that are spares for Dick's car also."

"What's missing?" I asked.

"The steering rack. The dive plane. The upper A frame. And that's just the worst of it."

Rex Hutton and Harold Sperb were Vollstedt's best fabricators, but of course that was why they had remained in Oregon—to finish Dick's new car. They wouldn't get to Indianapolis for another two days.

I slid down from my favorite perch on the workbench that ran along the rear of the garage.

"Jim Lindholm will be here tomorrow afternoon," I said. "Maybe he can help."

"These aren't taxicabs, Guthrie."

"I know."

In the morning I stayed in bed until noon, writing in my journal and musing over the Lightning's newly revealed personality flaw. The respite was welcome, and there wasn't much I could do at the garage area anyway. I had a fine case of what was called race-car rheumatism, and couldn't figure out how my back ribs, under the left shoulder blade, had taken such a beating.

That night I was on duty at Riley Children's Hospital, along with drivers Bobby Olivero, Larry McCoy and Jerry Karl. One of the most poignant aspects of the Indianapolis 500 was the way that hundreds of Indiana volunteers worked to spread the race's excitement into the gloomiest corners of life, arranging visits such as this one. We could see its effectiveness, but we left the hospital somewhat less animated than when we arrived.

For the second year in a row, Rolla had gotten me a room for the month at the Classic Motor Lodge, a well-worn motel across Sixteenth Street from the Speedway gates. After years of sleeping in the back of the decrepit station wagons with which I towed my own race cars, this was a fine luxury, and the prime location meant Rolla must have stretched his budget for it. I could almost ignore the brown shag carpeting, faded wallpaper, and olive upholstery with its glistening plastic fuzz.

Wednesday night, the hours passed slowly. I was waiting for a knock at the door, a knock that finally sounded at one in the morning.

It was Alex. He'd been a serious part of my life for just a couple of months. The moment he walked in, the dreary room was transformed, its disparate elements vanishing into a rosy glow.

Around dawn, I asked Alex about my ribs, since a bit of medical training was part of his background. He pushed and prodded.

"Does that hurt?"

"No ... yes ... no."

"I really don't think anything's broken," he finally said. I was relieved to hear it. The only sure way to tell was with an X-ray, of course, but that was out of the question. No way would I risk being barred from the track on the basis of injury.

Dick Simon's new car, the black Vollstedt/Offy, arrived at the Speedway at noon. Hal Sperb and the guys assigned to the new black car buzzed around it with enthusiasm, completing its preparation for the track.

Meanwhile, one of Rolla's precious new-style Offenhauser engines was being installed in my Lightning. Not only was it the most recent design, it had been assembled by Herb Porter, Goodyear's engine guru. We had high hopes for this powerplant.

The damaged right front of my car had been reassembled, but the right-hand side of the nose section sported a bright red dive plane significantly shorter than the green one on the left. I could only hope that the unequal downforce it generated at speed would have a minimal effect.

At the six-o'clock gun, the Lightning still wasn't ready.

Only one day of practice now remained before the first weekend of qualifying. Vollstedt's team had its hands full: one race car with untested repairs, and one car that had never turned a wheel on a track.

Up to this point, Vollstedt had pretty much ignored Jim Lindholm. That was about to change. Rolla had exhausted his resources. The California shop that built this year's crop of Lightnings had refused to fabricate any replacement pieces for the prototype. Rolla summoned Jim and me to his battered desk in the Lightning's bay of the garage.

"You know where Grant King's shop is, Jan, up north of the track, and you know Grant King," he said. King was a colorful Canadian-Chinese car builder and team owner; Sheldon Kinser and Gary Bettenhausen were his drivers this year.

"Here are the dimensions of the right front dive plane," Rolla went on. "Take Jim up to King's and see if you can get the aluminum to make it with. The specs are on the drawing."

Jim did more than ask for aluminum. He gained permission to cut the material and then, permission to use some of the other equipment. That was a pretty good trick in a stranger's shop. I watched him, knowing how good he was at twisting wrenches on a stock car, but not whether he could walk up to raw materials and a bending machine and fabricate an Indy-car part.

He could, and he did.

He finished it late that night, long after I left. Friday morning, Rolla had the wing in his hands.

"You were right, Jan," Rolla said. "He *is* a good man."

Meanwhile, the Wednesday and Thursday practice sessions saw speeds rise beyond 200 mph. Mario Andretti did it first, then A. J. Foyt, in the last minutes of Wednesday practice. Johnny Rutherford followed suit the next day. There was widespread scepticism as to whether the speeds were achieved with legal boost, eighty inches of turbocharger pressure. The calibrated popoff valves that limited boost wouldn't be installed by USAC officials until just before a car's qualifying run.

Andretti insisted his speed was legally achieved. Rutherford just smiled, "That's for us to know and everyone else to find out."

When the track opened on Friday May 13, my Lightning was ready to go. Its nose still sported the short red wing; they had run out of time to install the new one that Jim built. The new Herb Porter-built engine would need a careful half-hour break-in period. I went to consult with Herb about it, and hewed precisely to his instructions.

In mid-sequence, though, Phil Casey and Rolla came out to the wall. Both started waving, *faster*. I didn't need that, especially not in front of Friday's big crowd and all the reporters who were keeping an eye on my first outing after the crash. The previous evening's Indianapolis *News* had noted that remarks about my crash overheard on pit road included, "Now that she knows what it's really like, she'll probably quit racing," as well as the predictable witticisms about women drivers. I pitted.

"Look," I said with some heat, "I'm doing precisely what Herbie told me to do."

Phil and Rolla weren't convinced. We argued. My temper rose. But finally, the break-in was finished to everyone's satisfaction. Porter came to the pit and pronounced the engine ready to run.

When I stood on the gas, the nose flew—the front of the car had almost no grip on the track. It took me by surprise; it was a super-spooky lap. I brought it in. They fussed with it, but the car remained almost as spooky as before.

"Let's mount Jim's new wing," I said. While that was in process, I snooped around. Not only had the car been running with a short right-hand dive plane, I found, they had also flattened out the angle of attack on both sides. The problem was, they hadn't told me they did it. Forewarned, I'd have anticipated that the nose might fly.

As a driver, I was analytical and logical. In order to function well as part of the team, I needed to know the nature of the changes made to my machine. As matters stood, in the confusion of changes known and unknown, my sense of what the car was doing had become fairly well scrambled. Late in the afternoon, puzzled as hell, I asked if Dick Simon would take the car out. He had been at my pit on and off throughout the day.

He would. We stuffed padding into the Lightning's seat to suit Dick's shorter legs, and he made two laps.

"Check the caster," he said, "and the wheelbase too. It's automatically turning right, and it's unstable. It might not be square." Then he was gone. His new black Vollstedt car was at that moment being pulled out to the line for its maiden laps.

We took it back to the garage. Soon, they found reverse stagger at the rear—the left rear tire larger in diameter than the right, which accounted for the tendency to turn the wrong way. The six o'clock gun went off, and the track closed. I hung in with the guys while they checked the front suspension for bump steer—a highly undesirable configuration that caused a car to change directions as the suspension loads changed in the turns. They found big problems there.

I went to fetch supper: buckets of fried chicken, munchies, beer. A good many people at the chicken place and in the grocery store wanted autographs. Autographs were hard to give at the end of a day such as this had been. I couldn't help feeling that their admiration was misplaced.

On Saturday May 14, a fair-weather system lay on central Indiana like a comforter over the newly-planted fields, inviting race fans to come out and play. Three hundred thousand people were converging on Indianapolis Motor Speedway for Pole Day, the first day of qualifying, and lines ran for miles in every direction. The contest for pole position drew crowds akin to those for the race itself. The Speedway gates would open at 6 a.m. and, long before then, the greater part of the throng had maneuvered its vehicles to best advantage for a rush inside. So for more than a mile around, the previous night's atmosphere was that of America's biggest—the world's biggest—county fair.

Makeshift stands along Sixteenth Street and Georgetown Road sold cotton candy, popcorn, hot dogs; and those aromas mingled with the smoke from thousands of grills and Hibachis. Race fans cruised and partied through the night, in RV's and pickup trucks and cars of every description. Motorcyclists ripped the air to shreds as they accelerated toward Georgetown Road, only to turn and accelerate back the other way. The quantity of beer consumed might have floated a battleship.

A scattering of rowdies and drunks made eddies in the huge sea of fans, but overall the atmosphere was benign. Whiffs of anachronism bound the first Indianapolis 500, in 1911, to this one, like musk in perfume. A ghostly image of once-rural America, where dirt race tracks served alternately for horses and cars, traced a palimpsest through the huge modern grandstands.

All night, the tide of motorized humanity flowed crackling and popping around the Classic Motor Lodge. Alex, who was also involved in racing, left at four in the morning. I went back to sleep. At seven, I walked over to the track. The line of cars waiting to drive through the gates still stretched out of sight. Qualifying would begin at eleven.

An hour and a quarter of open practice started at nine. My lap times were still slow. With each lap, the car got looser—lost more and more of its adhesion at the rear. I brought it in.

"Tighten it up, will you?" That could be done in many different ways, the simplest being to add air to the left rear tire, which increased its diameter. But no change was ever really simple. Journalist and race driver Pat Bedard once described his Indy car as "a 200-mph Rubik's cube." Dozens of chassis and suspension settings could be changed, each interacting with the rest.

No wonder the car had gotten increasingly loose: the left rear tire was leaking. They replaced it. Out again. The car still felt loose. I pitted, and they flattened the front wings. This time out, the nose flew.

Dick Simon was also struggling for speed. Shaking down a brand-new car in a day's time was like trying to climb Everest without oxygen. Simon was a certified whiz at sorting out a chassis, but he had his hands full with this one.

The pre-qualifying practice session ended, and the opening ceremonies began. The rituals were institutional gloss on an atmosphere so charged with energy that it could raise your hair if you opened yourself to it, like a purple-black thunderstorm before the first bolt of lightning.

The rules that governed qualifying for the Indianapolis 500 were of Byzantine complexity. Rolla Vollstedt knew the rules and their implications by heart. Competitors would place their cars in a line to qualify, one behind the other, against the inner pit wall. (Qualifying order was set on Friday night, as each of the drivers drew a numbered black marble from a sack.) The salient point at this moment was that, even though neither of Rolla's cars had the speed for a meaningful qualifying attempt, both would be placed in the qualifying line. This tactic preserved certain rights in the event of rain or other interruption. When we reached the head of the line, where pre-qualifying tech inspection began, we would "push through," or go to the back and start over.

The line was an ordeal that I could have done without. The packed grandstands were liberally laced with hecklers who thought a woman had no place here. Many of them had obscene ideas. An area near the tower was so bad that we had christened it "the zoo" the year before. Since most spectators gathered in the same seats from year to year, we could expect to endure the same barrage of insults and epithets in that vicinity. Not all of it was good-humored; my crew last year had detected enough real menace to feel uneasy.

Nevertheless, I stayed with my car. Technically, a driver's presence in the line with the race car was not required, but my mindset today was the same as last year: if the guys who worked on my car were subjected to this, I was damn well going to be there with them.

When the track opened for qualifying, A. J. Foyt's car was the first to run. Foyt turned 193.465 mph for the four-lap average, and was disgusted. "Only horses run slower than I did today," he grouched over the booming loudspeakers.

Sheldon Kinser came next. At the completion of his third lap in the 185-mph range, his crew waved a yellow flag and the run was classified as incomplete. Kinser would have two more chances to qualify for the race. It was always a guessing game what speed would be required to "make the show"—to be one of the thirty-three fastest cars. Grant King's team clearly didn't believe that 185 mph would prove to be fast enough.

George Snider was next, in Bobby Hillin's Wildcat/DGS. George took the checkered flag at an average of 188.976 mph. Since he had completed the full four laps, no further qualifying attempts would be allowed in that car. Snider was followed by Al Unser, who posted 195.950 in his Parnelli/Cosworth.

Tom Sneva was next up, in Roger Penske's McLaren/Cosworth. The Cosworth was a newly developed British eight-cylinder engine that offered formidable competition to the old four-cylinder Offenhauser. But Sneva had little practice, and had hit the wall on Friday, so the crowd wasn't too excited as he took the green flag. Forty-five seconds later, it was a different story. Stopwatches throughout the grandstands revealed Sneva's speed long before the loudspeakers confirmed it: 200.401 mph. A roar came from three hundred thousand throats. The 200-mph mark had officially fallen at last, to an easy-going, bespectacled ex-schoolteacher from Spokane, Washington.

Sneva's second lap was even faster, 200.535 mph. The third and fourth laps dropped to the 197-mph range as the tires heated up and the car got loose, but Sneva captured the pole position with a record four-lap average of 198.884.

So it went. We pushed the Lightning forward, as cars in front of us made their qualifying attempts. As our car crept closer to the zoo, the heckling mounted. All the guys were edgy. Pete Gross and Phil Casey looked disgusted. Paul Diatlovich, the "mad Russian," swore softly under his breath. Jim Lindholm was getting hot. Jim had a short fuse anyway, and as crew chief on my NASCAR Winston Cup stock car, he had become accustomed to the respect that accompanied our increasing success in the Deep South. Not that NASCAR was a more hospitable venue for a woman; quite the contrary. But it hadn't been two weeks since we qualified thirteenth out of sixty-five entrants for the Talladega 500, ahead of such established stars as Buddy Baker and Bobby Allison. NASCAR hecklers found themselves looking foolish.

The line came to a halt as the track closed for inspection. We were smack in front of the zoo. The animals had some big signs. One was left over from last year. JANET GRAB THAT POLE, it read. It was illustrated with a barber-pole striped phallus. Another placard showed a big, sloppy pair of boobs. A chant began.

"Janet sign the sign. Janet sign the sign."

We ignored them, elaborately casual. At my side, though, Jim was starting to growl and twitch. Jim had a black belt in karate. We didn't really need the mayhem he was capable of inflicting.

"Calm down," I told him. At NASCAR races, those were usually Jim's words, whenever I let myself get agitated over our most recent hassles with NASCAR officialdom. We flicked a look of faint amusement at each other.

Bryant's public relations man, a new guy this year, tapped me on the shoulder. "Some people want you to autograph this," he said, as if he found it quite normal. He had brought me the sign with the pair of boobs.

It had occurred to me previously that the new PR man lacked a certain amount of sense. "No, thank you," I answered, with a touch of frost. I had long since learned to take a look at the reverse of anything proffered for an autograph. Some of the most conservative-looking people would try to get a signature on pornographic materials, and I didn't have much of a sense of humor about it.

The line moved ahead, away from the zoo, and reporters moved along with us. "Does that stuff bother you?" one asked.

"No," I said, "I figure it's their problem or the Speedway's, not mine."

What a lie. My muscles were tense. It would have been easier if I had actually been waiting to qualify—easier on me, if not the guys. Then, I could have drawn on the concentration, the focus I developed for the track, so that everything else disappeared.

Eventually we reached the head of the line, and "pushed through"—pushed the car out of line, and hauled it back north to the tail end. A few dozen cars now lay between us and the next qualifier, each attended by crew members who pushed it forward by fits and starts.

Donna Snodgrass came to sit with us on the pit wall next to the car, as we settled in at the back of the line. A reporter for the Indianapolis *Star*, she covered mostly women's subjects. She was also a racing enthusiast, highly knowledgeable about the sport and its personalities. "You were under discussion in Billy Vukovich's garage this week," Donna said. Billy was the son of the famous two-time winner of the 500, Bill Vukovich, who died in a fiery crash while leading the 1955 race. Billy was an early, vociferous opponent to my presence on the track in 1976. His most widely reported claim was that after forty laps I wouldn't be able to steer a car and that if any woman could match his endurance, he'd eat his hat. Nevertheless, Billy was among the first to come around after actually seeing me drive a race. He was thinking of having a hat made up out of chocolate, he told Rolla.

Billy had put a car in the field at Indianapolis every year since 1968. In 1973 he had finished second; in 1974, third. This year he was driving a brand-new Lightning, a 1977 production version of my car. He had nothing but trouble with it.

"Somebody in Vuky's garage was claiming that you weren't going to make the field," Donna went on. "He said you didn't have the balls for it. And Vuky said, 'Well then, I'd better grow a pair of tits, because she's eight miles an hour faster than I am!'"

So we passed the time.

Tom Bigelow, formerly a driver for Vollstedt and still a good friend, began a qualifying attempt. He made two sterling laps at 190 and 189, then spun. We held our breaths until he was reported okay. Johnny Rutherford, Sneva's top challenger, posted 197, 196, 196.5— and his crew waved the yellow! The speed wasn't fast enough to beat Tom Sneva for the pole position, and it seemed that nothing but the pole would satisfy them.

Bobby Unser astonished everyone with a four-lap average of 197.618 mph. No one could figure out where he had found the speed. Danny Ongais posted 193.040, and I felt the sharp bite of envy. Earlier in the month, the middle 190s were where I had hoped to be today.

Johnny Rutherford came to the head of the line again, made a warmup lap, and coasted to a stop, the victim of obscure mechanical problems. His crew put their backup car in line, but tactically speaking, they had lost their high-stakes gamble for the pole. The line was now so long that a first-day attempt was out of the question. No matter how fast Rutherford ran on Sunday, his starting position would be behind every car that made the field on the first day. At six o'clock, the closing gun brought qualifying to an end.

Alex and I spent the evening quietly by ourselves, talking and dining on take-out food.

On Sunday, before morning practice started, I wangled the keys to the pace car and slowly circled the track. I scanned the subtle landmarks in the turns, imprinted on my mind's eye the apexes and exit points, and tried to get my head screwed on straight. After two days of nasty surprises with the Lightning, it was clear to me that I was spooked. You can't go fast if you're afraid of what the car might do next, so my mindset had to change. I would do whatever it took to accomplish that.

Was my happiness with Alex part of the problem? We had been together only a couple of months, and he brought warmth and light into my life. I thought, *I should have been alone this morning; should have set out in my running shoes on the back road to Turn 3 in the early grey light, to work at clearing my mind.*

When the track opened for practice at ten, the Lightning was as peculiar as ever. It was agony to approach 180 mph. I had no sense of what might be wrong. Meanwhile, my teammate Dick Simon lost an engine, and the black Vollstedt was hauled back to the garage. I asked Rolla if Dick would take the Lightning out. He would, and soon identified a problem with one of the spring perches, which destabilized the right front corner of the car. When that was fixed, he tried it again, and came in with a list of suggested changes.

"Yes, it's spooky," he said, mopping his brow. "The steering's peculiar. Put some more caster in it."

More caster should result in a more stable car. It would also make the steering heavier, the wheel harder to turn. My strong preference was for maximum caster, but it was often tough to persuade mechanics to set a car up that way. The stereotype of female weakness was hard to overcome.

While they changed the caster and redid the bump steer, qualifying began. Johnny Rutherford was first in line. He posted a four-lap average of 197.325 mph. Gary Bettenhausen accepted 186.596 in Grant King's Dragon/Offy, but veteran Jim McElreath took a wave-off after one lap at 185.300. Since no one was left in line, the track opened for practice again.

Indeed, the Lightning felt better. A shade of confidence crept back, confidence that the car would do what I had in mind. The immediate problem was that it was loose exiting the turns, the back end trying to sneak out from underneath as the hard white wall swept closer. I pitted to confer with Phil Casey and Rolla about this. Should we try softer rear springs? As we talked, the yellow light came on. More cars had lined up to qualify, and the track closed to practice.

Roger McCluskey put his 1977 Lightning securely in the field at 190.992. Clay Reggazzoni, the Grand Prix ace, lost it on the third lap of his attempt. He spun into the infield, hit a bank of earth that launched him through the air, and took out a good-sized section of sturdy steel-cable fence. The car shed a wheel, a wing, and much more before coming to rest on the grass, a total loss. Reggazzoni was shaken but amazingly unscathed.

It was after five-thirty when practice reopened. The Lightning was no longer loose at the exit but now seemed to stand on its right front through most of the turn. Within two laps, the yellow light flashed on: Lloyd Ruby had presented himself for a qualifying attempt. Since this would bring the day to an end, everyone scrambled for a position in line. Ruby put his Lightning in the field at 190.840.

My spirits were lower than a snake's belly, as they said in NASCARland. In fourteen years of racing, I hadn't crashed a lot, but crash I had. It had never affected me before, and I didn't think that was the problem now. Driving a spooky car was the problem, and it had bitten me hard.

The guys hitched the Lightning to the little tractor and hauled it to the garage. I walked back through the day's-end melee, the tangle of carts, drivers, crewmen, officials, VIP's, tools, spares, tires, TV crews and timing stands that filled the narrow space between pit wall and the spectator fence. Along the way, I ran into Mauri Rose. The three-time winner of the Indianapolis 500 had been exceptionally kind and helpful the year before, when flak over the first-woman thing was really flying. Mauri was gracious and witty, with a zest for life that hadn't diminished in the quarter-century since his retirement. We talked for a minute, as the hubbub swirled around us.

"How's it going?" he asked.

"Awful," I said. "The car doesn't seem to respond in a predictable way to any changes we make. The steering is weird. It's got me completely confused. What's worse, I think it's got me spooked."

Mauri looked at me for a moment, his eyes sharp and sparkling. "You'll get it back," he said.

I wished I could believe him. "Thanks," I said, and we parted.

Rolla gathered the crew for a conference in the garage. The big question was whether to continue debugging the Lightning with Porter's new engine, or change back to the "mule," the old-style Offy. The consensus was to let it be. An engine change meant disassembling the entire back end of the car. New mysteries might creep into the complex rear suspension.

We were all pretty grim.

Pete Gross offered dinner. "Thanks," I said, "but I'm going to go lick my wounds."

"Some of the guys are coming over to my house later," Pete explained. "Just to kick back and relax."

Pete was making a contribution to unity, in the face of a bad situation. I was grateful. Teams had been known to come unglued under a lot less pressure than what we had here.

Later that night, I talked with Alex. "I've been wondering," I said, "whether how happy I am with you may be part of the reason I can't get my head in gear to go fast."

Alex was sure it was the car. "When they get it figured out so that it's predictable again," he said, "you'll be able to run it just as fast as you did before."

In the morning, though, I knew I had to be alone; and told him so. It hurt like hell to ask him to go away.

"It's just for a little while," I said.

"When you're ready, you know where to find me."

He sat beside me.

"This is tough," I said.

"You don't have to tell *me* that."

Then he was gone.

On Monday May 16, the Lightning was ready around half past noon. Again, no matter what changes of set-up we tried, the steering was strange, unpredictable, and I still wasn't quick.

It was one of the worst days of my life.

Sending Alex away hadn't done any good either. I didn't have confidence in the car, and I didn't have confidence in myself.

It was a godawful night to have social obligations. Rolla, Dick and I had a mandatory appearance to make at a Bryant Heating and Cooling managers' meeting, where we made cheerful and optimistic noises that were somewhat at variance with reality. On the way back, we talked about my car. When it came to chassis-sorting, experience helped, and Simon had several thousand more Indy-car miles under his belt than I did. He had been busy with his own car all that day, but he had an idea.

"Rolla," he said, "how about taking the Lightning to the Bear rack tomorrow morning?" Bear provided a sophisticated suspension analysis system that was offered free to entrants. "I have a suspicion about the caster."

Rolla said he would do it.

By now we were running late for the Monroe Shock Absorber banquet that honored rookies of the previous year's race, held each year at the elegant Columbia Club on Monument Circle in the heart of town. The Monroe affair was for race participants only, making it an enormously popular insiders' event. Owners, drivers, crews, and their spouses and dates packed the banquet hall. The evening was relatively formal, and I had brought from New York a new dress of gossamer blue and white silk that drifted to the floor. I had hoped to be securely in the field by now, ready to celebrate. As matters stood, I didn't even want to go.

Pete, Jim and the guys were saving seats for Rolla and me. A few minutes later, someone tapped me on the shoulder. I turned to see Howard Gilbert, a grey-haired inner-circle member of A. J. Foyt's crew. They occupied the table behind us.

"Don't be a stranger," he said. "Our garage isn't closed to you."

It was an extraordinary statement. Foyt's garage was a *sanctum sanctorum*, a place no one dared enter uninvited. On the last epic weekend of qualifying a year ago, I'd been there once—to be fitted to Foyt's own backup race car, for a possible qualifying attempt. I wondered whether Howard was telling me the offer might be renewed. Our eyes met and held. I thanked him.

"You're one of the guys," Howard said.

Beleaguered as I felt by our calamitous loss of speed, Howard's words were balm to my soul.

Dave MacIntire, an owner of Monroe, wound up the evening with a few remarks. I was listening with half an ear when I heard, "I asked Tony Hulman what he was going to say if Janet Guthrie made the field."

Hulman was the owner of Indianapolis Motor Speedway, and of a substantial chunk of the rest of Indiana. He had been the saviour of the Speedway after World War II, when it was threatened with demolition. His was the yearly prerogative of saying, "Gentlemen, start your engines."

The question was hardly a new one. Girt with tradition as the race was, the prospect of change sent shock waves through the entire establishment. My initial position was that I couldn't have cared less what Hulman said, as long as one of the engines that started was mine. But over the past year, I had been dragged kicking and screaming into position as a symbol of the changing concept of women's abilities. So many people, men and women, had asked me, "Do you know what's going on in your wake?" Then they told business and cultural stories in which I figured as a proof. It was profoundly embarrassing to me when people said that I had changed their lives. Now I had to try to live up to it.

MacIntire continued. "Tony said, 'Well, I could say "Persons"...'" He paused for effect, and the audience tittered. "'Or I could say "Gentlemen" because after all, it's the mechanics who start the engines.'"

Clever, devious. It brought down the house.

Like it or not, something had to be done. I sprang to my feet.

"I'd like to comment on that!"

It got their attention, even at the other end of the room. A spotlight swept around to our table, the blue light dazzling. Faces turned in our direction.

"There's an archaic term that would be well suited to the occasion, and that is, 'Gentlefolk,'" I said, and sat down. The room responded with laughter and applause.

When dinner was over, we worked our way toward the door, amid the usual hubbub of conversation. Kay Bignotti intercepted us. A strikingly handsome woman, with long dark hair and a dress that set off her impressive decolletage, she was the wife of master mechanic George Bignotti and the daughter of three-time 500 winner Louis Meyer.

"I'll start your engine," she said.

Simple words, valiant offer. An Indy-car starter motor, attached by heavy cables to a large battery cart, weighed some fifty pounds. Wielding one was not without its hazards.

"I have a USAC mechanic's license," Kay went on, "and I've been around these cars all my life. We can't let Tony get away with this."

"That's wonderful," I said. "I'd be delighted. Of course, I have to get the car in the field first."

"I'm not worried about that," Kay said.

I woke the next morning with a hangover. It wasn't from drink; I kept close track of that, and was conservative. It was the toxic aftermath of an evening spent socializing. They say that shyness is a genetically inherited trait, and that even though you can develop a cover for it, and appear to be at ease, you never really get over it. For me, the stress of being with people I don't know very well, especially in large groups, generates biochemicals that leave me with a hangover worse than any residue of alcohol.

Fortunately, the car would be on the Bear rack for several hours. I placed a call to Ted Wenz in New York. Ted was a successful single-seat car builder and suspension whiz, and he generously shared his knowledge. When we hung up, I still felt awful. Hangover notwithstanding, it was time to get my head screwed on straight. The Classic Motor Lodge was no place to work at this. Set into an ocean of asphalt in a down-at-the-heels shopping center, it was as bleak outside as in. On a map of Indianapolis, Eagle Creek Park was tinted green. That's where I went.

The day was sunny and warm. A breeze riffled through fresh new leaves, dappling the shade. I sat on a picnic table near the lake. Schoolchildren played at the shore, their high voices and rambunctious energy evoking a normal world—a world that might as well be on another planet.

One big difference between the normal world and a driver's world is that a driver confronts mortality a little more directly than people are usually forced to do. But this morning's news had been of a helicopter crash on the roof of the Pan Am Building in New York.

Four people waiting to board were dead, and so was a passer-by on the sidewalk far below. Some poor bastard minding his own business, just walking down the street ... there's never any way to tell what the fates have in mind.

Sweet birdsong came from somewhere in the trees. A bullfrog croaked. Eagle Creek was a peaceful place. I felt myself flow into that, and it into me.

So you're scared. So? Go ahead, let yourself feel scared for a while. Let it out in the open.

A beautiful little caterpillar dropped onto my finger, swung from the leaves by an invisible thread. Its delicate translucent-green body bore traces of pale aquamarine at the nose and tail. It inched about my hand.

I hadn't realized how much emotion I'd been suppressing. Released, it was an icy flood.

Time passed.

The black flapping of ravens dissipated, clearing the air.

But, dammit, that car IS spooky. In my mind's eye, I replayed the Lightning's behavior in the turns. *The thing won't do what it's told, its response is non-linear.*

A small bird appeared among the leaves. It was grey, the color that belonged to the goddess Athena. Its clear song continued, exquisitely sweet. An impudent robin bobbed on a branch nearby.

I must find the space in my mind where there's joy in putting the car through the turns. I've been there before. I'll find my way back.

The caterpillar spun its thread and dropped from my hand.

Goodbye, caterpillar. I hope you turn into a beautiful butterfly.

An hour had passed. I rose to go. I felt as if, before, I had been submerged, swimming in greenish murk among dim carp-like creatures. Now I had found an opening into water as clear as gin. Brilliant tropical fish darted about, with a shark or two, and surf crashed on sharp coral reefs. But I was a strong swimmer.

There's something still wrong with that car. There IS something wrong with that car. And we have to find it.

Quite late in the day, the Lightning was ready to go. I felt my way gingerly into the new setup. The car had changed, all right: it had new problems, bad ones. It pushed so much I could actually hear the front tires screaming in the turns, over the engine and airflow noise. Worse, the steering was binding up. Phil Casey was inscrutable as he added some front wing. The engine had stayed hot, and I brought the Lightning up to speed on the back straight, running it hard through Turn 3.

At the exit of Turn 4, the engine hiccupped.

I shut it down, eased to the inside of the track, and coasted to a stop on the back straight two miles away. It was our fourth tow-in of the month; turned out to be the fuel pump. So much for Tuesday's running. The track would close before the pump could be replaced.

Rolla and I walked over to the Monroe hospitality garage to take a break. There wasn't much to be said. Such a mass of ill fortune boggled the mind, but the struggle must go on. We were sampling their beer and bologna when the six o'clock gun went off.

One of A. J. Foyt's crew came in, saw Rolla, walked quickly to us. "Rolla, did you know Dick crashed?"

Rolla didn't seem to take it in; didn't respond. It must have been overload. His senior driver, crashed?

"Rolla?" I said.

Foyt's man said again, "Did you know Dick Simon crashed?"

We grabbed the team golf cart, whipped over to the hospital. Dick was sitting up, his driver's suit rolled around his waist, a fine sheen of sweat on his pale, stocky torso. A blood pressure cuff gripped his arm. The doctors weren't thrilled with the numbers they saw. Dick's blood pressure was high under the best of circumstances.

As usual, Simon was talking a blue streak, and putting the best possible light on this fresh catastrophe. "It was handling so beautiful," he said. "I'd gone through Two and Four without lifting, and just lifted a little in Three, and just a hair in One. Something broke. I think it was a half shaft."

He had gotten about 185 mph out of it, before the crash.

Finally, the doctors let him go. He was cleared to run. Back at the garage, the black Vollstedt dangled by its roll bar from the wrecker's hook. The right front and rear suspension were both ripped off, the gleaming black side of its chassis scraped white. It didn't look like a salvageable machine.

The usual crowd had formed. It took a long while to drop the car onto a rolling table and drag it inside. The guys clustered around it like ants tearing apart a dead grasshopper, removing the broken pieces. Within an hour, they sounded as if they thought they could fix it.

Later, Alex phoned. He'd been hurting badly over our separation. By now, the premise on which it was based seemed in doubt. It was meltingly wonderful to see him again, a balm to my spirit. He left around midnight, leaving my morning to racing thought.

On Wednesday May 18, after a week of hot, humid weather, the track surface was greasy and everyone's times were slow. The fastest time of day dropped below 190 mph. We were now at midpoint of the second week of practice. The last weekend of qualifying loomed large. Eighty-five cars were entered in the 500 this year, the second-largest entry in history, and only the fastest thirty-three would start the race.

Dick Simon seemed to have bounced back from his accident, as chipper as ever. At Rolla's request, he took out the Lightning. He turned 174 mph.

"It's undriveable," he said when he came in.

Phil Casey, chief mechanic on my car, had been puzzling the hell out of me all week. In spite of his fine reputation, he seemed curiously unaggressive, slow to suggest changes and slow to make them. Friction had developed between Simon and Casey, as Simon vigorously suggested possibilities for improvement. It was Simon who discovered that the bump and rebound settings of the shock absorbers were wrong, and that the wrong bump rubbers were installed. Then he tried the car again.

"It's still undriveable," he said. "Something's binding up." The steering wheel was so hard to move, when the suspension was loaded in the turns, that even Simon's bull-like strength was taxed.

Late in the day, Phil Casey had an inspiration that made up for everything else. He disassembled the steering rack and pinion. The rack had been replaced after the crash. Something didn't match. Its hard, toughened steel was now chewed as if by a monster rat.

We had finally gotten to the bottom of the mystery.

On Thursday and Friday, we unscrambled all that we had done in the past week. Bit by bit, we reconfigured the car as it was in the first few days of practice. Of course, new problems sprang up to hinder our progress. Late Thursday night, a leakdown test on Herb Porter's killer engine revealed where some of our speed had gone. The engine wasn't holding its compression. With eighty percent leakdown on all four cylinders, its horsepower was way off. Only one more day of practice remained before the last weekend of qualifying, and the engine had to go.

Jim Lindholm was now well established with Vollstedt's crew, and leaped into the engine change with everyone else. Around two-thirty in the morning, unable to sleep, I joined them. In spite of my pass, the gate guards gave me a hard time. Women with garage passes were still such a new phenomenon that their presence in the middle of the night was automatically suspect.

Three or four other garages had all-nighters going as well. Their yellow light spilled through open doors, puddling warmth under the cool indifferent starlight. Tools clattered, voices rose and fell, tinny-sounding radios blared. Everyone was tired. No one would yield.

Friday's temperatures were in the 90s. The track surface reached 136 degrees, and was as slippery as anyone could remember it. A. J. Foyt turned the fastest time of day in his backup car at 190.396, 10 mph slower than the fast laps of a week before.

Late Friday afternoon, Dick Simon pronounced the Lightning fit for a qualifying attempt. He got 184 mph out of it, the fastest it had gone since the crash. I was nearly as quick.

"That's a one hundred eighty-eight mile an hour car," he said, looking me in the eye.

I understood. It was a threat. The black Vollstedt car was still an unknown quantity. If I couldn't make the Lightning go as fast as it ought, Simon would attempt to take it away from me.

Nevertheless, I was as close to being happy as I'd been since before the crash. For the first time in a week, the Lightning seemed to be a predictable, controllable machine.

Nothing but rain could improve track conditions. It came with Saturday's dawn, but only as a baleful tease. The brief, light shower delayed the start of practice for twenty-two minutes. That cut our practice session to a little over an hour. Qualifying would start at eleven. Still, with a few more refinements, we should have the speed we needed. I set out to get it.

No sooner had I brought the Lightning up to speed than the yellow light came on. Cliff Hucul, a likeable, mild-mannered Canadian, was testing the same piece of wall that I did. He found it equally impenetrable. His car shed its rear wing and some bodywork, but Cliff wasn't hurt. Twenty minutes later, the track was clear. Everyone dashed out to get the last precious minutes of practice. The Lightning had stayed warm, and I brought it up to speed after just one lap.

At the entrance to Turn 3, the turbocharger disintegrated. I coasted into the pits feeling nearly frantic. The turbocharger came from Herb Porter. If the craft of one of the Speedway's best mechanics wouldn't hold up for us, was there really any hope?

Practice ended, and crews rushed to put their cars in line to qualify. We pushed the Lightning up the line, completing the turbocharger installation as we went. When we reached the front, I used the warm-up laps of a qualifying attempt to check things out.

We weren't even close to being fast enough. The replacement turbocharger was weak, the boost far too low. I pitted without taking the green. Practice resumed.

A yellow light brought practice to a halt when Tom Bigelow placed his car in line for his third and final attempt, his last chance to make the field this year. What speed would it take? Estimates had dropped since last weekend, as hot weather made the track increasingly slippery. Tom took the checker with the fastest run of the day, at 186.471 mph.

At the six-o'clock gun, Dick Simon was on the track for a qualifying attempt in the black Vollstedt-Offy. He took the green; ran 183, 182. Vollstedt waved him off.

Qualifying would open for the last time at noon on Sunday, after a one-hour practice session. When it did, my green and white Lightning would be at the head of the line.

Black as the pit from pole to pole, night settled over the Speedway. Alex and I, restless, drove out into the soft May evening in my borrowed Corvette. A silver copy of the Indianapolis 500 pace car, it bore the gold-winged emblem of the Speedway. Such cars were lent to drivers by local dealerships for the month of May, absorbing a racer's mystique that later fetched a premium price. The huge engine growled under its breath as we drifted along two-lane country roads.

At a bluff over the White River, we stopped for a while. The grassy scents of Indiana drifted changeably past, and the river glimmered with the city's distant skyglow. The night around us was full of a wonder of fireflies. Their tiny chaotic beacons saturated the darkness with magic. We sat quietly in a strange place, separated from time and reality; yet nothing had ever been more real.

"If I don't make it tomorrow," I said, "I'll never get another chance."

Alex's strong hand moved in mine. It was a warmth and comfort that changed no facts. Indeed, I was up against it. The newspapers were brimming with innuendo that my effort was history. Some writers were hard put to conceal their glee.

"How are your ribs?" Alex asked. I hardly knew. To a driver, no pain compares with the anguish I had experienced that week. A drop into uncompetitive speeds, with its threat of an end to racing, represents a fate worse than death. The most traumatic crash seems but a temporary and annoying inconvenience; cars and bones can be mended. To a driver, the only thing that matters is getting the speed back again.

Maybe we're not too tightly wrapped.

In any case, on that magical night came the rare sense of being one with the universe—dispersed and yet whole, meshed with infinite time and space. It was as if I had crossed the boundary between life and death: a translucent self that permeated the earth and beyond, seeing clearly, free of the clumsy baggage of personality and appearance, corporeality and ambition and fear.

Tomorrow at noon, the month's events would take their decisive and final form. Some twelve hours hence stood a transparent wall; beyond it, chaos. When we reached the wall, chaos would resolve itself into order. What kind of order? Success, failure?

There was no sense feeling anxious, and I didn't. There were no options, there was no more time. Whatever happened, however the four-dimensional puzzle developed as tomorrow played out, I knew my part of it was a perfect fit.

It was late when we rumbled back to the Classic Motor Lodge. At five in the morning I called Vollstedt. He wasn't asleep. "Rolla," I said, "let's reconfigure the car just the way it was day before yesterday, Friday afternoon." He didn't hesitate; his voice was firm. "It'll be done," he said.

Sunday morning's hour of practice had hardly begun. The Lightning was darting again.

What does the little car want? The diminutive came naturally, as if that would force it to obedience.

The little car wants perfectly steady hands.

Steady hands, not so much as a millimeter of correction. The slightest motion of the steering wheel made the back end lurch toward the outside, a transient moment of oversteer. On entrance to the turns, you gritted your teeth as it lurched, then stabilized— provided your hands continued perfectly steady. Otherwise, the lurches upset the car, reduced its adhesion and therefore the speed. At the exit, you had to leave more space between the car and the wall, to compensate for the uncertainty of the lurch.

Meanwhile, at the front of the engine, some six inches behind my ears, an appalling racket had developed. It sounded like a bunch of big steel ball bearings being swirled in a coffee can. It might be the timing gears.

That wasn't all. The oil pressure gauge was fluctuating wildly, the needle flapping from 120 to 20 psi and back again.

Beyond the exits of Turns 2 and 4, the outside wall had landmarks—a crack, a smudge of paint—where I checked the tachometer. Its needle moved slightly higher at the completion of each turn. The reading enabled me to gauge the car's approximate speed. On the third lap, the tach told me we had reached the qualifying range. I pitted. Rex still held the board; it read 186.5. That was sufficient.

"I could show you a faster lap," I told Rolla, "but there's trouble in the engine. Whatever it has left, we had better save for qualifying."

An engine change before the end of the day was remotely possible—just remotely.

Rolla's voice was firm and composed. "Fuel it and we'll put it in line," he ordered.

"Keep the oil heater in it and the radiators covered," I said to Phil. "I'll take the green the second time around, not the third. There isn't a lap to waste."

Deep in the garage area was a secret hiding place, a tiny set of dark, musty rooms to which I had a key. The rarely-used suite belonged to Goodyear, and its private bathroom was the only such facility in the garage area. (Men used a long row of urinals in full sight of passers-by.) As usual, no one was there. I sat at an ancient wooden desk and gathered myself up. A one-way mirror set into the door framed desperate activity outside in Gasoline Alley, as crews rushed for their last chance to put a car in the field for the Indianapolis 500.

My old familiar butterflies were doing their worst. To call the feeling disagreeable is an understatement, but the butterflies were a necessary part of preparation for what was to come. Barring catastrophe, we were about to make the field.

I thought of all the people to whom I owed this moment. There was Ralph J. Farnham Jr., who for ten years had let me build my race-car engines and chassis in his small boat-moving shop in Oceanside, New York. Rolla Vollstedt, the only man in racing with the fortitude to let a woman drive his car at Indianapolis. Lynda Ferreri, who owned and ran the team I drove for in NASCAR; the education I got in stockers found invaluable application here. The guys on the crew, who had spent so many long nights struggling with the Lightning's problems. My parents, who raised their boys and girls to believe in achievement, the girls no less than the boys. The women's movement, for making it possible for a woman driver to be at Indianapolis at all.

No driver ever does it alone.

Some forty-five minutes remained before the noon starting gun. I gave myself over to the process of preparation, surrendering to floods of adrenaline and related brain-triggered biochemicals that raced through every cell. In the years since I first learned how to do this, I had gained a fair mastery of it; but never was the process so intense nor had so much depended on its effectiveness. One must reach a certain level and then hold it, neither overshooting nor backing down. It wasn't pleasant, this ... apprehension, but it was utterly indispensable.

I did laps of the track in my mind.

At a quarter to twelve, Jim and Pete tapped on the door. I joined them in the brilliant light outside. A noisy wave of cheers and boos accompanied our progress toward the car.

The green and white Lightning was just being rolled out of its final tech inspection. An aisle of ropes, hung with multicolored pennants, led to the spot where Chief Steward Tom Binford would deliver his formal instructions for the qualifying attempt. The guys pushed the car forward. I pulled on my helmet, slipped my glasses through the visor opening. Jim held the lap and shoulder harness as I stepped into the seat of the car, then slid down into its firm embrace. My feet found the pedals—brake, clutch, and accelerator—sensing their familiar outlines through the thin ballet-slipper soles of the Nomex boots. The world narrowed to a very small frame.

Jim reached in and gathered together the four ends of the safety harness. My three-inch lap belt was already set to length, and I squeezed down as he threw the lever that fastened the belts together. With your elbows pinned close to your sides by the narrow confines of the cockpit, it was impossible to do the belts yourself. I tightened the loose ends of the shoulder harness and settled into place.

Chief Steward Tom Binford leaned over to speak the qualifying rules. We both knew them by heart, of course; this was a ritual.

"You may take no more than three laps to warm up. At the end of the third lap you must either begin your attempt, or clear the course. Timing will commence when you have crossed the start-finish line under the green flag. If you wish to abort the attempt, you must enter the pits or your crew must display a yellow flag prior to your completion of the third lap. As you complete the third lap, a white flag will be displayed at start-finish. A checkered flag will be displayed upon completion of the fourth lap." He paused.

"Good luck," he said.

The noon gun fired.

The starter motor was in place. Rolla, standing at the front of the car, twirled his finger. I flipped the ignition switch, and the engine spun and fired. The gauges leaped to life, their needles quivering. Jim armed the onboard fire extinguisher and squeezed my shoulder for good luck. Rolla shook my hand. The guys set the car in motion. First gear engaged with a satisfying clunk. We were off.

Had they succeeded in keeping the engine warm? Before I was even out of pit road and onto the track, the gauges told me that they had done a good job. One lap in second gear should indeed suffice to bring the oil temperature back up to running level. Then I could stand on the gas.

In the short chute I caught second, and started working the engine. My right foot held the throttle partly down, while the left varied the pressure on the brakes. Loading the engine in this way would heat the oil as rapidly as possible. The water temperature was already where it needed to be.

It took half of forever to go down the back straight in second gear, crawling along at 60 to 80 mph. At about midpoint, I started scrubbing the tires—snaking the car back and forth to generate heat in the rubber. The tires wouldn't adhere well until the tread temperature reached some 200 degrees.

In order to take the green the second time around, I would have to start bringing the car up to speed as soon as I reached the front straight. Would the temperatures be high enough by the time I exited Turn 4? I loaded the engine a little harder, foot deeper on the throttle and harder on the brakes, the rpms varying rhythmically up and down. The boost gauge needle, measuring the pressure of air delivered to the engine by the turbocharger, started to lift from its bottom peg.

Meanwhile, I felt little that resembled emotion. My stored emotional energy was strong enough to topple small buildings, but altered, transmuted into something more useful. Its fruit was the infinitely sharp focus on each tiny detail of operation that would make this qualifying run succeed.

In the chute between Three and Four, at the north end of the track, the oil temperature reached its operating range. The Lightning was ready to go. I moved my left foot from the brake pedal to the solid brace on the firewall, let the car surge forward, caught third gear and stood on the gas. The turbocharger wound up and delivered, its howl trailing off behind. At the main grandstands I caught fourth, and eased into Turn 1 without taking it quite to the limit. No sense wasting the effort; this didn't yet count. Out of Turn 2 and down the back straight, my foot was on the floor. Turns 3 and 4 would have to be taken at full speed in order to cross the starting line, a mile away, with everything the car had.

The rattle at the front of the engine was as loud as ever, clearly audible over the engine's roar and and trailing turbocharger scream, and the oil pressure was fluctuating again. If the engine blew in a turn, the balance between centrifugal force and the power that drove the wheels would self-destruct. A crash would be hard to avoid.

Air swirled into the cockpit as my straightaway speed rose toward 200 mph. Its solid force buffeted my head. I settled my helmet firmly against the padded headrest. I was used to the way the Lightning blurred my vision, almost like opening your eyes under water.

The little car wants perfectly steady hands.

The caution-light fixture near the end of the back straight was a marker for the entrance to Turn 3. Approaching it, I nestled back up to the wall again. Scribing the maximum arc through each turn, from entrance at the extreme outside edge of the track to apex at the inside to exit at the outside, was the path that enabled the highest possible speed. I couldn't use up all the track at the exit, because of the Lightning's quantum lurches, but I could use it all on entrance.

Now.

I backed off the throttle a tiny fraction and eased the wheel left, felt the usual stomach-gripping sensation of an incipient spin. Then the suspension accepted its lateral load, and the Lightning stabilized. If I'd gotten it right, I wouldn't have to move the wheel by a whisker until the exit of the turn.

The noise level increased as the car scrubbed off speed. I was tuned in to each part of it: tire noise, so much louder in the turns; engine rpms; that rattle. We curled down the shallow banking toward the apex, grazed the yellow line at the inside of the turn, and hurtled toward the implacable white wall at the exit of Turn 3 under full power.

Done!

That was one. There were seventeen turns to go: one more before the green flag, and sixteen after.

In less than a heartbeat came the entrance to Turn 4. Left ... stabilize ... apex ... and exit at full blast, foot on the floor, swooping across the multiple black tire tracks where other cars had spun.

At the wall, I marked the rpms and boost. Good, I had what I needed. With five-eighths of a mile of straightaway ahead, I let the car drift away from the wall. The oil pressure needle held still for an instant, then resumed its wild oscillations. The temperatures were okay. A few yards beyond the pit entrance, Rolla Vollstedt leaned over the wall to wave our green flag. That cued Pat Vidan, the official starter, perched in his cage high above the start-finish line. I hardly noticed Pat's dramatic flourishes as I whistled past, except to verify that green was indeed the color of the flag he waved. My eyes were already full of the entrance to Turn 1.

The southwest turn seemed to narrow into a funnel—an illusion fostered by tall grandstands that curved around most of its length. I pulled back close to the wall again, the tiny lurch to the right exacting my most earnest attention.

No mistakes. There will be no mistakes, you will not err.

Left ... lurch ... settle ... and we swept down toward the infield grass. The left front tire barely touched the yellow line where the track flattened out. The yellow paint was slippery. Putting a full wheel onto it would upset the car's balance. Then we were off the apex and away toward the right-hand boundary, the south chute wall. The car stabilized at the exit without coming dangerously close to the white cement. If I sustained my grip on the lurching, we could go faster the next time around. I left my foot on the floor a fraction of a second longer on the entrance to Turn 2. Whatever speed I could gain here, I would carry with me all the way down the long back straight. It worked out well; I had fifty more rpms on the exit than in practice.

Out away from the wall, I checked the gauges again. Except for the oil pressure, all was well; but that horrible sloshing rattle, the unmistakeable sound of machinery trying to tear itself to shreds, hadn't escaped me for an instant. It was no better but no worse. Would the engine last?

Herb Porter had just delivered the second of his promised creations; his engine reposed at this moment in Rolla's garage. If this engine blew, could we change it in time to get back in line to qualify before the six-o'clock gun?

Here came Turn 3, and a glance at the tach showed that indeed, the car still carried the extra speed. The entrance to the turn would be faster, then, and the line on exit closer to the wall. As I bent into the turn, the lateral acceleration rose, but I had long since surrendered to that force. All that mattered was for my arms and hands to retain perfect freedom of movement. Fighting the side loads was an instinctive reaction that could only slow you down.

Turn 3 was done, then 4. At the outside wall I noted with satisfaction the rise in engine rpms, up by 75 now. Then I looked toward Rolla and the crew, at the far north end of pit road. Damn, he wasn't showing me a speed! I wanted to *know*. One of the crew could have clicked his stopwatch the instant I came into sight in Turn 4, with barely enough time to flip over the numbers and hold up the result for the current lap.

Don't sweat the small stuff. I knew from my tachometer that the lap was fast enough to hold a place in the field.

High in the starter's stand, Pat Vidan waved the green again as I whipped across start-finish.

One lap down, three laps to go.

No mistakes.

The tire temperatures would have risen significantly by now. How would the car respond as the heat rose? Would it push, going farther out toward the wall, unwilling to answer the wheel? Or would it get loose, the back end trying to overtake the front? Usually, there was a change of some sort as a qualifying run progressed. I bent into Turn 1 a shade faster than before, my nerve endings exquisitely in touch with the tire contact patches.

So far, so good.

At the exits of Turns 1 and 2, a few feet of space lay between the car and the wall. That space was my margin for error with the lurching. If I could calculate it more closely—and if I were ferocious enough—some speed could yet be gained.

In Turns 3 and 4, I gained another fraction of it.

Down the front straight, Pete Gross was holding up the speed board, 187.5. *Damn*, I wanted to be faster than that. But that speed was for my first lap, which was ancient history now.

No cars except A. J. Foyt's had touched 190 since five days ago, as the track grew slippery from heat and lack of rain. I didn't care: I wanted more speed than what Pete had just displayed.

Pat Vidan held up crossed green flags. Two laps complete, five miles; halfway there.

I was far beyond any sense of self. My senses were entirely meshed with the car. Its grip on the smudged black line through the turns was as intimate as my skin. Ahead of me, the next turn stretched toward infinity. Behind me, the two completed laps shrank to a microsecond, done and gone.

The entrance to Turn 1 had a caution-light fixture. The tiniest fraction of my mind noted that the light remained green. I curled into the turn, balanced ever so delicately on the edge, like a ballerina holding an arabesque on one toe.

At the exit of Turn 2, the rpms were higher yet, but the lurch was getting tougher to deal with.

The great marvel was, the engine hadn't yet come unglued. It could happen at any instant. Fourteen years of mechanical experience told me no engine could long survive the thrashing that resounded six inches behind my head. Deliberately, I kept my eyes away from the oil pressure gauge. Turn 3 loomed ahead.

Perfectly steady hands...

I came cleanly out onto the front straight, and Pete held up the speed: 188.3. Pat Vidan waved the white flag. One lap to go. *No mistakes.*

In each of the next four turns, the tach needle rose just a shade higher than on the lap before.

Out of Turn 4 and away from the wall, with nothing left but the flat straight run to the flag, I could see Rolla and the guys on the crew leaping and waving their arms. I knew better. I had stolen a look at the oil pressure gauge. The needle was bouncing off the bottom peg, zero, nada, nothing. If the engine blew now, I would coast across the finish line—but the average speed would be spoiled, lowered perhaps sufficiently to keep us out of the field. And once we passed under the checkered flag, blown engine or not, there were no more chances. Those were the rules.

I'm not sure whether the lump at the back of my throat was actually my heart, but I am utterly certain I didn't breathe until the yard of bricks at start-finish flashed under my wheels and the checkered flag swirled high overhead.

The world opened up again. My field of view expanded from the car and the track to take in grass, trees, grandstands, the sky and all the universe beyond. It was done, we had done it.

One minute later, I was rolling down pit road. All along the pit wall, guys on other crews were holding thumbs up, waving and clapping their hands. Rolla Vollstedt and Dick Simon, running, had nearly reached the flag-girt location of post-qualifying ceremonies when I pulled in. All of us were grinning from ear to ear.

For a while I was lost in a blizzard of hugs and kisses from Rolla and the guys. The team had held together, we had struggled through fearful adversity, and here was the result: with a four-lap average of 188.403 mph and a fastest lap of 188.957, we had put Rolla's car securely in the field for the sixty-first running of the Indianapolis 500. It would prove to be not only the fastest time of day but the fastest qualifying time posted the entire second weekend of qualifying.

Nothing in my life would ever be the same.

The vivid drama of the last day of qualifying continued. Rolla's black Vollstedt-Offy came to the head of the line. Dick Simon always joked about his "leaky skin," which was running with perspiration even before he climbed in. Four laps later, he was in the field at 185.615 mph.

Now my heart really sang for Rolla. Through all these days of awful trials and mishaps, he had kept his temper and a semblance of good humor. Yesterday, aeons ago, he had faced the possibility that neither of his cars might make the field. The world had turned around, and Rolla was walking on air.

We held a team celebration that night. Rolla Vollstedt said, "If I could sing, I'd sing *The Impossible Dream*."

Later, Alex and I held a celebration of our own.

The last weekend of qualifying at Indianapolis was followed by six days of associated folderol prior to the race itself—some of it pleasant, some serious, some just duty. I still had trouble getting a grip on the basic fact: we had made it, we were in the field. Each morning, the first thought that swam into my mind was: *something strange happened last Sunday.*

Oh, I know what it was; I qualified for the Indianapolis 500.

I did what?

Who, me?

The sign painter had lettered my name on the wall of our pit, in big red letters with the number 27, so it must be true.

There were more hospitals to visit, commercials to be taped for Bryant, and interview after interview after interview. The Lightning and I were on the front page of the New York *Post*, the Los Angeles *Times*, the Chicago *Tribune*, and the Detroit *Free Press*, as well as the Indianapolis *Star*. Jane Pauley flew out from New York to tape a piece with me for the *Today* show. She asked whether I would put on makeup the morning of the race.

"Of course," I laughed. "The men shave, don't they?"

Mail and telegrams came in heaps and stacks. There were letters from Austria, England, Venezuela, and all over the U.S. Wonder of wonders, hardly any were hostile. Such unpleasantness as there was came almost entirely from American women, apparently furious over the obligation I felt to have the starting call acknowledge the presence of a woman in the field.

But by far the greater part of the mail carried a much different message. Empathetic and touching, the letters came almost equally from men and from women. One woman wrote, "For fifty years I have hoped that I would live to see the day a woman would qualify for this race...", and another commiserated, "You have had to force a smile after endless jokes about women drivers ... I face similar situations in my career, and I can't yell, I can't cry, I can't even have the comfort of knowing someone understands..." One man, a father, let me know that "Yesterday our four-year-old son, Chris, observed that his hero was 'Janet Guthrie, race driver'."

Some of the telegrams were special indeed. From the widow of Ralph De Palma, who had won the Indianapolis 500 of 1915:

"CONGRATULATIONS ... I WANTED TO RACE BUT RALPH TOLD ME YOU WOULD BE AN OUTLAW. WOMEN ARE RECOGNIZED ABROAD BUT NOT IN AMERICA ... MARION DE PALMA."

It had been just four years since half the world and I watched Billie Jean King defeat Bobby Riggs in tennis' epoch-defining "battle of the sexes." She sent a telegram that read:

"AND THEY SAID THAT HAVING A HEAVY FOOT WOULD ONLY GET YOU IN TROUBLE. THE VERY BEST CONGRATULATIONS AND THE VERY BEST OF LUCK, BILLIE JEAN"

I felt both humbled and thrilled.

Kay Bignotti practiced with the fifty-pound starter motor. She lifted it from the battery cart, brought it to the back of the race car, fitted its drive gear into the matching aperture in proper alignment, and held it firmly engaged while the engine spun to a start. It wasn't a big deal, she said; she hefted fifty-pound bags of feed for their horses all the time. What I didn't know was that she'd had to fight with her husband over this. George Bignotti knew the hazards of starting an Offenhauser engine only too well, and wasn't thrilled with his wife's exposure to them.

Kay's father, Louis Meyer, who had won the first of his three 500s almost fifty years earlier, watched skeptically at first. "I just thought it was some kind of stunt," he said later, "but now I don't know. She's pretty good!"

Whatever other flak Kay might have been catching, she kept to herself. Something must have nettled her, though; there was a wonderful quote in the Atlanta *Constitution*:

"Women have been doing things like this since pioneer days," Kay said. "Do you think when they were crossing the mountains in covered wagons a man would have turned to his wife and said, 'Don't shoot that Indian and save our lives, honey, you're a woman?'"

Most poignant of all were words that my chief mechanic, Phil Casey, brought from a source beyond any reach. Phil offered to buy me a drink one night. We went to the heart of the Establishment, the Speedway Motel bar. He seemed happier now that the car was in the field, and the strain on our relations eased. After a while, he asked, "Did you know I worked for Mark Donohue?"

No, I hadn't known that; although I'd certainly known Mark. The winner of the 1972 Indianapolis 500 came from Philadelphia, and had started out on road-racing circuits in the Northeast in the sixties, just a couple of years before I did. Our paths crossed frequently over the years, and Mark had been kind enough to write a letter of recommendation when I staked my financial life and racing reputation on a Toyota Celica project early in 1972. Mark was a major good guy and a sensationally fine driver. He was two years gone now, killed in Austria in a Formula I testing accident.

Phil said, "Mark told me once that if ever a woman would make it at Indianapolis, it would be you."

It was so unexpected, so overwhelming, this ... voice from the other side ... tears slid down my cheeks. We sat silently. The hubbub of racing folk in the bar swirled all around us.

At the time of Mark's death, I was still just a minor-league road racer. How could he ever have dreamed of this?

Our garage was overflowing with flowers. I put my sister Anne in charge of keeping track of the accompanying notes of congratulations. Late Saturday morning, yet another pair of florist's boxes arrived, taped together. The uppermost contained a dozen long-stemmed red roses, tied with ribbon. In the second box, equally beribboned, lay a strung-out rubber chicken. Featherless and scrawny, it was an appallingly ugly object—both in itself and for what it had once represented.

It belonged to an elderly track guard, who stood near the trackside wall to help manage traffic on pit road. In 1976, he shook this chicken at me whenever I drove by him on my way out to the track. The insult had been renewed this year, during the black week when we struggled with the Lightning's repairs.

I took the chicken from its box. Its ribbon bore a message, in the spidery hand of an old-timer. "Who said she didn't have the guts and the will? I did, and my face is still red. Oscar is at your disposal. Good luck." A handsome letter of apology lay over the chicken's feet. Most of the track's volunteer officials lived in modest circumstances, and the roses were surely a major expense. The ribbon and the letter (though not the chicken!) remain among my souvenirs.

If a few faces in the crowd remained hostile, it was easy to ignore them. I didn't know for years, for example, that immediately after qualifying, when the Lightning was taken to be certified for conformity with the rules, the official whose turn it was to certify the next car refused to inspect mine.

Toward the end of the week came the actual, substantive drivers' meeting (as opposed to the public one), held in private. Chief Steward Tom Binford presided.

"We've had three great starts in a row," he said. "There's a great temptation to let down your guard because of that."

He didn't mention the catastrophic start of the 1973 race; he didn't need to. All of us carried a vivid image of the flames, the wreckage, the tires and wheels of crashed cars flying through the air like enormous black ping-pong balls.

"The start of the race here is one of the most difficult situations you'll face. The track is narrow, you'll be three abreast, and there's a wide variation in speed throughout the field because of the way qualifying is done.

"Just remember—a five-hundred mile race isn't won on the first lap."

Tom Sneva, Johnny Rutherford and Roger McCluskey stayed on for the rookie meeting that followed. There were seven of us this year, rather more than usual: Danny Ongais, Bobby Olivero, Jerry Sneva (Tom's brother), Cliff Hucul, Clay Regazzoni, Bubby Jones and myself. The senior drivers reinforced Binford's remarks, and added to them.

"For one thing, the track will be slippery," Sneva said. "You won't believe how much dust and trash is stirred up when four hundred thousand people pile into this place on race morning, and how much of it settles on the track. So you can't get through the turns as fast as you did last time out, not for the first dozen laps or so anyway.

"And make sure you have at least one extra tear-off over your visor, because the grunge really piles up at the beginning."

Tear-offs were layers of thin transparent plastic that fitted over the tough helmet visor. They weren't used in practice, since you could always pit if your vision became obscured. By bending up their corners when you fitted them to the helmet before the race, you could grasp and rip off one at a time, even when your fingers were made clumsy by gloves.

Johnny Rutherford spoke of another difficulty we would face. "You'll never encounter such turbulence as you will at the start of this race. With the field packed up tight, nobody except the first row gets clean airflow over their wings. Until the pack strings out, your downforce won't be a fraction of what it is when you're running by yourself. So that will keep your speed even lower in the turns."

He turned to a different topic. "Most races," he said, "you psych yourself up for. This one, you actually need to psych yourself down. There's so much electricity in the air—and you can't afford to let it affect your head."

It was an interesting point.

For my part, I had every intention of making a cool and collected start. My starting position on the ninth row (since I had qualified on the last day) gave me good reason for concern. Nothing could be more stupid than to get wiped out on the first lap, and I had seen it happen in more than one of the 500-mile NASCAR Winston Cup races that I drove. Particularly toward the back of the pack, not everyone kept his head.

Although there would be slower cars in front of me, I wasn't about to break my neck trying to pass them all on the first lap. In addition, I wanted room to deal with whatever problems might be generated by someone else. When the field was strung out, the serious work could start.

Traffic situations weren't going to be easy. Indianapolis was so narrow that opportunities to pass were limited. Drivers who had raced here before would have an edge in that respect. But all things considered, if the car held together, I figured I stood a good chance of finishing in the top ten.

Saturday morning's paper devoted a full page to the starting field, in rows and columns. I took a copy and walked through the garage area, making notes on the nose aspects of all the cars. In the quivering little mirrors of an Indy car, it could be difficult to identify the car behind. Was it someone faster, to whom you were obliged to yield? Or was it someone you'd just passed, to whom you wouldn't give an inch? The differences in car color and shape, as seen from the nose, were minor but critically important.

The public drivers' meeting, the big one at the start-finish line, was set for 11 a.m. We lined up on bleacher seats, in the order in which we were to start the race: the field for the 1977 Indianapolis 500. One by one we were introduced; stood and waved. A. J. Foyt ... Johnny Rutherford ... Mario Andretti ... row by row ... Janet Guthrie.

Me?

When the meeting ended at noon, I figured on having lunch with my family and Alex.

"Lunch!" said Rolla. "You have to go be in the parade!"

"Parade? What parade?"

I soon found out. It was a huge event, televised throughout Indiana and elsewhere, that wound through the heart of downtown. Elaborate floats and marching bands and motorcycle drill squads, the full panoply of an American Memorial Day parade, preceded and followed the drivers. Each of us sat on top of a replica of the pace car, again in qualifying order by rows and columns. Caught by surprise, I was overwhelmed.

I didn't enjoy the parade; no shy person could. But there was no mistaking the enthusiasm. Young guys with little kids picked them up and held them over their heads for a better view, almost shaking them, as if they thought I was a talisman for the child's future. The fathers of little girls had often expressed such sentiments, in the week past.

The parade also offered the most poignant possible view of the city's civic spirit. Although tens of thousands of spectators lined the route, the choicest curbside seats went to groups of the disabled, assisted by volunteers. Indianapolis did itself proud.

Saturday night, the eve of the race, was reserved for a quiet dinner with my family and Alex at the condo Rolla had arranged for them. I stopped at a little shopping center to pick up a bottle of champagne, and stumbled across an XK 140 Jaguar, the car I had cut my racing teeth on fourteen years before. The beauty and familiarity of its lines never failed to touch me, even though this one was painted an unfortunate shade of purple.

"Janet Guthrie! Janet Guthrie!" At the Jaguar's side, a little grey-haired fellow commenced leaping up and down, waving his arms. "You used to race a car just like this one! Will you come and sit in it? I've owned it for twenty-one years!"

So I did. It felt and smelled just like my old Jag, a serendipitous tie to my roots. *A good omen,* I thought.

By the time Alex and I got back to the Classic Motor Lodge that night, the bacchanalia on Sixteenth Street was in full swing. Most of next day's four hundred thousand-plus spectators were squeezed as close to the track gates as they could manage. For a mile around, anyone with ten square yards of land had rented it for overnight parking. The electricity of anticipation could have lit up a small city.

In spite of the raucous carousing outside, I fell asleep in a cocoon of exquisite contentment. In twelve hours, I would be competing in the Indianapolis 500.

Sunday May 29. *Seven a.m. Race morning. I feel calm—too calm? I've been following Johnny Rutherford's advice, psyching myself down rather than up. Could I have I overdone it?*

I peered out through the curtains of my dark motel room. The bacchanalia had vanished, like wraiths of a midsummer night. They were all inside the track now, waiting for the start.

Four hours until the green flag. Plenty of time to prepare. I would do laps in my mind, as I had taught myself years ago for sports car races. I would imagine driving down into Turn 1, fixing precisely the point where I'd ease off the throttle; imagine turning the steering wheel, and feeling the car's response. After a few such laps, I would alter the imaginary line for imaginary traffic. And meanwhile, the butterflies would gather under my ribcage for their physiological storm.

That was how it was.

Kay Bignotti was on the starting grid, ready to go. Of all the elements that made May of 1977 what it was, her contribution and its effect had the greatest symbolism. She showed plenty of gumption to carry it through. Much later I learned that in the Bignotti garage that morning, one mechanic's eyebrows and lashes had been singed when the car he was starting backfired. Another mechanic went to the infield hospital with a burned arm. Kay, who witnessed this, was undeterred.

Rolla Vollstedt and Jim Lindholm flanked me as we walked out to the grid. I stepped into the Lightning's seat, wriggled down into place. Tension ratcheted up to its peak as the pre-race ceremonies reached their concluding moments. In spite of the anomalies in and around my car, tradition was well served. Jim Nabors sang *Back Home Again in Indiana*. The bands played *The Star Spangled Banner*. Tens of thousands of red, white and blue helium-filled balloons soared out of their net toward a milky-blue Memorial Day sky.

Tony Hulman stepped to the microphones. That sly fox had thought of a way to stick with tradition as well as do the honorable thing.

"In company with," he slowly intoned, "the first lady ever to qualify at Indianapolis—gentlemen, start your engines."

We made two slow parade laps, then picked up the pace, holding our rows a hundred feet apart. My field of vision narrowed down to the only things that counted: the track, the cars, and the gauges on the dash. If all four hundred thousand spectators had gotten up and walked out, I wouldn't have known they were gone.

The pace car pulled off the track, leaving the field under the control of pole-sitter Tom Sneva. As he brought us down for the start, I scanned the rows ahead for telltale puffs of dust that would offer the first clue to an incident. None appeared. We swept under the green flag for a clean start.

Directly ahead of me, Billy Vukovich used the ample power of A. J. Foyt's backup car to pull smoothly away. Amid all the dodging and weaving, that left me a fairly clear path—until we reached Turn 1.

Someone at the back had jumped the start. He used his excess speed to pass in the Turn 1 entrance, then pulled sharply down in front of me and hit the brakes. My left foot was poised over my brake pedal, ready for just such an incident. Hard on the brakes, I missed him by inches, and braced myself for a hit from behind. Given the thicket of cars all around, it seemed certain that someone would nail me; but I got away free, and floored the throttle again.

That driver's move was about as aggressive as you could get. At best, it was inappropriate in the first turn of the first lap. It was just the sort of thing that Tom Binford had warned against. Not until I saw tapes of the race did I realize that the driver was my teammate Dick Simon. He wasn't picking on me; in subsequent years, Simon caught flak from most of the top drivers for dangerously aggressive conduct on the track.

It took three or four laps for things to sort themselves out. By then, just as I anticipated, I had dropped back a couple of places. Had I started closer to the front, I could have afforded to conduct myself in a more spirited fashion. The 500-mile races in NASCAR had taught me that up front you could run for it, and indeed I had done so. At the back, prudence was the word.

When the field was strung out, I started working my way forward. I passed John Mahler, an Iowan who'd done a good job of putting an uncompetitive car in the field with a banzai run at the last moment, and Eldon Rasmussen, a Canadian whose manners were as impeccable on the track as off. Just as I was setting up the next pass, disaster struck.

Many drivers would tell you that the first time they ever made the field for the Indianapolis 500, the race itself was like an anticlimax. On the fifteenth lap, my race became an anticlimax indeed. Snappings and cracklings from the engine—a partial loss of power—*what's wrong?* The gauges offered no clue. I went racing into the pits instead of the next turn.

"A misfire!" I yelled to Rolla as he bent over the cockpit. They tweaked the fuel system. In two minutes I was back on the track, but nothing had changed. Was it ignition failure? That was what they tried next. Twenty-four minutes later, I charged down pit road and my hopes rose: the engine sounded smooth. But when the turbocharger boost came up, at about 6,000 rpm, the misfire returned. *Poppity-pop-bang!* So it was back to the pits. Could it be the magneto? Unlikely, but...

"There's a race car in the garage," Rolla said to Pete, "and there's a whole ignition system on it. Go."

Meanwhile, I was soaked with fuel. The crew had filled the tanks as soon as I pitted, a normal move. But as the stop dragged on, the methanol expanded in the combined heat of the sun and the engine. It forced the overflow valve open, spilling fuel that drenched my back and pooled in the seat of the car. On the first of several long stops, I refused to get out of the car or even take my helmet off. I was holding the focus, staying ready to return to the track as soon as the job was done. The guys poured water down my back and into my lap, and it helped. On the second long stop, I climbed out, but the damage was done. Nothing would counter methanol's corrosive effects except soap and a change of clothes—driver's suit, Nomex long johns, everything. I wasn't going to leave the car for that length of time, when it might be ready at any moment. And I was so intent on returning to the fray that the discomfort was easy to ignore.

The third attempt at repair, when I roared back out toward the track, proved no more successful than the first. Despair and a growing sense of resignation mingled at the back of my mind.

Rolla Vollstedt said, "At your option, Jan, we'll pack it in."

"What does Phil Casey say?"

"There are a couple more things we could try."

"As long as you guys can think of something that might fix it, I'll keep checking it out." Not that I was enjoying the process; even a single lap out there in a malfunctioning car, while the rest of the field whizzed past, seemed to last an eternity.

While the crew worked on the Lightning, I watched Danny Ongais and his black Parnelli/Cosworth in my mirrors. They were suffering through a pit stop almost as interminable as my own. Finally, they pushed the Parnelli back to the garage. The other rookies had been dropping like flies. If the Lightning could be repaired, we might yet gain the rookie award, which traditionally went to the highest rookie finisher.

And meanwhile, I watched the track; watched the cars flying down into Turn 1, and burned with desire to be among them still.

Two hours into the race, we had checked out six attempts at repair. I could see on everyone's faces that they were out of ideas. As they changed the magneto cap and the spark plug wires, I said to Rolla, "If this doesn't do it, let's pack it in." It didn't, and we did.

It wasn't until long after, when the engine was torn apart, that the cause of our troubles came to light. Deep in the Offenhauser's lungs, a quarter-inch chunk near the stem of an intake valve had cracked, yielded, and disappeared. Rolla said that never in his years at Indianapolis had he seen a failure of that sort.

As we walked toward the garage, the crowd in the pitside grandstands stood to applaud. Somehow I mustered a smile and a wave. "Next year," I called back to them. "Next year."

The methanol was still eating its way through my epidermis. With my race now over, the discomfort got my undivided attention. There was just one shower in the entire infield: in the garage-area men's room, amid a long row of urinals. Earlier in the month I had responded to reporters' queries that no, I had no plans to integrate the men's room, it wasn't my style. Now, however, I could hardly wait.

Rolla devised a solution. The guys fetched huge sheets of aluminum from our garage, and hastily divided the room in two. Then they stood guard while I scrubbed the methanol away. By the time I was back in civilian clothes, the checkered flag was out.

A.J. Foyt won his fourth Indianapolis 500—the first driver in history to do so. Jerry Sneva, who finished tenth, was Rookie of the Year. Dick Simon fell out after twenty-four laps, and was classified in thirty-first place. I was twenty-ninth. Johnny Rutherford, the previous year's winner, had been the first to exit the race.

As the day wound down, I faced the inevitable press conference.

"What happened?"

"We still don't know." I talked about the symptoms, and the attempted cures.

"Aren't you frustrated?"

"After fifteen years in racing, you learn a certain degree of stoicism."

And so on, for quite a while. At the end someone asked, "Will you be back?"

"You betcha," I said.

I didn't know how very hard that was going to be. But quitting was inconceivable; the sport had long since become my passion and obsession. Although I favored the quaint notion that this was what I was born to do, there had been many twists in the road that brought me here.

PART II

FIRST CLASS ... In the 1970 Sebring 12-Hour International Manufacturers Championship race, we finished first in class. From left: Judy Kondratieff, me, Sharlene Seavey (who got to drive only in practice), Rosemary Smith.

GROWING UP

I grew up in Florida in the 1940s, south and west of Miami as the coastline falls west and south toward the island chain of Keys. The land around us was piney woods, flat and dry, but South Florida's true natural scenery towered overhead. Blinding-white peaks and purple canyons of cumulus clouds drifted through crystalline blue skies.

Most afternoons, fluffy flat-bottomed clouds formed a broken ceiling that stretched to the clear, flat horizon. And up above, beyond the puffy cloud tops, away out there, the blue! To go play in the blue, to bank into billowing cloud tops and pop out again ... I can smell the mist now, the scent of the clouds ... dreaming of playing in the insubstantial air, in the blue away out there beyond the pull of earth.

I was born, however, in Iowa. My grandparents were born in Iowa. Most of my great-grandparents were born in Iowa, their forebears having moved west with the frontier. Seven generations back, Lt. George Guthrie fought in the Battle of Yorktown that ended the Revolutionary War. Our family roots are Scottish and English, with some Austrian and a dash of German and Dutch. My family is about as Middle American as they come.

My father, born in 1912, was raised on the large Iowa farm that was homesteaded by his great-grandfather. A migratory buffalo run deeper than the height of a person passed through it. Ploughed fields often yielded Indian spearheads and arrow points. The farmhouse had neither electricity nor plumbing until after World War II; but its parlor held a piano and, more importantly, shelf after shelf of well-thumbed books.

My father was always drawn to the idea of flight, and experimented. Chickens that he tossed from the top of the windmill fluttered to the ground unharmed. Cats sent aloft on his kites were agitated by the ascent, but returned to earth astonishingly calm. These cats were the same hayloft mousers that stood eagerly on two legs to get the last rich strippings of milk he squirted to them directly from the cows.

My mother was born in 1913 and raised in Brazil, where her parents were Presbyterian missionaries. My grandfather's master's degree from Princeton Theological Seminary was signed by Woodrow Wilson in 1908. His doctorate came later. He and my grandmother built schools in Brazil that stand and serve to this day.

My mother was a winsome, adorable blonde child who grew into a tall and beautiful dark-haired young woman. At five-feet eight-inches, she acquired the hated nickname "Martinelli"—the tallest building (thirteen stories!) in São Paulo. It was a relief to her, however wrenching, to leave Brazil and her parents for Cornell College in Mount Vernon, Iowa, where she no longer towered above her peers.

My father also arrived in Mount Vernon to attend Cornell, unloading one of his father's cows from a trailer behind the family car. "The cow that went to college" was a family joke, but a practical one. At the height of the Depression, its milk helped defray my father's expenses, as well as his appetite.

Cornell, however, was no cow college. Founded in 1853, its first (two-person) graduating class was half female: Mary Fellows earned her baccalaureate in mathematics there in 1858. Cornell was also the first college in the United States to engage a woman as full professor with a salary equal to that of her male colleagues, in 1871. My mother enrolled in, and completed, its pre-med program, with a major in chemistry.

Jean Ruth Midkiff and William Lain Guthrie—always called Lain, his mother's family name—graduated from Cornell College in 1934, and were married in Seattle in 1935. When my mother came into a small inheritance from her mother, who died when Jean was nineteen, they spent it on flying lessons. By the time I was born, Dad was managing the municipal airport in Iowa City, Iowa, just across the river from the old state capitol building. He gave lessons, bought and sold airplanes which he ferried from as far away as Pennsylvania, and celebrated the birth of his first child, me, by flying loops outside the hospital windows. That was March 7, 1938.

By August of 1941, Dad was flying DC-3s for Eastern Air Lines. I had a baby brother, Stewart, born that April, and we lived in the steamy heat of Miami, Florida. For my fourth birthday the following spring, they gave me a bicycle. It tickled my father greatly that I learned to ride it—no training wheels—within two hours. I barely remember perching on the seat, Dad starting me off with a push, whisking away; but in the faded color pictures he took that day, my look is one of pure glee. Speed, independence, and machinery: the seeds of my passion were sown early, and fell on fertile ground.

A racing driver is always asked, "How did you get started?" My own answer is that I was born adventurous and grew up insufficiently socialized.

Within a year and a half, we moved out into southwestern Dade County, near the pioneer crossroads of Cutler. It was deep country back then, virgin piney woods for the most part. A determined kid could shinny up the pines, gripping the scratchy, flaky gray bark of the trunk between her knees, to where the branches began. There, the perpetual southeast ocean breeze blew more freely, making a soft soughing sound in the needle canopy.

At first, I played with the Saint-Gaudens girls. They were great-grandchildren of the sculptor Augustus Saint-Gaudens, carousing companion of architect Stanford White. Carlota and Penelope were a few years older than I, and when they set off on their bicycles, I had to pedal furiously to keep up. Possibly I followed them too far away and was forbidden to play with them, or perhaps they moved away; but after that there was no one close to my age for miles around.

My mother wrote letters to her father and stepmother in Brazil, and to Dad's parents in Iowa. May 28, 1944:

> Dear Folks,
> ... Lain would like to buy a few acres around here somewhere and start quarrying rock ... A swimming pool would occupy the hole. We have always wanted a stone house...

By July they had found their spot, on Mitchell Drive. Half of the ten acres was piney woods; the other half had been the original Mitchell family homestead. A ruinous little two-story pine house, almost half a century old, slumped within a neglected grove of mangoes, avocados, oranges, grapefruit, and limes.

The land was on a high point of the limestone ridge that runs for miles along Biscayne Bay, sometimes close to the water, sometimes a mile west. It was typical of my father's wide-ranging curiosity that he had learned this, and its implications. The ridge surfaced at the north end of the property they bought, and that was where my father planned their stone house.

It wasn't long before he had invented a quarrying system that cut the stone absolutely true, each surface parallel, in perfect rectangular blocks. The creamy stone was beautiful, full of the fossils of sand dollars and coral branches, permeated with little holes. Dad didn't think small. The trenches for the quarry were cut so that, when excavated, the hole that remained would become a swimming pool of exactly half-Olympic size.

Meanwhile, however, the little pine house was our home. Built around 1900 in Key West and brought to Miami on a barge, it lacked any vestige of plumbing, much less a telephone. My folks moved in nevertheless. In between wartime flights to Natal on the Brazilian coast of South America, Dad worked furiously to build a septic tank from scrap airplane cowlings, install a kitchen and bath, and otherwise make the place habitable. I was six, Stewart was three, my sister Margaret was nine months old, and my mother was four months pregnant with my sister Anne. When Dad was gone—a round trip to Natal took almost four days—Mom coped alone. The difficulty of it boggles the mind, but my mother's letters are amazingly matter-of-fact.

On August 17, 1944, she wrote,

Dear Folks,
We have been in our own house a whole week now. Things are still pretty much astir, books in boxes stacked in the living room...
A complicating factor is the leaky roof. There was a huge vine completely covering the roof and it rotted the shingles ... We will try to get shingles a little later, after the plumbing is in and our pocketbook catches up with us.

The Florida panther may be an endangered species now, but back then, we were the ones who felt endangered. One morning my mother found panther tracks outside the screen window of the room where we small children slept. Panther screams in the night were blood-curdling. What we really had to watch out for, though, were rattlesnakes and deadly coral snakes, both of which were common enough. In the bone-dry winters, wildfires that crackled through the woods were a serious threat. In summer, mosquitoes clustered so thickly and desperately on the screens, whining for blood, that one could barely see out.

My mother still lives on the land they bought more than half a century ago. The pine woods and palmettoes that once surrounded them have all but disappeared. Million-dollar houses with air conditioning and swimming pools sit amid fine landscaping on tidy green lawns. Threats no longer come from four-legged or legless creatures, but from the two-legged kind.

My parents might have put up with a leaking roof—for a while—

but we were never, ever poor. Poor was a concept that did not apply. Being short of money was not the same thing. My mother's version of the variable quote that goes back to Voltaire was, "You can do without the necessities—it's the luxuries that count!" Foremost among our luxuries were books. Always, there were books. My mother taught me to read at an early age.

For most of my childhood, our single biggest treat was a weekly trip to the public library in Coral Gables. Oh, the riches there! It occupied a rambling building of native stone, shaded partly by live oaks hung with Spanish moss. Even in the shocking heat and humidity of Miami's summers, the library always seemed cool. (Air conditioning was years away.) The very scent of the place was thrilling: mossy, stone-damp, saturated with the fragrance of thousands of books. Every week I checked out the maximum number of books—five, I think—devoured them, and came back next week for five more.

Mostly, I sought out adventure stories. These, of course, had heroes who were boys; but somehow that was no impediment to imagining myself in their place. I can't explain how that worked. It wasn't that I wanted to *be* a boy; my sense of gender has been clear as long as I can remember. The imagined liberty of action was what appealed. Best of all were flying stories, especially from the distant past.

Later, Antoine de Saint-Exupery's *Night Flight* became an icon. Tennyson's *Idylls of the King* could make me light-headed, almost faint. I still have my old copies of Scott's *Ivanhoe*, *Marmion*, *The Lady of the Lake*, and all the books in *The Three Musketeers* series. Richard Halliburton's *The Royal Road to Romance* seemed a plausible model for adventure. To swim by moonlight in the reflecting pool of the Taj Mahal ... ah!

Among the daily comic strips, I favored "Steve Canyon" and "Terry and the Pirates." "Brenda Starr" was good, too, though I knew I would never be as beautiful as its heroine. But there must be, I thought, some other way to attract a Mystery Man like hers.

Less than a month after moving into the Mitchell homestead, my parents enrolled me in Miss Harris' Florida School for Girls. The public schools had refused to accept me the previous year because, although I could read, I would not turn six until March. Miss Harris, white-haired, not *quite* intimidating enough to freeze me with fear, gave me a book to read; then another. She placed me in the second grade. I attended her school for all but one and a fraction of the next eleven years, mostly on scholarship (which Miss Harris and my parents kept completely secret). I graduated in 1955.

Julia Fillmore Harris had founded her school in 1914, when Miami and its beaches were little more than mosquito-infested sandbars. The campus as I knew it bordered Biscayne Bay, half a mile south of the Miami River and downtown Miami. Its plain frame classroom buildings were screened but had neither heat nor, of course, air conditioning. Palm trees and casuarinas lined the paths. There were tennis courts, playing fields, and a small swimming pool.

We wore uniform cotton dresses in solid pastel colors, with tucks and bands below the waist that made the most flat-bellied adolescent look four months pregnant. A fashionable designer was said to have created the style, and that was doubtless true—in the twenties, when those tucks and bands would have girdled the lower hips, with a bloused waist. Locked into a time-warp that extended from the Edwardian era into the 1920s, the school on Biscayne Bay was an enchanted place.

Having gotten me accepted at Miss Harris', my parents' next problem was how to get me there. It settled into this: I would walk or be driven to Chapman Field, a smallish wartime airfield that lay a scant mile east. An airport limousine shuttled the five miles to South Miami, where I caught a public bus downtown. My mother accompanied me the first time or two; after that, I was on my own.

One day after school, the airport limousine failed to appear at the South Miami bus stop. I suppose I was six. Presently, I set out to walk the five miles home, along the weedy edge of Red Road. (There was still no telephone at our house.) I had gotten about halfway when my parents found me, and while I was glad not to have to walk any farther, I remember being puzzled by their evident concern and relief. To me, it was nothing more than a simple problem with a simple if arduous solution.

For years, I came to school early, drawn to the water's edge. In the flat morning calm, Biscayne Bay lay lambent in opalescent blue-white and pink. The scattered clouds were edged in gold. My mind drifted through those colors out to the Atlantic and beyond—idyllic hours for Pisces, the dreamer, and I feel very lucky to have all that among my memories.

When my parents moved into the little house with no plumbing, they were already planning for a bulldozer and a trencher, the first steps in the quarrying process that would yield their big stone house. That house was to lie longer in the future than they thought. The first interruption came in the form of the hurricane of 1945.

My mother wrote, on September 21:

> Dear Folks,
> We have taken refuge at the Phillips' wine cellar ... The house is a wreck. The entire back room where the babies slept has vanished ... winds of 143 mph were clocked at a lighthouse a few miles away.

With World War II just over, building materials were not to be had. My parents had four children under the age of eight, the youngest just eight months old. Somehow, Dad obtained two Army surplus canvas tents. From the ruins of the pine house, he salvaged enough wood to make a floor and waist-high walls, and put the tents on top. So we "camped out" for more than eight months. We kids had no problem with this; what do kids know? My mother was clearly made of strong stuff.

After a while, as concrete and cement blocks started to come on the market, my father built a temporary house with the help of his older brother, Gerald. Uncle Jerry was just back from the war in Europe. I remember jokes and laughter, good humor in our household, which otherwise could be quiet if not somber. He and his wife Beryl, called Babe, and their small daughter lived with us for a while. My brother Walter was born, the last of the family, in March of 1949. I built model airplanes and crocheted dresses for my dolls and did the dinner dishes while standing on a box, enraptured by the wonderful deep voice of Brace Beemer as radio's Lone Ranger. Time went on.

My parents never went out to dinner with friends, never entertained. The only exceptions were relatives. My mother's older brother Carl had become a physician, and he and his family lived in an elegant suburb north of Miami. Aunt Florence was as much a social creature as my mother was not.

My mother was solitary by choice rather than necessity, even though the care of five children was certainly preoccupation enough. She was beautiful, well-read, with a clear and thoughtful intelligence; but the strongest element in her personality was reticence. Nevertheless, people were always drawn to her. She easily attracted friends, whom she tended to hold at arm's length.

When they first arrived in Miami, a socially prominent woman took her up. My mother was told that she "could do anything she wanted" in Miami society. But my mother wanted none of it. So while my aunt and uncle joined the country club and the fashionable, exclusive Bath Club, my mother grew exotic tropical fruits, shot the fox that was after her chickens, chopped the heads off rattlesnakes with a hoe. And read. Books in Portuguese and in English were always at hand.

My mother once remarked about my father that, while life with him could be difficult, she had never been bored. My father was inventive, restless, insatiable for learning—about how things worked, about language. A dictionary was always within reach of our dinner table, and rare was the dinner when it wasn't opened. Roots and derivations of words charmed him. He loved reference works, his favorite being the ten-volume *Century Dictionary* and *Cyclopedia* published in 1902. These awesome books have often answered questions for me when all others failed. Like many pilots, he wasn't much of a tourist; but he was familiar with all the second-hand bookstores in each city where Eastern flew.

He was critical, of the world at large, of his offspring, and most of all, of himself. Sometimes jovial but more often sardonic, he was highly intelligent and valued intelligence highly. He was often far ahead of his time. He began his war on air pollution in the 1960s, writing a dictionary of his own. Smokestacks were "long acid- and fume-resistant tubes vertically placed for dumping wastes into the air," wind was "air in motion that moves waste material from one place to all other places, causing identity and ownership disputes." Also, "there is no right to dump." He had much more to say about air pollution, and environmentalists are only now catching up with him.

He was born nine years after the Wright brothers first flew. When men walked on the moon, he was a senior captain on stretch DC-8 jets. He celebrated his seventy-second birthday by taking hang-gliding lessons at Grandfather Mountain in North Carolina. When winter brought black turkey buzzards to south Florida, he never failed to admire their skill at soaring. He would watch them and say, boy, they really know how to do it.

After the 1945 hurricane, when we lived in the wine cellar, I remember a day when I became aware of the extraordinary aroma my father brought home from a flying trip. It was a compound of great complexity. The top note was cigarette smoke, mixed with the way airplanes smelled in those days, of solvents and lubricants and paints for aluminum; electrical apparatus, wiring insulation ... planes don't smell like that any more. But there was more to the blend. The basic familiar smell of my father was overlaid with an acrid essence of power, the residue of some elemental struggle. (Perhaps the weather had been violent that day, or an engine had quit.) Fear wasn't part of the smell, nor was there anything stale about it. He had won the cryptic combat—there he stood, after all, in his midnight-blue uniform with gold-embroidered wings and four gold captain's stripes on the sleeves—but it had left powerful traces.

I seem to see myself looking up at him—I must have been seven— and wondering what that smell was all about. It was as mysterious to me as the contents of paperback thrillers that the wine cellar's owners kept in its upper story. I could read and understand the words, but the scenes and actions described were utterly incomprehensible.

At the end of 1950, my mother was diagnosed with tuberculosis. Modern drugs were barely on the horizon. By February, she was isolated at a sanitarium in Lantana, seventy-five miles north. When she left Miami, she had good reason to fear that she might never come back—a fear which she was able to conceal from her children.

For a while, my father's parents stayed with us; but as spring planting season approached, they returned to Iowa. After that, I stayed home from eighth grade on the days when Dad was away on trips. I was going on thirteen, and accustomed to cooking and baking and sewing and taking responsibility for my younger brothers and sisters; but the shift in authority-figure was a different matter. Stewart was almost ten, and not much inclined to do as I said. Margaret was seven, Anne was six, and Walter was barely two, still in diapers. We coped, but it wasn't smooth or easy.

Worse, I was on the verge of surly and slothful adolescence. By the time my mother was back from the sanitarium three and a half months later—still confined to bed full-time—I was, I fear, something less than a joy to be around. A couple of genteel part-time housekeepers came and went, though I usually did much of the cleaning and cooking, and boiled my mother's dishes. It was more than a year before she was permitted to be on her feet at all. They were trying times.

By the summer of 1951, I was chafing at my family's isolated way of life, far from the mainstream. I longed to be normal, to fit in. I asked to go to public school, and did, entering Coral Gables High in ninth grade that fall. But it was too late. My character had already been shaped. The notion of trying out for the cheerleading squad was repugnant (a feeling that at least I knew enough not to share). No matter how I tried, I did not, could not, fit in. I didn't have a clue. In addition, the classes were a dreadful bore, and I learned almost nothing. A year later, I fled back to the school on Biscayne Bay.

The summer that I was fifteen, my parents rented a wonderful big haunted house on Saint-Gaudens Road in Coconut Grove. A two-story Italianate villa that predated the Depression, it belonged to an elderly bachelor who spent Miami's unbearable summers elsewhere. The rent was $125 a month, gardener included.

The house looked toward Biscayne Bay across a neglected grassy terrace. Beyond the terrace, mangrove trees gnawed at the low-lying bayfront. Long ago, a boat channel had been dredged from the bay up to the house, but the channel was silted up, and mangrove roots arched toward each other from either side. The mangroves were thick with mosquitoes and reeked of saltwater decay. Little crabs left delicate lacy tracks in the mud at low tide. I thought the whole place was marvelous beyond belief.

We didn't know the house was haunted when we moved in. But the summer was full of thumps and bumps in the night, my youngest sister sobbing in terror. My mother, still recovering from TB, had a housekeeper who lived many miles away. After spending a single night with us, cowering in her room with the door locked and the windows shut tight in the summer heat, this woman refused ever to spend the night again.

I woke one night with an iron grasp around one wrist—a hand that would not let go. I screamed. I was not a person who ever screamed. Then I found that one of my own hands was grasping my wrist, and had lost its circulation. But no such thing had ever happened before, or since.

It wasn't until after we left the house that we learned of the multiple axe murder there, years before.

But it wasn't any fear of ghosts that concerned me in that summer of '53. My father had bought a Flying Fish, a fixed-mast sailing surfboard, and I quickly discovered that I was afraid of it—afraid of being on the surface of the water. It was puzzling: I loved to swim, loved to swim under water with the recently popular face mask; swam like a fish. Being *on* the water was something else. On the water, I felt a sense of menace and hostility. I still don't understand why.

From reading books, I knew what the cure was for fear. You must immerse yourself in the thing that was feared. One morning I dragged the Flying Fish to the channel and poled it out to the bay. The craft was perhaps three yards long and a yard wide, with a freeboard of three inches. It was flat on top except for short wooden rails at the midsection of each edge, which dipped into the water on alternate tacks.

I dropped the daggerboard, caught the wind, and sailed seven miles southeast across open water to the Cape Florida lighthouse. I was terrified all the way over. I was terrified all the way back. And the worst part was, it didn't do a bit of good. The failure of my cure (not that I ever mentioned it to a living soul) nagged at me for a long time. To put the best possible face on it, I had learned something. I was unlikely ever to make a happy sailor of myself.

My heart was actually not at sea, but in the sky; had been for years. Miami's sky was amazingly beautiful back then, crystalline, without even a trace of today's yellowish pollution, so that its blueness went all the way to the horizon. Towering cumulus clouds formed on most afternoons, brilliant white, bright enough to hurt one's eyes. They billowed up to unimaginable heights. I longed to go play in the clouds. From books, I knew what that would be like.

I had been a passenger in small planes often enough. Flying was part of my life since before I could remember. I was just a few weeks old when my mother carried me on her lap in a two-place Aeronca from Iowa City to my grandparents' farm near Bloomfield. Later, I sometimes handled the controls. Now, I begged for flying lessons. The first entry in my pilot's logbook dates from that same summer of '53: twenty minutes of dual instruction in a Piper J-3 Cub. My father signed it, with his pilot's license number.

Over the next year or so, six hours of flying time went into the logbook. The scenario remained the same: I would beg to go flying, my father would instruct, I'd do things wrong, he'd yell angrily, I'd cry. When I got over it, I would beg to go flying again. It was a huge relief when he turned me over to a pilot whose flight instruction certificate was current. I soloed when I was still sixteen, with eight hours and fifteen minutes of time logged over the better part of two years. Flying was the first great passion of my life.

My lust to make a parachute jump sprang fully formed from the pages of Charles Lindbergh's *The Spirit of St. Louis*, in 1954. The way Lindbergh wrote about flying went through my skin like that chemical, DMSO, carrying his experiences into my nerves and bones. He was twenty, and hadn't yet soloed a plane, when he saw a parachute maker's demonstration. Lindbergh wrote,

"... when I decided that I too must pass through the experience of a parachute jump, life rose to a higher level, to a sort of exhilarated calmness." And, "What gain was there for such a risk? ... It was the quality that led me into aviation in the first place ... It was a love of the air and sky and flying, the lure of adventure, the appreciation of beauty..."

Afterwards, his conclusion: "Science, freedom, beauty, adventure: what more could you ask of life?"

There are worse professions of faith for an adolescent to stumble upon.

I proposed the idea to my father. "I made a parachute jump once," he said thoughtfully. I hadn't known that. He resisted my idea, naturally enough, but I nagged him throughout the summer. Then he chanced upon a retired pro, a man who had parachutes and might teach me how to use them. Dad had a condition, though: he would only let me jump if he himself flew the plane. The sport of sky diving was as yet unknown, at least in South Florida. There were no schools, no specially equipped planes from which you could leap with a static line attached, so that your parachute opened automatically.

The parachutist had been a "bat man" in air shows—in the thirties? the twenties? He wore a suit with bat-like wings; leaped out, soared and swooped, then opened his parachute at the last minute. As he dragged his gear from a closet, I understood he suspected that this had been my father's idea; and I understood, as he spoke in a grave way, looking at me, that he would do his best to scare me out of it. But it wasn't my father's idea.

I was taller than the parachutist, over five eight, maybe five nine already. Doubtless he didn't realize that I was just sixteen.

He ran through a litany of disasters, what could go wrong. He brandished a long scar on his arm. He sang gruesome verses to the tune of *Battle Hymn of the Republic*. "There was blood upon the risers, there were guts upon the boots," with a chorus of "Gory, gory, what a helluva way to die." I took it in, it registered. It didn't affect my desire to do this thing.

He showed me how to don the parachute and its reserve. "I want you to pull the rip cord," he said, "so you know how it feels."

I pulled on the shiny D-shaped piece of steel at the center of my chest. Nothing happened. Finally, I yanked hard enough. The parachute, white, silky, flimsy-seeming, as light and susceptible to the air as wisps of dust, spilled out onto the living room floor.

The parachutist—his name was Sekman—said, "Be sure to bring me back the rip cord. Otherwise I'll have to buy a new one." But I already knew, I had read about it, that preserving the rip cord was supposed to be the big test of the jumper's presence of mind.

He showed me how to fasten the helmet he was lending me, doubling the end of its strap back through the outer ring so that one quick tug would free it.

"When you land," he said, "it's about the same as if you jumped off a twelve-foot wall. Here's how you absorb the shock." I followed his example, rolling about on the floor.

In that autumn of 1954, my parents were at long last building their big stone house on the property they bought ten years before. We lived in a rented house nearby, where I put a ladder against the eaves and started practicing: first, from a few rungs up, then higher and higher. Eventually, I could jump off the roof.

It was November before there was calm air on a day when my father was at home. We rented a yellow Piper J-3 Cub, N70372. My pilot's log book registered an hour and a half of dual in that particular airplane. I put the parachute into the back seat, climbed in, fastened the harness with scrupulous care. My father double-checked it.

The top half of the Cub's door swung up and fastened to the underside of the wing, the bottom half folded down. I always liked to fly with the doors open, especially on takeoff. You could see the ground rushing by, the blades of grass blurring as speed increased, and then the magic moment of liftoff, the earth falling away, the chubby little black wheel slowly revolving to a stop. In a moment you were above the treetops, and the wide world came into view.

We turned our backs on the shimmering pastel towers of Miami and headed south toward the tomato fields, a ploughed expanse without houses, cars, or deadly webs of utility wires. The beat of my heart was loud in my ears. Adrenaline chilled my fingers, ran its icy feathers up the back of my neck.

I had read about all this. I had read about being "paralyzed with fear." Just *how* adventurous would I prove to be? Quite objectively, I wondered: that D-ring, the rip cord, had taken a fair amount of

JANET GUTHRIE: A LIFE AT FULL THROTTLE

strength to pull, in the parachutist's living room. Would fear sap my strength, so that I couldn't get it out, couldn't release the chute?

My father yelled above the engine's noise, "Don't bother counting to ten before you pull the rip cord. I'll kick the tail of the plane out of the way."

The altimeter needle crawled up past 3,000 feet. I swung my feet out the door, into the force of the airstream, and braced them on the rear strut and the little step. With hands and feet, I would push as hard as possible away from the dangerous surfaces of the plane. My father throttled back, pulled the nose up to drop the airspeed, nodded. I jumped.

If the rip cord offered any resistance, I never knew about it. I must have had the strength of a gorilla.

A few heartbeats later, the canopy filled, the harness yanked me to a stop. I swung back and forth, with nothing under my feet but flights of birds.

The silence was the greatest surprise. The fields below smelled moist and fresh. The world was beautiful, this view of it as rare and beautiful as diamonds, emeralds, aquamarines.

I still had the rip cord in my hand.

The summer that I was seventeen, fresh out of Miss Harris' School, I earned my private pilot's license at a little grass airstrip where I had gotten a summer job to pay for flying time. In the clarity of that Florida sky, flying was like a child's dream. Cloud shadows on the Everglades were as dark and sharp-edged as lakes, the color of a blue-black bruise. Endlessly flat, the earth slid off to a horizon so crisp and clear that the flat underside of the cumulus never seemed to meet it, but passed over the edge of the earth like the parallel edges of a colossal clamshell, slightly ajar.

One of the pilots who frequented the airstrip was as close to a knight on a white charger as the mid-twentieth century could supply. His silvery open-cockpit Ryan low-wing monoplane came straight out of the romantic age of flight. He was blond, funny, handsome, with chiseled Germanic features. His name was Nick.

Somehow, I caught his attention. He must have asked questions. He knew that I would enter the College of Engineering at the University of Michigan that fall. He was a junior in civil engineering at the University of Miami. I was working on my private license; he sometimes rented the same Piper J-3 Cubs that I flew.

It began as a bragging contest, like the song in "Annie Get Your

Gun:" "Anything you can do, I can do better..." I don't even remember who started it.

"I'll bet I can take a J-3 higher than you can!"

"I'll bet you can't!"

Mary Tracy Gaffaney, my instructor, held the bets. (She later became America's first World Aerobatic Champion, and a legend in South Florida aviation.) We would each fly the same plane, in the same kind of weather.

On August 2, I hung at 15,000 feet for perhaps five minutes. The altimeter needle no longer moved. This was it, the ceiling. I added carburetor heat, cut the throttle, pulled the plane's nose up into a stall, kicked left rudder and spun lazily down to warmer air. Nick went the next day.

Mary opened the sealed envelopes we each had given her. I had beaten Nick by 2,500 feet.

"When I got to twelve five," he said, "I just thought, she wouldn't have gone any higher than this!"

I knew, I had read about it, that you weren't supposed to beat a man at any game. But five minutes later, he caught up with me.

"Would you like to go to dinner?" he asked. I thought my heart would stop beating. "My brother Blackwell and his friend Barbara are having dinner on Key Biscayne on Saturday, and I thought it would be fun if we joined them."

Never in my life had I been invited out on an actual date. Now it had happened—after I broke all the rules.

During the fall semester, we wrote each other letters, which he signed, "Love, Nick." I signed mine likewise, full of passionate yearning. We spent that New Year's Eve at the Bath Club, the exclusive private club on the ocean that my parents didn't belong to, though my aunt and uncle did. It was black tie, of course. His patent-leather dancing slippers had grosgrain bows. My ballgown swept to the floor, shaped by hoops and ruffles. Palm fronds rattled in the breeze. If there wasn't a moon over the ocean, there should have been. We waltzed through midnight and when I looked around, no mice or pumpkins were anywhere to be seen.

It lasted only a year, and left me broken-hearted. Probably, he was wise. Our attraction to each other was fierce, and neither of us had marriage to anyone in mind—not yet. But this first romantic interlude also left me with an enduring legacy, a lesson. Attractive men existed to whom my mind and my sense of adventure might appeal. No matter what the contemporary culture said, I needn't suppress my true nature in order to hope for love.

I had picked the University of Michigan out of a book, for its excellence in aeronautical engineering. It seemed the most promising way to make a living in a field I loved. Flying was not an option: the airlines didn't hire women, the military didn't let women fly, and other venues paid little or nothing. But after a year of mixing up batches of concrete and drawing pictures of the threads on screws, I transferred out of engineering into a major in physics. This was a far better fit. Physics offered adventures of the mind. "On First Looking into Chapman's Homer" had nothing over the first occasion of deriving Maxwell's equations for the propagation of electromagnetic energy. The elegance, the inevitability!

Outside of classes, Michigan was largely a disaster for me. The Dean of Women, while I was there, delivered herself of the opinion that any female undergraduate who wasn't smart enough to realize that she was there to catch a husband, wasn't smart enough to be at Michigan in the first place. My experience with sorority rush was captured by Groucho Marx: any sorority that would have me, I wouldn't want to be a member of. As a freshman, I met up with Louise Bogan's poem *Women*:

> *Women have no wilderness in them*
> *They are provident instead*
> *Content in the tight hot cell of their hearts*
> *To eat dusty bread.*

Equally horrifying were Daisy's words in *The Great Gatsby*, when she learned that her baby was a girl: "I hope she'll be a fool—that's the best thing a girl can be in this world, a beautiful little fool."

None of this was a good fit at all.

At the end of my sophomore year, I took a year off: earned my commercial pilot's license and flight instructor's rating, flew, and spent two months hitchhiking around Europe. Then I went back to school, graduating in June of 1960. Among all the job offers, the clear choice was Republic Aviation in Farmingdale, Long Island, New York. After decades of building legendary fighter planes, Republic was opening a new facility for aerospace projects. It was the most exciting possible frontier for a fresh new graduate, and New York City lay within easy reach. My job title would be Research and Development Engineer.

THAT FIRST FINE
CARELESS RAPTURE

The frontier of aerospace had drawn me to Republic Aviation, but my engineering job there was tied to the ground. When Republic's fighter planes shook the windows of the research and development center where I worked, I could only yearn for the physical challenge of flight.

One fine balmy evening late that summer of 1960, I found my way to a grass airfield far out the eastern end of Long Island. I was still driving the ratty 1947 Plymouth coupe that had been my father's airport car, given to me for my senior year at Michigan. It was almost dark when I parked next to an AT-6, the big two-place low-wing advanced trainer familiar to thousands of World War II pilots. An AT-6 was fully aerobatic. The owner of this plane had offered me a half share in it for $650.

It was silvery, muscular, beautiful. I walked around it in the dusk. The little airfield was silent, except for an imaginary roar from the AT-6's engine. Bugs hopped in the fragrant grass. I thought of outside loops and snap rolls. I thought of Long Island's heavy air traffic, both commercial and military, and its proliferation of heavily-regulated air traffic control zones. I drove away, pondering.

Not long after that, I spotted a tiny classified ad in *The New York Times*: "1953 Jaguar XK 120 M coupe, $1200..." with a Manhattan phone number. That evening after work, a sparkling fretwork of night lights laced the early autumn dusk as I threaded my way along the parkways and into the glittering city to see the car.

I had driven a Jaguar just once. The year must have been 1954; the owner was a family friend. Cars and driving meant only one thing to me back then: access to the rest of the world, a means to an end. For the pursuit of adventure, airplanes had it all over cars.

So when the dark green Jaguar XK 120 purred into our driveway that day, I had no visions of silver trophies at Watkins Glen and Sebring, no daydreams of Indy cars that lapped three times as fast as the airplanes I then flew. I hung back a little as my parents went out to greet their guest. What I saw was one of the most powerful, most elegant, sleekest, lowest, raciest sports cars ever designed, a car that even today turns heads. In 1954, it was a sensation.

The open roadster stood less than half the height of our family DeSoto, and its long curling lines had the fluid grace of meshed whorls on an Attic vase. The Florida sun drew a heady aroma from its sumptuous leather-bound cockpit and bucket seats, backed by a base note of hot fresh oil. Even at rest, the Jaguar fairly quivered with power.

"Would you like to drive it?" the owner asked. Silly question. The solid chunk of the gearbox and sweet deep sound of the XK engine went straight to the center of my nervous system. The thing was far more a work of art than a car, and it was a revelation.

The day passed, the friend and his Jaguar vanished, and for the next six years I pursued my aviation fantasies until many of them came true. But in September of 1960, I made a choice that proved to be a watershed in my life, a Continental Divide, of greater import than I ever could have dreamed. The gray Jaguar coupe was irresistible.

Thus with my wonderful new salary of $125 a week and my usual sense of moderation, I leaped from airplanes to sports cars. I had minimal savings, and supplemented the bank's auto loan with high-priced funds from a finance company; but there was the Jaguar, mine. I drove the '47 Plymouth to one of Long Island's huge junkyards, where they gave me eight whole dollars for it.

I was living in a minuscule studio apartment in Northport, a charming harbor town on the North Shore of Long Island about forty miles from Manhattan, and that winter I ranged as far as the Jaguar's mechanical peccadilloes would allow. The New York Philharmonic under Leonard Bernstein was doing a season at the Academy of Music in Brooklyn, and many nights I drove there. Afterwards, full of music, the Jaguar and I purred back along the Interboro Parkway that crested Long Island's terminal glacial moraine. Black winter-barren branches framed glimpses of the sea of lights that was Brooklyn, once the sea floor.

In the spring, I found out about gymkhanas.

The word derived from an Anglo-Indian trial of skill on horseback and was pronounced jim-ka'-na. In an extensive parking lot, rubber pylons delineated an intricate sports car course. One car at a time, each competitor went through as fast as he or she could; and the fastest car won. There were penalties for moving a pylon. Risk to the driver was practically non-existent, top speeds rarely approaching fifty, but gymkhanas were exciting contests nevertheless.

I sat in the Jaguar one Sunday morning and watched a gymkhana in progress, thinking, *I can do this. I want to do this.* The entry fee was modest, the strain on the car not great. *(What did I know then of blown engines and crumpled fenders, of scored crankshafts and fractured axles, of repairs still not finished at four in the weary morning, of the grime that sinks into your cuticles and your fingerprints and won't be scrubbed off but remains until the skin grows out...)* The participants were mostly my age.

By summertime I was a regular competitor, with enough success in hand to whet my appetite for the next step: a speed event, a hill climb. Hill climbs have nearly vanished now (except for Pikes Peak), prey to safety and insurance concerns, but in the 1950s and 1960s they were classic sports car events. The Ellenville hill climb in the Catskills was to take place in mid-June. I went.

The path of competition zigzagged up one side of a valley that lay between two long parallel folds of the Shawangunk Mountains. I camped in a meadow at the top with a few other budget-minded entrants. Soon a heavy rain chased me and my sleeping bag inside the car, where it was hot and cramped and the mosquitoes had a midnight picnic. By dawn, I was the only one left in the meadow.

Many years later, when the twists and turns of the hill climb route had been bypassed by a straighter, wider road, I found my way back to the old course. Tall grass rose through cracks in the asphalt, and little trees sprouted where our brightly colored sports cars had leaped and clawed up the mountain toward ... what? An engraved silver bowl, a best time in class? No, it wasn't the award that was the objective but the moment itself, in its setting: the still summer heat, the katydids, the long line of cars on the road edges waiting their turn, the faint snarls and screeches drifting down through the trees as, one by one, a hundred drivers threw themselves against the mountain, writhing up almost two miles toward the finish line.

Gymkhanas might have been riskless, but hill climbs weren't. Just before my first run up that mountainside, a Corvette driver had gone over the edge and upside down into the trees. An ambulance took him away, hurt but alive.

I had studied the line cars took through the different corners, how each was affected by steepness and banking as well as radius. Then I put the Jaguar into the queue of cars waiting to run. As we crept forward, I made mental pictures of the sequence of turns, trying not to be scared. Eventually, I would learn to make fear into an intimate servant, to use it, to send it away when there was no job for it to do. The learning process began at the Ellenville hillclimb.

The starter turned toward me, raised the green flag. The rpm's were steady at 3800, first gear engaged.

Go.

I rushed toward the first turn. The road was crowned but a straight shot toward the outside of Turn 1 kept you off that elevation, a foot of energy loss that you didn't need to give away. The old pavement was rough, the Jaguar notoriously heavy on the wheel. You had to know when to fight it and when to give it its head, let it go where it wanted for a fraction of an instant before reining it in again.

Briefly up into third gear, then back to second for the turn. Left, and up. My helmet bounced on the window frame. The back end of the car came around, squealing faintly as I squeezed on the power. I let the steering wheel spin almost free under my hands as the front wheels straightened out, then seized and stopped the wheel when the car's long nose pointed up where I wanted to go. The road bent slightly to the right. Six turns to go.

A fast left-hander, then the finish line. Done. Abruptly, the practice run was over. Abruptly, the mindset changed: from "do whatever it takes" to "easy, easy now, quietly find a parking spot in the meadow here." In the back of my mind, I perceived a state of being that was new and unimagined: a strange sort of detached self-control. With equal dispassion and objectivity, I noted the condition of the brakes and the violence of my heartbeat.

I had never read about anything like this.

Sunday was bright and sunny, my wild sense of anticipation delicious. My Saturday time had been faster than all the other Jaguars, and I felt certain of improvement with more knowledge of the course.

Wrong. The excitement of previous success got into my head and affected my judgment.

There was a right-hand turn near the top that looked simple; you could see the whole thing as you approached it, as well as the road beyond. Hay bales that buffered the stone wall on the left had already been smashed by other competitors. You could even see the water that ran across the turn, draining Saturday's rains. I knew about the water, but when I reached it, I screwed up. The back end of the Jag slithered out toward the wall. I caught it, but ran out of room.

Thud! The left rear of the Jag hit a dirt embankment just beyond the stone wall and hay bales. The instant elongated itself, filling enormous quantities of space and time. The engine complained, the wheels scrabbled on dirt, but the car still moved up the hill.

Do whatever it takes.

Up the steep section, building speed, around the corner for more level ground, now very fast over the bad bump and through the little corner. Up the finishing straight, under the banner—that's it. Now slow, slow ... what's this noise at the back of the car?

My fingers were none too steady as I undid the helmet. Other competitors, alerted by the radio phones, had come around to look. Someone got a jack handle and used it to pry the fender out. I stood and watched, feeling almost as if it were a wound to myself. There were the sleek lines of my car, the masking-tape number on the side, and the damage that I had wrought. It felt awful. I moved the car to the meadow, and noticed a tender spot on my arm—must have hit the door or window handle. A remembered echo of the impact drew my eye to the fine wood trim at the top of the door, where a smudge of white paint matched a small wood stain on my white helmet.

Over that summer, I began dating another sports car competitor. He was tall and lean, with curly sun-bleached hair and broad shoulders. He drove an MG-TD. One weekend in July, after a gymkhana on Long Island, we wandered together from one party to another in the summer afternoon. The sun descended into the haze, and the day grew cool.

Jaguar and MG, we chased each other through beachside communities toward the house of still more friends, and there, in the most mundane setting, I found with a faint unexpected sense of wonder that I had fallen in love. Walls crumbled, windows opened. The world became a different place from the world that I had known. I felt connected not just to him but to the others there as well, as if the transparent barrier that separated me from other people had melted; as if I had just joined the human race.

Our affair ended before the summer did, though as they say, first love is indelible. It was many years before I succeeded in banishing him from most of my dreams. Slowly, that invisible barrier went back into place.

By the following spring, my Jaguar had become one of the cars to beat in gymkhanas, and was widely rumored to have an illegal supercharger. Surely, they said, a *girrul* in a coupe couldn't be winning all these events without some sort of unfair advantage. Of course, I had no such device, and the rumor delighted me; I took it as a compliment. Then clutch problems laid the Jaguar up. I bought a leprous 1949 Oldsmobile for $25, and struggled nightly with the impenetrable British in which the Jaguar's shop manual was written.

Slowly the Jaguar came apart, in the garage of a house I'd moved into in Amityville: seats out, floorboards removed, Liquid Wrench applied by the canful to free up seized, rusty bolts and captive nuts. When I started, I didn't even know that Liquid Wrench existed.

By now I was an officer of the South Shore Sports Car Club, and several members volunteered the use of their cars at gymkhanas while the Jag was out of commission. Their generosity was often ungraciously repaid. ("New game," said the club newsletter, "lend Janet your car and let her beat your time in it.") For the Ellenville hill climb, a member lent me his Austin Healey 3000. The Healey was different from the Jag, and it wasn't mine. I made certain that I had it under control.

My second run up the hill was halted at Turn 1 by the worst accident in the history of the Ellenville hill climb. Up at Turn 7, a yellow Triumph TR-3 had gone off the road and into the trees. Scant information trickled over the phones: the guy is trapped in his car, he's bleeding profusely, get a cutting torch! Where's the doctor? It seemed aeons before an ambulance roared down the mountain and out toward town.

It was nearly a week before we learned that the driver would survive.

When the competition resumed, my time was neither faster nor slower than before. As I packed the Austin Healey with its tools and spares, a slight, gray-haired stranger came along, stopped, watched.

"You did very well," he said to me quietly. "I watched you all weekend, each time from a different place. Years ago, I raced on factory teams in Europe ... you have good style, a classic style." He moved on; I never learned his name.

On the long moonlit drive home, I thought of his words; and thought also of something else I had learned that weekend. In spite of the bloody crash, it had never occurred to me not to continue. I had processed the news like a computer. Its sole effect on me was a slightly more cautious regard for Turn 7. Concern for the injured driver was stored too, surfacing only when the competition was over. It seemed an inhuman sort of reaction.

Later I would recognize this as part of the characteristic makeup of a racing driver; but to confront it for the first time in myself was unsettling.

The possibility of road racing was already in my mind. The previous year I had seen my first sports car competition on a road racing circuit, at Lime Rock, Connecticut. Like a lot of Americans, I had thought of auto racing only in terms of the annual spectacle at Indianapolis. Lime Rock was different—entirely different.

Tucked away in a beautiful rural corner of northwest Connecticut, the circuit wound for a mile and a half around a hill and down the side of a stream, turning both left and right in the process. The paddock held brightly-colored sports cars much like those entered at gymkhanas and hill climbs, with a sprinkling of fenderless single-seaters and other cars built especially for competition. They all raced together on the track, which made this a giant step up from running one car at a time against the clock. Here there was fender-to-fender competition, driver against driver. Speeds rose well over 100 mph. It was a whole new world.

By autumn I was negotiating to purchase a race-prepared 1956 Jaguar XK 140 MC roadster that met the specifications set by the Sports Car Club of America. SCCA was the preeminent, internationally recognized sanctioning body for closed-circuit road racing events in the United States. SCCA competition was major-league stuff back then; *The New York Times* sent reporters to SCCA National Championship events. In order to compete in SCCA races, one had to be a member; and in order to become a member, one had to be recommended by two others. The club was made up primarily of wealthy men, but even for the wealthy, membership in the SCCA didn't come easily. Years later, Le Mans driver Bob Grossman told me how big an issue it had been in the 1950s for SCCA to admit him, because he was Jewish.

Fortunately, being a woman *wasn't* an issue. Denise McCluggage, Evelyn Mull, and a good number of other American women had been racing sports cars throughout the fifties. Internationally, road racing (unlike American oval-track racing) had a history of participation by women that stretched back to the turn of the century.

It is fair to say that I had nothing resembling a feminist consciousness at the time I started racing. Like so many young women, I was blissfully insensitive to sexual bigotry. I simply declined to identify with the women about whose driving men made jokes; *they weren't talking about me*, I thought.

I had a lot to learn.

Throughout 1962, I kept my feelers out for access to SCCA membership, and by the end of the year it was done.

PASSIONATE AMATEUR

On the last day of February, 1963, three of us who had cut our teeth on gymkhanas and hill climbs set out from our homes on Long Island for the Sports Car Club of America competition drivers' school at Marlboro, Maryland. Dick Mooney had an MGA, Bob Aymar a Volvo, and I had my "new" Jaguar, a light blue 1956 XK 140 MC roadster.

Today, a would-be racer can simply bring a large check to one of many professional racing schools, which will supply all that is required: car, helmet, and the rest. Back then, the commitment was personal and substantial. A fresh loan from the bank had financed my XK 140, which (unknown to the bank) was race-ready. The three-day school on Marlboro's winding sports car track culminated in actual races. If we were successful, we would become licensed SCCA novice race drivers.

Our race cars were hitched to large, elderly American sedans. Mine was the $25 Oldsmobile, on which I had painstakingly installed a bumper hitch worth somewhat more than the car. It had been tough to find enough metal, in between the rust, to bolt it to.

The night before departure, I wrestled with the Jaguar's brakes, laboriously following the shop manual's instructions for replacing the shoes. That is a hard and filthy job at best, one I had never done before, and I still didn't have much mechanical experience. A friend from work who stopped by early in the evening said, "You realize you're going to be staking your life on those things?" I did, and I was careful.

It was late when the three of us assembled on Long Island's North Shore. Evening rush hour was under way. We rattled through the pockmarked, cobbled streets of Manhattan at dusk; and the brilliant city overhead did not soar higher than our sense of great adventure. We were off to slay giants, though the word windmills might have occurred to some. Pressing against the desolate nighttime, we reached a dowdy motel near Marlboro at two in the morning.

Six hours later, we lined up at the race course entrance for registration and tech inspection: roll bars, fire extinguishers, and so on. A few unfortunates were turned away, their equipment deemed inadequate. The surviving candidates gathered in a corner of the grandstand bleacher seats for review of the General Competition Regulations.

A full set of brightly colored signal flags stood next to the chief instructor. Each flag had a meaning, which we already knew by heart. A green flag would start the race or signal the end of a yellow-flag situation. A yellow flag meant an incident ahead, or debris on the track: slow down, no passing until you reached the next flag station. A waving yellow, the same, but worse: be prepared to stop. Red: disaster, all stop. Blue: a faster car is trying to pass you. Yellow with red stripes: slippery conditions, oil or gravel on the track. White: emergency vehicle on the track—a wrecker, an ambulance. Black with an orange circle: the meatball, something is mechanically wrong with your car, report to your pit. Black: you've done something offensive, transgressed the rules of competition; report to the chief steward. And of course, the black and white checkered flag: the end of the race.

Next came a blackboard introduction to the layout of the course. Each turn (called a "corner" in sports car racing) had its own proper line, from the entrance at the outside edge of the track to the center point of the corner at the inside, called the apex, and on to the exit point.

We walked the course with the instructors: a mile and three-quarters of patchy asphalt that wound into swampland and back out onto a banked oval where local stock cars raced for money on Saturday nights. (Sports car racers were amateurs, in the old sense: racing for money was *infra dig*. None of us, back then, would have been caught dead in a stock car race.) The winter woods were bleak, the trees bare, the pale sun lacked warmth. Marlboro—long since defunct—had one long straight and eleven tight corners. Like bloodhounds searching for a scent, we examined its details.

"That looks rough," said Bob, pointing at a fifteen-foot patch of asphalt that covered the entrance to a turn. Its cobbled surface would change a car's rate of deceleration. Our eyes traced the line through the turn, and found something else: a three-inch drop off the pavement at the outside, just at the exit point. The instructor nodded.

"If you run out of road here and let yourself slide off sideways, you'll be upside down before you know what happened. If you see you're about to put a tire off here, go with it. Turn the wheel and *drive* off the track."

We marked it on the note-covered course diagrams we were sketching.

Out on the track in our cars, we followed the instructor for two laps. Then the green flag waved, and we slipped our leashes and went as fast as we could.

Faster than blazes! Nobody feels faster than a novice race driver. He—or she—may not make much noise about it, but in his heart he knows that he's the next Mario Andretti. What a disappointment it was to find, at the end of the session, that we were a whopping fifteen seconds off the lap record. Crestfallen, we checked our spokes—a xylophone tune played on wire wheels with a lightweight wrench, to make sure no spokes were broken—and tried again. Little by little, as we imposed order on the chaos of sensory and mental input, things started to slow down in our minds; and our lap speeds rose in proportion.

On Saturday, we went faster. We were learning how to behave in traffic—who owned the corner, when and how to pass. "Watch your mirrors!" was the mantra of the day.

Our crucial test came on Sunday: five-lap races, from a standing start. As the only Class C car present that weekend, my Jaguar was automatically moved up to Class B, to race against the more powerful Corvettes. As I eased the Jag into position on the starting grid behind the Corvettes, I had the same butterflies, the same awful sense of apprehension that I knew from hill climbs. The back of my head felt light, my heart shook my ribs. The starter held the green flag over his head as he backed away from the track. My butterflies vanished.

The flag went down. We were off.

Time stretched out to accommodate enormous quantities of data gathered and decisions made, so much more than would normally fit into each fraction of a second. *The driver of that Corvette's asleep—dodge left, you'll miss him well. Here's a space between a green car and a yellow one; fill it before it closes up. Shift, damn the gearbox, it's slow as molasses, wait for it to be ready to accept second gear; grinding the gears will do no good. Ease right, crowd the yellow car just up to the edge of the road, you want the best line you can manage for the first left-hand turn. Brakes now, early, twenty feet earlier than usual, when you're not on the right line you can't take it quite so fast.*

Hill climbs and the faster gymkhanas had demanded skill in placing my car for maximum speed. Racing added another layer of complexity: a fender-to-fender, door-to-door battle against others like myself. I could see their eyes in their mirrors, looking back for an instant as I gained on them; and once past, checking on their location with a glance in my own, I saw how intensely they tried to stay with me, tried to pass me back. But they couldn't! I was already hot on the trail of the next car.

Enmeshed in this fierce competition was responsibility for each other driver's well-being. A pass had to be clean, not touch or upset the other car. This game could have serious consequences.

I got past all the Corvettes except one, which I was gnawing on as the five laps ended, and I took the cool-off lap filled with glee.

This racing was ferocious! I loved it!

Two broken spokes required my attention. I was bending over the work when a pleasant voice said, "You'll have to put tape on the standing lights before the next race." Those were the Jaguar's auxiliary lights, an inch and a half in diameter. The headlights were already taped, to keep glass off the track in the event of incident.

I turned to see who it was as he continued. "They were going to black-flag you for it, but you were doing so well I said to let you finish." It was Bruce Jennings, many times national champion. When he left, I floated back to my pit on a little pink cloud.

We lined up for the second race. Presently, barreling through a blind corner, I came upon two freshly spun-out cars that blocked the track. It had happened within the instant, and I was right on top of them. Again, I felt time stretching out, a single second expanding into aeons.

The two cars formed a wide V, separated at the bottom. To the left lay a few inches of paved track, a few feet of grass, and then the flag station with its white-suited workers. If I went that way, the violence of the move would upset the Jag's balance so much that I couldn't be sure of missing the people. To the right, gravel ran into a swamp that bristled with solid trees. In a flash it was clear that between the two cars there was precisely enough space for a skinny Jaguar. I went through the space.

The whole episode, all my calculations of possible response, could have been measured in small fractions of a second, and yet it seemed to happen in the slowest of slow motion. There was no hesitation or doubt that I could go through the hole, though there must not have been more than three inches of clearance. Nor was I frightened—just busy.

I wondered about that afterwards. Surely one would have expected to feel some sort of fear? The part of my mind that was dealing with the situation understood its peril, and translated that into action, but my emotions had stayed out of it. Or seemed to. In retrospect, it was scary enough. The scene was seared in my memory as if by a branding iron. So the hazard hadn't gone emotionally undetected, after all; but the *feeling* of fear wasn't useful, and hadn't been there.

By race end, I had passed all but two of the Corvettes. The silver Revere bowl I got for third place has served as my sugar bowl ever since.

As I peeled off my driving gloves, I found a half-inch blister on my hand. From what? The steering wheel caused no pressure at that point. I moved my hands around the controls as I did on the track until I found the cause.

The Jaguar's transmission was so slow on the upshift, the pause between gears so interminable and the gain by other cars while it lasted so vexing, that I had squeezed the shift knob with all my might while I waited. The wait might have been half a second per shift, but it added up. The suppressed emotional force that powered my run to the front had found an outlet after all.

At day's end they gave silver trophies for win, place and show. Bob, Dick and I each had one. But would they give us a license? We stood fidgeting as those who had been successful were called to pick up their log books. One by one, each of us was called.

We had been observed, judged, and certified; we could enter any race open to novices. The whole racing world lay waiting. We looked at each other with big silly grins on our faces, and then we went to pack for the long trip home. Good thing there weren't any more races that day; none of us could have gotten our heads back in our helmets.

Early in May, the three of us headed to Vineland, New Jersey, for our first full race weekend. This track lay at the western edge of the Pine Barrens, which were settled in colonial times. A legacy of lilacs marked abandoned clearings. The closer you got to the race track, the sweeter the scent of lilacs.

Dick Mooney and I finished second overall in a two-hour relay race. All three of us won trophies that weekend: gleaming, graceful pewter pitchers. I filled them all with lilacs. The cloud that we floated home on this time was perhaps less of a pink and more of a pale and fragrant lavender.

Two weeks later, we were back at Vineland again. The course had long straights followed by sharp, second-gear turns, and that was hard on brakes, which were not the Jaguar's strong point. By mid-race, I had no brakes left, but I was determined to stay in front of a brand-new Jaguar XKE I had been dicing with. That was a mistake. You could slow a car by using progressively lower gears, but it took caution and a sharp eye on the tachometer. I was too intent on the competition. An ominous cloud of smoke followed my Jaguar back to the pits.

One thing you learn about racing mishaps that will keep you off the track for a while: you always feel a great deal worse the morning after, when the euphoria of competition is gone and the magnitude of a catastrophe becomes clear. The damage to my engine proved to be disastrous. Over-revving on the downshifts had snapped the head off a valve, which tore one cylinder to shreds. The prospect of not racing opened like a black hole in front of me.

Never, ever again would I abuse an engine.

Dick Mooney knew of a Jaguar engine for sale, in a car that had been wrecked. I could have it sooner and cheaper if I pulled it out of the wreck myself. That was how I spent June, in the heat after work, a slow struggle, long golden evenings alone with the wreck in the weedy yard behind its owner's auto repair shop.

Races at Watkins Glen were scheduled for the last day of June. As the date rushed closer, my nights of work on the car grew later and later. It was ten at night on the eve of practice before the engine installation was complete, but there was cause for alarm: the oil pressure gauge showed erratic readings. "The trouble must be in your gauge," the owner said. In auto racing as in aviation, those are famous last words.

I reached Watkins Glen in a red-eyed dawn, but when the track opened for practice, my new engine sounded somehow wrong. I sought Dick Mooney's advice. "I think you've wiped a bearing," he said. "I wouldn't run it any more."

I snapped the tonneau cover over the Jaguar's cockpit, took lap times for Dick's practice, and retreated to a cheap hotel in the village to lick my wounds. Maybe, I thought, I'd better set this expensive madness aside for a while. Not that I had much choice. My checkbook was bare.

It was a sociable, easygoing summer after that, full of civilized pleasures. There was sailing on Long Island Sound, swimming at the Lawrence Beach Club with Peter (a young Republic engineer who sometimes crewed for me), dancing at Susan Lippman's wedding at the old Garden City Hotel, long amusing afternoons on the Atlantic beaches with Bob Aymar.

One of the guys I was dating was a sandy-haired, freckled engineer at Grumman named Tom. I had met him the weekend I blew the engine at Vineland, where he was crewing for another Grumman engineer. Tom was funny, smart, and had the same streak of steel down his backbone that I did, which made for occasional conflict. He liked my cooking, which tended to be ambitious, and I liked his enjoyment of it.

Slowly, I got caught up on my bills. I had moved to a small apartment in Great Neck, in a marvelous crumbling ruin called the Tuscany Gardens. Its arched windows looked out over wrought-iron balconies into a cobblestone courtyard, and it was cheap. It was also unfurnished, and from June through mid-August I slept on a pile of old clothes under my sleeping bag. When Peter invited me to a black-tie dinner dance at the Lawrence Beach Club, I wore a long white dress I had made from designer fabric bought for next to nothing on Orchard Street, and golden sandals found on sale at Bergdorf Goodman. As my mother always said, you can do without the necessities; it's the luxuries that count.

Yet through all the good times that summer, something vital was missing: the bloody, salty taste of competition at speed. As soon as I could, I knew I'd have at it again.

By October, after many fits and starts, the Jaguar was ready to go. I went to a Long Island Sports Car Association race at Lime Rock to check out the engine, and I won.

The following weekend, there was an SCCA Divisional Championship race at Thompson in the northeast corner of Connecticut. Tom, the Grumman engineer, offered to crew.

That weekend had everything, and all in balance. Tom had tickets for the Bolshoi Ballet at Carnegie Hall on Friday night, and we savored it afterwards over blinshiki at the Russian Tea Room. Then, back to my apartment in Great Neck, where we left his Porsche, hitched the Jaguar to my old Buick, added his tent and sleeping bag to the rest of my camping gear, and cruised companionably through four hours of moonlight to Thompson.

Saturday practice went smoothly, and that evening Dick Mooney joined us for steaks broiled over a makeshift fire. When our easy conversation had run its course, we spread our sleeping bags on the soft pine needles and fell asleep next to the dark, poignant shapes of our race-ready cars.

At dawn there was fog; the night had been cold. Tom jacked up the back of the Jaguar and removed the rear wheels so that I could adjust the brakes. I hadn't yet quite mastered the art of postponing fear until it was useful, and little wavelets of it riffled occasionally through my veins, sharpening every sense.

At the instant the green flag fell, the butterflies metamorphosed into a different kind of thing, on the far side of fear. Excessive adrenaline became useful now that action was at hand. And there was plenty of action in this race: two competitors flipped their cars upside down, and one caught fire—miraculously, without injury to the drivers. But when you committed yourself to competition, any fear of harm became subservient to the desire to win. What you did on the track was in your own hands. You weren't passive, you weren't helpless, and that made all the difference.

I finished second in class, for my first Divisional points.

On the first weekend in November I was back at Vineland, with Peter crewing. The Jag was fast in practice, and I felt hopeful of a good showing that would complete the necessary six races to qualify for an SCCA National competition license. It was not to be. The car's oil pressure had continued iffy, and a telltale clanking sent us early on the road for home.

A friend at work knew of cheap storage space near Republic, in an old barn behind a farmhouse. There I abandoned the Jaguar to the winter dark.

WHATEVER IT TAKES

On a cold brilliant day in February, 1964, when the flat farm fields of central Long Island were covered with snow that squeaked underfoot, I tackled the Jaguar again. The barn that sheltered it had neither heat nor electricity, and I was still using flat wrenches. It took a flashlight to get them solidly around the deeper nuts and bolts.

Getting an engine ready for removal without the use of a ratchet wrench, sockets, and extensions is something like cutting up a chicken with fingernail scissors: it's an exercise in frustration, although it can be done. I had the benefit of ignorance; I didn't know that the project was entirely unreasonable.

It took two months for me to tear the engine apart, down to the last nut and bolt, and rebuild it. A 1956 Ford station wagon ($95) replaced the old Buick, and served as my makeshift garage as engine assembly progressed. The Ford had room for the engine block, crankshaft, rods, pistons, and myself, if I knelt or sat cross-legged. I borrowed tools here and there: a torque wrench from the gas station across the street, a piston-ring compressor from another Republic engineer. The oil pump got intensive scrutiny, as the clear suspect for the most recent failure. Nearly every page of the shop manual bore my blackened fingerprints.

There was so much to learn! How to lap in valves, and what a properly lapped valve seat looked like when it was done, and how to check it for the slightest trace of leakage. How to check the clearances of the new lead-indium bearings, by laying a thin strip of Plastigauge on the crankshaft journals, tightening the bearing cap bolts to the right number of foot-pounds, then undoing the assembly to examine the width of the crushed strips. And on and on.

It was enjoyable, in a way, to explore the geography of a whole new world, to feel in my hands the shape and heft of each carefully machined component of my engine-to-be. If I'd had the money to engage a competent mechanic, though, I'd never have started the job. Some of my friends figured I'd never finish it.

Besides the engine, the car needed bodywork. A bright shiny

JANET GUTHRIE: A LIFE AT FULL THROTTLE

appearance ought to go with the new engine. I did the bodywork in the rented barn—hours of puttying and sanding, to smooth out old damage to the Jag's voluptuous fender curves. But a fine coat of paint required spray apparatus, and that meant the use of an air compressor. I started asking around.

It was a mild, windy day in April when an acquaintance from my sports car club introduced me to Ralph J. Farnham, Jr., at his shop on New Street in Oceanside. "Farnham Marine, Founded 1917" was neatly lettered on the door of his truck (1917 was the year of his birth). Ralph's main living was in the boat-moving business.

At first glance, the shop and its environs looked like an eclectic junkyard that had somehow suffered the effects of an oil-well blowout. Surrounded by weedy boatyards and a small-time auto wrecker or two, his concrete-block building sloped down from the street, its far end sinking slowly toward the water table. It was not a great deal bigger than a one-car garage.

My friend and I stepped inside, squinting against the gloom. At an ancient workbench, a powerfully muscled man bent over a vise that clenched a thick slice of iron plate. The five-pound steel mallet in his hand struck sparks that flew to the far corners of the shop. The blows were loud enough to pain our ears.

My acquaintance off-handedly introduced us. Farnham acknowledged me with something like a grunt. Just under six feet tall, he had a ruddy complexion and a neatly trimmed, inch-wide beard that made nearly a perfect circle of his face. His wrists were three times the size of my own, and his forearms and biceps made his wrists look small.

"Bring your car down on Saturday," he said brusquely. "I should be back from City Island around noon."

He turned back to the vise, readjusting his work. "Never use force," he said, as he smote the work another mighty blow. "Get a bigger hammer."

At half past eleven on the appointed day, I towed the Jaguar down New Street. Near the door leading into Ralph's shop, a twelve-foot section of five-inch diameter steel pipe lay propped up at an angle on remnants of heavy machinery. Ralph was wielding the arc welder. A blazing fountain of sharp sparks poured from the apparatus in his hand as he blocked off the butt end of the pipe with a plate of quarter-inch steel. He put down the welder's face shield and saw the Jag.

"Be with you in a minute," he said.

Scrounging around the shop yard, he packed a one-pound coffee can with stones and sand, tamped it into concrete-like solidity, and dropped it down the pipe like a cannonball. Then he squinted along the pipe's length, adjusting its direction.

"If you hit that bucket," he said, pointing to the scoop of a mammoth construction crane that dangled high in the air a few blocks away, "you can hear it ring all over the neighborhood."

He lit an acetylene-oxygen welding torch, then snuffed it out on the pavement. Through a hole near the base plate, he filled the bottom of his newly-built cannon with the hissing, explosive mixture. He lit it off with a match.

BOOM!

My mouth fell open as I watched the projectile sail upward. It vanished perhaps a quarter-mile away. The bucket did not ring.

It occurred to me that with a friend like Ralph, one might not need enemies. Within his shop, however, lay all the apparatus needed to paint my Jaguar in a professional way, and he showed me where everything was. I fetched in my gallons of enamel, and set to work.

By Sunday night, the Jaguar was an elegant shade of blue. So were my fingernails and eyelashes. I was truly proud of the results; there was only one little run on the whole car, and no orange-peel texture anywhere. It looked beautiful. With a light heart, I picked out a blue dress to go with my eyelashes and the streaks in my hair, and went blithely off to a party at Tom's big house in Lloyd Harbor.

It didn't seem impossible, back then, to keep life somewhat well balanced. Somehow there was time, that spring, for strolling among the weeping cherries at my favorite haunt, Planting Fields, a grand old North Shore estate and gardens that had recently opened to the public. There was time to go see Richard Burton's sensational, brooding *Hamlet* on Broadway (twice, even), where it took a platoon of mounted policemen to keep order among the nightly crowds eager for a post-performance glimpse of Dick and Liz. There was time to plant roses and zinnias and bachelors' buttons in the neglected courtyard beneath my apartment windows. And I was still seeing something of Peter, the young engineer at Republic who sometimes crewed for me, as well as Tom and a couple of other guys, though less often as the Jaguar became more demanding. The racing season was already under way.

May wore on, and the pressure grew as my engine neared completion. Ralph Farnham had once crewed for a driver at the Indianapolis 500, and he started to take an interest. When I finished assembling the engine, Ralph helped me drag it out of my station wagon and drop it into the Jaguar. It was a fine fair Saturday when I spun up my engine for the very first time.

There was no oil pressure.

I took out the spark plugs, hitched the Jag to the Ford, and towed it up and down New Street in gear. That brought the rpm's all the way up to 4000, much faster than the starter would turn the engine over. There was still no oil pressure. Ralph helped me check each component of the oil delivery system. Nothing explained the problem.

Monday morning early, I hauled the Jaguar to a shop where two British mechanics specialized in XKs. If anyone could figure out why there was no oil pressure, it would be they. By Wednesday, they had given up.

Thursday passed. Friday. Saturday. Sunday. Monday. I read and re-read the shop manual, asked questions of every mechanic I knew.

On Tuesday after work, I took the Jag back to the British shop and put it up on their lift, drained its twelve quarts of oil. A plethora of little bolts held the pan in place. As I undid the bolts and pulled the oil pan down for the fifth time, my frustration teetered toward despair.

It was a mild sunny evening in early June. Golden light slanted through the surrounding woods, deep green now that summer was truly under way. Tom would be sipping a martini about now, I thought wistfully, on the flagstone terrace by the apple trees, a few miles away.

I carried the oil pan outside and set it down on the white gravel drive. I stared at it glumly—and suddenly, there was the answer, as if I had been blind. Without visible dents or scratches, the bottom of the pan had been uniformly pushed up, subtly distorted, so that when the pan was fitted to the engine, the oil pump intake sat in a blind alley amid the baffling. It must have happened when that XK 140 coupe was wrecked. The pump couldn't possibly suck up any oil!

Quickly, I salvaged a pan from my old, blown engine; brought the car down off the lift, started the engine, and there it was—oil pressure!

I whooped and skipped like a five-year-old. Gleefully, I hitched the Jaguar to the Ford, dashed home and popped open a can of beer. As I filled out an entry form for my first race of the season, I thought the plain gold liquid to be the nectar of the gods.

Driving the Jaguar to work for the rest of the week put easy break-in time on its engine. At day's end, I pointed its long nose east and north among Long Island's great estates. The Jaguar purred gently through green meadows and shadowy woods toward Planting Fields, where hundreds of rhododendrons neared their peak of bloom. In the late spring dusk, masses of flowers glowed lavender to cream to crimson under the pines. Far away, out over Long Island Sound, a summer thunderstorm rumbled south.

Soon, other thunder would fill my ears: the urgent, exuberant roar of sports cars at speed. The Jaguar was ready. So on this peaceful evening, as the little racing windscreen brushed back a bug or two, I was most peacefully content.

In 1964, that first engine I ever built with my own hands was to power the Jaguar through twelve races. Foremost among them was the first-ever 500-mile SCCA National Championship race at Watkins Glen, in the Finger Lakes region of New York, scheduled for late August. Anticipation of it set my heart on fire.

Watkins Glen was to American road racing then what St. Andrews was to golf, or Wimbledon to tennis. It was home to the Grand Prix of the United States, held at the beginning of October when the hills above Lake Seneca flamed with color, and low clouds full of rain fled before the wind. The Grand Prix cars of those days carried no commercial signage, and their pure colors showed their country of origin: dark British racing green, Italian red, German racing silver. Briggs Cunningham had established the American colors at Le Mans: white with a blue stripe. Small, fenderless, and fierce, the Formula 1 machines screamed past onlookers in the pits to whirl over a hill against the dark and turbulent sky, the leaves on the crest red and gold, rain flying from under the wheels of the racers.

American drivers were our special heroes: Dan Gurney, Walt Hansgen. There were no women Grand Prix drivers at that time, although Maria-Teresa de Filippis of Italy had competed in the Belgian, Portuguese, and Italian Grand Prix races in 1958.

The mystique of Watkins Glen was complex and powerful, like a grail, and I pressed toward it with all my strength. Given the Jaguar's heavy demands for maintenance and improvement, this meant more and more time spent at Ralph Farnham's shop. His generosity in allowing me access to the facilities of his shop, its chain hoist, bench grinders, drill press, and lifetime accumulation of ancient but invaluable odds and ends, was the cornerstone of my life in racing. Without his help, I could never have reached the upper levels of the sport.

Ralph started coming to the races in mid-June—mostly spectating, sometimes lending a hand. His endlessly fertile, creative, original, mischievous mind made him entertaining company. He had a passion for history, and a gift for recounting it. His immense strength was often good to have at the races, and like many strong men, he took great care to be gentle.

He lived with his mother, who was the same age as the Brooklyn Bridge, and his daughter, on whom he lavished all the affection of his generous soul. From time to time, Ralph took me home to dinner, which his mother prepared and served with 19th-century formality. Their house was a small 1920s bungalow which they shared with a six-foot iguana and which had also sheltered, until recently, a sizeable boa constrictor.

"The boa used to wrap itself around the base of a lamp," Ralph said, "where the light made it warm. A neighbor's daughter who happened to sit next to it said, 'Gee, that lamp sure is realistic.' About that time the snake moved. You know, she didn't even bother opening the door on her way out—she went right through the screen."

Questionable humor aside, the resources of Ralph's shop were a treasure beyond price. Grime and disorder seemed to reign, but that was deceptive. The essentials were there, ranging from an ancient, rusty arc welder to a huge fifty-year-old lathe. The place was a jungle of antique engines, steel girders, thirty-foot boat trailers, and oddball machinery. Ralph had a standing offer of a hundred dollars to anyone who succeeded in running full tilt through the shop yard at midnight. I never took his bet, but long before my ten years there were out, I knew that yard like the back of my hand.

As the summer of '64 wore on, and the race at Watkins Glen loomed larger, work on the Jaguar left little time for pleasant evenings with Tom. A 500-mile race at Watkins Glen would run some six and a half hours. The logistics were formidable. Among other things, I needed a co-driver to share stints behind the wheel. Dick Mooney accepted my invitation. His girlfriend Pam would help crew, and so would Ralph. Once again, we pulled into Watkins Glen in a red-eyed dawn.

There was rain, mud, and trouble. Half an hour before the start of the race on Sunday, Dick and I were furiously at work in a repair shop down in the village, changing the Jaguar's fuel pump. We rolled it out with no time to spare. An SCCA National Championship race, back then, was the biggest thing in road racing after a Formula One Grand Prix, and the road from the village back up to the track was thickly jammed with spectators. Dick roared past them on the wrong side of the road in the Jag while I kept the Ford's nose tucked in right behind him. When we reached the track, the grid was already forming. As the pack moved off on its warm-up lap, we were still changing tires. *The New York Times* photographer came looking for me, and captured something resembling a snarl.

Dick drove the Jag off to chase the pack around for the start, and I turned my attention to setting up the pits. Our first fuel stop and driver change would come in a little over an hour, and somehow I had to shift my mindset from fuel pumps and toolboxes to what lay ahead, on the track.

There would be no room out there for any extraneous thought. The concentration required in racing obliterates everything else. At any given instant, the focus is: can I extend my braking point at that fast right-hander a little deeper into the turn, say five feet beyond the 100 marker? Or, if I move my apex six inches down the track, can I get 50 more rpm's at the exit? Or, if I set up the driver of that Corvette three times in a row for an outside pass in the hook, and he is used to blocking me there, can I fake to the outside the fourth time and take him with an inside dive to his right? And so on.

No matter what else is going on, you can't miss a yellow flag. You may be intent on your prey, on passing at over a 100 mph—a different line through a turn, the wobbling of your target as the distance between your door handles drops to inches and he tries to stave you off—but if a yellow flag waves at the edge of your peripheral vision, you mustn't miss it. It means trouble ahead.

The frame of mind that enables all this is beyond the confines of everyday experience. You can't drive well in competition if your mind is muddled. You must find your way to a different place. It's a crystalline state, like when a saturated solution of some chaotic liquid is lowered a hundredth of a degree in temperature, and instantly reorganizes itself into a geometric structure of infinite precision. That is what enables the soaring sensation of committing yourself to fly through a turn at the highest speed your machine will bear, with only the most tenuous grip on the pavement. There may be serious penalties for error, and you must acknowledge that and accept it.

When Dick brought the car in for its first refueling, I had found my way into the right place.

Some five hours later, we took the checkered flag in sixth place overall behind a Ford Cobra and three Corvettes, and second in class by ten feet. The prize was a big silver bowl of classic Paul Revere design. We filled it with champagne, drank it empty, and filled it again. Jaguar enthusiasts descended out of the woods, patted the Jaguar, caressed its fenders. They talked about Jaguars that they had watched in races on the old road course that used to run through the town, and proffered their race programs for autographs.

Night had fallen, and a chill wind blew beneath the stars. Pam and Dick were ready to head for the Seneca Lodge, where there was warmth and food and drink. I sent Ralph with them. I craved a few moments alone.

How to gather up, connect the entirety of this endeavor? Weeks of labor, intricate mechanical preparation; wild anticipation illuminating our plans. Tense last-minute crises, and their desperate resolution. Then, that other state of being, on the course, that had been my locus for the past few hours; and last, the swirl of congratulations and happy enthusiasm that enveloped us at the end.

The Jaguar stood still in the starlight, reflecting the flicker of campfires, seeming to quiver with silent echoes of the day's violent passage.

We did it, I thought. *We did it.*

CHANGING
PERSPECTIVES

Some people are fortunate enough to find their calling early in life, and to pursue it without false starts or interruption. Many more of us, I suspect, cast about for their direction like hounds seeking the trail of a fox. Flying might have become my calling, since it was my first great passion, but the times weren't right. Had I been of age in 1942, I would unquestionably have volunteered for the WASPs, the Women's Airforce Service Pilots, who flew the hottest planes of that era. (And I would then have been heartbroken, as most WASPs were, when their distinguished service was summarily terminated at the end of 1944 because enough men had been trained to take their place.)

In 1964, I thought I had the best of two worlds: an intellectually challenging occupation, and an avocation that addressed my lust for physical adventure. My identity was split between "aerospace engineer" and "SCCA racing driver." The rest of the decade was to see that balance shift.

I loved my job at Republic, of course, and was always glad that engineers whom I respected asked for me to be assigned to their projects. But the sport had scored its first casualty as early as 1963: under the pressure of engine-building, I dropped an evening course in electromagnetic theory, the first step toward a master's degree in physics. Each coming race weekend beckoned seductively, seeming to shimmer in rainbow hues.

Somehow, I also found time for an active social life. Some men were serious in their pursuit; some were just friends. Quite a few were roped into crewing for me, which could be a mixed blessing. Tom had already proposed marriage, and I didn't respond in a straightforward way. Although I couldn't have articulated it at the time, I believe I felt threatened by the prospect of a conventional life, and was balking at any steps leading toward one. Certainly I felt conflict over this; Tom was so ... *suitable*. He was a good companion; yet my relationship with him wasn't the totally transforming experience that I had felt with just one man three years earlier, when I was twenty-three.

By the end of October, 1964, Tom was discouraged enough that he called less frequently. By the end of that October, Dick Mooney and Pam were married. (Dick gave up racing for the next thirty years.) And by the end of that October, I had met the second man who was able to turn my world upside down. From the moment our eyes met, I went right over the cliff. The only problem with our brief time together was that he didn't see it my way. A few months later, he married someone else.

At twenty-six, I still expected, as I always had, that I would marry and have children—didn't everybody? But each of the two men whom I would have married in a heartbeat proved unattainable; and I fear I left more heartbreak among the others than I like to think about.

November of 1964 brought an unexpected twist to the direction I sought. NASA announced the Scientist-Astronaut Program. Rumors of it had circulated in the industry for some time. A friend at Republic handed me the published requirements to apply.

"Look at this," he said. "You're a pilot, you're not taller than six feet—unless you have those high heels on, maybe—you have a degree in physics, and you've been working in our space program four and a half years. It says a doctorate or equivalent experience. If you'd done this work at a university, you'd have the doctorate. So why not?"

Surely he was teasing me ... but the leap into space was the great adventure of the twentieth century, the ultimate challenge, the chance to make a contribution right out at the frontier of human experience. Night and day, it obsessed me.

"Doctorate or equivalent." I leafed back through the papers I had written for Republic. "The Far Field of a Dipole Antenna Mounted on a Conducting Sphere," page after page of spherical Bessel functions and Legendre polynomials. "Electromagnetic Wave Interaction With a Plasma"—more math which, as I look at it decades later, I can no longer follow. And on and on. It might not add up to a doctorate, but perhaps it might be enough to make the case for equivalency. Quietly, I bounced the idea off some of my friends and colleagues. The response was unanimous: go for it!

I applied, sitting for the required Graduate Record Examination in physics early in 1965. I hit the 94th percentile on achievement and the 99th percentile on aptitude. NASA soon advised me that my application would advance to the second round of evaluations, conducted by the National Academy of Sciences. Now there was nothing to do but wait. And dream. The wild excitement of it was tempered only by my feeling that acceptance was unlikely, mostly because of the doctorate.

At home in Miami for Christmas, I let my family know what I was up to. As usual, my mother didn't say much, though she must have been alarmed. My father's reaction was more direct: "First you go out and try to break your neck at a hundred and forty miles an hour, and now you want to sit on top of one of those things and let them light a match to it?"

Uh, well, yes, I did. Intensely.

On February 11, 1965, the *Long Island Press* printed a wire-service item: "Four women are among the 400 applicants being considered for the new scientist-astronaut program, the Manned Spacecraft Center said yesterday." It didn't give any names.

Meanwhile, I worked on the Jag, preparing it for the coming season. I was also pitching Ford dealers throughout the metropolitan area for sponsorship in the year-old Trans Am professional racing series, which had sparked a great deal of excitement across the country. Factory-backed Mustangs, Camaros and Barracudas set the pace in the hands of some of the country's top drivers, but a privateer might make a mark. How I wished I were rich, and could field a Trans Am car of my own!

Late in the evening at the end of April, I was elbow-deep in the Jaguar's innards when the phone rang. It was Roger, a racing driver whom I had been seeing since December.

"I was just listening to the radio," he said, "and heard that all four women applicants for the astronaut program were rejected."

Well, there it was, a little kind of death. I dove back into the Jaguar and tried not to think about it.

On Monday May 2, the letter came from NASA. "I regret to inform you ... it is commendable that you were among those considered ... We anticipate that we will conduct other Astronaut Selection Programs in the future. We will retain your application..."

Don't call us, we'll call you.

It was signed by Donald K. Slayton, Assistant Director for Flight Crew Operations—one of the original seven astronauts.

I put the letter away.

The rest of 1965 was dark and tangled, a dismal year. The Jaguar seemed endlessly prone to failure. Endlessly, I worked on it. My journal holds day after day of entries like: "Balanced pistons. Two of the rods don't match." "Oil pump and timing chains in." "Into the heart of darkest Newark at midnight to leave the crankshaft for Tufftriding. Dark men bent over a bubbling cauldron, flames leaping from a forge at the cobbled edge of the street."

Long late-night trips across the Bronx in an unreliable old car, alone, were enough to make a woman feel ... well, apprehensive. But racing had sunk its hooks into me more deeply than ever. The sport had become the driving force in my life.

Mid-May brought the most frightening moment I was ever to experience in racing. It didn't take place on the track, but in Ralph's shop. Having carefully lapped in a new set of valves, I was busy installing them in the Jaguar's beautiful aluminum cylinder head. I was doing it the hard way, because one of the many expensive tools that I didn't have was a valve spring compressor. Instead, I had carefully chosen two socket wrenches that rested, one inside the other, on the wide flat valve spring retainer and the pair of small tapered keepers. When I struck the assembly a mighty blow with a five-pound steel mallet, the springs compressed, the keepers dropped into their slot on the valve stem, and the valve settled into place.

Midway through the job, with five valves installed, I hit the next assembly a glancing blow. It came apart, and the powerful springs, recoiling, propelled some sharp portion of machinery toward my face. It struck my right eyebrow, cutting to the bone. Blood flowed copiously. Worse, it was immediately clear what the outcome would have been had the piece struck half an inch lower. The terror of that moment can bring sweat to my palms even now.

Pressing a rag against the cut, I walked outside, opened the door of my station wagon, and got in, pulling its steel shell around me. Then I burst into tears.

Presently, I finished installing the rest of the valves.

My social life that year was nearly as complex and distressing as the misbehavior of the Jaguar. I declined yet another proposal of marriage. I still expected marriage and children, but not as contemporary culture directed, an end in itself.

My erstwhile suitor Tom called now and then. He had a new sailboat, he said cheerfully, and a ski house in Vermont. Then, inevitably, came the question. "Are you still racing?"

"Yes."

And there the conversation would end.

On the work front, the storied history of Republic Aviation Corporation was drawing to a close. Grumman had clearly won the race for aerospace contracts, including the Lunar Excursion Module. Republic's Farmingdale plant and its runways, where Republic Thunderbolts had taken off for the theatres of World War II, were sold to Fairchild Hiller late in the year.

The Advanced Orbiting Solar Observatory program, where I worked as one of two Experiment Coordinators, was cancelled in mid-December, 1965. Some employees were laid off immediately; the rest of us had a short grace period in which to wind up our reports and consider our choices.

My involvement with auto racing was hardly a secret, and I was offered a spot on the Experimental Safety Vehicle that Fairchild was developing for New York State. The alternative was a transfer to the Maryland suburbs of Washington, D.C., where most of our dwindling aerospace work was located.

Some of my colleagues were headed to Grumman, where the action was, and I wondered whether I should go there too. The satisfactions of work in the yeasty, intoxicating atmosphere of the space effort were considerable, but my passion for my sport again interfered. If I moved to Grumman, the new job would demand late hours. And I needed to resume the after-work courses toward a master's degree that I had dropped in the face of racing pressure two years earlier. There'd be precious little time for engine-building, precious little energy for midnight trips bearing crankshafts into the heart of darkest Newark.

I mused over these things in the gloom and depression of the half-dismantled AOSO offices, and at the beginning of January I followed the path of least resistance, to Maryland.

Three weeks later, I found a telegram at my door. It offered me a ride in the first-ever Daytona Continental 24-Hour, America's new answer to Le Mans! I thought the top of my head would come off. This was to be a major international event; practice would begin on February 2. The details, when I learned them, brought me down to earth. A team of five women drivers would be assigned to two Sunbeam Alpines sponsored by Macmillan Ring-Free Oil. An Alpine was a smallish, low-performance car with a smallish engine. There would be little chance of even a class win with this vehicle. We were to be called the Ring-Free Motor Maids. Worst of all, as the last driver to come on board, I was technically relief—not even guaranteed a stint at the wheel.

Would I go? Of course I would go. I would go if I had to collect the

Alpine on Long Island and carry it to Daytona on my shoulders.

In Florida, I met the other members of the team. Rosemary Smith was an Irish rally driver. Smokey Drolet was from South Florida; her background included stock car racing and an all-girl auto stunt show. Suzy Dietrich mostly drove open-wheel formula cars. Donna Mae Mims was at that time the only female winner of an SCCA National Championship, in her famous pink Sprite. I was the youngest of the five, with the fewest years of experience: three seasons. We happened to be the only women in the race, but as usual in sports car racing, that wasn't an issue—except to the press, which loved it. While there had been women competitors in several of my SCCA races, a women's team would be a new experience for me.

Problem was, the women's team had no cars. The Alpines were late arriving, and needed work when they got there. I studied the course on foot, then got three laps of the track on Thursday night. At the eleventh hour, the Alpines qualified for the starting field.

And what a field it was! Ford Motor Company had entered five ferocious GT Mark II Prototypes. One of them was to be driven by Mark Donohue and Walt Hansgen, another by Ken Miles and Lloyd Ruby. Mario Andretti and Pedro Rodriguez had one of a dozen Ferraris. Jochen Rindt of Austria, Lorenzo Bandini of Italy, Baron Huschke von Hanstein, and Phil Hill were also at the helm of fast machines. As *The New York Times* said in its pre-race coverage on February 6, 1966, "No finer field of cars and drivers has ever been assembled for a race of this length."

The sixty-car field included Corvettes, Jaguar XKEs, and Cobras; but also Triumph TR-4s, Corvairs, and even a Rambler Marlin. Those of us in the lesser machines would be running a race of our own. In truth, our task at the wheel of slower cars was tough: we had to drive looking backwards as well as forwards. We would put our cars through the turns as fast as they would go, gnawing away at some suitable competitor, while at the same time keeping out of the way of the more ferocious and exotic machines.

Race day dawned sunny, windy and cold. The green flag sent the pack off at three in the afternoon. Each time one of the Alpines pitted for gas and a driver change, I was there, hopefully anticipating a turn at the wheel. It was after midnight before one of the women finally called for relief. At last!

Faster cars overtook the Alpine like sharks in murky water. I kept well out of the way. It was easy to stay clear of them on the wide, high banking; trickier in the narrow infield turns. My three laps of practice left me with a lot to learn. But then came the luscious sensations of figuring out each turn, finding the line that was smoother and faster, converting my initial clumsiness into something that vaguely resembled art. How I had lusted for this!

I stayed in the car for several hours, two or three tankfuls of gas, then reluctantly yielded the wheel. Back in the pits, a contingent from my old sports car club, South Shore, who had clocked my laps, showed me how gratifyingly fast they were. We finished thirty-first, with a leaking head gasket the last few hours. Never again, I promised myself, would I agree to be a relief driver only.

By April 1966, I was back at work on Long Island, at a tiny aerospace company formed by colleagues from Republic, within easy reach of Ralph Farnham's invaluable shop. The Jaguar continued to tantalize and frustrate, its potential for victories clear but maddeningly elusive. The elegant creature would show its strength for part of a race, then break, in yet another new and unanticipated fashion. But when Bridgehampton hosted the new Canadian-American Challenge, which attracted a full field of international hero drivers in some of the fastest race cars in the world, our SCCA races were a curtain-raiser. I took second place in a good race against tough competition.

Texas oil millionaire Jim Hall unveiled his revolutionary winged Chaparral that weekend, an aerodynamic innovation that was to change race car design forever. Its huge airfoil, mounted over the rear wheels, dramatically increased downforce, and therefore cornering speed. Dan Gurney won, however, and it was a great thrill to accept my silver trophy from Gurney's hands.

The Jaguar's tally for 1966 came to two firsts, a second, and two thirds. It wasn't what I had hoped for; but I had learned a few things, and would persevere.

January of 1967 was dominated by the prospect—the question, really—of driving for Ring-Free again at the Daytona 24-Hour International Manufacturers Championship race. Emotionally, I was desperate to be there, to be in the action, even if it had to be at the wheel of uncompetitive equipment. Intellectually, rationally, I was more sensible. Why undertake those significant risks without a chance of winning at least in class?

It is a question that haunts drivers at every level of the sport. Should you accept a turkey in the hope that you can make it sprout a few eagle feathers, go faster than it has any right to? Maybe someone will notice, and you'll get a better car next time. Or should you wait for a competitive car, knowing full well that you may never in your lifetime get your hands on one?

My own beautiful Jaguar was not a particularly rational choice. At the beginning of 1967, though, it still seemed to have the potential for wins in its class.

American sports car racing was in its glory days in the late sixties and early seventies. The model may have been European, but American movies with American stars portrayed the peak of the sport: 1966's *The Grand Prix* with James Garner, 1971's *Le Mans* with Steve McQueen. The major American enduros—Daytona's 24-Hour, Sebring's 12-Hour, the 6-Hour at Watkins Glen—commanded the media attention that NASCAR was to hold three decades later. Many if not most top sports car racers were wealthy, sophisticated, passionate amateurs like the Texas oil tycoons Hap Sharp and Jim Hall, who drove his Chaparral onto the cover of *Newsweek* magazine in 1966.

In 1967, I still saw myself as a passionate amateur, absent the wealth. All through my sports-car racing years, I had worked hard at keeping up a front. I was playing a rich person's game, and could blend in fairly well if I hid all evidence to the contrary. I might be building my engines with my own hands, but on race day my manicure was as perfect as I could make it. I might be sleeping in the back of my tow car, but by sneaking into the Circuit Club at dawn for its hot water, I could still pull on a pair of Lily Pulitzer tropical-print jeans and a lacy white shirt and blend into the blazer-jacketed crowd.

What I dreamed of then, hoped for and worked toward, was twofold. First, I sought a sponsored car for the domestic Trans-Am series, a Camaro or Mustang. I had put a lot of fruitless effort into this. Second, I dreamed of a ride at Le Mans or in Sicily's legendary Targa Florio, races that epitomized the glamorous history of the sport. Meanwhile, the Jaguar was the most car that I could afford, and Ring-Free Oil was the only sponsor in sight.

Ring-Free promised the women's team two Shelby-American Mustang GT350's in the Grand Touring class at Daytona in February 1967. I went. Once there, however, the picture changed. When the dust settled, Anita Taylor Matthews, Smokey Drolet and I had an ordinary Mustang in the Touring class. It had been someone's street car until the previous week.

Whatever the setbacks, we soldiered through. I got seven hours at the wheel, which was enough to scratch my itch. At the finish, in spite of forty minutes fixing an electrical bug, we were fifth in class and twentieth overall, out of sixty at the start.

In spite of the grip racing had on me, the core of my self-image was still as a professional in some aspect of science. I still loved the elegance of science, its intellectual rigor. Of the choices open to women at the time, earning a living in science seemed best. Then, early in 1967, our little aerospace company was notified that our main contract would not be extended. I would soon be unemployed. Maybe it was time to get that master's degree in physics after all. I applied for a teaching fellowship at the University of Miami, where I could cut expenses by living with my parents, and by mid-April my acceptance was in hand.

As the winter dark receded, I fitted the Jaguar with a three-carburetor cylinder head and an overdrive transmission, seeking every advantage that the rules of competition could provide. This season was likely to be the Jaguar's last; it was eleven years old. Then what would I do? I redoubled my efforts toward finding sponsored rides, the racer's dream: just show up and drive.

March of 1967 brought news of a possible ride for Ring-Free at the Sebring 12-Hour in central Florida, America's other International Manufacturers Championship race, and my world started sparkling again. An international race had first been held at Sebring in 1950, making it one of the oldest and certainly one of the most glamorous road races in America.

The French manufacturer Matra was to supply Ring-Free with an 1108-cc coupe for the GT6 class. It was said to offer at least the possibility of a class win, though it had the second-smallest engine in the entire field. (The smallest was a 1098-cc Sprite.) There were also hints that the Matra might lead to a ride in European endurance races. The 24-Hour race at Le Mans in France, first held in 1923, had mythic allure for any sports car driver. Le Mans was the Everest of my aspirations. Anything that led in that direction was worth pursuing. The end of March found me in Florida.

Sebring! The scent of orange blossoms ... the sound of so many languages ... swampy trees hung with festoons of grey Spanish moss. Race cars streaked freely along the public roads from their garages in the small, sleepy town to the race course at the airport five miles away, licenses and mufflers be damned.

My memory drifted back to the first time I saw Sebring: not as a racing driver, but from the air. Nine years earlier, I had landed there for fuel, in a Stearman crop duster. I was ferrying the big open-cockpit biplane from Miami up toward the spring crops farther north. There was no control tower at Sebring back then—the Stearman had no radio anyway—and the few airplanes in sight were corroded World War II relics with grass growing between their toes. Except during race week, Sebring was a quiet place.

Like any good short-field pilot, I set the Stearman down in a nice three-point landing at the very end of the runway—only to realize that my objective was barely in sight! Sebring had been a bomber airfield in World War II, and its white concrete runways were over five thousand feet long. So I advanced the throttle and flew over to where the gas pumps were, feeling rather foolish.

During race week, two of those long runways became part of the 5.2-mile course. The rest of it wound through service roads and taxiways. While Ferraris and Porsches shrieked down one runway, aircraft rose from the next. The juxtaposition could get confusing at night; but that was all part of the fun.

My co-driver in the Matra was to be a young Dutch woman, Liane Engeman. She and I met in New York a week before the race. Liane was blonde, good-looking, with the kind of presence that could stop conversation when she entered a room. She was completely at home with the international stars that congregated at Sebring. She also proved to be a smart, perceptive, capable driver, and we hit it off quite well.

Four teams of women drivers were entered in this race. Suzy Dietrich and Donna Mae Mims would share the same Ring-Free ASA they drove at Daytona. Smokey Drolet and Anita Taylor Matthews had an independent Alpine. In a considerably faster category, there was a beautiful yellow Ferrari Berlinetta 275. The well-known driver and journalist Denise McCluggage had come out of retirement to share it with Marianne "Pinky" Rollo. Denise had first driven the Sebring 12-Hour, paired with Ruth Levy, in 1958.

It was Denise who introduced me to astronaut Wally Schirra, as he watched the action from behind our pit. Of course I mentioned my unsuccessful application for the Scientist-Astronaut program some two years before, as well as the pending fellowship at Miami.

"You ought to go ahead and get your graduate degree," he said. "When we find a qualified woman, we'll take her."

Could this be true? I had put everything I had into the Scientist-Astronaut application, and had failed. Now, I was more guarded. Our conversation was interrupted when Liane pulled into the pits, and I leaped back behind the wheel.

The Matra proved to be no streak of lightning, but Liane and I gave it our best. A relatively small car in a major enduro like Sebring demands the same attention as the faster machines—judgment, balance, desire, commitment, endurance—plus the Janus requirement, to keep just as sharp a lookout behind as in front. You must know who is overtaking you, precisely where they will pass, and how best to place your slower vehicle to give them a clean shot on through. And whatever the machine, the driver's pleasure lies in keeping it balanced on its own edge of adhesion in the turns.

We took first in the GT6 class, twenty-third overall out of fifty-eight starters.[1] Dietrich and Mims were just two positions behind, so our women's team's unusual streak of finishes remained intact. Drolet and Matthews spent hours in the pits and were classified thirty-fifth. Denise McCluggage and Pinky Rollo drove the Ferrari to seventeenth overall and second in GT12 class. Mario Andretti and Bruce McLaren, the fastest qualifiers, took the overall victory for Ford. A. J. Foyt and Lloyd Ruby, also in a Ford, were second.

Next morning's victory banquet filled Harder Hall, a pink relic of the 1920s boom. Liane and I were called to receive a prize for the top-finishing car of French manufacture, offered by René Dreyfus, the former French racing champion, owner of the fashionable Manhattan restaurant Le Chanteclair. As we left the podium, John Baus, who managed the North American Racing Team of Ferraris, intercepted me.

"Might you be available to drive the Matra in the Douze Heures du Reims in June?"

My heart leaped. The Reims 12-Hour, a road-racing classic in itself, might lead to Le Mans.

As casually as possible, I answered, "I plan to be in Europe then anyway." This was true. My parents were taking the whole family to two months in Europe. I didn't mention that we'd be camping in a Volkswagen Microbus. International racing drivers were more likely to stay at the Ritz.

Baus said, "Call me in Paris..." and I did, but the ride at Reims never materialized. Even so, the European trip turned out to be a magical, epic adventure. We gathered in Zurich and headed south to

---

[1] For years I thought we were second in class, but apparently a 1300-cc Lancia was reclassified, leaving us first.

luminous Venice, then down the Dalmatian coast of Yugoslavia. At night, a tent attached to the bus' side sheltered the younger generation's sleeping bags. We bought crusty bread from village bakeries, blushing gold cherries at orchards tucked into the hills.

Skirting forbidden Albania, we turned south toward Greece. It was in Macedonia that I sat on the steps of the Roman amphitheatre at Stobi and put on paper my decision not to go to graduate school. Where the stage had been, blood-red poppies blew in the golden grass.

This watershed choice was as definitive as the one seven years earlier, when I walked away from the AT-6 (and from flying, though I didn't see it at the time). The XK 120 Jaguar that I bought instead of the airplane had set me on a different path. And the choice I made in Macedonia proved to be the end of physics and the beginning of my life as a professional driver, in unforeseeable ways.

The ingredients of my decision were complex. Partly, it was "*cherchez l'homme.*" "Luke" was the new man in my life, and two months away from him were proving more painful than I had anticipated. But there was more. In spite of Wally Schirra's encouragement, I suspected that even a master's degree wouldn't suffice to get me into the astronaut program. Partly, there was my old reluctance to be cooped up indoors. And part, I think, was my own reassessment of such talent as I had for science. Certainly I was clever; but I had slowly begun to suspect that I wasn't original, at least not in the field of physics. I had found great pleasure and delight in studying the classics of physics; but without invention and originality, joy would surely prove elusive.

Maybe the remoteness of ancient Stobi lent perspective. I wrote to the University of Miami, withdrawing, with my apologies.

We reached the cobalt Aegean near Platamon. The voluptuous, gushing spring of Daphne resupplied our bus' water tank for days. The Acropolis in Athens held me spellbound. For some reason beyond thought, I took a little pair of scissors from my satchel and cut a lock of my hair. Then I scattered it on the site of Athena's oldest temple, at the Erechtheion.

By August I was a full-fledged bum, supporting the Jaguar on unemployment insurance. Goodness knows, it was easier to keep the beast in operating condition without simultaneously holding down a full-time job. I had high hopes for the 1967 SCCA Nationals at Watkins Glen, but without a decent set of rain tires, I finished fifth.

The Northeast Division of SCCA, mine, was perhaps the most competitive in the country, with the possible exception of California. Competition rules allowed you to go cherry-picking elsewhere, for a maximum of two out-of-Division races. Two of the doggone Triumphs had done just that, accumulating more points toward eligibility for the end-of-season runoff races for the National Championships at Daytona. It was time for a little cherry-picking of my own. I chose the October Nationals in West Palm Beach, Florida.

On race day, I had a single overriding objective: to finish first in class. When the checkered flag fell, I had my essential victory.

It had been a laughing, dancing day in the sun, and the finish meant that I would go to the Daytona runoffs as first alternate. If one of the top three in the Northeast Division couldn't start the race for some reason, I would be added to the field.

The Daytona runoffs took place during Thanksgiving week. I went without crew. It was Ralph Farnham's busy season, taking boats out of the water. Luke didn't want to take more time off from work, or away from his classes. So I set off by myself, into the teeth of a typhoon of calamities, as it turned out. It didn't help that my bank account contained just about enough money for fuel; definitely not enough for hotels or restaurants.

My latest $135 station wagon, a Mercury, had no particular interest in going to Florida. By Virginia it was developing vapor lock, for which the fix was a bag full of ice on top of the fuel pump. In South Carolina the starter motor gave up. In Georgia a wheel broke, and so did the jack on the Jaguar's trailer. When I finally rolled into the infield at Daytona, the Mercury fuel pump quit for good. Inspired, the Jaguar's fuel pump quit as well. I was practically moved to tears when some hospitable competitors offered me space on the floor of their hotel room. I think there were six of us in it. Somehow I got the parts, fixed the cars, presented the Jaguar for technical inspection, and headed out onto the track for practice.

This was what I had been waiting for. The race for our class would use the 3.1-mile road circuit, which included almost three-quarters of Daytona's huge bowl. If ever a course was made for the Jaguar, this was it. Its sleek lines and big long-stroke engine, the good breathing enabled by its double overhead cams, should give it the high-speed advantage it needed over more modern cars. On the fast Watkins Glen circuit the year before, I had qualified faster than all the well-supported Triumphs. Even if no one from my division fell out before the race here—even if I didn't start—I hoped at least to leave the Jaguar's mark.

It was a year too late. At 143 mph on the high banks of Daytona, while the Jaguar's mirrors were still full of Triumph, my beautiful engine threw a rod, turning most of itself into scrap metal. It broke my heart. My Jaguar racing was at an end.

The trip back north was even more nightmarish than the trip south. The Mercury wagon left Daytona running on seven cylinders. By Jacksonville, it was down to six. The Virginia tollway was a particular torture, with four thousand pounds of Jaguar and trailer to pull. Each time I brought the rig to a stop to hand over an endless succession of quarters, I was on tenterhooks as to whether I could get it rolling again. The end came on I-95 near Quantico, as a few more cylinders gave up the ghost. Trailing dense clouds of smoke, I coasted off at the next exit, through a stoplight, and into the first service station, half a mile away.

It was my great good fortune to fall into friendly hands. The service station owner was a NASCAR racing enthusiast, an easy-going, capable, no-problem sort of guy. He said I could leave the rig with him, and that it would be safe, until I could come back with another tow car. And the bus north stopped right at his door.

TURNING PRO

Life without the Jaguar was a life I could hardly imagine, but the 1967 Daytona runoffs made it intolerably clear that the XK 140's competitive days were over. By April of 1968, the elegant creature that I knew so intimately was gone, sold to the friend of a friend somewhere in the deep South. I never saw it again.

Life without the Jaguar was, however, considerably closer to normal. For four years I had no race car of my own, no relentless drain on my salary. A handful of rides kept my hand in and my hopes up. I went back to work as a technical editor at Sperry in November 1968, and slowly became solvent again. Luke wasn't quite as solvent as I; but we went skiing in Vermont, adventuring across Haiti by tap-tap truck and DC-3, diving the coral reefs off Jamaica.

I acquired a handsome white Plymouth Barracuda fastback that was only a year old, and found it extremely agreeable to have reliable transportation for the very first time. It was comforting to have a stylish fur coat, proof against Manhattan's winter winds; lovely to slither into a silk-knit Pucci minidress, to peruke my hair and saunter in to the Madison Avenue Sports Car Driving and Chowder Society at Sardi's in Manhattan with money for lunch. In the Jaguar years, lunch was a glass of wine, on the pretext of dieting.

In 1970, Luke and I spent three weeks in Japan. My brother Stewart and his wife, Marty, were living there while Stew did the field work for his doctorate in anthropology. The four of us set out to a remote mountain festival, and later Luke and I struck off by ourselves. We made our way to Kyoto, to Nara, and to the sacred island of Myajima; to Hiroshima, across Hokkaido to the Sea of Japan and its hot springs, having fine adventures along the way.

A normal life had much to be said for it.

But something was missing.

Certainly, enough people had lectured me on the wisdom of giving up my obsession with motorsports. You don't have the money for it, they said; that was perfectly true. You have so many other things going for you, they said, why risk your life? I didn't have an answer for that. But I never stopped looking for rides, sending out sponsorship proposals, trying to find my way into the seat of any race car I could. My files are crammed with old letters and proposals for racing. So well written! So well reasoned! So unsuccessful.

In March of my first year without the Jaguar, 1968, it looked as if Ring-Free was finally going to give its women's team a more competitive car for Sebring. American Motors was making a big push with its Javelins, which would join the Trans-Am Mustangs and Camaros to take part in the 12-Hour. A young mechanic independent of the factory effort, we heard, was building a Javelin to Trans-Am specs for Liane Engeman and me. As a bonus, Ring-Free would have a Formula Vee for each of us, for one of the curtain-raising races there. These were the Volkswagen-engined single-seaters that were extremely popular and hotly competed in at the time.

What could be better?

A lot could have been better, as it turned out.

Registration and tech inspection opened at Sebring on Wednesday March 20. No Javelin appeared. There was only one Formula Vee, not two. The Vee got through tech on Thursday morning. There was still no Javelin, though we heard a rumor it was around somewhere. I borrowed a car and went looking for it, out in the huge ancient hangars and around the infield. As I crested a humpback bridge toward the center of the course, I spotted the thing, dead ahead, and my heart sank.

The big coupe with our number on it, 26, was up on jacks in a great state of disassembly, right there in the middle of nowhere. Not one element of the picture looked professional. Clearly this particular young mechanic had bitten off a great deal more than he could chew.

He needed parts. He needed a lot of parts. I flew into action, drawing heavily on the kindness and resources of Ronnie Kaplan, who ran the official, factory-backed Javelin team. With the help of the parts he provided, we managed to hide from the tech inspectors the fact that the Javelin had brakes on the front wheels only. Liane and I squeaked into mandatory night practice at the last minute, and each made the required number of laps.

Practice the following morning, the last available session, made clear just how bad the situation was. For openers, the engine ceased to function in each turn. The slightest lateral load caused an immediate interruption of power, which didn't resume until the car was once again proceeding straight ahead. This was obviously a fuel-starvation problem, yet somehow it couldn't be fixed. The tachometer—a driver's primary instrument—didn't work, and there was no speedometer from which the rpm's might be calculated. The rear brakes were finally hooked up, but since they were drum brakes fitted with ordinary street linings, their only contribution was to fill the car with the fishy odor of overstressed material.

As the final qualifying session opened, we got a word of advice from the young mechanic. "Don't take the corners too hard," he said. "With these big wheels and tires, there's a good chance the axles will snap and the wheels fall off."

Ye gods and little fishes.

We did what we could in the Javelin, then leaped immediately into the Formula Vee for the curtain-raiser race. A good many of the hottest Vee drivers from around the country were in the field, in extremely competitive, well-prepared cars. All the smaller-engine cars, including ours, were gridded at the back. Liane started the two-hour race, handing it over to me in the middle. It was my second-ever time at the wheel of a rear-engine single-seater, and while it was different, I rather liked it. We finished eighth out of twenty starters in class, sixteenth overall in a field of thirty-eight.

By the time the Vee race was over, the grid was posted for the 12-Hour. Our Javelin wasn't—quite—the slowest car in the seventy-two-car field. We had been turning faster laps with the Volkswagen.

Hindsight is a great thing. Never again would I agree to start a race with so badly crippled a car. At the moment of decision, though, it seemed almost reasonable. We were accustomed to being backmarkers in the Ring-Free cars anyway, in sixty hours' worth of competition to date. This had been the company's first actual attempt to provide something intended to be competitive. If we walked away from the Javelin, we figured it was likely to be the last car we got from them.

It was small consolation that, despite the vexing fuel-starvation problem, we were never the slowest car in the race. (According to the official race records, eleven cars posted slower race laps than we did.) By the end of the third hour of the race, we had gained twenty-five positions; by the end of the fourth hour, an additional eight spots.

None of it was fun.

At half past the fourth hour, 2:25 in the afternoon, Liane pitted. Something had to be done, she said, about the fuel starvation problem. It had gotten worse; the car had come to a complete stop before the engine came back to life. They fiddled with it and sent her out a couple of times, unfixed. Then the Javelin spent an hour and twenty-one minutes in the pits.

About that time, we started hearing rumors: something about one of the Fords, its Australian driver claiming Liane had forced him off the course.

Liane was puzzled. "There was a French Porsche 911," she said. I knew the one. It was one of the squirrels that you had to be careful of. It had qualified fifty-fifth in the field.

"About half an hour before I came in," she said, "the driver was trying to pass me in the esses. I was right at the edge of the road, making as much room for him as I could. He brushed my left rear fender anyway. I hardly felt it, but he spun."

I went to look at the left-hand side of the Javelin; saw nothing. Then, as I looked more carefully, I saw faint rubber marks at the back of the left rear fender, and a cracked taillight lens.

It hardly seemed anything to be concerned about.

No assessment was ever more wrong. The incident turned into one of the biggest brouhahas in the history of Sebring.

As it turned out, a photographer in the infield had caught the whole sequence of events on film. The Javelin's position on the track was just as Liane said. The French Porsche 911 was first shown just behind our Javelin, at a forty-five-degree angle to the track. Liane continued on her way. Paul Hawkins, an Australian driver in a Ford GT40 sponsored by Gulf Oil, entered the esses behind the spinning Porsche. The GT40 drove onto the grass, avoiding the Porsche, then back onto the track.

The Porsche continued to the end of the race. The Ford pitted, then continued for the next four and a half hours, usually in second or third place. A little after 6 p.m. its suspension broke, putting it out of competition.

Hawkins returned to his pit spitting nails. The Australian had a tempting target: not the Frenchmen in the Porsche, nor any flaw in the Ford, but the "bloody birds" in the limping Ring-Free Oil Javelin. The Gulf Oil team's PR man, Al Bochroch, wasn't slow to seize his chance. He escorted Hawkins directly to the press room, where the frustrated driver vented his considerable spleen. Needless to say, more than one reporter lapped it up.

The officials couldn't enlighten us: they knew nothing about any incident involving our car. The crew of the flag station where the Porsche spun hadn't perceived any contact at all between the Porsche and the Javelin—never mind the Ford.

When rumor of the accusation reached the Director of Competition, Jim Kaser, he immediately ordered that special attention be paid to our car by all observers and flag stations, for the duration of the race. Afterwards, he wrote, "All reports indicated the car was being properly driven and was staying out of the way of faster cars."[1] So we continued, finishing thirty-second out of thirty-six cars still running at the end. Jo Siffert and Hans Hermann won, in a factory Porsche prototype. No official complaint was ever made, though the rules specified the procedure for it. No other driver complained of our conduct; on the contrary, several later defended us.

It was all done in the headlines next day, and that was enough.

"Bloody Birds' Knock Ford from Race"—Miami *Herald*.

"Porsche Sacks Sebring; Ford Blames Woman Driver"—Palm Beach *Post-Times*.

"Watch Out: Those Women Drivers"—Tampa *Tribune*.

It seemed nothing could stop the media juggernaut—not the letters from top drivers in the race, defending our conduct; not the availability of photos of the whole thing; not the winner's version. (Jo Siffert: "I didn't see any girls.")

Only one motor sports magazine chose to print the pictures of the actual incident. Photos of Liane, however, appeared everywhere. The accompanying text always implied that her beauty disqualified her from any possibility of competence. Leon Mandel, then editor of *Car and Driver*, relished the vitriol enough to add significant doses of his own.

Even now, more than three decades later, Hawkins' accusation is allowed without rebuttal into histories of the sport. It "shines and stinks like rotten mackerel by moonlight," as John Randolph famously observed.

I had just gotten my first major lesson in where the edge was—not the racing edge, the edge to find in the turns, but the sharp edge of society's attitude toward women and the use to which it could be put.

By November of 1968, the wolf was at my door. Unemployment insurance and savings and the proceeds of selling the Jaguar had all run out. I went to work for Sperry Systems Management Division of Sperry Rand. The job required a degree in science or engineering, and it paid an engineering salary, but as "publications engineer," I was

---

[1] Letter in my possession.

basically a technical editor. That was how I earned my living for the next four years.

At Sebring in March of 1969, Liane Engeman and I and Donna Mae Mims shared a Sprite Prototype, a tiny 1293-cc coupe designed by Donald Healey. The Hawkins fracas reverberated unpleasantly in the headlines at first, but faded as we went about our business with a well-prepared little car. Ring-Free had at last contracted with an experienced, capable outfit, and the event was notably free of stress.

Our race went so smoothly that I would not answer when people asked how it was going, for fear of jinxing it. We finished second in class (Prototype 7) and twenty-third overall, out of seventy starters.

Back at Sebring in 1970, we won the Under-2-Liter Prototype class for Ring-Free with a slightly faster version of the same little 1293-cc Donald Healey Sprite. Rosemary Smith, Judy Kondratieff and I finished ninteenth overall out of sixty-eight starters. It was a memorable race.

The field that year held fifteen formidable factory-backed cars designed exclusively to win races of this sort: Ferraris, Porsches, Alfa Romeos, and Matras. All were in the hands of internationally famous drivers. Mario Andretti took the pole, in a Ferrari 512. The top independent car in qualifying, fifteenth on the grid, was a Porsche 908 driven by Peter Revson, nephew of the Revlon cosmetics mogul, and movie star Steve McQueen. Everyone in the pits, of course, had their stopwatches on this pair. McQueen's right foot was in a heavy cast, the result of a motorcycling accident, but even so he was just a few seconds slower than Revson, who was a world-class driver.

After leading for most of the first eleven hours of racing, Andretti's Ferrari broke. That put a Porsche 917 in first place, one lap ahead of the Revson/McQueen Porsche 908. A team Ferrari 512 lay in third, another lap behind. Mario Andretti got into this Ferrari, and set out to do the impossible.

I was leading our class to the checkered flag then, and had the closest possible view. There was no way in hell that Andretti could make up such a distance—but he did.

Rarely have I seen such driving as in that last hour of that Sebring race. On a pitch-black course strewn with wreckage, Andretti turned laps as fast as the car had *qualified* at *in the daytime*. Revson was extracting the utmost from his smaller Porsche. Then the leading 917 broke with only a quarter-hour to go, putting Revson/McQueen in first place.

Andretti overtook the smaller Porsche just minutes from the end. The melodrama intensified when he pitted for fuel. At the checkered flag, Andretti was ahead by 23.8 seconds. It was a night to remember, and a feat that is talked of to this day.

Toward the end of the 1971 season, the Sports Car Club of America scheduled a three-hour endurance race at Bridgehampton. It was a compelling opportunity: a fast, challenging circuit that I knew by heart, close to home where I knew people who could crew. I set out for the National Championship races in Watkins Glen with a single cold-blooded objective: to line up a ride for the Bridgehampton 400, in a car capable of winning it.

For two days I scrutinized the entrants there, and by Sunday the deal was done. With $500 from Ring-Free Oil and a set of tires from Goodyear, I got a seat as co-driver of an ex-Trans Am Camaro. Its new owner, my co-driver Kent Fellows, had prepared the car well.

At Bridgehampton, our primary competition came from former Ring-Free driver Ray Cuomo, who shared a similar Camaro with George Lisberg. They qualified on the pole for the race, but Kent seized the lead on the first lap. He was still leading when I took over, and I kept it first overall.

What a different world! I had sought a ride in the Trans-Am series for years. This Camaro suited me to perfection. Bridgehampton was perhaps the most challenging track in the country, and I knew it well. Its long front straight lay on golden sandy heights that looked out over Sag Harbor and Peconic Bay. At the end of the front straight lay a breathtaking pair of top-gear downhill turns, blind until you were hurtling over the crest. I was good at those downhills; loved them, in fact. The rest of the circuit, almost three miles long, was equally demanding. It wound its way up and down the scrub-covered dunes, every turn a fast one, most of them blind. The Camaro ate it up. Three hours from the start, we led the field under the checkered flag.

It was so simple. All I had to do was get my hands on a winning car. And all that took was ... money.

Many years later, a wealthy friend told me that when he, too, came to understand how the fastest car was acquired with the most dollars, and the fastest car usually won, he lost interest in racing. Purchasing the fastest car was no problem for him; but if victory was less a matter of skill and desire than of money, the sporting element diminished and his interest did, too.

It is an eminently rational perspective. But along with the

physical traits that I inherited from my father—fine hair, long narrow feet—came a generous dash of Don Quixote syndrome. That victory at Bridgehampton at the end of 1971 got folded into my passion for racing like egg whites into a soufflé. It formed part of the background for what became the decision of a lifetime.

That winter, my thirty-fourth, my midlife crisis issues surfaced. They were the usual suspects: what was my life all about? Where was I going? Where could I—where should I—apply my strengths? Where did the requisite passion lie? Should I return to physics? Flying? One day, a friend who knew of my interest in history called to say that a small pre-Revolutionary house in Huntington, New York, was on the market for $15,000. Two centuries earlier, it had been the patriots' secret armory. What a place to live! But a mortgage would tie me to a full-time job for at least fifteen years; my life would perforce become conventional. That prospect was daunting. Still, wasn't it about time for a life that seemed more secure?

Or was it? Only one endeavor had ever taken me completely outside myself, had required all I had and then some, had propelled me to a different level of existence. That endeavour was racing.

Racing was irrational. Racing was dangerous. It would have seemed far more prudent to buy the historic little house. But not long after I turned it down, a car lost control on the street in front of it, and killed the owner in his bed.

My choice had already been made. In January, I gathered all my savings and most of what I could borrow, got commitments from a few solid, knowledgeable volunteers whom I knew, and threw myself into the construction of a new race car of my own.

Meanwhile, I had finally broken off with Luke, ending a problematic four-year relationship. Then I learned that the man who had so shaken my existence eight years earlier, but who had married another woman, was now divorced. We started seeing each other again.

So at the beginning of 1972, I lived in bliss, my imagination running wild. All I most wanted in life seemed within reach: the man who had captured my heart, and a nationally competitive team of my own.

My objective was to field a Toyota Celica in the newly announced professional Two-Five Challenge series. Datsun (later called Nissan) was already a sizeable presence in sports car racing, and a driver named Bob Sharp had built himself a Connecticut racing empire with Datsun cars and factory-level support. Toyota was just now introducing its first sporty model, the Celica. Could a Toyota racing program be far behind?

I pitched this idea to local dealers, to the East Coast distributor, to the importer in California, and to Japan. A handful of individuals showed interest. Letters of recommendation undoubtedly helped. Among them, those from Indianapolis 500 winner Mark Donohue and Sebring impresario Alec Ulmann were standouts. I was grateful indeed. In mid-February, I was offered a Celica at dealer invoice cost.

The Celica was the first new car I had ever owned. One of my volunteers and I broke a bottle of Piper Heidseck over its engine block, in a howling gale of snow and rain. The Celica had less than seventy-five miles on it when we pushed it through knee-deep snowdrifts into an ancient wooden factory building and commenced tearing it apart, down to the last nut and bolt.

Within six weeks, my little group and I had made a great deal of progress. The chassis, stripped, was fitted with its stiff and intricate roll cage—designed by Charlie Gresl, cut and fitted by Tom Carren and myself. Engine design was under way. Then Dave Reilly, who had offered the space in the factory building, and whose knowledge and experience were essential, ran out of money and took a job driving trucks. The Celica had to find another home. Ralph Farnham obliged, and his minuscule shop again became the place where I spent every waking minute that I wasn't at Sperry.

Along the way, my relationship proved to be almost as short-lived the second time round as it had been the first time. I had imagined I could have it all. I was wrong. Sometimes I wondered whether the Celica's demands were a cause; but most likely, it just wasn't meant to be.

The Celica slipped behind schedule. So many things had to be designed and built from scratch. My volunteers grew weary. My bank loans became ominous. I crushed my fingers, scraped and blistered my skin. There wasn't an inch of that car that didn't have my blood on it.

Early in the summer, the rent for my charming ruin of an apartment in Great Neck was raised by one-third. I had been there nine years, but the squeeze was too much. I moved to a tiny, cheap hole in the wall behind a storefront on a busy commercial thoroughfare in Floral Park, Long Island. Access lay through a padlocked gate in a chain-link fence.

On a typical day, I went straight from Sperry to Ralph's shop, worked on the car until the small hours of the morning, slept a little and was back at Sperry before 8 a.m. Late in the summer, I went for the medical exam required to renew my racing license. I had known the doctor for a long time. He saw ominous effects of stress, and queried me. At the end he said slowly and gravely, "You have to give up."

"I can't," I said.

Hundreds of small delays obtaining or fashioning parts prolonged the completion of the Celica until autumn, and then the Two-Five Challenge series, for which the car was designed, was cancelled before it ever put a wheel on the track. The gesture that launched the Celica, on that snowy February day when I broke the bottle of champagne over its nose, looked in retrospect like a swan dive into a black and dismal swamp.

Life breaks everyone, it is said and, after, some are stronger at the broken places. I can't claim that I was ever stronger after that ghastly year. I *can* say that the job got done. The price I paid was long-term damage to the gift of joy.

In mid-October, the Celica had its first trial outing. I took third place in an SCCA race at Lime Rock, Connecticut, beating three Corvettes and a Porsche in the process. One week later, at an SCCA race at Bridgehampton, I won: not just first in class, but first overall. The re-energized crew completely exhausted the supply of cold champagne at Baron's Cove, the traditional locus of post-race celebrations in Sag Harbor.

The week after that, the last SCCA races of the season were scheduled at Pocono International Raceway in Pennsylvania, a track I had never seen. Its road-racing circuit wound through the infield, then climbed out onto the high-speed oval used by Indy cars. I started in twenty-seventh place. Light rain was falling through fog so thick the oncoming turns were invisible. Braking and turning points were set by what could be seen out the side window.

It was a sprint race, giving me twenty minutes to work my way through the field. Within six laps I was first in class, and held that position to the end. I had no idea that one other car lay ahead in the fog, putting me second overall. Later that day came a four-hour enduro. My co-driver and I were first in class for much of the race, finishing second. Among the cars behind us were two Porsches, a Ford Cobra and a Ferrari.

It was good, but it was SCCA, not the now-defunct professional Two-Five Challenge series for which I had built the Celica. So it was a bittersweet ending to a nightmarish year, both personally and professionally.

I campaigned the Celica for the next three years, entering it in fifty-two races. For a while, it was the fastest Toyota in the country. A-1 Toyota of East Haven, Connecticut, became a generous sponsor at the dealership level. I owed the dealership owners, Dom Galardi and Tony Buglione, a great deal of thanks for the successes we had.

The demise of the Two-Five Challenge series left me without an appropriate professional venue for the car, so I chose targets of opportunity. We gained our class championship in the North Atlantic Road Racing Championship series in 1973. I then flew to California with a full-blown proposal to Toyota USA for a racing program under the auspices of A-1 that might challenge the Datsuns on a national basis.

They heard me out, but I remember puzzling over the look of faint amusement on their faces. Even though 1973 was the year of Billie Jean King's "Battle of the Sexes" tennis match against Bobby Riggs, it never occurred to me that those men at Toyota might not have been prepared to support a racing program with a woman driver. In any case, all we ever got from Toyota USA was a request for artwork which they could, and did, convert into a poster trumpeting our NARRC victory. They sent it to their dealerships nationwide.

I kept on racing. Having finally quit my job at Sperry, I drove Ralph Farnham's boat-moving truck to keep the rent paid. This was great fun. Ralph had all the expertise about moving boats, but he didn't like to drive, and while he was still immensely strong, he had a bad back. So I would hitch up the trailer, back the rig under the boat, sling the huge jacks and concrete blocks around, and we would set off down the road with some thirty- or forty-foot vessel behind. These trips were a great relief from the never-ending pressure to maintain and repair the Celica.

And there were other compensations as well. As it happened, actor Paul Newman, at age forty-seven, was just beginning his racing career in these years, in a Bob Sharp Datsun that ran in the same class as the Celica. Of course, I had quite a close view of what he was doing on the track, and often found myself defending him against envious grumbling that he was just a rich star who had bought himself a top-notch ride. (He was later to demonstrate his talent beyond any doubt.) It was quite a thrill to have him around. When his name had appeared in the top twenty on the Nixon White House enemies list, Newman's response, solicited by *The New York Times*, was: "I'd like to thank Bob Haldeman for making this award possible, and I'm sending John Erlichman to pick up my award."[2]

I thought he deserved immortality for that remark, and one day in the paddock I told him so. Newman was always reserved, if not remote, but at this he smiled.

"Making that list is the greatest honor I've had in all my years as an actor," he said.

Understandably, Newman kept to himself. But one particular moment lodged permanently in my heart.

I had gone to a race at Bridgehampton without any crew at all, and lost yet another differential in practice. Race time was forty minutes away. I was sliding dejectedly out from under the back end of the Celica, when a shadow fell. It was Newman.

"What happened?"

I told him.

"Can you fix it in time?"

"I don't think so."

He bent over to peer at it, then turned those famous blue eyes toward me with a look of sympathy that penetrated all the way to my fifth dorsal vertebra.

"I'm sorry," he said.

It's a wonder I didn't melt into the sand on the very spot.

The end of the 1974 racing season found the Celica badly damaged. I had been helped into a bridge abutment during the season's last race. My outlook on life was as bleak as the winter darkness that gnawed on each diminishing day. Then late one night, I came home from Ralph's shop to find a message on my answering machine.

"This is Rolla Vollstedt in Portland, Oregon," the voice said. The name rang no bells. "Please call me about a possible ride in the Indianapolis 500."

Oh, certainly. Very funny. But the next morning, I called Chris Economaki, the editor of *National Speed Sport News*, to ask who Rolla Vollstedt was.

As Chris filled me in, my pulse began to race. Vollstedt was real. Three hours later, when it was time to call the West Coast, my hands had quit shaking and I was calm enough to have an objective

---

[2] Haldeman and Erlichman were two of Nixon's main Watergate henchmen. If memory serves, those were the two whom Newman specified.

conversation. Vollstedt said he was seeking the best woman driver in the country, and had gotten my name from several sources.

We talked at length. Nothing came of it. I was not surprised. The last three years had drained me of optimism. I no longer believed that my efforts would lead to a top-notch ride. From time to time, I thought of the words of a tough-minded auto executive at Sebring in 1968. This man had admired my prowess, and had offered what help he could. But his voice was slow and emphatic as he said, "You will never be a winning driver, *because* no one will ever give you a winning car, *because* you are a woman."

I hadn't believed him, at the time.

Not long after Vollstedt's call, I was invited to compete in the first Women's Superstars, a decathlon-like television event that pitted athletes against each other in sports not their own. The event was a minor milepost in women's sports—Superstars for men had been going on for a couple of years—and we welcomed the chance to make each other's acquaintance. Of the twenty-three women who gathered in Houston for the preliminaries, only Billie Jean King, gymnast Cathy Rigby, and stakes-winning jockey Robyn Smith could be said to have name recognition. Ten Olympians, six of them gold medallists, seemed nearly unknown. Speed skater Diane Holum, with 1972 Olympic gold and silver medals among her credits, was nearly penniless and about to be evicted from her home when the Superstars invitation threw her a lifeline. Almost none of the competitors had been able to make a living at her sport, and several noted that this show-biz event offered women athletes a rare touch of the spotlight, a rare chance to make more than pocket change. Would it lead to better things for women in sports? No one knew, but an irritating condescension was evident in some of the press coverage.

Walt Cunningham, one of the early astronauts, was among the honorary judges in the Houston Astrodome. A couple of days into the competition, he and I struck up a conversation. Of course, I mentioned my Scientist-Astronaut application of a decade earlier.

He said that it would be a cold day in hell before women were accepted into the astronaut program.

Startled, I said, "Why is that?"

"Well," he smirked, "it took us $270,000 to figure out a way for a man to go to the bathroom in space, and remind me to *explain* to you sometime how women are different." He half turned away, as if he thought the conversation closed.

Not quite. "How come," I said, "the Russians can put a woman in space and we can't?"

He twitched. "Oh," he said, "the Russian space program is entirely different from ours. They don't even *need* men. They could just as well send up *monkeys*."

I couldn't think of anything to say after that.

The remark was, of course, a classic of its kind, freighted with contempt and sexual innuendo, and reflecting the cultural attitudes that, by that time, had fueled feminism to white heat. But in 1974, I had yet to give these matters much serious attention. The politics of feminism were proceeding without me. Cunningham's comment seemed the product of a warped mind. I thought him to be an anomaly in a mostly rational world. I still had a lot to learn.

By 1975, the International Motor Sports Association (IMSA) had established a new series of professional races in which the Celica had a chance of success. Although the rules of preparation were profoundly different from the specifications to which I had built the car, I set my cap for the IMSA race at Lime Rock, to be held at the end of May. An enormous amount of work lay ahead. I hauled the Celica south to my parents' home in Miami, where I set about making the necessary changes with the aid of my father's shop equipment. The 1968 Barracuda fastback that made such elegant transportation when I bought it in 1969 was now, six years later, my tow car and camper.

Early in 1975, I had proposed to Dom Galardi and Tony Buglione that their dealership, A-1 Toyota, take over the maintenance of the race car. To my surprise and relief, they agreed. In the second week of May, I hauled the Celica to East Haven on the Connecticut coast. But Dom and Tony didn't really understand what an enormous amount of work was required to support a race car. They gave me keys to the shop, and I worked late and alone there nearly every night. East Haven was a long way from Long Island. More often than not, too tired to drive home and with too much work still to do, I slept in the Barracuda in the dealership's parking lot. I didn't let Dom and Tony know about this.

Practice for the big race at Lime Rock was scheduled for the third week of May. It was after midnight Thursday when I hitched up the trailer, loaded the race car onto it, and pointed the Barracuda's nose northwest toward Lime Rock. I was fatigued to the point of smelling like rubber tires, and my nostrils were full of it, the reek of two days of hard, hot work. My clothes were dark with automotive grime. I was not altogether sane. A little way out of New Haven, I spotted a shabby motel. It cost me eight bucks to get cleaned up and sleep for two hours. I pressed on as the sun rose.

Some new volunteers turned up at the track, lured by an ad I had placed in Competition Press, so it was necessary to be light and cheerful, and to persuade them that this was all great fun. We soldiered through trouble with the carburetors and the front suspension, both newly installed to suit IMSA's rules.

We qualified on Saturday, worked on the car all day Sunday, started the race on Monday, and promptly sheared all the flywheel bolts, thus disconnecting the engine from the rear wheels. It was a new and different failure mode, entirely unanticipated, and an occasion more bitter than can be described.

I was about five thousand 1975 dollars in debt at this point, with no prospect of climbing out. My career in physics was eight years gone, hopelessly out of date. I had no savings, no pension plan, no house, no health insurance, no stocks or bonds, no jewelry. My living situation was intolerable. And I was fresh out of engines again.

It was the nadir, the pits, the bottom of the black and dismal swamp. Carl Orff's *Carmina Burana* was suitable music. "*O Fortuna ... vita detestabilis.*"

I had no reason to think that this might not be the end of the world—of my racing world. I could never have foreseen that it was, instead, the winter solstice.

The dark seemed endless. My great gamble with the Celica—I had bet almost four years of my life, and all my resources, on it—had failed to attract the kind of funding necessary to succeed on a national level. "Really," I said to myself, "you are going to have to come to your senses, and start making some provision for your old age." It was long past time when a sensible person would have quit spending every penny she made on race cars. My heart ached over this.

How could I give up that white heat, that ferocity without malice, that infinitely sharp focus on each infinitely small segment of time? How could I renounce that mysterious access to abilities beyond what the conscious mind or will could accomplish? For thirteen years, racing had been an obsession. The prospect of giving up loomed like a kind of death.

The first sign of light was a new place to live, in the city itself. One of my Lime Rock volunteers had a friend named Marianne

Magocsi, who was soon to marry T'ing Pei, son of the architect I. M. Pei. Her studio apartment in Manhattan (in Kips Bay Towers, a building of I. M. Pei's design) was vacant. She let me have it for a nominal amount.

I transferred the Celica to Orangeburg, near Nyack on the Hudson, to an exceptionally beautiful nineteenth century industrial park with tall trees and well-tended green lawns. There was a great peacefulness to the place, and I drank it in like one dying of thirst. My garage there was shared with a young graduate student named Doug Schirripa, who became one of the best volunteers I ever had. He was brilliant, irreverent, cynical, witty, completely reliable, and made terrific crew at the year's remaining races. When we rolled out of our sleeping bags to see six guys polishing Bob Sharp's tractor-trailer full of factory-backed Datsuns, our competition, at least we could joke about it.

Then fortune's turn upward gathered speed. Out of the blue came a phone call from a big Manhattan public relations agency. Would I be interested in representing Toyota on a national media tour concerning small cars and safe driving? They wanted a woman racing driver, and one of my friends had given them my name.

They would book me onto TV shows, radio programs, and set up newspaper interviews, and I would talk about small cars, safe driving, and of course Toyotas. When they learned I had been racing a Toyota Celica for the last four years, they were amazed. No one had told them that.

By late September we had a contract for a part-time, one-year program. On the strength of it, I signed a lease on a bigger apartment in Kips Bay, beginning just as Marianne's lease expired at the end of October. With its floor-to-ceiling, wall-to-wall windows looking north to the United Nations and the necklace lights of the Queensboro and Triborough bridges, it was the aerie of my dreams.

Thoroughly tired of being underdogs, Doug Schirripa and I went back to Bridgehampton at the end of September to face better odds. The Vanderbilt Cup races were no longer part of a major series; the factory teams with the tractor-trailers weren't there.

I started the five-lap qualifying race near the back of the twenty-seven car field. In four and a half laps I passed twenty cars, working my way up to second place. The fellow who was leading, in an ex-factory Huffaker MGB, had never run against me, and wasn't prepared to accept defeat at my hands. As we came off the last turn and started toward the checkered flag, I was right behind him. Our engines were evenly matched, but I had come through the last turn faster than he. The incremental speed would carry me past him before the finish line. He didn't want that to happen. We were so close that I could watch his eyes in his mirrors as he checked on my location. When my nose was almost even with his tail, he violently swerved in front of me.

He expected, of course, that I would back off; even a moment off the throttle would kill my momentum enough to give him the victory. I thought it a contemptible move, left my throttle foot on the floor, and swerved violently onto the chewed-up asphalt at the edge of pit road. Doug told me that a gasp went up along the pit rail; we were doing well over 100 mph at the time. I was a car length in front of him at the finish line.

The next day, I led the Vanderbilt Cup race from start to finish. I never drove the Celica again.

Altogether, the circumstances of my life were improving with bewildering speed. My first priority was getting out of debt, so my apartment remained sparsely furnished except for books—and the glorious panorama of autumn in Manhattan that filled the huge windows. With the Celica in limbo, the civilized pleasures of that autumn of 1975 and the luxuries of the media tour seemed rootless. Maybe it was just as well that I drifted through them; it was a breathing space.

In December, not long after the winter solstice, I called Rolla Vollstedt again.

THE CHANCE OF
A LIFETIME

In the year since I found Vollstedt's initial call on my answering machine, I had learned a little more about his background. He had entered cars at Indianapolis since 1964. His best finish as a team owner had been ninth, but one or more of his cars had always made the field. That alone was a significant achievement, in those decades when as many as ninety cars were entered for the thirty-three-car race.

Vollstedt's position on the United States Auto Club Board of Directors was also reassuring. USAC was the sanctioning body for all of Indy-car racing (properly called USAC Championship racing, a fine point carefully observed by the participants) and for venues such as Sprint car racing that traditionally led to Indianapolis. As such, USAC governed the highest levels of professional open-wheel racing in America.

Always an innovator, Rolla Vollstedt had been the first builder to run an Indy car with wings, the first to mount an Offenhauser engine in the rear. Somewhere along the line, he decided to be the first to bring a woman driver to Indianapolis.

Nevertheless, I was wary. As I had learned at Sebring with the woefully underprepared Javelin, driving for someone unfamiliar to you could put you in a situation fraught with peril. Of course, Vollstedt knew little about me, either. Since there were no women in oval-track racing, he had queried his road-racing friends and acquaintances. The name he kept getting was mine.

One week into the New Year, Rolla Vollstedt and I again explored the possibility of my joining his team for the 1976 Indianapolis 500. Vollstedt had already engaged veteran Indy-car driver Dick Simon for the full racing season. Like many owners, he would enter two or more cars at Indianapolis, so I might become the junior, rookie driver. I restated my initial position: there must be time for familiarization, and it must take place in advance of any publicity.

"You understand that publicity is necessary," Vollstedt said. "That's the reason Bryant Heating and Cooling puts money into racing."

I said I understood that, but testing would have to come first. If it was successful—if the car could go fast enough, and if I could drive it fast enough; if I liked them, and if they liked me—then they could go ahead and make whatever noise they felt they needed to.

I had reasons for a guarded approach. It had finally gotten through my thick skull that a woman driver might not be taken seriously, and that the consequences could include a reputation left in tatters. I would take every possible precaution to avoid such a foolish position, when the stakes were so high.

"Ontario would be the right place for testing, if we do it," Vollstedt said. The 2.5-mile speedway near Los Angeles was comparable to Indianapolis, and Dick Simon would doubtless welcome the chance to check out his new ride. "But track rental alone is a thousand dollars a day, and then there's wear and tear on engines and chassis, crew expenses and salaries, ambulance and fire truck costs. I don't know whether Bryant will cover those expenses on speculation, without some sort of publicity payback."

I stood my ground. I wasn't telling anyone about this, and my condition on it was that no one else did, either.

"I'll talk with Bryant about it," he said.

Two weeks later, I learned from a mutual acquaintance that Arlene Hiss intended to declare for Indianapolis. When we first met in the '60s, Arlene Lanzieri was campaigning a Sprite in the Sports Car Club of America. She was tall, slender, attractive, and entirely serious about the sport. Her Sprite was professionally maintained and competitive. We didn't know each other well, and when she married Indianapolis 500 driver Mike Hiss and moved to California, we lost touch. After he and Arlene separated, she took up driving again. She had won two regional championships in the smaller SCCA Showroom Stock classes.

Arlene had tested an Indy car at Ontario the previous Friday, January 16. It was a fast car that Lloyd Ruby drove the previous year. Ruby, who had raced in every Indianapolis 500 since 1960, would be her teammate, and the well-regarded Mike Devin was crew chief.

Would Vollstedt and Bryant cave in at the appearance of another capable woman driver with competitive equipment and a well-organized team? I kept the news to myself.

Next day, I flew out to Los Angeles to represent Toyota at the Los Angeles Auto Show. Vollstedt and I talked again. Then came a call from Roy East, Vollstedt's main contact at Bryant Heating and Cooling. East and I talked for three-quarters of an hour. He was checking out my seriousness of purpose; and I his. It went well. "The next step," he said, "will be for you to come to Indianapolis and meet the management here. How about early next week?"

I hung up feeling as if tiny champagne bubbles effervesced through every nerve. This couldn't be happening, could it? Just two months before, I had faced the bleak collapse of my dreams of running a professional sports car racing team. Now, a door was opening toward ... the greatest race in the world.

The wonderful secret lit up my weekend with dazzling intensity. I was out at dawn exploring Mulholland Drive, legendary to generations of motoring daredevils. Then, the La Brea tar pits: mastodons and sabre-tooth tigers and the one human female who had left her bones with the huge wild ones, thousands of years before. Tar-dark and eerie, their skeletons stood elegantly reassembled, fleshed out only in the mind's eye.

On Monday morning, the phone rang. Vollstedt had learned about Arlene Hiss, and thought the Bryant executives might indeed change their minds. Phone calls flew back and forth. Nevertheless, that night I stepped off the plane in Indianapolis to meet Roy East, a pleasant, soft-spoken man with grey hair and a gentle manner. He seemed earnest, sincere, solidly behind the idea of bringing a woman driver to the Speedway. I liked him.

The next morning, East was perceptibly nervous as we circled through Bryant headquarters toward the plush offices of the top brass. As executives of an Indianapolis-based company that had sponsored cars in the 500 for years, these men were completely familiar with the taboo against women and the extent to which it was woven into the rituals of the race. I had never been to the Indianapolis 500, and while I was aware of these issues, I hadn't personally experienced their force. The Bryant officers had. So they needed to check me out carefully, and they did.

When they left, Roy East reached over to touch my hand—a gesture of relief and approval. "Would you like to see the track?" he asked.

Of course I would.

We took his Pinto.

Near the Bryant plant the fields were bright with snow, the golden stubble of winter breaking through here and there. We angled east and north to 16th Street at the heart of Speedway, Indiana, population 15,056.

The street was lined with small, neat homes. Snow brightened their tidy yards. Dozens of street-light poles bore brightly colored silhouettes of race cars. No two silhouettes were the same. They were the winners of Indianapolis 500 races since 1911, each with its driver's name.

At the end of the residential area, 16th Street was crossed by railroad tracks. The race cars at one time travelled by train, and all the old ovals—Trenton, Milwaukee—had train tracks nearby. Opposite the tracks loomed the great grey backside of the Turn 1 grandstand. Seeing it at first, I didn't quite comprehend: such a huge structure, not industrial, not office, not a power station nor an oil refinery, and yet it was so ... big ... and then the understanding grew.

We drove past white-painted, well-groomed nineteenth century houses that served as track offices, toward the new tunnel under the south chute. Through it we entered the heart of the track.

Oh, the austere, empty beauty of Indianapolis Motor Speedway, on that late January day! It was like the beauty of dry shocks of corn in the farmed fields and the black leafless branches, under the wintry blue sky. The empty stands were skeletal, as beautiful as the mastodon bones of La Brea. Only in one's imagination could the Speedway be fleshed out ... the screaming cars, the colors, the heat of summer and of passion, the swirling flags, the crowds ... flesh and blood and flame.

Roy opened a gate, and we drove out onto the track itself. Now, the vastness of its volume became more clear. But the pavement was so narrow! As the little Pinto crept along, I felt schizophrenic: in breathless awe of the legendary Speedway, yet simultaneously taking it in with a driver's eye, objectively evaluating the racing surface. Roy glanced over, and smiled.

The back straight seemed interminable. I had flown small planes out of many an airport where the runways were less than half the length of the straightaways here.

We angled out of the northwest turn toward the pit entrance. The front straight grandstands towered far overhead. A quarter of a million people would fill numbered seats here on race day, another hundred and fifty thousand thronging the infield grass. It was hard to imagine. I was glad of our solitude.

Roy turned the Pinto into Gasoline Alley, where the great winged symbol of Indianapolis Motor Speedway hung suspended over the center aisle. The double row of garages resembled well-tended stables on a traditional estate: white wooden clapboard trimmed in dark green, double doors that swung outward, small paned windows hung with curtains or discreetly painted from within. There was a reassuring homeyness to it; and yet over each pair of doors was blazoned the name of last year's occupant and his qualifying speed.

A. J. Foyt, 193.976 mph.

Gordon Johncock, 191.652 mph.

Star tracks.

Tom Bigelow, 181.864 mph.

Tom was Rolla Vollstedt's driver in 1975, and the speed was for car number 17, the Bryant Heating and Cooling Special.

I kept trying to take it in; I felt as if I'd been let out of a cramped little closet into limitless, dazzling space.

We left the abandoned garages behind, waiting for spring and the spark of life. Roy drove me to the airport for the plane back to L. A.

Out at the gate, the terminal's glass walls reflected the crimson disc of the setting sun. I stared at the brilliant image while the real world of airplanes and runways dissolved.

From the virtual sun streamed the memory of Athena's most ancient temple, where I cut my hair and left it eight years before. Athena, goddess of wisdom and learning, counselor and companion in antiquity, her helmet and aegis...

Guide me and protect me.

The sun's burning image sank, reached the horizon, slipped, and was gone; and that became my talisman.

Bryant gave their stamp of approval, and Vollstedt mailed me a contract. He would furnish transportation and lodging for the Ontario test, and for Indianapolis if the test was successful. If we made the field, I'd get forty per cent of the purse, the usual driver's share. There would be no salary.

My driving services would be exclusive to Vollstedt on those terms for 1976, and he had the right to renew for 1977. Bryant and any other sponsors Vollstedt might obtain had permission to use me in advertising, publicity, and personal appearances, for which I would receive expenses only. It was understood that Dick Simon was Vollstedt's number one driver and that he would have the choice of race cars; mine would be a backup for his. If required, I'd be obliged to relinquish my car to Simon at any time up to halfway through an actual race.

Rolla told me later that all he got from Bryant to bring me to Indianapolis was $10,000, which was used up before we ever left Ontario. Lella Lombardi, the Italian Grand Prix driver, was widely reported to have turned down a $50,000 offer to come to the Speedway, but I had no complaint over the terms. When you get the chance of a lifetime, you don't fret if it doesn't come on a golden platter. Rolla engaged Ontario Motor Speedway for the 17th through the 19th of February, three weeks away.

With a break in Toyota's Los Angeles schedule, I borrowed a Celica from them and started north on the coast road for San Francisco. The last four years had taxed me to the limit; my soul needed a respite. In the pure Pacific light, the coast seemed one long existential moment. The air was clear and cool, scented by hillside herbs and flowers. Long green curls of surf lifted into transparency, then whitened and fell luminous on the shore. Cove followed headland to the north; the mountains dropped into the sea and lay there fragmented while the Pacific surged all around, patient and sure of its next bite of earth.

I was thinking at every moment of Indianapolis. I was filled with it, and gathering strength all the time.

Thanks to my old friend Bruce Wennerstrom, I had reservations at the Stanford Court, perhaps the most luxurious hotel on Nob Hill. Pushups and running had become my initial prep for Indy cars, but I wasn't sufficiently inured to a jogger's life to go out and run through the streets of San Francisco's poshest turf. So I was running barefoot in the room, knees high, from one corner to the other, when I landed askew on my right foot. It rolled under with a sharp crack. It hurt so much I could hardly see or think.

I'd never broken a bone in my life. *A broken foot—with Ontario two weeks away—it couldn't happen, it hadn't happened.* I made the feeling of terror diminish, and squeezed it out of my mind. I limped through Muir Woods, had dinner at Le Trianon—and woke in the morning to the certain knowledge that I couldn't go on ignoring the problem.

My borrowed car had to be returned to Los Angeles, and I took the coast road south again, my right foot propped up on the passenger seat. The Interstate would be faster, but it was infamously ugly. I couldn't cope with that much ugliness when my emotions were in danger of getting out of hand. By now I was thoroughly frightened, as the heat and swelling crept up to my knee. How fast would this heal? *Could it heal in time?*

None of my family nor I had a regular doctor, but my return ticket to New York featured an optional $5 detour to Miami, where I went to the emergency room of a small hospital near my parents' home. By now my foot had turned dark purple and green and yellow, with various tints of salmon. They X-rayed it, slapped me into a wheelchair, and rolled me up to a door marked "Cast Room."

No way! Not a chance!

They were *not* letting me out of the hospital without a cast.

I was not having any cast.

We were at stalemate when they remembered an orthopedist due in that morning, a fellow associated with the football team. *Aha,* I thought, *someone who knows about athletic injuries and athletic drive and desire.*

At this point, no one in the world knew of the impending Indy car test except Vollstedt, myself, and Bryant—not even my family. Partly, I hadn't wanted them to fret about it; and partly, I was nurturing my old superstition that if something absolutely wonderful is going to happen, if you tell someone about the possibility, it won't come true. But when the superstar orthopedist perfunctorily ordered a cast two hours later, I coughed it up, told him that the chance of a lifetime was at stake. It made enough of an impression that he explained the situation.

The fifth metatarsal, the long bone on the outside of the foot, was cleanly snapped in two. That was the bone, he explained, that enabled you to put pressure on the ball of your foot. When I stepped on the brakes, he said, the tendon would only pull the broken end of the bone toward my ankle. A cast was mandatory. There was no way I was going to drive a race car in ten days.

They wrapped my foot in plaster from toes to knee while I watched in mute dismay.

I went home through the dazzling Florida noontime in a state of shock. My brother Walter was there, sitting at the big claw-foot oak table in the kitchen. I propped my foot on a chair and told him what was up: my never-dreamed-of chance at the ultimate race in the world, and now this.

There wasn't much to be said. My mother came downstairs and found the two of us staring into space, looking as if we were contemplating the end of the world. I told her, and then there were three of us staring into space—though she was probably more shocked that I might race at Indy than that I might not. Then my father turned up. I told him. He headed out the kitchen door, slamming it. For a while after that, doors slammed at various points around the house, while Mum and Walt and I sat glumly at the table. My family excels at non-verbal communication, and Dad's position was clear: he wasn't thrilled over the prospect of his eldest daughter's running the Indianapolis 500.

It made for a sleepless night.

Next day, I called Mary McGee, the motorcycle racer with whom I had shared a Toyota pickup truck in the famous Baja 1000 off-road race the previous November. Motorcycle racers knew all about broken everythings. I told her I was entirely ignorant of what might be physically required of the right foot in driving an Indy car.

"Should I tell Rolla, and try for a postponement?"

"No! Don't do that." She questioned me more closely about just what was broken, and how badly, and where. "What kind of cast is it? Is it plaster of Paris, or is it one of these new plastic casts?"

"Plaster of Paris."

"Well," Mary said, "that's easy. Leave the cast on until—when are you going to California?"

"Monday a week from tomorrow. We have the track Tuesday through Thursday."

"Leave the cast on until Friday, then just get in the bathtub with it. It'll soak right off."

"Really?"

"Really."

I was content with Mary McGee's advice; but there was still plenty to worry about. Double-clutching, for instance: if those cars had gears, and if downshifting was necessary as it would be on a road circuit, and if the pedals were as stiff as in some cars I'd driven, I didn't see how I'd be able to execute that combined push and twist, the ball of the foot on the brakes and the heel reaching over to zap the accelerator.

Next day, I went back to New York on crutches. Rolla soon called, with news of Arlene Hiss. She had run some four hundred miles under observation by USAC drivers at both Ontario and Phoenix, and they planned to enter her in the first Indy-car race of the season, March 14 at Phoenix. Rolla said that, contrary to his original plan, he might have to enter a car for me at Trenton in April, even though it meant substantial extra expense for him. I was tremendously pleased with this news. The more time and experience I had in this radically different machine, the better our chances would be.

All that week I beat the bushes for a doctor who might fabricate some sort of lightweight splint to substitute for the cast. There were plenty of blind alleys. I took a cab out to Brooklyn, where a doctor who treated boxers had a seedy, dirty office in a shabby neighborhood. He wouldn't touch the cast.

On Saturday I took the plunge. Off with it! I was soaking in a tub full of bubbles when the door buzzed from the lobby. Leaving a trail of plaster and puddles, I hopped to the intercom. Mary McGee and a friend had unexpectedly arrived from California.

"Your timing is exquisite," I said. "Come on up, I'll leave the door ajar."

The remains of the cast made quite a mess. There was advice and inspection, comment and good cheer. It was wonderful beyond words to have this support at such a critical juncture.

Sunday. One day to go. A small gathering of friends and relatives at my place. The phone rang. Someone I knew had been killed on takeoff in his new miniature BD-5 jet. Beyond the pools of light in my living room, full of warmth and affection, dark wings brushed closely by.

At dawn, as I packed my helmet bag, I was ready for whatever Ontario might bring. Doug Schirripa, my excellent Toyota crew volunteer, drove me to LaGuardia. I kept the crutches until the last minute, handing them to him in exchange for my helmet bag at the door of the plane. I put the helmet bag on the empty seat next to me, and my foot on top of that, and when we landed in Ontario the swelling was no worse.

Ten minutes later, as I stood scanning passers-by for signs of recognition, a distinctive voice behind me said, "Are you who I'm looking for?" I turned into an embrace and a kiss.

"They dared me to do that," he said, gesturing at two young men who laughed as they reached for my helmet bag. "I'll bet it's the first time in history that a USAC car owner has kissed a driver when they met."

Vollstedt was just under six feet tall, lean, with fine grey hair, rimless eyeglasses, and impish good humor. He introduced his two blond crew members, Roger Thrall and Al Kissler.

"Dick Simon's plane won't be in for another half hour," Vollstedt said as we walked toward a distant gate. The warmth of his personality soon set me at ease. It enveloped the crew, myself, and our plans for the next crucial days.

While we waited, chatting, in the smoggy night that reeked of jet fuel, I was intent on the impending arrival. What would the attitude of Rolla's number-one driver be?

The first-woman issue was already making waves, and it was clear that plenty of people would be glad to see the entire endeavor sink. The first fan reaction to Arlene's announcement had appeared in *National Speed Sport News* on Feb. 4. "I hope that all the he-men ...

boycott the race if Mrs. Hiss is allowed to drive," wrote Mrs. C. Bowman of Ossian, Indiana. "They have enough to think about out there on the track besides a woman. If there was a terrible wreck … just what would she do, faint?" If Dick was even a fraction that narrow-minded, the next couple of days could be awfully tough. Besides, he had veto power: Rolla had promised his new driver that if my performance didn't meet with his approval, the project would end then and there.

Just as Dick Simon's plane pulled up to the gate, Rolla noticed my limp. I told him that I'd turned my ankle in one of New York's infamous potholes the day before.

Slowly, the jet disgorged its passengers. "There they are," Rolla said.

Dick Simon was an inch or two shorter than I was, I guessed, but built like a bull: broad-shouldered, athletic, and bursting with vitality. He was wearing a brown polyester double-knit suit with white stitching in a vaguely Western style, and white patent-leather shoes. He was then forty-two years old, and quite bald except for a fringe around the back. His girlfriend Melanie, some twenty years his junior, was a perky, pretty blonde.

While we waited for the bags, Dick queried Roger and Al about the car. I listened intently. They talked for a while of the tires, and then of "stagger." I'd been following everything until that. "I'm going to have to learn a new vocabulary for USAC, Dick," I interjected. "What's stagger?"

At first, he told me too much—stuff that any driver knew. But it seemed that "stagger" was the difference between the diameters of the inside and outside rear tires.

"Does it mean anything else as well, like asymmetry in suspension settings?" Sports cars were set up to turn both left and right; Indy cars, just left. There were a lot of implications to that.

"No, just the tires."

So far, so good. Dick Simon had put a car in the field at Indy every year since 1970, but he wasn't talking down to me. He seemed willing to accept what I knew, and was generous with his own knowledge. Our eyes had met, and something strong flowed between. I saw no sign of prejudice, no hidden agenda there.

Rolla took us to register at the Sixpence, a small, cheap, trucker's motel, then to supper. By the time I got to bed my watch read nearly three a.m., New York time.

Four and a half hours later, I was wide awake. The hazards of this undertaking flashed randomly through my mind, like lightning in a dark sky. It wasn't fear; it was rational, an acknowledgement of risk. I imagined again the Greek goddess, imagined her there in the dark with her helmet and shield. *Who else, indeed, is there for me?*

We left for the track around nine.

This was the day, then, that had saturated my being since January. In the enormous infield, spacious garages of pale-blue corrugated steel stood in well-constructed rows. We turned into the second alley, and like a zoom lens, my eyes filled with the car.

It was pulled halfway out of its garage, sitting there in the sun that seeped down through the Ontario smog ... the quiet car, dark blue. This car should approach 200 mph, this car that I was going to attempt to put in the field for the most important, the most historic race in the world ... beginning today.

Other images flashed through my mind's eye: the fearful start of the Indianapolis 500 in 1973, cars catapulting through the air and across the straight, flames like a gas pipeline blowout ... Swede Savage dead of it, the blond, shaggy-haired driver who'd had the Trans-Am ride back in the sixties that I tried so hard to get...

Harold Sperb, Rolla's chief mechanic, came out of the garage and stood by the car. I went straight to him and introduced myself. Some drivers ignored their mechanics, or condescended to them. That was a foolish thing to do in a sport where one loose nut could spell catastrophe.

Sperb was a grizzled man in his late fifties. When he spoke, which was rarely, it seemed to hurt him. One of the guys commented later that week, "Sperby don't say all he knows."

Rolla, Dick and I turned to the car. Originally built in 1971-72, it had been modified several times. In 1975, it hadn't been fast enough to make the field at Indianapolis. After that, they made improvements. A new car that Rolla was building wasn't yet ready. Dick would run this blue car at Phoenix.

In profile, the car resembled a spawning salmon, with a concave curve from the nose up to the windscreen, then a back that humped over the intake log of the tall Offenhauser engine. From above, the bodywork's outline was more like that of a hammerhead shark. Its nose spread out to the sides, with blunt tips where a shark's eyes would be, ahead of the front wheels. Then the body narrowed to clear the front suspension, before bulging around the cockpit and engine. Streamlining—low drag—was as vital to an Indy car as to a fish. A central unibody portion, the "tub," formed the seat and contained the fuel cells. Aft of that, the four-cylinder turbocharged Offenhauser engine was itself part of the load-bearing structure.

I turned my attention away from the engine compartment (what an unaccustomed luxury!), looked over the rest of it, put a hand on the little chrome-plated roll bar for support, and stepped in. Finding it hard to catch my breath, I put my weight on my hands on the tub and slid down into the seat, wriggling my bare feet past the unfamiliar crossbars and barriers hidden in the nose until they touched bottom somewhere forward of the front tires. My toes groped for the essential parts: accelerator pedal, brakes, clutch. I pressed them gingerly, then harder, snapping my injured foot on and off the accelerator, standing hard on the brakes. It seemed as if I could push hard enough. But I wouldn't really be able to tell until I started thrashing around, out on the track.

As I moved my feet on the pedals, my shins and knees, which were bent up into the cowling, tangled with the dashboard and other bits of structure. The car was too short, the pedals too close. Rolla had asked me beforehand what my inseam length was, but no one ever believed how long my legs were. Otherwise, the car seemed to fit me well enough.

I had the guys rock the car back and forth to rotate the gears inside the transaxle, so that I could engage each gear in turn, feel its position. The tub was a tight fit, allowing only the minimum essential motion of arms and legs. I moved the stubby little gearshift lever through its range with my fingers and a twist of the wrist. The gates to the gears were narrow, close together, and not spring-loaded, so that in neutral the lever flopped blindly about; your hand had to learn where each gear was.

"Let's get that pedal assembly fixed," Rolla said. "Stay where you are."

They measured what they had to do. I climbed out then, and Dick said, "Come on, I'll take you for a ride around the track." Rolla gave us the keys to his rental car.

Like Indianapolis, Ontario was so vast that you couldn't take it all in at first. A few hundred sheep grazed in one quadrant of the infield, a cost-effective way to keep the grass mowed. We drove a couple of laps while Dick pointed out markers; they were few. Instead of the well-defined geography I was used to on road circuits—a clump of shrubs here, a patch in the pavement there, the apex of each turn marked by a chewed-up area—the infield here was just one big nebulous soup. How could you find the apex? I wondered, and how did you keep track of it while setting up for the turn?

"By the way," Dick said as we cruised down the back straight, "make sure you don't stand on the gas in first or second gear. Just use part throttle until you're in third. I sold a Champ car once to a kid who'd been doing good in Sprint cars, and when we came here to get him checked out, he didn't listen to me. He spun it three times before he ever started down the back straight, and sold the car on the spot."

Meanwhile, on each lap I became more conscious of the omnipresent wall. Road circuits didn't have walls like this one. White-painted concrete, four feet high, it harshly defined the outer edge of the track—an unyielding boundary to the playing field of this new game.

Dick's running commentary was crammed with valuable stuff. "When you warm the car up," he said, "you stay down on the inside flat part of the pavement in the turns and on the chute, the short straights—below that white line."

"What does it want for a warmup?"

"Stay in first gear until..." He went through the specifics.

"I expect to be excruciatingly slow at first," I said. "I've never destroyed a car in my life, and I don't propose to begin with this one. But it's going to be embarrassing."

"That's fine, make sure you're comfortable ... but if you stand on it going down the straight past the pits you'll look as fast as blazes, and nobody in the pits can see what you're doing in the turns."

I laughed; it was nice advice.

They hooked the car up to an electric golf cart and towed it out to the pits. I took my helmet bag into the women's room to change. There were urinals along one wall. Rolla had noted that when the track opened in 1970, there weren't any women's rooms because, of course, women weren't allowed in the garage area.

Slowly, deliberately, I put on my racing gear—the soft knit Nomex long johns, thick Nomex socks, the driver's suit that I'd made myself eight years before from Nomex fabric cadged for free from DuPont. Nomex, a spinoff from the space program, is a cousin of nylon that won't support combustion and doesn't melt like nylon, which can cause especially nasty burns by adhering to the skin. Nomex has a lovely creamy color when new, but a well-worn suit of Nomex looks distinctly grungy. The stuff has a great affinity for motor oil and the carbon blacks carried by it, which never completely wash out. My suit was quite well-worn.

The change of clothes was a ritual, significant on several levels.

One of them was that I shed, with my feminine clothes, any of the feminine aspects of my personality that could interfere with my competence as a driver. There would be no residue of helplessness, dependency, or passivity—learned behaviour that was historically part of our culture's feminine identity. The subtle body language that said "female"—the shrug of the shoulders, the lowered gaze—disappeared. It wasn't consciously suppressed; it simply vanished, like so much useless baggage. The driver part took precedence over everything else.

I tucked my gloves and glasses into the hollow of my helmet, and carried them out toward pit road. There was a chilly grip around my heart and a light-headed chill at the back of my skull as the blue car was made ready for the track. I perched on the pit wall, out of the way of the action, and watched.

Dick Simon took the car out for its warmup, stopped in the pits for a brief checkup, then stood on the gas. We heard the engine wind up on the back straight, a distant howl of purposefully increasing pitch. When he came into sight in Turn 4, he was running fast and hard. The blue car's velocity was incomprehensible, the engine's scream underscored by the rip of torn air. In a flash the thing was gone, the very sight of it blurred, the machine quivering with speed.

In a few laps he ran it up to an average speed of 171 mph. Then he pulled in. He made some adjustments which, he said, would result in more "push"—the USAC word for understeer. Extra push would be better for a novice than the more neutral setup that enabled faster speeds. Meanwhile, as I sat on the pit wall, the apprehension had vanished. I was feeling detached now, objective. My turn would come. I was gathered up, all of one piece, ready.

Dick took the car out for a few more laps. The changes slowed him to 169. When he stopped, I watched the tentative air of a few words exchanged among Vollstedt, Simon, and Sperb; then saw the consensus as clearly as if spelled on a billboard. When Vollstedt turned toward the pit wall, I was already reaching for my helmet.

Into the car, still clumsy at getting my feet past all the obstacles. The world contracted to a very small frame: the instruments, the steering wheel, the blue nose of the car pointing down pit road to the open track.

"Ready?"

"Ready."

They spun the engine and it caught and fired, sensitive to the slightest throttle movement. The sound was strange, the four big organ pipes of the engine's exhaust muted by its turbocharger. My eyes watered as acrid fumes from the alcohol-rich exhaust drifted forward. I checked the gauges, ran the rpm's up and down a thousand or so, flipped my helmet visor down and snapped it into place. The guys put their weight to the car and set it in motion; I disengaged the clutch and tickled first gear with the shift lever. It stuttered lightly as transaxle speed approached engine speed. When my fingers told me it was ready to yield I pressed harder, and it dropped neatly into gear. I was on my way.

At the end of pit road I eased back on the throttle until the drive train was free of strain, the engine neither pushing nor pulling, and slipped it out of first gear. I dropped the engine rpm's some more and pulled the shift lever down toward second; it went in with a satisfying plunk. The whole process took a fraction of a second. I had never used a gearbox without synchros before, nor shifted without the clutch except in emergencies, and was surprised at the ease of it. Then I was out on the track.

Gingerly, I felt it out, gentle on everything—particularly the throttle, mindful of Dick's warning. It took only the slightest motion of the accelerator pedal to send the car rushing forward, the leap of the tachometer needle confirming the rising pitch of all that machinery thrashing around three inches behind my head. It was a long time since I had driven an open car; I felt shockingly exposed. The wind rushed noisily past, licking through the bodywork and over the plastic windscreen to brush my head and shoulders like an industrial-strength vacuum cleaner in reverse.

I took another lap in second gear, shaking the car left and right like a terrier with a rat, getting the feel of the steering. I watched the tires go left and right as I turned the wheel. Somewhere out in front of them, my feet lay hidden in the nose. When I wound the engine up to 7000 rpm to catch third and then fourth gear, it began to show its strength.

Then it was time. I came out of Turn 2 under power and gave it full throttle down the back straight. The turbocharger wound up and delivered: 700-plus horsepower applied to a 1,500-pound car.

My eyes must have been as big as the tachometer face.

The car hurtled toward Turn 3, the vibration phenomenal, the airstream trying to lift me out of the seat by the helmet strap, the acceleration unbelievable. I shut down early for the turn, feeling it out, working my way into this unknown territory.

On the front straight, Roger hung out a pit board with the lap speed. One-thirty, the first one said. One-forty, the next. Up it went.

I came in, breathing hard, to think about it. I had done that for years at a new track: take a few laps, come in and mull it over, doing laps in my mind. It was efficient, and it saved wear and tear on the car.

Everyone was smiling.

I stayed in the seat and went over my impressions. With this four-cylinder Offy, the power arrived all at once; the torque curve had a segment that must have been nearly vertical. When you reached it, you thought you were headed straight for the moon. That was the fun part, planting your foot on the straights. The hard part was in the turns.

Rationally, I knew that I hadn't even scratched the surface of the car's potential. Emotionally, I felt like I had a tiger by the tail, a tiger that could easily turn and bite. But the good news was that my foot did what was required of it. That huge burden of worry vanished as if it had never existed.

"Everything all right?" Rolla asked.

"Fine, except the pedals are really still too close." Holding my knees bent up so my feet didn't hit the pedals at the wrong time was a strain. They pulled the cowling and said it wouldn't take long to fix, but it seemed to take forever.

Out again. In six more laps I was at 157. The buffeting and vibration from the airstream were hard to get used to; the world turned to jelly, almost like opening your eyes under water. Two more laps, and in.

As I rolled into the pits, I covertly scanned the little group at the pit rail. What were they thinking? Everyone was still smiling. But I still didn't feel I had the handle on the situation; and I had expected to go faster than that.

Indy cars of that era had no telemetry or gauges for lateral acceleration, but two to two and a half lateral G's in the turns is a conservative guess. What's that like? Suppose you weigh 150 pounds, and you lie down on your right-hand side on the floor, and someone puts two 100-pound sandbags on top of you. That's the force that would be pressing you against the right-hand side of the cockpit in the turns. Nothing in ordinary life can prepare you to believe the car will get on through.

One more time. It took six laps to get to 161.5; the increments of speed were coming harder as I came closer to the car's potential, about 169 in this configuration. This time in, I saw that they were looking uneasy. I felt discouraged; I was still doing a lot of things wrong. I hadn't developed an eye for the right line, and was taking the turns a little differently each time, so that there were more surprises at the exit point near the wall than seemed healthy. What I didn't know—Dick told me later—was that Rolla hadn't planned to allow me over 150 on the first day. I was actually going faster than they were comfortable with. But next time out, I didn't need the pit board to know the speed had dropped off a little. My learning curve had temporarily crested.

Later, the group assembled for drinks in Rolla's room. I wasn't drinking. "How'd you really feel about it?" he asked.

"I wish I'd gone faster."

We went to dinner. I was learning more about Rolla Vollstedt. His racing involvement dated from 1947. His livelihood was in the lumber business, where he was a successful executive, but his heart was in oval-track auto racing. He had built race cars of his own design in the garage of his home in Portland, Oregon, and campaigned them to West Coast championships. He had brought his cars to the Indianapolis 500, and watched them come heartbreakingly close to the front. Never heavily funded, he operated his teams on minimum dollars, but with maximum savvy, dedication, and hard work.

He was comfortably well-off, but hardly rich. That translated into conflict between his racing activities and his family, wife Irene and two young sons.

"Do you know what a racer is?" he would ask new acquaintances. "A racer is someone who has four hundred dollars in the bank, a mortgage that is overdue, kids who are hungry, and a race car that needs parts. Guess how he spends the four hundred dollars."

Rolla was a racer. I could relate to that.

The track opened at ten the next morning, and Dick continued working with the car. It gave me plenty of time to do laps in my mind. I was determined to get a grip on this thing. It would help to mark the apexes of each turn. I found some orange rubber cones at the track office and set them out. Rolla didn't like that.

"You won't have any cones when you get to Indianapolis," he said gruffly. I argued that it would help me make the transition, and that when I had developed an eye for the turns, I wouldn't need the cones any more. The cones stayed—briefly.

At twenty past one I took the car out for the first time that day, and in four laps was at 168.5 mph. Ha, that was better. Halfway down the back straight on the fifth lap, the engine blew. It sounded like a high-speed military tank surmounting a heap of steel wreckage.

In a flash I killed the ignition and flipped the car out of gear. The noise diminished somewhat. For a moment I thought I hadn't gotten it out of gear after all, that so much noise had to mean the engine was still rotating. But the source of the noise was speed: tires on pavement, air against chassis. The car coasted over a mile to pit road and still had momentum to spare. I braked it to a stop.

"Engine," I said. "I'm afraid it's pretty bad." I was grateful for the "telltale," the needle on the tachometer that remained at its highest reading, proving I hadn't over-revved it.

They pulled the spark plugs, and on the third one found evidence of disaster. It had swallowed a valve. There would be no more running today.

The engine they installed that night wouldn't be quite as strong, Rolla said. It was almost noon the next day before Dick took it out, and indeed, the maximum rpm's had dropped from 9250 to 9100. Nevertheless, I hit 170 my second time out. This was our last day, and the chips were down.

"You're still not using up all the track," Dick Simon said at a pause in the proceedings. "You need to exit your turns right against the wall, not four feet away from it."

I'd certainly thought I was closer than that. Besides being hard and immovable, the wall presented an optical problem. It was crowned with a fifteen-foot chain-link fence; on top of that, four sturdy rows of barbed wire slanted inward overhead. As you sighted on your exit point from the apex on out, the slant deceived your eye, and the overhang seemed threatening as you came underneath it. This was a problem that I had to solve. The means flashed quickly into my mind.

While everyone else was eating lunch, I scrounged through Sperb's toolbox for welding rods. Rolla's rental car stood nearby. I clamped a welding rod into the passenger-side door, bending half a foot of it back at an angle.

Out on the track, eighty miles an hour in the rental car was fast enough to get the sight lines right. I lapped the track until a single arc through the turns swept me right up to the noisy point, where the welding rod scraped the wall. Sure enough, the optical illusion faded.

Dick was walking through the garage area when I returned.

"What did you do?" he asked, staring at the side of the car. Its right-hand side was covered with a swath of white dust.

"Just nestled up to the wall a little. The car's okay."

He saw the protruding welding rod, and understood. "Better wipe it off before Rolla sees it or he'll have a heart attack."

Out at the pits, they were warming the race car again. As they worked the throttle, it made nervous little howls that ended in a yip. Rolla had a plane to catch this afternoon. There wasn't much more time. Back on the track, I brought the temperatures up as fast as I could, then stood on the gas. I was finally starting to get the rhythm of the thing.

I came down the front straight at full speed, maybe 190 mph. Out away from the wall, I checked the gauges, then flicked a look at the pit board. Then I focused on the turn ahead. When I thought about it afterwards, I remembered how my rib cage tightened as my eyes found the caution-light box that marked my turn-in point. I snuggled back up close to the wall again and eased gently off the throttle.

I pressed the wheel left, lightly at first, then harder, and came back on the power enough to keep the car balanced fore and aft. The white line that marked the inside edge of the track was blurred like chalk on a powered-up grinding wheel.

The apex lay out beyond the pit-road exit. The orange cones were gone, but the framework of reference points was familiar enough by now. When the left front tire grazed the white line, my eyes were already out at the big red letters painted on the wall. Ontario Motor Speedway, they read. One of them marked my exit point, the spot where I would come closest to the wall.

The path of the car through the rest of the turn was already determined. Had I come in too fast, or apexed too early, I would find myself not next to the wall but in it. I watched the wall come up like a bird watches a snake, making little adjustments with the wheel and throttle, finding out how much adhesion I had left to maneuver with.

Done! Foot on the floor, and out away from the wall—but just for an instant. In the short chute, you had time for one breath before you had to do it all over again. Then you were out on the back straight, with maybe ten seconds to relax, check the gauges, and think about Turn 3. At last, I was starting to feel fierce.

I ran a 172.4. When I came around on the next lap after that, Dick Simon had climbed over the wall out onto the track and was standing in the middle of it with the board. He was so close that even at straightaway speed, I could see his grin.

"I thought you were going to get white sidewalls," he said when I came in.

"White sidewalls?"

"That's when you've used up more track than there is, and the paint comes off on your tires."

Rolla was orchestrating a photograph. We pushed the car out onto the track while Al set up his Hasselblad. The mood of the group had been light all afternoon; still, Rolla was a complicated man who could keep you off balance. He had that mysterious something that bound a group of disparate individuals into a smoothly functioning unit, and he was a gentleman; but working with him could be puzzling. Sometimes he'd tell you things he'd told you twice already, as if he'd forgotten he said it; then sometimes your mind and his would run on the same track through some fairly intricate matter, and you'd get that thrill of knowing only a word had to be said here and there, a signal light—no explanations required.

But now, I needed more than a clue. He hadn't yet stated his position. He hurried us through the photos, one eye on his watch. Finally, the words came.

"As far as I'm concerned, this program is a go-ahead. Dick, I'll talk to you when I get to Portland." Then he was gone. When they took the next picture, the classic shot of the driver standing in the race car, helmet cradled in one arm, I was grinning like Alice's Cheshire cat.

THE HEAT ISN'T IN
THE KITCHEN

Overnight, clear air swept away the smog, unveiling the splendor of the San Gabriel mountains, craggy, frosted with snow. The clarity of their emergence felt like an exhilarating metaphor for the outcome of my recent ordeal.

As my flight from LAX climbed east, Ontario Motor Speedway drifted into view.

Had I lapped that track at 172 mph in an Indy car?

Had I taken the first steps toward the Indianapolis 500?

Indeed, it was true.

But had I known what my life would be like in the weeks after that fact was made public, I might not have been all that cheerful. Bryant's press conference to announce our entry in the Indianapolis 500 was set for March 9 in Indianapolis. None of us, I think—not even Rolla—anticipated what a sensation we were about to create, what a hornet's nest we were stirring up. Dick Simon may have suspected it; certainly in supporting my presence on Vollstedt's team, he had put himself in the line of fire. The night before the press conference, after having dinner with Frankie Del Roy, USAC's respected Technical Director, Dick said Frankie got the secret out of him with one question: "Is it Lombardi?" Lella Lombardi was the Italian Formula 1 driver.

"No."

"Then it's Janet Guthrie."

At dawn, I went over my notes. I thought of the press conference as just another hoop to jump through, one of many that lay ahead. My own reality was on the race track, at the wheel of a car. I would jump through any hoops necessary to get there.

Bryant's PR man was waiting for us—Dick, Rolla, and me—on the steps of the Columbia Club. He whisked us up a back elevator and hid us behind a heavy curtain, on the other side of which a sizable room buzzed with excited voices. Even Dick looked nervous. One by one, we were called and introduced.

Flashbulbs flared, TV cameramen and reporters jockeyed for

position. It was a media mob scene like something out of the movies ... only here I was in the middle of it. The three of us were swirled apart.

My path crossed that of Dick King, USAC's Executive Director and Director of Competition. King was some six-feet-five inches tall, powerful, and formidable. His decisions on my eligibility for licensing and competition were of crucial importance. He made his position clear immediately: hoopla notwithstanding, none of this was a sure thing. It was no longer optional for me to enter the Trenton race in April, it was a requirement, and my performance there would be closely scrutinized. King also wanted me to sit in on rookie indoctrination for the race at Phoenix, five days hence.

At lunch, served in the adjoining banquet room, I found myself seated at the dais next to Tony Hulman himself. Hulman was the owner of Indianapolis Motor Speedway, which he had rescued from near-oblivion in the aftermath of the Second World War. A blueblooded graduate of Yale, he was one of the richest men in the country, and it was his prerogative each May to utter the words, "Gentlemen, start your engines!" *Who, me, sitting next to the legendary Tony Hulman in front of a hundred and some reporters?*

After the requisite formal remarks by the Bryant executives, Hulman, King and Rolla, it was my turn. I talked about the Ontario test: "It wasn't until I read the obituary page next morning and found my name wasn't on it that I started to feel okay," I said. "But then you start to enjoy the capabilities of the car..." After that I touched on the grimmer moments of the last thirteen years of fielding my own cars. Vollstedt had summarized the high points, my accomplishments; I wanted to specify that I had paid my dues.

The questions that followed were mostly on the sceptical side, as if my experience on road circuits, even in the international fields at Sebring and Daytona, didn't count. I stood on the high points of my record nonetheless, smiling all the while.

When lunch broke up, there was more to do: talk here, pose, stand there. Toward the end of it, Dick Simon and I found ourselves momentarily side by side. It was great to exchange a look with him, one note of solid reality in this incredible three-ring circus. Simon was a normal racing driver, with the normal giant-size ego, yet he showed no sign that he was disturbed by my encroachment on his limelight. I was relieved and grateful.

It was almost 4 p.m. before we walked down the steps of the Columbia Club, and the Blue Streak edition of the Indianapolis *News* was on the streets. Our picture was on the front page. It gave me a foretaste of the weeks to come.

The initial reportage was straightforward, but by the end of the week there were stories like this one, from the Boston *Globe* on March 14:

> *Concoct, if you will, your own bizarre picture of the Indy start. Have Ms. Guthrie fishing in her three-feet-by-two-feet handbag for her keys, with bobby pins and Max Factor beauty aids and hair brushes and ballpoint pens and clipped newspaper recipes flying through the air. Have her still working on her eyelashes in the rear-view mirror as the other 32 drivers angrily blow their horns.*

My education in the more virulent strains of sentiment toward women was under way. I had had the great good fortune of being brought up to believe that a woman could do whatever she chose. It was startling to discover how widespread was belief to the contrary.

From the moment I got back to my apartment in New York, the phone didn't stop ringing; TV crews followed news magazines, right through the doors. It seemed to me easier to cope with the press at home than to meet them elsewhere. I didn't enjoy the spotlight, but if it came with the territory, I would do my best to reflect credit on Rolla Vollstedt and his team.

The biggest trouble with all the fuss and feathers, what kept me awake nights, was that it would be weeks before I could deliver the goods. The Trenton race at the end of April would be the first public proving grounds for our heretical endeavor. Until then, I had little power to refute the naysaying. And little did I know how the upcoming race at Phoenix, a race I only observed, was to set the stage for a truly agonizing seven weeks.

On the eve of practice in Phoenix, Friday, Rolla took our team to dinner at a restaurant jammed to the rafters with owners, drivers, crews, and hangers-on. Whatever anonymity I may still have had when we walked in the door didn't last five minutes. Rolla introduced me as we worked our way toward the bar. It was clear enough that not everyone was thrilled. Some were hard put even to be polite. It was also clear that Rolla commanded enough respect to keep most of them in line, but I was all too conscious of cold stares from various corners of the room. No sooner were we settled at a table in the bar than a stranger attached to another team started in.

"So you're gonna drive at Indianapolis." The sneer in his voice belied the smile on his face. "I don't believe in it myself. I hold to the old standards." The man pulled on his beer. "But you never know what's gonna happen next. Maybe I'll put my wife in a race car ... or my girlfriend."

He couldn't have flaunted his contempt for women more clearly: wife, mistress, me—indistinguishable. I hadn't a clue how to deal with it. I looked him down, and kept my mouth shut; but the encounter preoccupied me throughout dinner.

Later I learned that the fellow was a hanger-on of no particular account; and later still, I saw that hangers-on were among the most bitterly, venomously resentful of a woman's encroachment on Big-Time Auto Racing. The hangers-on were macho only by association; therefore a woman's participation posed a grievous threat.

Rolla remained cheerful throughout the evening, dancing and joking and continuing his introductions. I was grateful that he was such a mother hen, but I couldn't stay under his wing forever; and I didn't know which animals in the jungle would keep their claws sheathed, or even which ones had claws.

In the bright morning we pressed toward the track, along an ill-maintained road that wound through tall, dusty scrub. I was apprehensive to the point of faint nausea. We crossed a dry wash and fetched up behind the scruffy main grandstand, where a long line of men waited for credentials. Again came the hostile stares.

Equipped with our passes, we were waved through the gate in the battered red and white steel Armco barrier that served as the track wall. There was a lot on my mind. Never having seen an Indy-car race, I was most intensely concerned to see what the protocol was in traffic situations—how passing was accomplished, and how the passed and lapped cars positioned themselves. I had asked Rolla and Dick about it, and they had given the same answer: a lapped car should hold its line, let the faster cars find their own way around. I couldn't believe that was true. It was at variance with all my experience.

The entry list boasted almost all the stars of USAC Championship racing, and of course Arlene Hiss would be making her Indy-car debut. At the rookie meeting, officials and veterans spoke of race procedures and of the peculiarities of the Phoenix track. Meanwhile, out in the pits, crews were starting to warm their engines. One, then another, more: WEEEEE-YAH, WEEEEE-YAH. The sound of it was hair-raising. Then practice began.

Phoenix was a relatively short track, a one-mile oval of notoriously rough and irregular surface. The sound of a single turbocharged Offenhauser in the vast flatlands of Ontario had been impressive enough; but in this small space bounded by hills, the noise echoed and redoubled, a force of its own. Two and three at a time, the cars shot down the short front straight, each pushing and trailing its Dopplered blast of sound: EEEEE-NYOW, EEEEE-NYOW, EEEEE-NYOW, without respite. So many cars, so little room; stunning acceleration as they shook and sought their direction off the turns.

I watched intently, studying, making notes. Traffic was heavy, closer than anything I'd experienced except at the starts at Sebring and Daytona. The distance between the cars—the margin for error—seemed minuscule; and given so much power and cornering force, the drivers' control looked superhuman.

Qualifying was held late in the afternoon. On the road-racing circuits that I was used to, cars qualified with everyone on the track at once, in a session that might last half an hour. The fastest lap turned by each car at any time in the session was the one that established its starting position. Qualifying here was different, and much more intensely pressured: one car at a time. Drivers drew for position in the qualifying line by pulling marble-sized numbered balls out of a sack.

Arlene was first in line for qualifying, but you couldn't have seen that by looking: her car was invisible beneath a three-deep ring of reporters, photographers, cameramen, and hangers-on. The time she posted, 27.92 seconds, was a full second slower than her practice laps. At day's end she was on the last row of the twenty-two-car field, twenty-first out of the twenty-four qualifying attempts. Al Unser was on the pole with a time of 25.56 seconds, and Dick Simon was eighteenth in the blue car with a time of 27.32, just six-tenths of a second faster than Arlene.

On Sunday morning, with race time coming on like a freight train, it struck me that there was something sinister about Phoenix, and I have felt that way about the track ever since. Wild little hills loom over it, dotted with cactus and scrub. Isolated figures on horseback stood here and there on the steep slopes, perfectly still. They were physically quite close, yet so distanced; it was like one of those Clint Eastwood spaghetti westerns. I felt a sense of foreboding.

Marks of violence, certainly, were everywhere. The pits and paddock were full of damaged men—men with burn scars, missing limbs, men in wheelchairs, men with limps—casualties of this kind of racing.

One of these men introduced himself that morning, a spectacularly damaged man. Burns. His left hand had no fingers, was just a thin pink stump. His nostrils were scalloped and cheeks marked by fire. It was Mel Kenyon, one of the winningest drivers in the history of USAC Midget racing. He had beautiful eyes, and his gaze was clear and direct as he wished me good luck in our endeavour. It was too bad, he said sympathetically, that I didn't have better equipment.

Then I talked for a couple of minutes with Steve Krisiloff, a well-established name in Indy cars. It was a tenth-rate team that I was associated with, he said, the car a piece of junk. "That shitbox," he called it. I was taken aback by the assertion and the language. Shitbox. It rang in my ears. Surely the team and the blue car weren't that bad.

Meanwhile, Arlene was suffering a wretched excess of pressure and attention. She was smiling, but she still looked nervous and miserable. There was some dreadful ceremony at the base of the timing and press tower in which she was presented with a huge bunch of long-stemmed red roses, for the benefit of the assembled photographers, at a time when she must surely have wanted to be gathering herself up in private. Someone dragged me over for a photo; I wished Arlene good luck and got out of her hair.

Rolla had arranged for me to watch the race from a tower in the infield that offered an unobstructed view of the entire course. As the pace car drew the field out onto the track, the tension was almost unbearable.

Twenty-two Championship cars howled at full throttle toward the green.

Into the first turn they crowded with sharp deceleration, feinting and passing. Then, hot out of Turn 2 and onto the back stretch, the pack began to string out. Leaping and twitching over the rough spots, darting toward the inside to try a pass, they were still on the first mile. There were 149 miles to go.

Of course, I focused on Arlene. For the first half hour, I didn't take my eyes off her, slowly rotating there in the tower to follow her progress all the way around the track.

Arlene blew it.

She was lapped within ten miles, and she held to the fast line, the "groove." There's only one fastest line, and two cars can't occupy it at once. One must yield, giving up a little speed in the process. Drivers of the fastest cars kept finding Arlene on their line. The worst moments were when a pack came upon her, scrapping among themselves. I felt a lump start to form in my stomach, and after a while, I picked out a few other relatively slow cars and focused on them instead.

What I saw was that, contrary to the advice I'd been given, the slower cars did in fact yield the line to faster drivers. At the entrance and exit of the turns they stayed down, toward the inside; on the straightaways, against the wall. It got complicated in between, or when there were several cars, and I absorbed it all with greedy intensity.

Spins and crashes brought out the yellow repeatedly. Although Arlene was nowhere in the vicinity of any incident, she was black-flagged after the gestures of the other drivers left no doubt as to their sentiments. She said that no, she hadn't tired, and they let her out again. By the end of the race, however, her neck had given out and her head was bending toward the outside of the turns at nearly a forty-five-degree angle. By then, she was running more than ten seconds a lap slower than the leaders.

Bobby Unser won. Dick Simon was seventh. Arlene was fourteenth, the last of the cars still running at the end.

I climbed grimly down from the tower, found Rolla, and told him I was getting the hell out of there. I knew I couldn't defend Arlene's performance, to the media or anyone else, and I wanted no part of condemning it.

Arlene had been a fine, competitive sports car driver. What happened? What had cut her speed so far below her practice laps? How could she have lost a normal racing driver's judgment of position and relative velocity?

And why hadn't anyone devised a head support for her? She couldn't have known—nor did I then—that 150 times around a one-mile race track in an Indy car will tax the neck of nearly any driver. For that reason, A. J. Foyt used a solid structural support, thickly padded, to lean his head on. Gordon Johncock preferred a shoulder strap, a strap that was fastened to the side of the helmet and ran under the left shoulder, so that the driver's head was actually forced to the left. Then, in the turns, the strap took the strain.

But her crew must have known about this. They'd been around. Why the omission?

It was months before I talked with Arlene. Eventually, I heard that there had been problems with her crew. Between that and the three-ring circus that surrounded her debut, Arlene had lost her composure. And she had been firmly instructed not to yield the line: "It doesn't matter how slowly you go," they'd said, "the important thing is to finish. Let the other drivers find their way around you." They hadn't shown her any lap times. Arlene had done as she was told.

As I came to know Championship racing, I saw rookies do worse things, and I saw some of the top drivers do dumb things too. But in the Klieg-light glare of a woman's debut, no mistakes were allowed. Arlene never got another chance; she never drove a Championship car again.

One thing was clear: Arlene's debut at Phoenix was going to step up the heat coming my way. "Gal Flops in Race Debut," screamed the Monday morning headlines. "Male Drivers Hint Boycott If Woman Enters Next Race."[1]

My own feeling, of course, was that I wasn't any more like Arlene Hiss than rookie Bobby Olivero was like rookie Gary Albritain. I was just a rookie, period. However, Phoenix had given me a close-up view of the pressures I could expect, which would have given pause to any thoughtful person.

The extent of the damage was apparent within the week. There was a serious possibility that our Trenton entry would be refused. Drivers had been in Dick King's USAC office, Rolla said, pounding on King's desk, demanding that he keep me out.

As a countermeasure, I was to provide USAC with a complete racing history: every race I had ever driven, with engine displacement, kind of car and class, and finishing position. It took a while to dig it all out. The hundred and twenty races included a dozen major international endurance events. There was the class win at the Sebring 12-Hour in Under-2-Liter Prototype and the overall win in the Camaro at Bridgehampton. There were heavy, powerful front-engine cars (Camaro, Mustang, Jaguar, Corvette); small single-seat rear-engine cars; and the Chevron B-16, a fast rear-engine prototype. I had raced the Daytona and Pocono two-and-a-half-mile speedways at night and in the rain. For good measure, I threw in the pilot's license: commercial rating, with 400 hours in twenty-three aircraft types.

Nine days after Phoenix, Arlene Hiss renounced her Championship ride, citing lack of sponsorship.

[1] Detroit *News*, Des Moines *Tribune*, March 15, 1976

For the next six weeks, the media had ample opportunity to snipe, and snipe they did. I wrote to a friend, "I'm getting so tired of fielding hostile questions that when a bull-ring stock car driver came up yesterday and sounded sincerely enthusiastic, I nearly burst into tears."

That letter understated my feelings. I remember a moment, on a grubby, oil-smeared propeller plane droning toward Milwaukee—weary of Bryant's and Toyota's tours, the endless smiles and photos; haunted by the knowledge that the least mishap at Trenton would precipitate a deluge of scorn and derision and end my racing forever—when I almost wished the plane would crash, so it would be over with.

The fuss wasn't really about me, of course. The fuss was about the cultural mindset as to what women could and should—or couldn't and shouldn't—attempt. The women's movement had made this opportunity, this chance of a lifetime, available to me. I was in the right place at the right time with the right background of experience, dedication and passion. Having found myself, by historical accident, on the cutting edge of women's incursions into traditionally male fields, I had become the flash point, the lightning rod for the volatile emotions that festered in the aftermath of the legal successes of the women's movement.

By now I had learned enough about the blue car's competition history to understand how precarious were the chances of getting it into the field at Indianapolis. The best that Sprint-car ace Tom Bigelow had been able to do with it the previous year was at Milwaukee, where he qualified twelfth out of twenty-one starters, finished ninth of twelve cars running at the end. On the big, fast tracks (Pocono, Michigan) he had qualified last of thirty-three and two spots from last, respectively. And of course, at Indianapolis the car had been withdrawn. For whatever reason, it just wasn't a competitive car.

Meanwhile, Rolla was negotiating with the Trenton promoter to use the track for testing prior to race weekend. The outcome was this: our team could have it on April 16th and 17th without paying the usual rental fee, provided I attended a New York press conference on the 15th, plus a press conference at the track in the middle of practice on the 16th, plus whatever media turned up on the 17th. I was desperately eager for more track time, and embraced this bargain with open arms.

Four days before our Trenton practice date, Dick Simon and I were on PR duty in Indianapolis for Bryant. After dinner at the Speedway Motel, Dick said, "I hear that Hurtubise is in the bar. Let's go see!"

Jim "Herk" Hurtubise was a legendary driver who, though still active, was slipping down the ranks. Three sheets to the wind, he rose from his table in the bar and embraced me. In the dark, as I shook his hand, I was shockingly reminded: this was the man who, burned within an inch of his life in a crash at Milwaukee twelve years earlier, had told the doctors to mold his fingers so they could grasp a steering wheel. His hands were not like anything I had ever touched that was human. A long time later, I asked Herk whether it was true about his hands. "Nah," he said, "I told 'em to fix me up so I could hold a beer can."

Early next morning, I pulled on my jogging shoes and trotted off, paralleling the back straight of Indianapolis Motor Speedway toward Turn 3. The steps of the grandstands there were slippery with frost. At the top, sunrise burst over the gray-painted ziggurat. I turned and looked back at the track, the narrow dangerous track, so quiet now. Distant morning sounds drifted past: faint barks of dogs, hasty traffic, chickens crowing, life at the edge of a midwestern town. In my mind's eye, brilliant race cars howled down the track into Turn 3, ghostly images streaking past the infield's neat lawns and greening trees.

Thirty-eight drivers had been killed here so far.

It was necessary to make peace with that: to open my heart to this place and its history.

The sun moved higher. The hazard was there, was here, and lay ahead. My heart had its reasons, wordless, in which logic played no part. And presently, heart joined mind and spirit to say, yes. Satisfied, I jogged back again.

Later that morning, Dick King announced that he would indeed issue me a conditional Championship license, in spite of the pressure on him not to do so. Mostly, the contention was that I hadn't enough experience. No such taint followed Sheldon Kinser, for example, who had been a rookie at Indianapolis the previous year, 1975. Kinser's background was on the southern Indiana dirt tracks. When Kinser drove out onto Indianapolis Motor Speedway on the fourth day of practice for the 1975 race, one year earlier, he had never sat in an Indy car before, never driven a rear-engine car, never driven a turbocharged car, and had never driven on a track over a mile long.

Trenton Speedway's mid-town Manhattan press conference on Thursday April 15th, was held in the Autopub on Fifth Avenue at 59th Street. The place was jammed. Before long, a photographer was agitating USAC racing star Johnny Rutherford for a photo of us together. My stomach clenched. I looked at him and said, "Are you going to sit still for this?" JR looked, smiled, then put his arm around me! It was a gracious move, one that astonished and delighted me.

The hubbub continued. My formal remarks were almost routine by now. Then there were questions from the floor, most of them on the incredulous side—the same kind of stuff I'd been dealing with for the last month and a half.

"How old are you?" The tone of voice made the subtext perfectly clear.

"I'm thirty-eight, A. J. Foyt is forty-one, and Bobby Unser is forty-two."

"Don't you think that's too old to be starting at the top level of racing?"

"Juan Fangio was thirty-eight when he came out of the stock car tracks of Argentina, and he won his fifth World Championship in Grand Prix when he was forty-six."

"So many drivers have been killed at Indianapolis—what's your greatest fear as you look toward that race?"

"Not qualifying."

"Are you going to take up Bobby Riggs' challenge to race you or any other woman driver?"

That was news to me. "I wouldn't even dignify that with an answer."

Finally, Chris Economaki put the hot one: "What do you think of what the other drivers said about Arlene's driving?"

I made a politician's reply, the same thing I'd been saying: she practiced well in heavy traffic, she qualified well, she did well in trials, it's not the first time the top drivers have had harsh words for a rookie, I didn't know why she drove slowly in the race but there may have been a good reason.

Chris said, "That's not what I asked you. I asked you..." He repeated his question.

Pinned to the wall. And Johnny Rutherford sitting right beside me.

I said, "I think the comments were exceptionally harsh and that if a man had driven the same way they wouldn't have said the same things."

There was a sort of snort and a noise that sounded like "No kidding" from Johnny. I flicked a glance at him and saw him nod his head.

Later, as the affair wound down, a reporter for *The New York Times* beckoned from a phone booth, the receiver to his ear. He put his hand over the mouthpiece. "Bobby Unser," he said. "He just told me he could teach me how to drive better than you. I told him I didn't drive. He said he 'could take a hitch-hiker, give him a Corvette off a showroom floor, and turn him into a faster driver than her.'"

Bobby Unser had never seen me drive anything. It was too much of a muchness, and it cracked me up. "A hitch-hiker!" I laughed. "You're kidding! He really is a male chauvinist pig, isn't he?"

All that made headlines on the front page of the Sunday *New York Times* sports section.

Finally, trailed by photographers and cameramen, we were outside—outside where my car, my Indy car, sat in its neat little package of a trailer, right there on Fifth Avenue. The splendors of the city stood all around: beyond the fountains, the fabled Plaza Hotel; Bergdorf Goodman, full of women in mink; A La Vielle Russie, with its Fabergé eggs in their original Cyrillic-lettered cases; Tiffany, where diamonds peeked coyly from heaps of sawdust in the windows. Central Park opened up on the right, and horse-drawn carriages waited at the curb.

I felt like Alice gone through the looking glass.

Amid the Fifth Avenue cops and the curious, my crew opened up the trailer and there it was ... Vollstedt's blue car, my car, reality. I hungered for it like a person starved.

At long last, we were on our way to Trenton.

TRIAL BY FIRE

TRENTON [April 16]—It's a shame USAC officials couldn't fit a tent over the Trenton International Speedway and include lion acts, the fat lady and a few clowns ... Yesterday the wraps were taken off Janet Guthrie.[1]

The place was a circus, all right. A hundred reporters and photographers fidgeted in the pits as Dick Simon took the blue car out onto the Trenton track for its first laps. He warmed it up, stood on the gas, and pitted. The big Offy was backfiring, belching orange.

The crew worked on the car for the next four hours, while the press grew increasingly restive. When Dick brought the blue car in with its turbocharger on fire, the guys could hardly get past the photographers to put out the flames.

Vollstedt's team had spent the night in a Quality Inn blessedly isolated from Route 206 by a half-mile of woods. In the morning I jogged through the trees past a placid creek, soaking up the scent and sight of fresh spring greens and pink dogwood as a buffer against what lay ahead.

Trenton Speedway was an archetype of American racing, and an anachronism even in 1976. It lay within the New Jersey State Fair Grounds northeast of Trenton; the railroad grazed Turn 4. Even its entrance was obscure. A big corner of the fair grounds had been turned to profit, with a scruffy-looking shopping center set in acres of shoddy, pot-holed asphalt. Dick Simon and I cast about for the way in, finally spotting it behind the stores. It was like finding a gate into another time. Shabby and worn but still striking, the fairgrounds buildings embodied a civic pride as outdated as the architecture itself.

Trenton Speedway had been a classic one-mile oval until 1972, when an ambitious promoter extended it to a mile and a half. The peculiarity of the extension was that houses notched into the back

[1] Burlington County *Times*, April 17, 1976

stretch, creating a blind right-hand bend known as the dogleg. The dogleg was the only right-hand turn anywhere in Indy-car racing at that time, and it scared the heck out of the roundy-round boys. I viewed it with ironic contentment. *At least*, I thought, *I know how to turn right.*

The dogleg wall was concrete, but steel guard rails bordered most of the track—the cruel Armco-type barriers on which François Cévert had died at Watkins Glen. The rough and irregular surface of the track was spotted with patches. At least these offered some landmarks, some visual check points for the line.

Four drivers were testing: Johnny Rutherford, Tom Sneva, Dick Simon and myself. Simon was shaking down his own Eagle for the Trenton race, since Vollstedt's new car remained in the final throes of construction in Oregon. He had sponsorship from Lan Hairpieces for Men, and with a rug on he looked a bit like a toy badger. Intent on testing his Eagle, Simon was nevertheless courteous to the media that flocked around me, though they infringed on his time and space. Rutherford and Sneva stayed well away.

Simon had no sooner started his warmup than the Eagle's engine blew. Vollstedt immediately offered a deal: if Dick would shake down my blue car on the track, Rolla would make Rex Hutton and Roger Thrall available to change the Eagle's engine that night. Rex was my new crew chief, a young man in his twenties. Shy and soft-spoken, he had a fierce desire to see the blue car do well. When Dick accepted, I was greatly relieved. It was clear enough how the media would play it, if I took to the track in a seriously malfunctioning race car.

I walked over to the rail to check the star drivers' lap times, and the media troops fell in behind. It was peculiar and disconcerting to hear the pat-pat and whisk through the grass of dozens of trailing feet. In the ladies' room, I realized I had almost forgotten to unplug the wireless microphone, tied around my waist, that was broadcasting every sound to the NBC television truck. A circus, yes.

It seemed perfectly appropriate, then, when trucks full of elephants and tigers rolled into the fairgrounds. Grey trunks swung out of side doors, sniffing the methanol fumes that drifted over from the track. The effect was surreal.

Rutherford left around noon. "If I can be of any help," he had said, "let me know." I was beginning to understand why they called him "Gentleman Johnny."

At 12:30 there was an intermission for the press lunch. Now the photographers closed in: stand here, do this, put on some lipstick for us. ("No.") I was mortified at being the center of the fuss when Tom Sneva, a genuine racing hero, stood twenty feet away.

Sneva, driving for one of Roger Penske's teams, would be in contention for the win both here and at Indianapolis. Just a year before, he had been at the vivid center of a seemingly unsurvivable crash. Midway through the Indianapolis 500, he touched wheels with another car, launching himself in a cartwheel of flames up to eye level with the expensive private suites in Turn 2. People fainted on the suite terraces, but Tom came through with little more to show for it than a thick band of scar tissue around one wrist. He had once been a high-school principal and kept something of a pleasant, teacherly demeanour; he was perhaps the only driver besides Rutherford who thought Arlene Hiss should have had another chance.

I was starting to get a grip on the media pressure—a strange but necessary transition. I couldn't help being nervous about press conferences; they say that public speaking ranks right up there with death among most people's fears. But that was what I was there for, to be displayed, to increase the promoter's gate. It was the price of our using the track for this crucially important shakedown. It was crystal clear that the bugs in the blue car were bad enough to have prevented my qualifying, had we gone to race weekend cold.

It was almost 2 p.m. before the blue car was halfway ready to run. The suspension still needed setting and the turbocharger wasn't cured, but the promoter was getting frantic.

Dick Simon came close and spoke quietly in my ear. "Leave your foot on the gas pedal in the turns," he said, "about halfway down. That keeps the turbocharger spun up, otherwise the engine quits cold. You have to really stand on the brakes with your left foot to get it slowed down, but they'll take it."

Wonderful.

As I worked my way down into the seat for the first time since Ontario, two months before, all I could see was camera lenses. Photographers at the back were holding their cameras over their heads to grab what they could. Would this raucous, sceptical uproar affect my ability to concentrate on the track? The question had haunted me since Phoenix.

The guys pushed me off through a dense thicket of photographers. Their shins barely cleared the front wheels. I could only hope they realized that the car was wider at the rear. Running over their toes would be what Ralph Farnham used to call a fox pass.

Then I was out on the course. Like a door slamming shut, the fracas in the pits was obliterated. There were real problems to deal with. The car was indeed a handful. Power wasn't reliably available at the rear wheels when you wanted it, which upset its balance in the turns. Half its total braking force was chewed up by the contradictory input at the back—power and brakes simultaneously—which necessitated an early brake point. On this short track, with lower gears installed in the transaxle, the amazing thrust forward when the turbocharger boost came on was all the more dramatic. My helmet rattled against the cowling, blurring my view of the instruments and the track. I had no head support.

In ten laps I got down to 39.63 seconds—fast enough, someone said, to have put the car in the field the year before. It worked out to 145 mph. That was enough, and the crew signalled me in. They hadn't been in favor of running the car anyway, before it was fixed. That was fine with me.

On Saturday the media crowd dwindled, the engine problems were mostly resolved, and we got down to serious business. I sank my teeth into the workings of the blue car and the track, and my lap times dropped steadily.

What scared me was the mirror situation. The blue car had just one small mirror, on the right. Vollstedt and Simon repeated, "Don't worry about it. The faster cars will find their way around you." But their well-intentioned remarks contradicted what I had seen at Phoenix. Most of the slower cars had yielded when overtaken. Arlene Hiss didn't yield, and was crucified. If you couldn't see who was overtaking you, you couldn't do anything about it. I wanted as much mirror as I could get.

Late in the day, I asked Dick Simon to follow me around the track in his Eagle so I could do a mirror check. As we howled over the rough pavement into the turns, all I could see was a blur of color. Part of that was my own blue car: the rear tire, the wing, pieces of engine. Mirror adjustments were a guessing game. At speed, as the big rear wing forced the back end of the car down, you could find yourself with nothing in view but the rear suspension and the pavement. I begged Vollstedt to add a mirror on the left, and he said he would.

My other concern was that the side loads had begun to tell on my neck. Vollstedt said he would arrange for a shoulder strap to be installed on my helmet that week. I didn't even know what they looked like; it was a device used only on the ovals.

The car was no heavier on the wheel than any of a dozen cars I had raced in the past; strength simply wasn't going to be an issue. The level of concentration and commitment it required, though, drew on every ounce of experience I had.

The infamous dogleg was delicious. I went through it flat out. Gradually, the rest of the turns fell into place. When I ran 155 mph, they called me in. At 34.7 seconds, the lap time was just one second off what star driver Tom Sneva was turning in Roger Penske's state-of-the-art machine. Considering that I was running on the same worn tires Dick had raced on at Phoenix, Vollstedt felt it was time to call it a day. We couldn't afford to use up the blue car before race weekend.

The hot laps raised my spirits, which had undeniably sagged under the relentless pressure of publicly expressed scepticism in the previous weeks. It was a good thing, because the heat rose all that week. All I had to do was pick up a newspaper. The day after practice was Easter Sunday, and *The New York Times* article opened with a line from Rodney Dangerfield: "My wife drove into a tree but she told me it wasn't her fault, she honked her horn first." Bobby Unser took it from there, with his hitch-hiker quote in bold-face italics.

I drew consolation from the brief UPI clip in a box right up front: "Janet Guthrie exceeded 155 miles an hour today in practice at Trenton International Speedway. Her time was one second slower than that of Tom Sneva, who was also testing at the 1 1/2 mile oval."

No matter what Bobby Unser might say, so far, I had delivered the goods.

Dick Simon was also quoted in the *Times*, to somewhat more cheerful effect. "'I thought she was going to be just another woman,' said Simon, 'but within a couple of minutes we were carrying on a conversation on a driver-to-driver basis.'" The *Times* piece was reprinted that week in Chicago, Houston, St. Louis and a dozen or so other cities, under such headlines as "Are Women Drivers a Menace to Racing?"[2] And the chorus rose higher. "Guthrie Has Racers Fuming," one story began, quoting driver Pancho Carter, the 25-year-old son of an eleven-time Indianapolis 500 competitor: "She doesn't have the experience or the background ... I think there is some politics involved."[3] Pancho Carter had never seen me drive anything.

And from driver Johnny Parsons Jr.: "Women aren't built to drive that kind of race car. It takes too much strength in the arms ... Janet will probably cause more problems than Arlene, [she] doesn't have the car Arlene does ... we don't want her to put us between the sheets

[2] Little Rock (Ark.) *Gazette*, April 19, 1976
[3] Terre Haute *Tribune-Star*, April 18, 1976

in a hospital..."[4] Johnny Parsons Jr. had never seen me drive anything.

From Billy Vukovich, who had finished second at Indianapolis in 1973: "Indy racing is too demanding physically for women. ... After 40 laps, Guthrie won't be able to steer a car..."[5] Billy Vukovich had never seen me drive anything.

Mario Andretti took a more balanced view. Under his own byline "as reported to" Len Haas, he said, "I think she is being unfair to herself by striving to run the Indianapolis 500 this year, no matter how badly she wants to do it. I believe she should run the whole Championship season away from the super speedways, and then approach Indianapolis ... after she has had a thorough acquaintance with this equipment in competition which is not so severe and does not create so much pressure."[6]

Mario was a critic I could agree with. I'd have loved nothing better than to approach Indianapolis with more Champ car experience under my belt. But that wasn't the hand I'd been dealt. I could either go for Indianapolis, or walk away

Bobby Unser was quoted everywhere: "People say it's giving racing a shot in the arm. I just hope they don't do it at the expense of someone's life."[7]

Fortunately, I didn't see the one from Johnny Rutherford until much later. It went out on UPI: "I don't think any woman has the necessary credentials to drive Indy cars."

The stresses of the last six weeks reached their peak. Bobby Unser's comments were thrown in my face at every turn. "What makes you think you can handle one of these big Indy cars?" was a standard opening query, delivered with a jocular sneer. And I'd grit my teeth and summarize my record one more time.

Flying back to New York from Chicago, I caught up with my journal.

Every Indy-car race brims with mishaps. We've joked that any incident within half a lap of me—in either direction—will be chalked up to my account; but what if I do make a mistake? A bobble, an oversight—like all those men who spun out in the Phoenix race. What if I don't see someone coming behind me, and move to pass another just as he gets there? The car is so blind toward the back; I'm used to a mirror that spans the whole width of a sports car. So easy not to see someone, to make a wrong move. What if...

[4] Fort Wayne *News-Sentinel*, April 22, 1976
[5] Trenton *Trentonian*, April 25, 1976
[6] Cleveland *Plain Dealer*, April 23, 1976
[7] Philadelphia *News*, April 23, 1976

I turned my mind back to the team. The guys had been great. Something of a siege mentality had developed, and they were on the inside of it, with the car and with me. Not one of them had run for cover. Rolla set the style; he was as protective as if my honor were his own. On Friday, the day we had so much trouble, he specified to the mob of reporters just what was wrong with the blue car, and suggested they make an allowance for it. That was a rare thing for an owner to do.

How can I not succeed, supported by each member of this team? That's where it's at, in the middle of all this: with the people, Rex and Roger and Carl and Dick and Rolla, and with the track. With that white patch in Turn 4 that mysteriously vanishes in the afternoon light—the patch that you want your wheels on the right-hand side of.

I stared out the window for a while, as the necklace lights of New York's great suspension bridges tilted into view.

If I fail, they'll cut me into mincemeat and feed me to the sharks.

If I succeed, my life will never be the same.

If I fail, I'm going to change my name to Mildred Schabowsky and move to Brooklyn and clerk in a dimestore.

If I succeed...

I couldn't even imagine what the changes would be.

The day was at hand.

Twenty-eight cars were entered at Trenton. It was the second-largest field of USAC Championship cars the track had ever seen. The fastest twenty-two would start the race.

Behind the wheels would sit the finest race car drivers in the United States: A. J. Foyt, Johnny Rutherford, Gordon Johncock, Bobby Unser—each a past winner of the Indianapolis 500—and Tom Sneva, Wally Dallenbach, Roger McCluskey, Mike Mosley, Tom Bigelow, and Billy Vukovich. All the stars were there save Andretti. Everyone was tuning up for Indianapolis.

Official practice opened on Saturday April 24. All went well. Rookies, eight of us, were segregated from veterans for the first two practice sessions. (USAC blandly stated that this was not unusual, but everyone knew the real cause.) Then we were thrown in with the rest, sink or swim. Rookie Gary Albritain, a star of high-powered Super-Mod racing, sank. He stuffed his car into the wall, which he had also done in practice at Phoenix, and Dick King quietly sent him home.

God knows I was tense; I think the unrelenting pressure had

caught up with me at last. My times weren't quite as fast as on the test days, partly because of the traffic and partly because of some problems with the car. Still, at about 152 mph I was faster than seven others.

Johnny Rutherford turned the fastest lap of the day. Shortly after, he stopped by our pit, flushed and rumpled from the track. "You're doing fine," he said, and then: "I just wanted you to know that the newspaper accounts of what I said were wrong."

When he left, Roger and Rex and I looked at each other and smiled. "Quite a guy," Rex said. I was as glad for them as for myself. The night before, the three of us had worked on the blue car until late at night, in a fairgrounds Quonset hut from which the circus elephants had just been evicted. It was littered with straw and smelled of elephant. We joked a bit as we held the pieces of the blue car in our hands. If Johnny Rutherford had kind words, Rex and Roger had certainly earned them.

On Sunday morning, I was ready to face my fate. Then the rains came. Championship cars don't race in the rain. Hour by hour, the tension grew. I brooded in the RV that had been lent to our team—as usual, at a price. It bore a sign on top four feet tall, "JANET GUTHRIE MOTOR HOME, SUPPLIED BY —— MOTORS." There was always a crowd outside trying to get in.

I burrowed as deeply as I could into the armloads of pink and white dogwood I had propped behind the windshield. The flowering branches were my only protection and refuge. Too many strangers were inside, wanting something: interviews, conversation, comments, autographs, some little piece of me for their own. A week later, my brother the anthropologist would observe this phenomenon with professional interest, muttering about *mana* (in Polynesia, inherent supernatural power) as he made notes on a lined pad.

There was enough on my mind without an RV full of strangers. The blue car still suffered from turbocharger lag. There was a problem with the oil cooler, too. And the shoulder strap on the helmet hadn't worked for me. The geometry was wrong: my neck was longer and my shoulders narrower than Simon's or the other drivers who used one. The strap pulled my head down, but didn't support it well against centrifugal force. I was plenty worried about that.

Around noon, Dick Simon burst into the RV with a shout of "They're running!" He was teasing, but I thought my heart would leap out of my chest. Dick had been even more cheerful than usual that morning; he was the first to spot an account in the Trenton *Times* of what A. J. Foyt had said. "She looked good out there today," Foyt was quoted as saying, "and if she can do the job, I'm behind her a hundred percent." Dick's voice, as he read it to us, was full of enthusiasm and pleasure. It came like a brief ray of light into a murky and uncertain day.

A. J.'s powerful voice on our side may have been even more important to Simon and Vollstedt than to me. They were both established figures in the sport, with reputations that were unquestionably at risk in this endeavor. The garbage aimed at me was hitting the rest of the team as well, especially its veteran driver. He consistently defended my ability—after all, he had recommended me for a license—and I had been getting jumpier and jumpier about that. Simon's positive attitude hadn't yet flagged, but he wouldn't be human if it wasn't affecting him.

After an eternity of waiting in the rain, the race was postponed for a week. Jackie Stewart and Jim McKay were there for ABC-TV; it was the first time I had ever met the former World Champion, and I was delighted to hear him say on-camera that "male chauvinist pig may be the nicest thing said about Bobby Unser in years."

"What will you do this week?" they wanted to know.

"Hide," I said. "Maybe pull the phone out of the wall."

But I couldn't, of course. Next day I was on duty in Chicago for Bryant, our sponsor. The last item on Monday's agenda was a late-night radio show of exceptional hostility. On the plane back Tuesday evening I wrote:

I think the strain is starting to tell on everyone. Rolla was trying to say goodbye at Trenton Speedway in the middle of a gigantic crowd of reporters; he looked at least ten years older than when we met, and couldn't concentrate on what he wanted to tell me.

I put down my pen and stared out the plane window, remembering: the reporters jostling each other, desperate to hear what we said; the last spatters of rain.

"I'm taking the turbocharger and the oil cooler back to Portland in my suitcase," Rolla had said, struggling to collect his thoughts. "We'll see if we can't get those taken care of."

Roger waited at his elbow. "We'd better go, Boss," he said. Newark Airport was forty-five miles away.

"I'll call you in Chicago tomorrow," Rolla said to me.

"Okay, Boss." I reached out to touch his arm for a moment. "Safe home." He turned to go, and I headed for my old Barracuda to drive back to Manhattan. We had been staying in close touch by phone—he in Oregon, I in New York or wherever. There was so much pressure, so much hostility. Rolla had steel in his backbone, but his voice on the phone sounded more and more beset. I suppose I sounded the same way. At some point in each conversation, one of us would ask the other, "How're you doing?"

The answer, whichever of us said it, stayed the same. "Oh—got my head above water. How're *you* doing?"

There was more media stuff to do in New York. By Friday I was wiped out, not willing to twitch a muscle, and real fear was seeping in—the kind that incapacitates. I fought it down. It didn't help when a sports car driver I knew stopped by on Saturday with a copy of Keith Johnsgard's academic work on the psychology of racing drivers. His study pointed out in passing that "one out of three of the full and part-time professional racers [who participated in the study] has been killed or forced to retire with serious race incurred injuries ... Risk of death assumes rather alarming probability as one moves from amateur to the very highest levels of automobile racing."

I was struggling with the impact of that as I packed my stuff for the race. Rolla had caused a professional driver's suit to be made to my measure by Hinchman in Indianapolis, of heavy, gleaming cream and blue Nomex. On it were all the embroidered patches of our sponsors, and the United States Auto Club patch as well. It was more beautiful to me than any fashion designer's outfit, and no garment ever so became me in my life.

Sunday May 2. Dawn. The day of the trial by fire. In the morning dark I sought Athena, but I didn't sense her there in the dark room as she had been before the trial at Ontario.

The butterflies were giving me fits. I drew open the curtains. South Jersey was brushed all over with the pale greens of early spring. Ethereally delicate leaves unfolded in the trees. And she was there, the grey goddess, at the meadow's edge, shadowy, as tall as the trees.

"This is your battle," she was saying. But she was there.

She was there at the track, too, by the infield pond.

After the morning's last, abbreviated practice session, I climbed out of the car. "They're drawing for position in the qualifying line," Roger said. "Get your buns on down there."

I drew the last spot. That gave the grandstands plenty of time to howl, whistle and jeer, in between the deafening qualifying runs of the other cars. Shouts of "Go back to the kitchen" (and worse) rained on us like the spears of hostile natives in a '50s jungle movie. I managed to tune it out, and get my head together for qualifying. It is such a curious process. The butterflies do their worst, stomping around on your diaphragm, making the back of your head feel light. God knows what your heart rate is, but it shakes your rib cage. You do laps in your mind. Each patch of pavement or rusty juncture of steel guardrails marking your line through the turns is vividly superimposed on what your eyes actually see: the cars in front of you creeping inexorably toward the moment of truth.

I would have two laps, just over a minute, eight left turns and two passes through the dogleg, in which to make the field ... or fail, which, as Mark Twain said, "would astonish no one and gratify the rest."

With about four cars left in line, I stepped into the blue car's seat and wriggled slowly into position. I felt remote, thinking out each placement of hand or foot as if I were directing a robot that might drive its arm or leg straight through the bodywork if not correctly instructed.

As the guys pushed the blue car to the head of the line, the sense of horrid apprehension reached its peak. The feeling was ghastly. Nevertheless, I knew I was in the right space.

The chief steward knelt beside the car, bracing his elbow on the bodywork that covered the fuel cells. Ritualistically, he spoke the qualifying instructions, then paused.

"Good luck," he said, "and Godspeed."

They fitted the starter to the back of the gearbox.

"Switch on?"

"On," I said.

The big Offenhauser caught and fired. I armed the fire extinguisher system by pulling its safety pin, and gave the pin to Roger. The last car in front of me screamed into Turn 1, the decreasing pitch of its engine telling that the checkered flag was out. The butterflies gave a final stomp, and left. The trick with butterflies, someone has said, is to make them fly in formation. Mine had been rivalling the Blue Angels.

I watched the steward with his clipboard and stopwatches, a few feet away. The steward watched the starter on his stand across the track, behind us. The starter watched the previous car. The signal came, the track was clear.

Go.

Out onto the track, swerving left and right to warm the tires, steering clear of the slippery bits of rubber and chewed-up race track that littered the inner apron and the outer parts of the course. Check the engine temperatures, okay.

Stand on it through the dogleg, ease into Turns 3 and 4 with some room to spare. Down the front straight and into Turn 1 at about eight-tenths, then give it everything I've got. The next two laps would be for real.

There are writers of fiction who have laid out wildly exciting descriptions of the imagined physiological responses of a driver on the track. It's interesting reading, but you don't actually feel like that at all. When the time has come to qualify the car, your body becomes part of the machine. You have no interest in a readout from your nervous system; it's not useful and it's not wanted and it's not there. Your emotional steam, superheated, is harnessed, entirely at the service of your will. If you're sweating profusely enough to turn your driver's suit a darker shade of blue, all the way through the double-layer Nomex skivvies, you won't know it until after you've stopped the car. The only readouts you want are from the tachometer, to tell you with its minuscule variations how well you've gotten through the turns, and perhaps, on the straights, from the oil pressure and boost gauges, to tell you that the engine is in good health.

That's the kind of space I was in when I made the qualifying run. I was entirely "in the moment," as the current description goes, and I also knew in the moment that the run was a good one. When I saw the guys, I knew it must have been good indeed. Their glee lit up the pit like fireworks. Roger beamed and sputtered with joy as he undid the belts. For a moment, I was too weak to move. Then I was out of the car and they were hugging me and Rolla was shaking my hand, and I saw the other crews staring at us and heard the roar from the grandstands.

It would be splendid if this were fiction, and I could write that I qualified on the pole, fastest of all. But it was real life; what I did was exact from the blue car just about everything that it had to give. With a lap of 34.42 seconds or 156.886 mph, I qualified fourteenth, in the middle of the field. Behind us were a driver who had competed five times in the Indianapolis 500, three drivers who had run close to a full season of Indy-car races in 1975, and every other rookie at Trenton that day.

If the blue car was capable of such a solid showing here, maybe there was real hope of making the field at Indianapolis after all.

A. J. Foyt had the pole at 32.47 seconds, and Johnny Rutherford was second. Dick Simon, thirteenth in his Eagle with a time of 34.40

seconds, would start on my left. The horrible pressure of the last six weeks decompressed. It's a wonder that I didn't get the bends.

Shortly before race time, driver introductions were to be held in front of the grandstands. As we walked that way through the pandemonium along pit road, I must have looked tense again, because an oldtimer said, "Remember, eight hundred million Chinese don't care what happens here today." I thought that was the funniest line of the weekend, and it helped. "God be with you," he said in the end. It was something I heard often that day, and in the days ahead.

Meanwhile, the guys were pushing the cars out onto the starting grid. Bobby Unser's car was not among them. He had damaged the front suspension in the closing minutes of practice, and was out of the race.

Over the PA system, the promoter called our names and car numbers in reverse order of our positions in the field. In that order, we lined up next to the track. No hype or PR could change anyone's position in this line. It was simply what we had earned, who was faster than whom. And so, I took my place.

Soon it was time. The butterflies were back at work. The head-support problem had been solved by a thin, resilient luggage strap that ran forward from the chrome roll bar to the edge of the cockpit, a brace against centrifugal force. The turbocharger lag was something I would have to live with.

I was drawing on everything I knew, everything I'd learned in my life, and bringing it to bear on this race.

The Star Spangled Banner blared scratchily from the loudspeakers.

"... and the land ... of the ... brave..."

"Janet and gentlemen, start your engines!"

The words were swallowed as twenty-two 800-horsepower engines sprang to life. Rolla shook my hand, Roger squeezed my shoulder, and they were gone.

It was good to be starting next to Dick Simon, to have justified the effort he had made in my behalf; but I was glad to have been a whisker slower rather than faster. I feared increasing the burden on him beyond what he could bear.

The pace car moved off, and we pulled out behind it. The pre-race jitters vanished like snowflakes into fire. When we took the green flag, I had long since found my way into that clear white heat without malice, the crystalline focus on car, competition, and track.

At Turn 1 I tucked in behind Simon, figuring I could learn the most by following my mentor. What I learned was that he wasn't nearly as concerned about race-track etiquette as I was. When Spike Gelhausen put a move on me, I gave him a clean pass, then watched as Simon gave him a very hard time indeed. I dropped a couple more positions in the first few laps, then started gaining them back.

The consciousness of what's going on during a race is a funny, complicated thing. Part of you knows that your car leaps and scrabbles, roars out of the turns, dances and twitches on the rough parts. Part of you intensely respects your proximity to the edge—the hairline that separates the fastest transit of a turn from losing it, a spin, a crash. Part of you knows the toll taken on your physical self by all that thrashing about. Part of you knows how critical are your neuron-quick calculations, and the penalty for error. But none of this is anywhere near the surface of your mind. Your focus is on the details that will carry you past the car ahead.

After a while, the lapping began. Lapping was what had kept me awake nights. How much of the overtaking traffic would I be able to see in those quivering little mirrors? To my enormous relief, I could see it all. At a maximum speed differential of only a second or so a lap between myself and the very fastest of the cars, I had time enough to spot who was coming, and to get a good fix on the moment when they'd be in a position to pass.

The hardest part was figuring out who was who—which driver was coming up on me, and which was the driver I'd just passed. The noses of the cars were small, often a different color than the sides. In the mirror, all you could see of one was the nose and the wheels. I had spent some time before the race memorizing car numbers, the driver of each, studying what the noses looked like. While I didn't have them all down pat, it helped.

Of one thing I was sure: any driver who came up to lap me was not only going to have plenty of room to do it, he was going to have so much room that there wouldn't be any doubt in his mind. At Phoenix the slower cars had yielded the line, and in spite of all the well-meaning advice to the contrary, I now did the same. Each time, it cost me maybe a second. Most of the overtaking drivers gave me a wide berth when they went by. The only exception was an orange-red car that slid past with just inches to spare: Gordon Johncock, who seemed not to share the fear that I would do something strange. I had to admire his nerve. Johncock led the race for much of its distance, then ran out of fuel a lap from the end.

We were maybe fifteen or twenty minutes into the race when I felt a sudden clarity, almost a moment of epiphany. I was coming out of Turn 4 against the inside rail, leaving all the room in the world for a couple of faster cars on my heels to go by, and balancing that need against concern over a buildup of rubber bits and track grunge that would stick to my tires if I got too far off the line. The blue car was leaping forward off the turn as the boost finally came on, my foot having been on the floor for what seemed like forever—a second or two. Ahead lay the front straight and the pits, the bulk of the grandstands, a car I was overtaking. Turn 1 was a long way off. I'd have six or eight seconds to check the instruments and the mirrors and read the pit board and position myself for the next turn. And in that instant it flashed through my mind:

This is just like any other race I've driven.

It gave me new verve.

The yellow came out on Lap 33; it was Vukovich with a blown engine. The timing was perfect, and they brought me in for fuel. Someone handed me a cup of water. I didn't want it, but, mindful of all that had been said about the physical endurance needed to complete an Indy-car race, I tried to drink it as a precaution. I was soon to regret that move.

On Rolla's signal, go, with a light screech of the tires. The trick was to keep the wheels just short of spinning in first and second gears, meanwhile dodging the crews and anyone else in pit road who might be just as intent as I was on regaining the track—sort of like a drag race through an obstacle course, with moving obstacles. Then I was back in the pack, getting ready for the green.

We'd had no more than two laps at speed when my helmet strap came undone. The parachutist's quick-release redoubling of the end of the strap that I learned when I was sixteen had not failed me in thirteen years of racing. But my attempt to get that cup of water inside the full-coverage helmet had loosened the strap, and in the beating of the wind inside the cockpit, it came apart. For a couple of laps I considered leaving it that way, but air turbulence inside the blue car was so pronounced that the helmet started to move and lift. There was nothing for it but a pit stop—under the green! The crew flew around in a flurry of consternation, not understanding, as I pulled off one glove and refastened the strap, my fingers fumbling in haste. No redoubling of the strap this time; nor did I ever fasten it that way again. Once had been costly enough, putting me a couple of laps down.

We refueled under the yellow again, but this time, back on the track, a vibration shook the car. Maybe it was buildup on the tires, maybe one had originally been out of balance. The pit stop to change tires extended into the green. *Damn.*

Off again, in hot pursuit. The yellow came out almost immediately—what wretched luck, we could've changed those tires on the yellow—when A. J. Foyt's engine blew.

Ten laps later, Dick Simon was out of the race with a burned valve. Trouble came for me on Lap 73. A handful of fast cars, Tom Sneva among them, was breathing down the back of my neck in Turns 1 and 2, and I held the blue car low as we pulled out onto the back stretch. Too low.

At the edge of the "marbles"—the bits of rubber and chewed-up race track at the bottom of the turn—the back end of the car broke away. I had slowed, anticipating an insecure surface, but not slow enough.

Oh shit.

When the back end of an Indy car starts out, with the weight of the engine and transaxle to give it momentum, you're in trouble. I knew that, though this was the first time it had happened. Dick had told me, "Help it on around. Turn left and lock up the brakes. If you try to save it, you're likely to go into the wall nose first, and that's bad."

But I couldn't do that, the other cars were too close.

If I spin, I'll spin right up into them.

Back in the Jaguar days, I used to play with the XK 120 coupe in the winter—going through an icy corner too fast, letting the back end start out, feeling it go, and getting it back again. Sometimes I'd let it continue to where it wasn't saveable any more, where it would snap all the way past. It was fun to do 180-degree spins. Later, when I raced the XK 140, it was sometimes useful to hang the back end out in a turn, making a skinny car into a wide one for whatever period of time seemed desirable. Those were front-engine cars, though; they would sit down and write you a letter before they went all the way around.

Rear-engine cars were different. In my first race in an open-wheel, rear-engine car, at Sebring, I'd gone into one of the high-speed airport turns too fast. I got off the throttle and the back end immediately snapped out. Against my urgent desire to slow down flashed the understanding that unless I got back on the gas, the car was headed backwards or sideways into the haybales. I planted my foot, hung the tail out the other side, aimed between the haybales, and came back onto the course without ever losing a place.

All this experience was stored somewhere, in distilled form, and I brought it to bear and got the blue car saved. It took perhaps a second. Sneva was safely past.

In the process I killed the engine—probably by depressing the clutch as the car came straight again. That was another ingrained reaction, which should have had the opposite effect. But with the turbocharger acting up, it didn't work.

I'm a mile from home and too slow to coast there and the engine's dead and I don't have an onboard starter. I'll end up parked at the back of the infield. That won't do.

All that took another couple of seconds.

So I stuffed it back in gear and popped the clutch. It started right up, and I was off and running again.

Four laps later, fourth gear failed. The gearbox made noises of distress. I grabbed third gear, which seemed okay. But if fourth gear was screwed up, bits of metal would be flying around inside the housing, chewing up everything in sight. That would cost Rolla a lot of money in a short time. I pitted.

According to the next day's reports, I was eleventh at the seventy-ninth lap, and nine laps down; most of those laps were due to our green-flag pit stops.

"Fourth gear is gone," I yelled in Roger's ear. Emotionally, I must have felt it could be fixed, which made no sense. A hand reached into the cockpit and killed the engine. "I've still got third!" I shouted. But Rolla Vollstedt was shaking his head, and his look was one of sad resignation. When I climbed out, I saw why. The transaxle case was fractured, and dark thick oil dripped into a widening puddle on the ground.

I remember the depth and width of that crack—not so deep as a well, nor so wide as a church door, but 'twould serve—watching the oil drip out of it, and thinking at first only, *Can't it be fixed?* Though the evidence of my eyes told me otherwise. Denial, it's called.

I looked out at the track, the cars whistling by, the race going on without me, and felt suddenly ripped from life, watching while life went on.

Reporters and photographers, of course, had come down pit lane at a gallop. I ignored them until the finality of the damage settled in, as Rolla, Rex, Sperb, Dick and I talked. Then I took a deep breath, and turned to deal with it.

I knew damn well how I'd done while I ran. This hadn't been

I still have the teddy bear.

Graduation from Miss Harris' Florida School for Girls in 1955 was an elegant affair. My flower girl was Bunny Kreeger.

My family in 1971. From left: me, my mother Jean, Anne, Stewart, Margaret, my father Lain, Walter.

The Stearman PT-17 was my all-time favorite airplane. I especially loved aerobatics. This photo is from 1956.

I was sixteen when Charles Lindbergh's The Spirit of St. Louis inspired me to make a parachute jump in 1954. It was my first big adventure.

In the anechoic chamber at Republic Aviation, 1961. I was a research and development engineer.

In my Jaguar XK 140MC, at a Sports Car Club of America race at Thompson, Conn., June 1964. I started last and finished second.

Ralph Farnham and Jim Hancock complete a victory lap with me at Bridgehampton, N.Y., August 1966.

The Celica that I built with the help of volunteers, and raced from 1972 through 1975. Here, at Bridgehampton, N.Y., in 1974.

In 1974, I paid the rent, in part, by helping Ralph Farnham move boats.

We took first in class (Under 2 Liter Prototype) in this tiny 1293-cc Donald Healey Sprite in the 1970 Sebring 12-Hour.

Ralph Farnham's shop, where he let me work on my Jaguar and my Celica, was sometimes under water.

The first big step: successful completion of testing at Ontario, Calif.,
February 1976. From left: Bertie and Hal Sperb, Roger Thrall,
Melanie and Dick Simon, me, team owner Rolla Vollstedt, Al Kissler.

Rolla Vollstedt
at the Ontario
test. I took the
picture.

The great thrill of meeting
A.J. Foyt at my first Indy-car
race, Trenton, N.J., 1976

—Pat Singer

—www.greenfieldgallery.net

On the last day of qualifying for the Indianapolis 500, 1976, A.J. Foyt let me take
his car out in practice. Talk about pressure!

—Courtesy Motorsports Images & Archives

I have just completed the qualifying run that will presently put us in the field for the 1977 Daytona 500. Jim Lindholm, left, and Ralph Moody.

Lynda Ferreri was my NASCAR Winston Cup team owner in 1976, 1977, and part of 1978.

—Courtesy Motorsport Images & Archives

—Tom Franklin

Right after I qualified for my first Winston Cup race, the Charlotte World 600, May 1976. Track General Manager Humpy Wheeler offers his congratulations; Roger Thrall is happy too.

−Stewart Guthrie

With teammate Dick Simon, after qualifying for my first Indy-car race, Trenton, N.J., May 1976.

−Hugh Baird

Pit stop in the Indianapolis 500, 1978

−Hugh Baird

Kay Bignotti on the grid, ready to start my engine for the Indianapolis 500, 1977. Because of Kay, Speedway owner Tony Hulman was obliged to modify his starting call from "Gentlemen, start your engines."

Paul Newman had recently won his first SCCA National Championship when we talked before the Winston Cup race at Ontario, Calif., November 1976. I got a big hug!

With President Carter in the White House, supporting Title IX for the Women's Sports Foundation, September 1979.

Quizzed by World Champion Jackie Stewart in the pits at Indianapolis, 1978.

Jane Pauley came out from New York to her home state to tape an interview for the Today show, Indianapolis, 1977.

like Phoenix.

"What happened?"

"Fourth gear disintegrated under power. The transaxle housing is cracked."

"How do you feel?"

It didn't even occur to me that the reporter was asking about my physical condition. (One wrote, "When she climbed out of her car, she surprised her critics by checking out the rear end of the car instead of collapsing.")

"Frustrated," I said.

When the press was mostly satisfied, I headed for the RV. The race was done.

Johnny Rutherford won. Johncock, even with the time he lost coasting in for fuel, was second, and Tom Sneva third. Dick Simon was classified sixteenth, I was fifteenth. A quick calculation showed that without the extra pit stops and the cracked gearbox, I'd have been in the top ten at the end. But then, the road back from the races is often paved with might-have-beens.

Before the crowd had a chance to spill out of the grandstands, the promoter sent someone to hustle me over to the press box. It hung over the very top of the grandstands, and reeked of cigar smoke. Johnny Rutherford was up front, going over the race. His compliments on my driving were widely reported the next day, and Sneva's as well. When he was gone, it was my turn.

"How did it feel?" they asked.

"It felt great while it lasted," I said. "I think I ran strongly while I was in there, and I hope the other guys feel the same way about it."

"How do you feel physically? Were you tired?"

I laughed. "The most physically taxing part of the day was the climb up the grandstands to the press box here."

"There's been so much attention focused on you, did that have any effect?"

"No, after thirteen years of racing, you develop a certain power of concentration, and I was able to put it out of my mind. But I'll be glad when the fuss dies down."

"What did you think of the way George Hamid called the start of the race?"

"I'd have been happier to hear, 'Championship drivers, start your engines.'"

"When are you going to Indianapolis?"

A trap. It wasn't official yet. Two of the Indianapolis 500 stewards,

Don Garner and Art Meyers, had been watching at Trenton. They and Dick King would confer with Indianapolis 500 Chief Steward Tom Binford before announcing their judgment.

"I haven't spoken with any USAC officials yet, but Rolla Vollstedt said he was satisfied with my performance. If we receive their approval, we'll be there Thursday or Friday."

"How will you feel if they turn you down?"

Uh-oh. I saw a couple of wolfish looks as they waited for the answer to that one: eyes especially bright, mouths a little ajar.

I took a deep breath. "Surprised," I said.

And that was in no way boast, but truth.

They'd smelled blood, though, and pressed it. "What action will you take if they turn you down?"

I could almost see the word "lawsuit" forming in their heads. Not a chance.

"I really couldn't comment on that."

"Do you feel any special satisfaction that you beat both Bobby Unser and Billy Vukovich, who said you didn't belong here?"

I hadn't beaten them; they'd just been forced out before I was. "No," I said, "I don't feel anything special. It's just the breaks of the game."

Finally it was over. At the door, an armed guard was waiting.

"They told me to get you back to the motor home," he said.

An armed cop, how extraordinary, why in the world would I need an armed cop? Then we went out the door.

I've no idea how many hundreds of people were waiting, but as we made our way down the stands and across the track the crowd grew even larger, so that we moved foot by foot with great difficulty. I was amazed and confused, and signed the proffered programs and scraps of paper as we went, the guard trying his best to dissuade me. He was clearly relieved when we reached the RV and his duty was discharged.

Waiting at the door of the motor home was Dick Mooney, with whom I had shared that wonderful ride in my Jaguar at Watkins Glen twelve years before. He had his young son by the hand. I pulled them inside. It had been years, and I was so glad to see him now, to touch reality again.

I've always had a taste for deserted race tracks, after the race is over and only the shades and the trash blowing around and the passions still permeating the air are left, like the aftermath of lovemaking. And so I was content when all the demands were finally satisfied, long after the other teams had gone, still to be there, to walk out onto the track in the dusk with Rex.

As crew chief on the blue car, he carried a lot of responsibility—especially for so young a man. The day had been his success as well as mine. It was a good thing to share.

"What was it like?" he asked. And I did my best to tell.

I remember the red of the evening sky, the whiffs of rubber among the earthy smells of spring, and our peaceful talk of the quirks and habits of the blue car.

We had done what they said was impossible. We had run a race that was just like any other race in my life, but incomparably more important. "Women can't do it," they'd been ranting and raving. And now it was done.

A huge burden had been lifted off all of us on Vollstedt's team. I'd walked barefoot over the hot coals and my feet were not blistered, nor was anyone else's hide. We were on our way to the Indianapolis 500.

INDIANAPOLIS, MAY 1976

In the rosy five days between Trenton and the opening of practice at the Speedway, anything seemed possible. Media stuff came in torrents: the *Today* show, *Good Morning America*. Coca-Cola called me, and set a date to talk about sponsorship! Could this get us a better car, improve our chances of success?

I flew out to Indianapolis on Thursday May 6. My teammate, Dick Simon, had cheerful news: driver Billy Vukovich, a harsh critic before the Trenton race, had positive words about my performance there. He was impressed, he'd said. But if I'd had any notion that the Trenton race would clear the air and make it possible for the oval-track world to accept me on my merits as a driver, I was soon disabused of it. That night, Rolla Vollstedt took Rex Hutton, Roger Thrall and me to dinner at the Beverage, a scruffy bar and grill on 16th Street near the track. It was a racing hangout, mostly for crew members, and it wasn't five minutes before I heartily regretted Rolla's choice of turf. Hostility hung in the air thicker than the cigarette smoke, which was thick enough to choke on.

It was the first time I saw clearly how much pressure the guys on the crew were going to be under, and my heart ached over it. The usual camaraderie of the racing game was absent; in its place came glares and insults. It was just like the cattlemen versus the homesteaders in the classic movie *Shane*. When a couple of crew members from another team joined our table, the move was as deliberate, as ritualistic and as gallant as when Shane walked into the cattlemen's bar to order a soda pop for the homesteader's son.

If ever medals for valor were deserved by anyone, it was the guys on my crew. Next day they built a tiny enclosure in one corner of Rolla's garage so I could change into my driving gear with a modicum of privacy. On it they hung a neatly lettered sign. It referred back to a Citizens Band radio "handle" that they had chosen for me, which I had declined, so far, to accept (hubris, I thought). "Indy Lady is OUR Indy Lady," it said. The sight of it nearly reduced me to tears.

There were incidents they protected me from, things I didn't learn about for a long time. Parts, for example. Borrowing and lending of parts, tools, and spares among teams had always been part of the game. It was a couple of years before Rex told me that when Vollstedt's crew went out to borrow something, they faced a question: "Is it for his car or for hers?" My blue car, it seemed, was not to be aided in any way.

Practice opened on May 8. Rolla had asked Dick Simon to shake down the blue car before I took it out. They fired it up in the garage— and the clutch tore itself to bits. Fixing that took most of the day. Half an hour before closing, Dick set off on his warmup laps, and promptly blew an oil line off the turbocharger. Clouds of dense smoke billowed from the hot compressor, and Dick was towed in on the end of a rope. Next day, things got worse. He pitted almost immediately with a burned piston. A spare engine went in that night. It had been a godsend for Dick to shake down the car, to run interference. The atmosphere around our efforts was as highly charged as a mine full of coal gas. Had I been at the wheel for those first two days of mechanical failure, things might have turned ugly indeed.

By Monday May 10, my turn was coming up. I'd been holding myself ready for this for the last two days, tension building inside. As I walked back from the public women's room, trailed by the usual crowd, two sunburned young men veered toward me.

"Hi, Janet," one of them called, friendly, waving his beer can. "Ya gonna run today?"

"Looks like it."

"Ya gonna qualify?"

"Hope so."

"Well, we don't," they grinned. "We hope you crash on our corner."

I kept on walking, but after I closed our garage doors behind me, I kicked some handy tires while steam came out my ears. Still, no residue of this unpleasantness would follow me out onto the race track. I knew that I could shed it as a snake sheds its skin.

A wave of cheers and boos greeted my first appearance for practice at Indianapolis Motor Speedway. The Offy roared to life. Rolla scanned for traffic, waved me out onto pit road. "Remember," I whispered to myself, "it's just like Trenton, only bigger." I don't know who I thought I was kidding.

A proper warmup; third gear, then fourth, foot to the floor. As a rookie, I was obliged to use only the inner half of the racing surface, never approaching the outer wall. In a little over a lap, the engine went soft.

Not a piston again!

What a sickening sensation. No matter how fast I killed the ignition and disengaged the clutch, the damage was already done.

Reporters and cameramen were crowding into our pit. "The thing you have to remember," I said, "is that this happens to everyone, not just us." A. J. himself had come in on the end of a rope that day. Bobby Unser and three other drivers trashed their engines as well. The track was closed for a forty-five-minute sweep-up when Steve Krisiloff's turbocharger came unglued, scattering sharp little pieces abundantly on the line. None of those woes, however, made the evening news— just ours. A spotlight had its drawbacks.

Rolla was now out of engines, and the pain of it showed clearly through his customary cheer. Even a used Offy would cost some $10,000. He was already $60,000 in the hole this year, he had told me, and no extra sponsorship was in sight. Coca-Cola's proposal had been appalling. The promotion was to be for their Tab diet cola, which came in pink cans. They would require my driver's suit, helmet, and the clothes that I wore to the track and race-related social functions to be that shade of pink, with Tab logos. For this, they offered $300 a day. At Indianapolis, a pink driver's suit would be like waving a red flag in a ring full of bulls. Rolla and I turned it down.

By nightfall Rolla was smiling again, albeit feebly. Goodyear had lent him an engine, one of the "mules" they kept at the track for tire testing. And the presumptive cause of the melted pistons had been found: a cracked fuel fitting. I changed into work clothes and dived into the engine change with Roger and Rex. We had hoped to get through the two-phase rookie test the first day the track was open, and pressure was mounting. Rolla was the one whom I really felt for. I had come to admire and respect him: he was smart, he kept all the bases covered, he was thoughtful and thorough. Besides that, he was funny, considerate, and he loved the sport. He was taking a lot of heat in the press; more than one article pointed out that the blue car hadn't made the field the previous year. I hated to see that happening to the only man who had the imagination and the fortitude to give a woman a chance to drive his car.

Next morning, Tuesday, I looked at the heap of laundry in the closet, the dirty work clothes on top, and thought: I can wash those tonight ... if I'm still alive.

We were back on the track again just after two. I set off to shake down Goodyear's replacement engine. Every flicker of a needle on one of the gauges caused a little extra squirt of adrenaline to flash through my veins. If we lost this engine, the outlook would be bleak indeed. After seven attentive, careful laps, all seemed well. Rolla notified the official timers that we would attempt the first phase of the rookie test: twenty laps, a hundred miles, at a speed no less than 159 mph and no greater than 164, using only the inner half of the track. Judging my speed from the rpms at the exit of each turn, I clicked off a first lap of 164.414. Too fast; but it beat the hell out of being too slow. The subsequent laps were right on target.

At our pit, I fended off congratulations. "When you're trying *not* to go as fast as you can, you lose your concentration—and you're not going all that slow that you can afford to lose it," I said.

With any luck, we could get through the second, high-speed phase of the rookie test as soon as the blue car was refueled. Four veteran drivers were required to observe the second phase, one on each turn; but Eddie Miller's second-phase test was under way, so observers were already in place. Then the loudspeakers boomed, "Yellow light."

Miller, a Super Vee road racing star, had crashed. He lost control in Turn 1 and slid 325 feet into the infield, where the edge of a ditch launched his car 200 feet through the air. Tumbling end over end, it came to rest upside down and burst briefly into flame. It took nearly twenty minutes to cut him out of the car. He broke his neck, but was neither paralyzed nor dead.

Reporters drifted back to our pit. "Did you see the accident?" one asked me.

"No."

"Have you ever seen anyone killed?" His eyes probed obscenely.

"Yes."

"Where—who was it—what did you feel?"

"You accept the risks in this game. It's like anything you do in life; you evaluate the risk and decide whether or not it's worth what you're getting out of it."

But what *did* I feel about Miller? I was sorry that he had crashed, not so much for his injury as for the end of his effort. He was out of the game. It was as if some part of myself had crashed.

By the time the track reopened, it was "happy hour," the last hour of practice, when most drivers tried for their fastest speeds. My second phase would have to wait.

Next morning's papers, May 12, carried USAC rookie test supervisor Shim Malone's compliments on the first phase. "It was one of the better rookie performances I've seen," he said. "And it was even more impressive when you realize she only had six hot laps prior to the test."

Out in California, though, the widely syndicated columnist Jim Murray had a different perspective. "At long last, Indianapolis is acting on a suggestion made long ago in this space that they add a woman driver to the field to more nearly approximate the perils we other motorists brave over the Memorial Day weekend ... I would expand the field still further to include: a) a drunk driver..."[1]

Wednesday's practice was lost to ignition problems. So was most of Thursday, when rain brought practice to an early end. Rain continued on Friday morning, giving reporters plenty of time to pounce. Was George Snider going to file a protest? Had USAC reprimanded me?

What in the world were they talking about?

Slowly, it became clear. During our brief track time on Thursday, Snider had overtaken me as we approached Turn 2. I made what would have been the courteous move on a road-racing circuit: to the outside, onto the pale gray slippery area, to give him the best line through the apex of the turn. Snider, not understanding my intention, clamped on the brakes, and we both exited onto the back straight. This non-incident was now in headlines across the country— "Guthrie's Practice Nearly a Disaster," for example, over a story that claimed we had both been "left with pounding hearts." A quote from Snider described the moment closely enough, but the embroidery was amazing.

On the whole, though, I couldn't complain about the press. You won some, you lost some; and the race at Trenton had quieted a lot of the scepticism. Most reporters had been considerate and fair.

Ironically enough, there had in fact been a serious transgression by a rookie on that rain-shortened Thursday. Spike Gelhausen was banished from the track for an hour after a series of offenses. His official rebuke from USAC reaped no more than a mention in the trivia column, "Pit Pass," of the Indianapolis *Star*.[2] Imbalances in the press were like mosquito bites compared with what those in power might have done. Thursday's events reflected USAC's scrupulous objectivity.

[1] Los Angeles *Times*, May 12, 1976
[2] May 14, 1976

The rain finally stopped on Friday afternoon, and out I went. After just one lap at speed, I was back. "There's a rattle," I said. "It sounds like it's coming from the right front. The oil pressure is down to one-ten, and it could be the chains or gears rattling around in the engine. But I think it's a right front wheel bearing."

Given Friday morning's stress, Vollstedt might have been justified in thinking that the problem was nerves, and I knew it. The moment was tense. A look at the wheel bearings would cost us a lot of time, time we didn't have. If I didn't pass the rookie test today, I wouldn't be allowed back on the track until Monday. Rex, normally so mute, was the first to speak. "Take it back to the garage," he said. It was an order, and it couldn't have been easy for him, with the boss standing right there.

They hauled it away. Half an hour later, it was apart. The outer wheel bearing was okay. The inner one was crumbling. Rolla whistled softly. "I gotta hand it to you, Guthrie," he said. "You've got a damn good feeling for the machinery." Later, he told reporters that most rookies would have driven it until the wheel fell off.

That evening, Rolla introduced George Snider, who immediately told me he had never claimed that I cut him off. He shared a bit of insight, too. "If I see somebody fast coming, I stay right against the wall on the straight but lift a little, so they pass me there." It was excellent advice.

Saturday May 15, was pole day—the first day of qualifying. Since I hadn't yet passed the second phase of the rookie test, I couldn't go out in practice, much less make a qualifying attempt. The complexities of the rules nevertheless made it important for the blue car to remain in the qualifying line. When we reached the head of the line, we would "push through," go to the back of the line and start over. Rolla was with Dick Simon at the head of the line; Dick's new silver car, too, would be pushed through.

About 175,000 people were on hand—not a large crowd for the Speedway, but impressive nevertheless. Pole day was an institution second in importance only to the race itself. As I came up to the blue car, Rex Hutton was looking even more tense than usual. "You might want to stand somewhere else," he said. "There's a bunch of assholes in the stands above us here." Indeed, the hooting and hollering seemed unusually persistent. "They've got a sign," Rex continued. "Don't look."

I did look, of course, but I've forgotten what the sign said. It was directed at me, and it was obscene. Eventually they started chanting in unison. I couldn't make out the words, except for my name in it.

Stubbornly, I stayed with the car. For one thing, I wasn't going to flee a bunch of jerks; and for another, if this was what it would be like next weekend when I had to face that qualifying attempt, I'd better get used to it; and for a third, if the guys were subjected to this on my account, I was damn well going to be there in the line of fire with them.

It made for a long day. A mob mentality seemed to be at work. Not all the hectoring was exuberant cretins' idea of fun. Some of it was serious, and seriously ugly, like a few of the letters I had gotten. Part of a three-page opus read, "You are clearly either a neuter or a lesbian ... a phony, ugly, non-talented inarticulate, man-hating, money-grubbing, hypocritical bitch."

Was there an unstable creature in the stands here, someone with a gun, ready to be swept over the edge by the next wave of shouts? At exactly that moment, having pushed through and gone to the back of the line, we were again approaching the area we called "the zoo." Bob Sowle, one of Rolla's volunteers, eyed it and said, "We're all a little gun-shy." His metaphor for disliking the crowd was ordinary enough, but an eerie echo of my thoughts.

Did all of us feel it, then? I turned to Roger, a strong young man who mostly drove logging trucks in Oregon and whose life included bar fights that he called "having a good time." Lightly, almost as a joke, I expressed what was in my mind. The muscles at the back of his jaw tightened. His customary good cheer was utterly absent from the look he flicked at me. He didn't say anything; he didn't need to.

Late on Monday afternoon, we hitched the blue car to the little tractor and hauled it backwards up pit road to the far north end, the rookie-test spot near the entrance to the pits. Dozens of reporters and photographers trailed along; I felt like the Pied Piper. Dick Simon, who had put Rolla's new silver car securely in the field with a banzai qualifying run on Sunday, had tested the blue car earlier in the day. "It's not right," he said. "If you take your foot off it, the front end will wash right out toward the wall. You're a driver, you can handle it. Just make sure you don't lift in the turns."

A car that mysteriously headed for the outside wall if you backed off the throttle could be unhealthy, but time was running out. I stepped into the seat, awash in the soft clicks and whirs of a myriad of motor-driven Nikons. The ghoulishness of that had diminished since last week, as more and more of them realized they weren't so likely as they'd thought to get the last photo before my spectacular demise.

I made two laps in succession at second-phase speed, over 165 mph, feeling it out. The handling wasn't great, but it would have to do. When I brought the blue car to a stop in the pits again, Rolla was there. Our eyes met. I nodded.

He turned to Rex. "Tell USAC to round up their observers."

The crew hauled the car back to the garage area for a full load of fuel. I sat on the pit wall doing laps in my mind, under a sullen grey sky. Fog, rain and high winds had kept the track closed until mid-afternoon. It was cold, too, in the forties. That strong wind promised to make the execution of twenty perfect laps especially entertaining. Gusts that came between the grandstands could move the car around quite a bit.

Refueled, the blue car returned. I wriggled down into the deep shelter of its seat, a buffer against the crowd. Word came up the line: the observers, the four veteran Indianapolis 500 drivers who would sit in judgment, were on their way out to their stations above each turn. USAC wouldn't tell Rolla who they were.

Shim Malone, the USAC official in charge of rookie tests, knelt beside the car. "Twenty laps at any speed at which you're comfortable over a hundred and sixty-five miles an hour..."

On the warm-up laps I tried unsuccessfully to identify my four observers in their wire-mesh cages out above the outer wall. They might be friend, foe, or neutral. Eight or ten cars were out on the track—moderate traffic, not too bad. The next fifty miles were going to be smooth, consistent, smooth, fast, and smooth. If the blue car held together for the full twenty laps, that would be a pleasant novelty. When the gauges showed operating temperature, I stood on the gas, and Rolla waved the green flag. Let the trial begin.

Very tense. No fun. *Smooth, keep it smooth.*

I hit a high of 171.429 mph. It was the fastest lap I had done here, which wasn't saying much. The slowest car in the field so far was Jim McElreath's at 179.122. I eased the blue car to a stop within a forest of microphones and lenses. Rolla and the guys were grinning from ear to ear. Roger couldn't even wait until I was all the way out of the car to hug me. At last, the rookie test was done.

But celebration was premature: the veterans' critique was yet to come. It was their prerogative to say whether I had passed or failed—whether I looked smooth, how I handled traffic. Who had they been? Did they see clearly, or had they watched through a distorting lens of preconceptions?

Shim Malone and I waited for them in a cramped back room behind USAC's offices under the pitside grandstands. "Now that it's over," I said, "will you tell me who they were, so that it won't be a shock when they come in?"

"Bettenhausen."

"Ohmigod." Gary Bettenhausen had been among the more vocal objectors to my presence at Trenton.

"No, he said he'd give us a fair shake. And Tom Bigelow, Al Loquasto, and Graham McRae."

Bigelow I could count on to be fair. Rolla Vollstedt's former driver had remained his friend. Tom had been amiable and open with me, without the woman thing getting in the way. The other two were unknown quantities.

They entered the room. I looked appropriately grave. Malone said, "Gary, do you want to start?"

"Well, no, I was on Turn Two. Al was on One."

"Okay, Al, you begin, then."

I looked at him.

"Well, Janet, I'm afraid you looked sorta shabby in One. Your line wasn't too good and you looked pretty ragged."

My eyes must have gotten huge. How could he say that? The one thing I hadn't been was ragged. I just stared at him, and swallowed. He returned the look steadily, and continued in the same vein. Then it was Gary's turn. He said that I entered too wide and my line varied a lot. Well, from him I rather expected it. Bigelow, who was on Turn 3, said I wasn't using up all the track.

They all looked stern and dubious.

I fell for it hook, line and sinker.

Before McRae even had his chance, they burst into uproarious laughter. Their spoof had been a royal success. I was brimming with fight-or-flight biochemicals, just about to spill into fight mode, and as the stiffness melted out of my joints, it was a good thing there was a chair to hold me up.

Gary was the first to stop laughing and speak. "I think you did a fantastic job. Your line didn't vary more than six inches the whole twenty laps." One of the others said it was the best rookie test he'd ever seen. One by one, they shook my hand.

We came out of the USAC offices to face a swarm of reporters—and Tony Hulman, the owner of Indianapolis Motor Speedway. Tony had a sense of occasion, and he shook my hand at considerable length while the cameras flashed. "I admit I never thought I'd see a woman driving at Indy," he said. "But it's okay, if she's able to drive out there, she should."

We moved off toward Vollstedt's garages. It was time for the ceremonial removal of the rookie stripes, the three strips of yellow tape on the rear wing of the car that alerted overtaking drivers to the presence of a newcomer. It was a huge relief to see them go. But we were still some nine or ten miles an hour shy of the speed it would take to put the car firmly in the field for the race.

"What now?" a reporter asked.

"Now the serious work begins," I said.

Two days later, the blue car was still giving us fits. Mario Andretti paused while we were setting tire pressures at Goodyear, on our way out to the track. He looked at the car and at me and at the hordes around us; asked how things were going. "I really feel sorry for you," he said. Subsequently he told UPI, "She has two strikes against her, but with a competitive car she can do it. She has a lot of class."[3]

Roger had given me a necklace that I didn't wear but sometimes put into the pocket of my driver's suit where I could run my fingers over the letters of its pendant. "Oh shit," it read. We found it humorous, which might tell you how bad things were. Touching it helped me keep up a dispassionate appearance, and make hopeful statements to the reporters who still trailed our every move.

By Thursday evening, May 20, the facts of the situation were inescapable. Our chances of putting the blue car in the field were next to nil. I was sitting beside Rolla on the workbench in the garage while yet another failed engine was hauled out, both of us as bleak as could be, and he made some feeble joke, and I put an arm around his shoulder.

"That's a switch, Guthrie," he said, his nose suddenly seeming stuffy. "It's not usually the driver trying to console the car owner."

Rolla's next move was truly extraordinary. Sometime that evening or Friday, I don't know when, he went to see Leo Mehl, Goodyear's main man at Indianapolis. Mehl was entirely responsible for Goodyear's enormously complex and extensive racing program. One of the really good guys of the sport, he wielded his formidable power with grace, wit and style. Rolla asked Mehl to serve as intermediary in approaching good teams with a spare car—a car for me to qualify for the Indianapolis 500, a car that wouldn't be Vollstedt's.

[3] San Francisco *Examiner*, May 22, 1976

It was an astonishingly generous step for Rolla to take, a move perhaps without precedent for a car owner. The customary procedure would have been, as the saying went, "when you've changed everything else and it doesn't work, you change the nut behind the wheel." Nor would I have jumped ship myself, even though Johnny Rutherford had told me quietly, "It doesn't hurt to walk around"—the Speedway words for seeking another ride. Owners often acquired a driver for their backup machines after their first one had qualified.

But Rolla Vollstedt had brought me to the Speedway; had been accused of exploitation as our troubles mounted, had remained steadfast and kind under the most appalling pressure. None of us expected the uproar, the strong emotions our effort would arouse, and we weathered it with a sense of unity that sprang from Rolla himself. Had he been a different sort of man, these last two weeks could have been one long nightmare. Instead, it was an incredible adventure, with high points and low—but an adventure that now seemed on the verge of heartbreaking collapse.

That fact had not escaped attention elsewhere in the country. Rolla told me there was interest down in Charlotte, North Carolina, the heart of NASCAR land, where the World 600 Winston Cup stock car race was to be held the same day as the Indianapolis 500. If I didn't make the field at the Speedway, there was a possibility down south. I didn't want to hear about it—not yet.

By Friday night, Leo Mehl's search had born fruit and Rolla had his answer. A. J. Foyt would consider putting me in his second car.

A. J. Foyt. The sense of unreality that permeated May was now complete, bursting into my never-never land like the top of a thunderstorm blows its anvil head into the stratosphere. The one, the only, the legendary ... I could hardly believe it when he even spoke to me, or smiled at me across a room. Drive his *car*? The car that carried the number 1, the mark of his national championship the year before?

Rolla had summoned me into his back garage to tell me his news—the garage with the minuscule dressing room the guys had built for me, and the sign they had put up to claim me as their own. His voice was none too steady, and my throat had a lump in it the size of a baseball.

"Let's give the blue car one more day," I said.

So we agreed, and so Saturday went. We had the usual spate of problems, mostly with the turbocharger. Back and forth we went between garage and pit, while the intermittent melodrama of qualifying and bumping played itself out on the track. Drivers and cars were shuffled like a deck of cards, in a desperate search for speed. In between qualifying attempts, we ran the blue car. Whatever speed it had to offer, I was going to get. I owed it to Rolla. I was talking to myself by now, in the car where no one could hear; and on this mild spring day, my driver's suit was almost as wet with sweat as if I were doing laps in a pool instead of on a race track. But at day's end, we weren't even close. USAC's clocks had me at 173.611. Rolla smiled faintly at that, when we were alone in the garage. He had wanted me to exceed the women's record with his car, and even though a speed posted in practice was unofficial, it pleased him to have done so.

"You gave it something extra, didn't you?" he said, and I nodded; though in fact I cared nothing about women's records. My competition was all the other drivers seeking a spot in the field. And try though we had, our game was now at an end.

When the six o'clock gun went off, Rolla took me to A. J. Foyt's garage.

It was Cinderella time.

A. J.'s crew was waiting, and as I slipped into the seat of the orange-red Coyote they were ready to do all that was needed. Foyt was two inches taller than I, but my longer legs posed the usual problem. They moved the pedals and heel stop deeper into the nose, then re-padded the seat for my narrower girth. They cut a deep slice off the plexiglas windscreen, bringing it to my eye level. I sat there as long as I could, feeling it out, engaging the gears, flicking my eyes from one gauge or another up to an imaginary track and back to the gauges again.

When you're a kid you sometimes have dreams in which your childish wishes are granted beyond imagining: the fabulous candy store, where all the luscious foil-wrapped treasures were yours to choose ... or how you stood before scores of the most beautiful dolls, each more exquisite than the next, and you might have any you pleased. Those dreams are always of the moment before choosing, when all possibilities are open, filling your world with wonder and a sense of peace. On the eve of driving A. J. Foyt's car, I lived that dream.

Not that I didn't feel the weight of responsibility. Foyt's Coyote/Ford was worth, in dollars, more money than I'd ever seen, hundreds of times more than every thing of value I owned in the world. The cost of it would fully cover a six-bedroom house in the best part of town, with a country-club membership thrown in. And I was to take that ... house ... and drive it around Indianapolis Motor

Speedway at three-digit speeds, as fast as I could make it go—fast enough to do the thing justice, and without doing it an iota of harm.

I went to bed that night with a full heart, and slept like a child.

In the morning I was at the garages well before the track opened. With the moment at hand, I felt like a traitor, and fought back tears as I walked along the outside row of garages toward Vollstedt's, near the end. No one was there. The blue car sat lifeless, like the intricate husk of a beetle from which the living insect had burst and gone away. The sight of the guys' sign on my cubicle made my throat ache. It was hard not to think of how much we'd been through together, what we'd survived, what we had accomplished. Now I was leaving them behind, the guys who had supported me through so many trying days and sleepless nights. It felt awful.

I tried to think of other things as I shed my silk shirt and jeans and slid into the soft Nomex long johns. So many poignant moments, so many small kindnesses, so many people saying, "God bless you, God be with you." I thought of Johnny Rutherford, who had recently gone far out of his way to follow me through a couple of turns; then came to Vollstedt to suggest changes in our suspension setup. Sure enough, it helped.

At the other end of the spectrum from J. R. was Bobby Unser. Not that he lacked a sense of humor. When Bobby's car was hauled out to the track for the first time that month, a poster was taped to its nose. A head shot of a truly ugly hog, most swinish, bore the caption "Male Chauvinist Pigs Need Love Too." The poster remained taped in his garage-door windows all month.

I thought of Mario Andretti and Jim Hurtubise, he of the burned hands. I had read once how the worst thing for Herk, after his terrible fire, was that so many people couldn't bring themselves to shake hands with him any more; and that he had wept over that. Hard, rough, curved, and scaly, Herk's hands were like claws. To grasp them was an intimate reminder of the nature of our game. I had watched Mario cross pit road to shake hands with Herk, unflinchingly and without hesitation.

It was time for the brief practice session to start. I walked out to the pits, on the last day of qualifying for Indianapolis, 1976. A dense, deep tangle of people and TV equipment surrounded Foyt and his machine. At the center was Foyt's crew, in their red and white checkered shirts, standing off the crowd. As I stepped into the seat there was a surprise: the whole dashboard—every instrument in the car—was covered over with silver tape.

"We didn't want you to get confused," Foyt said cheerfully. He couldn't possibly have expected me to believe that; I knew his secrets were his own. Not having the gauges made me uneasy. I was accustomed to monitoring an engine's health. But this was Foyt's game, and he made the rules.

"Use third gear," he said. That was another surprise. Had he dropped the boost? Or did he simply expect that I would be slow? Whatever, I could only do as I was told.

Foyt and his crew were perceptibly on edge. "I've never destroyed a car yet," I reassured them, "and I don't propose to begin with this one."

Foyt's guys had been quite open about their feelings. "We don't want him to run the backup car here," they'd told me the night before. "We came to see A. J. win his fourth Indy and we don't want to do anything that would undercut the effort." Nevertheless, what the boss said, went.

They tucked me in. The track went green.

On the warmup laps I felt it out, shook it. What was the nature of this beast? What was the response to steering input, to on-throttle and off-throttle? What did it communicate that was different from Vollstedt's machine?

Nearly everything, that was what. My third lap at speed was faster than I had ever gone in the blue car. I was balanced on a knife edge between the urgent requirement for speeds approaching what the car could do, and the absolute necessity not to spin or crash. Pressure? If I'd been made of carbon black, I'd have turned into a diamond on the spot.

I went faster every lap. Foyt's Coyote felt like a blindingly fast caterpillar, a creature with hundreds of sticky, suction-cup feet that could somehow move with supernatural speed. If a giant hand were to turn the track upside down and the car with it, like a caterpillar on a branch, we wouldn't fall.

Yellow light!

Jim Hurtubise, out in his old front-engine roadster, had lost it in Turn 2. I was on the back straight, and pitted without seeing Herk's car at all. But in Foyt's pit, someone yelled, "It's Herk!" and Foyt turned pale. What he thought he heard was, "It's her!"

"Did she spin, Frankie?" he yelled at Del Roy. "Did she hit anything?"

"No ... no, she's fine, it was Hurtubise."

Maybe the moment of fear that I had crashed, that I had harmed his car, lingered in Foyt's mind. "It scared the hell out of me," he said later. "My heart quit beating."

The yellow was long. Foyt's pit became unbearable; the reporters were totally agog. Foyt, Vollstedt and I stepped across pit road to the grassy margin by the track wall, where the press couldn't follow. I was glad to get my breath, and sort out my impressions.

It had been like getting out of a Model T and into a Ferrari, though I wouldn't say that out loud for fear of hurting Rolla's feelings. In the short chutes, between Turns 1 and 2 or Turns 3 and 4, stepping on the gas was like squirting a watermelon seed out from between your fingers: quicker than you could even comprehend.

What a car.

Time was pressing hard on us when I climbed back in. Soon the track would close and qualifying would begin. On the green I shot out of the pits; babied it for a lap, then hit 179.037 and 180.796. The third lap was down a hair, as I tried to get organized in my mind. There was a lot of difference between 173 and close to 181, especially in just nine laps. Then the yellow light went on. Practice was at an end.

Excitement in the crowd was at fever pitch. Would Foyt let me qualify the car?

The first thing A. J. did was pull up the edge of the tape covering the tachometer, holding it so I couldn't see. Almost imperceptibly, he twitched.

"Next time," he said sharply, "use fourth gear."

I couldn't have felt more pleasure if I had just been knighted by King Arthur. It meant that the telltale needle showed him high rpms: that I had driven his car a lot faster than he expected me to.

They took the car away for fuel. Foyt's face was full of thought. "That was fast enough to get into the field as it stands," he said, "but maybe not by the end of the day." Foyt himself was on the second row at 185.261. "If we put the car in line right now, can you qualify faster than what you just ran?"

Could I?

Only once in my life had I been in a one-shot qualifying situation. That was at Trenton, three weeks before.

By the end of that year, I was to establish myself as a good qualifier, one who could always squeeze a couple of extra miles an hour out of the metaphysical space-time of a qualifying run. But when Foyt asked the question, I didn't know that yet; had to look inside for an answer. It took maybe three heartbeats.

"Yes," I said.

I didn't say, "I think so." I knew I could.

We parted then, escaping the pandemonium. Foyt told his guys to refuel the car and put it into the qualifying line, and vanished into his garage. Rolla and I went with Leo Mehl, who had set all this in motion, to Goodyear's tiny unmarked "office" just inside the garage gates. Leo sank into a chair behind the decrepit desk, Rolla and I found space on a cracked vinyl couch. I think it was 1977 when Leo gave me a key to this little-used space, where a creaky passage led to an antique toilet and washbasin. The key was my most precious possession at the track. It meant I no longer had to use the women's room in the spectator area.

Leo said, "I had a phone call from my boss. He wanted to know what the hell was going on down here. He told me he didn't care what I did as long as it had nothing to do with you and Foyt. He told me to go see an X-rated movie."

Ordered by Goodyear management to butt out, Leo had been explicitly referred to a view of the role of women at the crassest level.

Rolla and I retreated to the Vollstedt garages to wait it out. The first man into the field when qualifying started at noon was our friend Tom Bigelow, posting a secure 181.965.

Time passed. There was no word from Foyt. Rumors were flying: that Goodyear was putting up money for the ride, and that they had indemnified Foyt for $50,000 should I wreck his car before it could be purchased. Foyt hotly denied this, later in the day.

Rolla went to see him. I stayed where I was, guarding like a wolf the mindset that I had used to drive Foyt's car and would need in spades for a qualifying attempt. In a few minutes, Rolla was back. Things didn't look promising, he said.

Meanwhile, the fate of the blue car remained to be decided. One option, that I begin a qualifying attempt with it in order to put an official stamp on the speeds, had little appeal to any of us, although Rolla might have been wistful to have that women's record locked up.

Presently, he stepped outside, where half the garage alleyway was filled with waiting reporters. Some noted that his eyeglasses didn't conceal tears at the corners of his eyes.

"The No. 27 Bryant Heating and Cooling Special is officially withdrawn from competition," he said. We're parking it. We've run out of time to bring it up to qualifying speed.

"But I don't look upon this as a failure, not as though it's the end of the world. I think you should all keep in mind that we've accomplished a helluva lot here this month. First of all, I had the pleasure of working with an intelligent race car driver who happens to be a woman. And don't lose sight of the fact that I have another car in this race."

The minutes ticked interminably on. News trickled in: Mike Hiss, Arlene's estranged husband, made his first attempt and was waved off; a second attempt, and spun. Lloyd Ruby took the Eagle that Arlene drove at Phoenix and qualified it at 186.460 for his seventeenth Indianapolis 500, seventh-fastest in the field.

There was still no word from Foyt.

At ten past two, Bryant's Bill Hall burst through the door.

"It's over," he said. "Foyt just came out of his garage and told the reporters he wasn't going to let you run it."

Grimly, Rolla left. He was back in ten minutes.

"A.J. says the guys on his crew don't want him to run a second car, and that Jim Gilmore [part owner of Foyt's team] doesn't favor it either. They want him to focus on winning his fourth Indianapolis 500. He says it's the car he plans to run at Pocono, and he doesn't have time to rebuild it.

"But the last thing he said," Rolla went on, "as I was going out the door, he called across the garage and said, 'I just might change my mind and come get her before the end of the day.'"

I hope that never in my life do I spend another four hours such as those were, hoping against hope, not for an instant letting go of the mindset that would enable me to put Foyt's car in the field. Each time the garage door cracked open, my heart leaped in anticipation of the sight of a red and white checked shirt. Each time, it was not that messenger.

Toward the end of the day Jackie Stewart came by, with kind and complimentary words of understanding that perhaps only a champion could bring. I don't remember what he said. I was still holding that focus. There was still time.

At five-thirty, it was no longer reasonable to hope. Yet there was still a chance; even at quarter to six. After that, nothing remained but the six-o'clock gun. Deep in Vollstedt's garage, the sound was muffled, but I can feel it still: it went straight through my heart.

There were no tears then, though you could see tears at Indianapolis at six o'clock of a fine May evening every year. Big macho guys who never heard of sensitivity training were walking back through Gasoline Alley with tears streaming down their cheeks. They were the drivers who hadn't made the field.

Someone from the Speedway press office sought my attendance there, for a formal windup to the month. The room was full, the session long. When it was done, the reporters did something strange: they stood, and applauded.

It was nearly dusk when I walked back to Rolla's garage to clean out my stuff. The task was so poignant I felt weak from it. In my tiny dressing room were the fan mail and telegrams, the leftover bits and pieces and my racing gear: helmet and head sock, Nomex long johns and driver's suit, all saturated with strength and apprehension, doubts and power. I packed them up, emptying the space where I'd— how many times?—made the metaphysical transition from "woman" to "race driver," shielded behind the guys' bold inscription: Indy Lady is OUR Indy Lady. A huge bouquet of flowers stood on the workbench. I left them there, but not the card. It read, "Respectfully—the entire Gilmore-Foyt racing team."

The grandstands were empty, the chain-link gate out to pit road closed and locked. Most of the crews were dispersed and gone. Not a wheel would roll here until Thursday, Carburetion Day. The ebb of day drew me out toward the track, as surely as a receding tide. I climbed the gate, dropped onto the other side, and walked out to the trackside wall.

I looked down toward Turn 1, where the work of a lap begins, and up toward Turn 4, where it ends, where nothing is left but a straight hot run for the finish. All the passions of the month were there, quivering through the dusk. Behind me rose a sound I'll never forget.

The grounds-keepers were cleaning the pitside grandstands. From one step down to another they pushed the trash, a broad, inexorable avalanche of noisy debris. Slowly it cascaded down, the cans and beer cups and crumpled programs, with a sound of waste and conclusion. It was suitable music for the end of my dreams.

NASCAR WINSTON CUP, CHARLOTTE, MAY 1976

Tuesday morning, a day and a half after the devastating end of my great adventure at Indianapolis, I found myself standing in a different world. The garage area of Charlotte Motor Speedway (now called Lowe's) was at the heart of big-time Winston Cup racing, NASCARland.

Stock-bodied race cars nestled flank to flank under a long open shed, sheltered from the North Carolina sun like sleek fat Easter-egg colored cattle. Noses to the bench that ran down the center, as if feeding at a trough, they jostled and bellowed with the unmuffled force of five hundred-plus potential horsepower. The massed engines were loud enough at idle, but when a mechanic ran the revs up into the power range, the noise transcended into pain. It reverberated through the soles of your feet and resonated in your lungs and brain. Anyone not busy kept his hands clapped over his ears. Conversation was impossible.

If the garage-area sheds looked like bright cartoons of a surrealistic farm, the crews completed the picture. They polished their machines as a farmer might groom prize livestock for a county fair. Some wore crew uniforms bearing richly embroidered sponsor patches, some sported bib overalls. No other woman was anywhere in sight. In appearance and language, the Deep South was a world apart.

Practice was under way. Out on the distant high-banked turns, full-size Chevrolets and Fords looked like flies on a wall. But my car, a Chevrolet Laguna, was in the final throes of engine installation back at Ralph Moody's shop, and my impatience and frustration were growing harder to contain.

I had known for days that the offer of a ride in the Winston Cup race at Charlotte was floating around Indianapolis, but I didn't want to hear about it. I just wasn't going to contemplate the possibility of failure, or expend emotional energy considering an alternative race. Not until Indianapolis, my Indianapolis, was over with. Rolla Vollstedt, however, had kept his finger on the details of the Charlotte deal all along. With his help, it came to pass.

The Charlotte World 600, held the same day as the Indianapolis 500, was the longest-distance race on the NASCAR calendar: 600 miles, 400 laps of a 1.5-mile high-bank race track. Completed in 1960, Charlotte was one of the superspeedways that ushered stock car racing off the dusty half-mile dirt tracks and into modern times. NASCAR racing in 1976 was twenty-seven years old, rich, mature, and more sophisticated than it looked. Stars like Buddy Baker, David Pearson, Cale Yarborough and Richard Petty were in their prime. Many of the races were shown on network TV, and the Winston Cup series already drew more spectators than any other racing series in the world.[1,2]

It was a long time before I learned how the Charlotte plan had coalesced. The new General Manager—that is to say, promoter—of Charlotte Motor Speedway was Humpy Wheeler, a puckish blond man with a highly developed sense of fun and mischief. His Charlotte race was one of the main events on the Winston Cup circuit, but the Charlotte newspapers were devoting their headlines to my adventures at Indianapolis. When my chances of making the field for Indy dwindled, he pounced on the idea of transferring all that attention to his own fiefdom, by bringing me into it.

The key to his plan was Lynda Ferreri, a high-powered banker who was Vice-President of the Charlotte Chamber of Commerce. Humpy's inspiration dovetailed with Lynda's civic intent to help upgrade his race's image. "It would be good for the city," she said, "good for the economy." Later she confided another motivation: "So many people were saying you were a hoax, that it was impossible for a woman to compete in Winston Cup. And I thought to myself, *wouldn't it be fun to be part of disproving that?*"

Within twenty-four hours of her conversation with Humpy, Lynda Ferreri became the new owner of a Winston Cup race car. She had a lot to learn, but she was gutsy, pragmatic, creative and an extremely quick study. The Chevrolet Laguna that Lynda bought was alleged to be the very car that A. J. Foyt had put on the pole for the Daytona 500 that year, only to have NASCAR disqualify it when they found an illegal nitrous-oxide injection system. Unlike horses, though, race

---

[1] As of 2004, "Winston Cup" has become "Nextel Cup." In 1976, almost everyone called the series "Grand National," which had been its name for years. In the early 1980s, NASCAR put a stop to the use of the historic name by assigning it to the next level down, formerly called Sportsman.

[2] Goodyear survey for 1976, quoted in e.g. *Road and Track*, March 1978

cars are not tattooed, and reporters said the provenance was dubious. We never knew for sure.

Humpy lined up the legendary Ralph Moody to supply the engine and run the effort. A former driver, Moody had been half of the fabulously successful Holman-Moody team that operated Ford's racing program in the 1960s. Moody had a smallish race car shop in the Charlotte area, and wasn't otherwise engaged.

Rolla Vollstedt persuaded his old friend Tom Nehl, one of the South's largest GMC truck dealers and a racing driver himself, to come up from Jacksonville to supervise affairs at Charlotte as a kind of Rolla surrogate. Rolla would send his crewmen Roger Thrall and Gary Gale with me as well. And perhaps the most critical ingredient of all: Rolla spoke with NASCAR star Cale Yarborough, who had driven Rolla's car at Indianapolis in 1967, and Cale had agreed to take my car out in practice. Unless Cale approved the machine, I wasn't to touch it. Is it any wonder that I'll always be grateful to Rolla Vollstedt? I have a very great deal to thank him for. He made only one condition: come what might, they must return me to Indianapolis in time for his sponsor's banquet on Sunday night after the race.

So everything was set: owner, chassis, engine, and crew. All they needed was a certain lady driver, who up until 6 p.m. on Sunday was doing her very best not to be there.

On Monday, all the details for my ride at Charlotte fell into place. And I felt something like a mountain climber who, nearing a longed-for summit, has tumbled instead into the shattering abyss; only to find myself, as if in a dream, magically reassembled on the path to a different peak.

Early Tuesday morning, the restaurant of my Charlotte hotel already held a small crowd of reporters. "David Pearson says he hasn't thought nothing about your chances in the race because he don't really think you'll make the field," one began.

It looked as if Charlotte would be like Trenton all over again. But I was in a stronger position now. There was a ton of difference between thinking you could do what everyone called impossible, and having actually done it in front of the skeptical world.

"Just wait and see," I smiled. "If people can just remain objective until they see what I can do, that's all I ask." The articles that ensued over the next few days seemed to match what I felt in the garage area: a bell-shaped curve from hostile to skeptical, heavy on the skeptical, with a little open-mindedness at one end.

We were out at the track early, and Cale Yarborough drove me around it in a street car, pointing out its features. He was cool, formal, and kept his distance; he seemed to be making it clear that the help he offered was for Rolla, not for me. When I shook hands with Richard Petty, I thought I'd get frostbite. Later, he would be quoted as saying of me: "She's no lady. If she was she'd be at home. There's a lot of difference in being a lady and being a woman."[3]

Actually, a handful of women had raced in NASCAR's early days. Sara Christian and Louise Smith, among others, competed on NASCAR's flat dirt tracks; but only one woman had driven in one NASCAR race since 1955.

No woman had ever competed in a NASCAR race on a high-banked superspeedway, or at a distance longer than two hundred miles. The preponderance of opinion, endlessly repeated, was that no woman could.

By mid-afternoon on Tuesday, while Charlotte resounded with the roar of stock cars at speed, mine was still nowhere to be seen. Track time, seat time, was desperately important to me. Tom Nehl, Rolla's surrogate, applied the necessary pressure to obtain the use of a journeyman driver's car in which I might learn the track. Suited up and ready, I climbed in.

Strange, strange. You got in through the window, the sheet metal of the door being permanently welded shut over the bulky roll cage. So much room! Like a living room, compared with an Indy car. I liked what lay under the skin of the door on the driver's side: braces of heavy steel tubing, sturdily protective. The big upright seat seemed loose as a sofa after the narrow confines of the Indy car, but a similar "granny" curled around my rib cage from its right-hand side. I sat there feeling it out, imprinting its gauges and controls. Soon I was out on the track.

The pavement at Indianapolis had been smooth as a bowling alley. Charlotte Motor Speedway was bumpy all over, and the car felt disconcertingly sloppy. I warmed it up at the bottom of the steep banking, then gradually brought it up to speed, gauging its responses to a turn of the wheel, to the throttle, to the bumps.

The noise! That big V-8, unmuffled, was deafening. The engine was ahead of you, not behind, and the huge exhaust pipes exited at the doors. Your best grip on traffic behind you came not from the

[3] *Autoweek*, June 5, 1976

mirror—there was just one little passenger-car mirror, at the top of the windshield—but from the noise the traffic made.

I brought it in after three laps to think about it, getting organized in my mind. Many drivers here had asserted that I wouldn't be strong enough to handle one of these 3,700-pound beasts—they had no power steering—but it was clear to me that the issue wasn't going to be strength. While an Indy car responded instantly and with great precision to the slightest pressure on the wheel, the stocker exhibited all the flaws of the passenger-car steering and suspension design it was born with. On this rough track, you had to chase it all the time, and it seemed to take a couple of yards of steering wheel for corrections.

Out again, and faster. Another pause to mull it over. One more time. After a total of twelve laps, I was at 143.927 mph, and pushing hard on the limits of my experience. An Indy car went down the track all in one piece. Here, I felt like a sheep dog chasing sheep—running around nipping at the heels of a bunch of loosely connected parts, trying to keep them all headed in the right direction. Then the yellow came out, and practice ended for the day.

As I walked out the garage-area gate, autograph seekers besieged the driver in front of me. A youngish woman pressed her way to the front, preceded by an endowment along the lines of Dolly Parton's. She was clad in shorts and a thin white T-shirt, and as she held up a pen she made the most of her assets.

"Sign here," she ordered, and pointed to the swelling expanse below her left shoulder. The driver did as he was asked.

So this was the stock-car racing South. I remembered some of the shouts that had floated over from the grandstands earlier. "No tits in the pits, get the tits out of the pits!"

At dinner that night, Lynda Ferreri was disturbed to learn the car hadn't arrived yet. "I wish I had known about that," she said. "I drove to the track to see you this afternoon, but they wouldn't let me in. They said no skirts were allowed in the garage areas, and of course I was in a skirt, I had come straight from the bank."

Late next morning, my car finally reached the track. The red Chevrolet was parked like an outcast by the garage-area fence, its hood up, eyed by tech inspectors. The legendary Ralph Moody stood nearby.

Moody was some six feet tall, lanky, erect of bearing, fifty-eight years old. His face remained rather expressionless as I thanked him for accepting this role. He was agreeable enough, but uncommunicative. The man working on the car was his assistant, Will Cronkrite.

Roger, Gary and I watched, awash in the smell of rich exhaust; the burning rubber that drifted down from the track; the funny taste that carbon monoxide leaves in your mouth; the lump-lump sound of big V-8's at idle. Cronkrite and the NASCAR inspectors didn't seem to be in much of a hurry, and I was practically twitching with impatience. Finally it was done.

"Okay," said Moody, "she's all yours, get in and check it out."

It was awful. The engine skipped and missed, and the handling compared poorly with the borrowed car I'd driven yesterday. Pushing it hard—I was dead serious now—I barely ran 141 mph. Three laps were enough. When I brought it in and explained what it felt like, what the car was doing, Moody was indifferent.

"They're all like that, you'll never get 'em to quit doin' that," Moody said. "Will, check the float level." At least that might be the carburetor problem, the skipping and missing.

Anger and frustration welled up in me. Thank God for Tom Nehl. Presently he appeared with Cale Yarborough at his side, flushed and ruddy from his recent practice laps. Cale's manner was still reserved, but he was ready to honor his commitment to Rolla by testing the car for me. As I described to Cale what the car seemed to be doing, Moody wasn't listening.

Cale ran a handful of laps, and came in. He didn't say much, and looked speculative. His only timeable lap had been in the low 140s. Qualifying speeds would lie in the 150s. I was trying to query him as to which aspect of the suspension setup might affect which of the car's problems when Junior Johnson joined us.

Junior Johnson! One of the greatest stock-car racers of all time, retired from driving since 1964, now running the most successful team in Winston Cup: the team that Cale Yarborough drove for. Junior had a penetrating gaze, and I returned it.

"What's goin' on?" Junior asked Cale.

The two held a brief, low, incomprehensible conversation. Then Junior looked at me, looked at the car, looked at Moody, and said to his chief mechanic, "Give 'em the setup."

I knew perfectly well what a huge gift that was.

Stock car suspension setups weren't as complex as Indy-car setups, but they had to be right. Variations in caster, camber, spring strength, weight distribution, and so on interacted to make a car fast as blazes—or out of the field. Setups differed from track to track and from driver to driver. A qualifying setup was different from a racing setup. Good setups were a closely guarded secret, the fruit of experience and constant testing. I fully appreciated what Junior Johnson's words had meant.

It took until Thursday morning to install the new components and change the settings. Practice time was evaporating like drops of water on a hot griddle. Some ten minutes of practice remained when I hit the track. No time to stop and think it over between laps, no time for the quirks of the car to sink in. I brought it up to speed as fast as I dared, the oil and water temperatures just barely warm enough.

It was a different animal.

It was great!

My speeds leaped up to 150 mph. Then the yellow light came on. Practice was at an end. Time to get the tires changed, and line up for qualifying. I wasn't out of the woods yet; I'd have to find a few more miles an hour. So far, I had a grand total of seven laps in this machine. Forty-eight cars would be attempting to make the forty-car field.

At a vantage point in the garage area, Ralph Moody and some of the crew watched my qualifying run, stopwatches in hand. In fact, there were a lot of stopwatches in a lot of hands. Several drivers had publicly suggested that the only way I could make the field was if the official timers falsified my speed—bumped it up a couple of notches. That had even gotten into the papers, and people's backs were up.

My first lap was 152.310. My second lap was almost a mile an hour faster, 153.282. The two-lap average of 152.797 put me on the inside of the fourteenth row. The row directly ahead of me would consist of the future superstars Dale Earnhardt and Bill Elliott, only a hair faster than I had been.

Lynda, who had arrived just before qualifying, this time in pants, was ecstatic, as were the crew and I. Even Ralph Moody perked up, expressing what for him was almost jubilance. "I have never seen anyone—man or woman—adjust to driving a stock car racer as quickly as Janet did."[4] The trouble was, he couldn't acknowledge assistance. It was as if Junior Johnson hadn't existed, hadn't changed everything. "I knew she could do it, but we had to win her confidence," he went on. "We told her she had to have confidence in what we were telling her."[5]

When I walked out the garage-area gate that night, I was besieged

---

[4] Charlotte *News*, May 28, 1976
[5] ibid

by autograph-seekers with hats, programs, bare hands to sign. A large, muscular young man in a white T-shirt presented his shoulder as he handed me a pen. He curled his arm up into a perfect Charles Atlas pose, pointed to the cloth stretched over his bulging bicep, and said, "Sign here!"

I did as he asked, and laughed all the way home.

On Friday, in spite of a broken valve spring that cost painful repair time, I got in a few more laps and gained another gratifying three miles an hour. Veteran race winner Donnie Allison offered valuable tips. During Saturday's supporting races, I studied traffic. Also, I agitated for a crew meeting. There was still so much I didn't know, and too many loose ends: how pit stops were done, how often to expect them (especially as it related to yellow-flag situations), what the signal to go was and who was to give it. I had a long list, and there was sure to be stuff I didn't even know enough to ask about, that could be elicited from guys who'd been around for a while.

"A crew meeting?" Moody shrugged. I'd had to pry information out of him with a crowbar. I wondered whether Ralph Moody was burned out. The breakup of Holman-Moody in 1971 had been notoriously acrimonious, and the drive and initiative that must have powered his rise to the top in racing were nowhere in evidence. Nevertheless, a crew meeting was essential. If I had to arrange it and run it myself, I would; and I did.

What about a relief driver? Not one person in the garage area thought I could go the distance, and I wasn't sure of it myself. Two and a half to three hours, yes; I'd done that before and I could do it again, without any diminution of speed. Four hours or more—well, we'd see. Considering that a handful of the men used relief drivers here each year, I couldn't see how it would be any disgrace if I did, too.

By race day, every seat in the grandstands had been sold. They filled the infield to overflowing with cars and campers and people, and then they filled the fields outside and walked the people in. Traffic backed up for nineteen miles. Half an hour *after* the start of the race, cars were still lined up for two miles on Route 29, creeping toward the track. The ticket sales records that were set every day since my arrival topped out on race day at a record 103,000. The previous record, the year before, was 90,600.

Humpy sold television rights to ABC, the first time ever at Charlotte. "*They* called *me!*" he said later. "What did I know, this was the first race I'd promoted—TV people *never* call you. You call them."

Maybe ABC helped make up for the grief he'd gotten from NASCAR headquarters at Daytona. "When the news first got out about you coming here," Humpy told me in June, "Bill France called me up, but he needn't have wasted his money on the telephone. I could hear him yelling all the way from Florida."

Half an hour before the start, I poured cupfuls of water down the neck of my driver's suit. Roger helped me pat it onto my shoulders, back, arms and legs, until the thick Nomex was saturated and dripping everywhere. It was an old trick of mine for endurance races. The cooling effect of evaporation wouldn't last four hours, but it would be a start. The temperature was already 85 degrees in the shade, and the heat inside the car was estimated variously to rise to 130-150 degrees.

Out on the track, the pre-race show was winding up. It featured the prancing steps and high-tossed batons of the West Texas Strutters. Then came a surprise. Moody said, "You better get on out there, they're about to start driver introductions."

"Do what?"

He explained.

"Do I have to?" This last half-hour before race start was when the butterflies were at their most manic. Nothing I wanted less than to face a crowd of 100,000.

On the wide grass D in front of the main grandstands, forty West Texas Strutters in spangled short shorts and cowboy boots faced the members of a marching band, forming a gauntlet that led to an elevated platform. The platform held an announcer, two race officials, and Miss World 600, who was almost wearing a white jumpsuit without legs.

"Starting in fortieth place," boomed the loudspeakers, "driving the Miller Chevrolet, from Rossville, Georgia—BOB BURCHAM!"

Bob Burcham sprinted through the gauntlet while the trumpets trumpeted, the Strutters leaped and screamed, and the crowd thundered its applause and cheers. He took the steps two at a time, kissed the beauty queen to the accompaniment of whistles and Rebel yells, shook hands with the officials, and raced down the other side.

"You gotta be kidding me," I said.

One of my guys quit laughing long enough to say, "You don't have to kiss her."

"Starting twenty-seventh..."

Through the gauntlet I went, to the sound of 50,000 cheers and 50,000 boos. I shook hands with the official, ignored Miss World 600, was grabbed and kissed by the Winston cigarettes representative, and got the hell out of there.

It was getting uncomfortably close to 12:30, starting time. Moody brought foam-plastic cups which he cut in half lengthwise and taped, two deep, to the heels of my shoes. The bare floor pan of the car would get hot enough to blister your feet. I climbed through the Chevrolet's window, fastened the belts, and Roger tightened them. The strains of *The Star Spangled Banner* floated down from the loudspeakers, and the very memory of it, after all these years, sends the numbing tingle of adrenaline to the tips of my fingers and toes. The words of the starting call, "World 600 drivers, start your engines" were lost as forty massed, unmuffled V-8 engines simultaneously shook the earth with inconceivable force.

It was after 3 p.m., 350 miles into the race, with 250 miles to go. We were loping along under the yellow flag in a ragged line behind the pace car. It was going to be a long yellow. Buddy Baker's and Dave Marcis' cars were both stuffed into the wall near Turn 4. Oil and metal bits were strewn all over the area. The drivers were okay, though, and the safety crews were cleaning up.

It was time to inventory what strength I had, how much was used up and how much was left in reserve. Would it carry me through to the end of the race, or would I have to hand the car over to the would-be relief driver waiting in my pit?

The assessment was as remote and objective as a scan of the instruments on the dashboard.

The heat had been brutal. My driver's suit was saturated everywhere except the shins and elbows. The fresh water had long since evaporated, replaced with sweat. My head was filled with the reek of hot rubber dust and the raw exhaust that had begun to seep in from the engine compartment. My right forearm ached from the strain of throwing the car into the banking, four turns every thirty-some seconds. Sweat stung my rib cage where the skin was raw from the granny's harsh embrace. The radios were working badly or not at all. I heard orders for hot dogs from the infield stands, communications to and from other cars, and intermittent cracklings that nearly blew my eardrums out.

The pace car slowed as we approached the wrecks. Clearing and cleaning the track would take a while longer.

Well?

I had long since gotten the knack of distributing the steering load in the turns, using not just my forearms and biceps but the muscles of my right shoulder and back, then diagonally down to the brace of my left leg against the floorboard foot support. With most of the force spread out that way, I had more than enough power to juggle the wheel over the rough parts, to position the car where I wanted it. Strength was not an issue. Endurance was an issue. I let my body tell me what it had to say. Then I reached for the radio button on the transmission tunnel.

"I'm going to go the distance," I said.

Four laps later, the track was clear. The starter, on his perch above start-finish, held up one finger as we passed underneath, and the rotating yellow lights on top of the pace car went out. It meant we'd get the green next time around, and it also meant forming two columns out of the single line of cars. Those of us who were a lap or more down stayed to the inside; the faster cars doubled up to our right. The luck of it put me opposite Donnie Allison. I looked over as we accelerated down the back straight, and Donnie put his hand up, thumb and forefinger together, with a barely perceptible smile. There could have been no better sight in all the world.

David Pearson, leading at this point, held the field back as the pace car dropped below the yellow line leading to the pit entrance. From now until the green came out, the choice of speed was his. I was at the midpoint of Turn 4 when the field burst into full voice. We were off—thrashing, jousting, feinting, passing, in a maelstrom of sensation and sound.

Half an hour later, as I backed off the throttle at the entrance to Turn 1, the transmission jumped out of gear. It was a good thing no one was close by, as the sudden loss of power at the rear wheels upset the car. I stuffed it back into gear again and held it there until I was out on the back straight. I knew from experience that a transmission that popped out of gear when you lifted wasn't likely to do so when your accelerator foot was on the floor.

Moody had warned me this might happen. "They all do that," he said, though I came to know this wasn't so. (It never, ever happened to me again. That particular transmission had at some point been abused.) He told me they had a rubber strap to fasten around the gearshift lever, to help hold it in place.

As I entered Turn 3, I held the gearshift lever with my right hand; I could feel it struggling to jump out again. All the turning had to be done with my left hand. This wasn't a viable situation, at least not for long.

The radio was ineffective, but the guys heard bits of my voice, and after a couple of laps acknowledged with a "PIT" sign. A fully suited-up, helmeted driver was the first person to arrive at my door, eager to relieve me. I pushed him back, got Ralph, pointed at the gearshift lever, yelled. In a flurry of confusion, they found the rubber strap and hooked it up. Annoyed, I departed with a squeal of rubber, holding the gearshift lever hard forward in first and third, against the pull of the strap.

As the race wore on, the windshield became pitted and sandblasted, obscuring vision especially as the sun dropped lower in the sky. The exhaust leak worsened; I could feel the effects of carbon monoxide more and more. The radio was a constant strain, BRAPP-P BRAP BRAP inescapably amplified into my ears.

We were under the green flag from Lap 238 until just before the end, 240 miles without a yellow-flag break. I had learned something every minute I was on the track.

I'd been cautious at first. There was no sense doing something brash before I properly understood the way the game was played here, especially as dense as traffic was. At Trenton, which like Charlotte was a 1.5-mile track, the field of Indy cars had been limited to twenty-two. Charlotte's high banking enabled stockers to run just as fast as the Indy cars went on that flatter circuit, but there were nearly twice as many cars, none of them familiar to me.

As I gained a better idea how things were done, I could mix it up with more verve. Even so, I had to be careful. There was no doubt at all that I would be held to a higher standard of behavior and courtesy than any other driver in the field. When lapped, I moved to the bottom lane, no matter how many cars I myself was passing at the time. I was caught in heavy traffic once, trapped on the high side, and properly stayed there; but once, balked by slower cars, I moved down just as the overtaking car—Pearson—did also, in an Alphonse/Gaston routine, *après vous*. The rest of the field wasn't nearly so concerned about staying out of the leaders' way. On almost every lap I saw faster cars balked by slower ones, worse and longer than anything I was guilty of.

As the race went on, I became bolder about passing. The famous NASCAR "slingshot" was enormous fun. I would draft up to the back of a marginally slower car, extracting every bit of extra speed I could get from his wake, then pull out and around at the last moment. So when we came down to the final laps, I was running quite a bit faster than I had at the start.

Two laps from the end, two of the slower drivers tangled on the front straight. David Pearson, leading by seven seconds over Richard Petty, encountered a web of spinning, crashing cars. For a moment it appeared that Pearson couldn't get through, that his victory was lost; but he dived for the grassy D, fishtailed back onto the pavement, and kept his lead. We passed under the checkered flag with the yellow flag hung beside it, four hours and twenty-two minutes after the start.

Slowly we rumbled down pit road and into the garage area. By the time I had cut the ignition, the Chevrolet was surrounded. Lynda was at the door, almost too happy for words. "You did it," she cried. "You did it!" Tears were trickling into Roger's mustache from behind his sunglasses. Someone unfastened the window net, but I wasn't about to move. Now that the race was over, waves of nausea rolled through me. Carbon monoxide from a broken header had caught up at last. I pulled off my helmet, gulped water, poured water down my neck. All around the car, there was pandemonium.

When I mustered the strength to climb out, Lynda hugged me, ignoring the sweaty mixture of rubber and grit that covered my driver's suit, and I hugged her back. We had finished fifteenth, she said.

ABC-TV got their stuff first, down in the infield. Then I was shepherded up to the press box, just as they were finishing with David Pearson. I stayed at the back of the room, trying unsuccessfully to remain inconspicuous until the winner had gone. Pearson, flushed with victory, was feeling expansive.

"Really, she did a good job," he said. "I've been joking a lot about her this week, but she did a fine job of driving. I wouldn't mind racing with her any time."[6]

With Pearson gone, it was my turn on the hot seat. Someone kept asking how I felt about this or that "as a woman." I gave him neutral answers for a while, but he persisted. Finally I said, "I don't feel *anything* as a woman driver. I feel things simply as a driver."

"What did you think when Richard Petty cut you off?"

I had already forgotten the incident, and tugged hard to bring it out of memory. Sometime during the first half of the race, a small pack of the leading cars had overtaken me. I saw them coming and moved out of the way, down to the bottom lane, as we entered Turn 1.

[6] Nashville *Tennessean*, June 1, 1976

Midway through the turn, one car broke out of the little group, cut down to the bottom, chopped right across my nose. Day-glo red and blue, a big white No. 43. Petty.

It was attempted intimidation. I was surprised by the move, and amused. The man just didn't know me yet. I lifted for an instant, he missed me by inches, and we went on.

So what was I to say? Unsportsmanlike, discourteous? Well, he'd been those things, but...

"Racing is an aggressive sport," I smiled.

Finally it was over. A little glass-bubble helicopter waited on the grassy D in front of the pits. It would be hours before traffic cleared between here and Charlotte's airport, and the track was keeping its bargain to get me back to Indianapolis in time for Rolla Vollstedt's sponsor dinner. In spite of the assistance of several large Southern police officers, an enthusiastic crowd made for slow going before I was finally on board.

I had never been in a helicopter in my life.

All around us, race-goers were waving, cheering; there must have been thousands of them. The pilot twisted the collective, the pitch of the rotors changed, and slowly, magically, we rose from the ground.

When you're a kid you dream of flying, sometimes: of flapping your arms and rising into the air, over the tops of the trees, light as a bird, and you feel a sense of pure elation that, once grown, you may never feel again. Lifting off from Charlotte Motor Speedway in the helicopter was like that dream of flying. In the high-banked ring of the track, the circle of upturned faces, waving arms and tossed caps, inaudible cheers—all receding as we rose over the grandstands and tilted southwest—dreamlike, but this was real.

BIG-TIME AUTO RACING

Janet Guthrie drove the car they said she couldn't drive, endured the strain they said she couldn't endure, and completed the race they said she couldn't complete. —Nashville *Tennessean*, June 1, 1976

"I'd race with Janet Guthrie anytime," said winner David Pearson, one of a million or so—this reporter among them—who said she wouldn't be able to stand up to 600 miles in a stock car on her first try.
—*Autoweek*, June 5, 1976

In the single month of May, my world had turned upside down. The scorn and disbelief that weighed so heavily on us in March and April had been dealt with in the only possible way: on the race track. First at Trenton, then at Indianapolis and finally at Charlotte, May's developments had shaken up conventional wisdom in the oval-track racing world. The shift wasn't universal, but it was a beginning. Perhaps the most remarkable evidence of change was this: reporters at the Charlotte race, mostly weathered veterans of NASCAR, had voted to award me the Curtis Turner Award for outstanding achievement in that event. Named for the legendary driver who co-founded Charlotte Motor Speedway, the award was symbolic of a seismic shift of thought. The only question was, could this upheaval help secure a foundation for more progress on the track?

In the tumultuous days after Charlotte, would-be agents besieged me with rosy scenarios of endorsements, movies, books. Most wanted a large chunk of all my presumed future earnings from any source whatsoever, beginning immediately. More serious—much more serious—was an encounter with Pat Patrick that left me reeling. Patrick was the multimillionaire owner of Patrick Petroleum and of Patrick Racing, one of the most successful teams in Indy-car competition. George Bignotti was his chief mechanic, and his drivers in 1976 were USAC stars Gordon Johncock and Wally Dallenbach.

Nine days after the Charlotte race, on my way to Chicago to meet with one of the would-be agents, I sat down to talk with Patrick at a coffee shop in the Detroit airport. He was a short, chunky, florid man with all the human warmth of a pneumatic drill. We slid into a booth upholstered in cracked grey vinyl, a worn wood-grain table between us.

"Rolla Vollstedt's a loser," he began. "His cars are junk. You ought to have a shot at something better."

"Nothing would please me more than to get my hands on better equipment," I said, "but Rolla gave me the best he could. He incurred heavy expenses to do it, and he took a lot of heat for bringing me to the Speedway." That was an understatement if ever there was one. "What I'm hoping is that you, Rolla and I could find some way to cooperate."

Patrick looked both surprised and incensed. "There's no way in hell I could work with Rolla Vollstedt," he said, his voice rising as he launched into a diatribe that went on at length. "Your contract with him can and should be broken," he said. "If you don't get out of it, you're throwing away the greatest chance you'll ever get."

I said again, I wasn't going to walk.

"You're screwing up," said Patrick, then slid out of the booth and walked off down the concourse without another word.

I flew on to Chicago feeling thoroughly ill,

But I didn't regret what I'd done; I didn't even see it as a choice. I owed my whole chance at Indy-car racing to Rolla, and I wasn't going to abandon him, especially now when it seemed that funding for major improvements might be close at hand.

Bryant Heating and Cooling had come through with enough money for Rolla to confirm entry for me in the Pocono 500, scheduled for June 27, and a new flurry of Bryant media stuff was under way. I was optimistic. The blue car's fuel delivery system had been shipped out to California for testing, where a defective sensor was found. That, presumably, was what had caused all the burned pistons at Indianapolis. Besides, with Trenton, Indianapolis and Charlotte behind me, I felt I could step up the heat.

Up to this point, caution on my part was mandatory. Any slip-up would have been a major, possibly terminal setback for our program. Reports from the Charlotte race reflected that fact. David Pearson was prominently quoted as saying I'd gotten in his way a couple of times. And indeed I had—like nearly every other driver on the track, as Pearson had also said. Benny Parsons at least put it all in one sentence, "She looked smooth to me. I had one close brush with her, but that happens with dozens of drivers every race."[1]

In point of fact, at Trenton I had given the other drivers enough room for a Mack truck. At Charlotte, I had minded my manners better than anyone else I saw. Now, I thought, I had earned the right to take a few more chances. But when practice opened at Pocono on Friday June 18, our mechanical problems were a replay of Indianapolis. Then, even worse, qualifying for the field of thirty-three was rained out. USAC officials filled the field according to the rule book. Top drivers were placed in the front half of the field, and names were drawn by lottery from among the rest. Two unfortunate teams would have to pack up and go home. The luck of the draw put me in twenty-second position, and the grumbling and dirty looks that followed were a harsh reminder that I wasn't yet regarded as "just another driver," my fondest wish. USAC fined car owner Grant King $500 for "abusive and obscene language" concerning my presence in the field.

On race day, the stands were filled with a record 120,000 spectators, making this the largest single-day sporting event in Pennsylvania history. I had the inside of the eighth row, directly behind our friend Tom Bigelow. That was good. If I could stick to his heels I'd be fine. To my right was Larry Cannon, who claimed that "if it wasn't for the heavy congestion on the first turn, she'd probably finish the first lap last."[2] Behind me was George Snider, flanked to the right by Eldon Rasmussen. Both Snider and Rasmussen had impeccable manners on the track. Directly behind Rasmussen was Bill Simpson, a major antagonist at Indianapolis who had been equally vocal and hostile about my presence here at the Pocono 500.

When the green flag fell and we hurtled toward the first turn, I tucked in behind Bigelow and squeezed through it in good shape. A few cars behind me, all hell broke loose. Grant King's driver, Sheldon Kinser, chopped off Eldon Rasmussen, who spun. Lee Kunzman's car cut a tire on the debris. Jan Opperman's turbocharger ingested some shrapnel and choked on it.

Who exactly was the menace here?

We crawled around under yellow for six laps. On the restart, I held my position, passing a few cars, losing ground to a few others. It was hard work, as intense as the sun's fire focused through a convex glass.

Twenty laps later, Bobby Unser melted a piston and brought out the yellow by choosing to stop on the pavement. He did me a favor: the

[1] Atlanta *Constitution*, May 31, 1976

[2] Levittown-Bristol (Penn.) *Courier*, June 27, 1976

blue car was out of water and leaking fuel. I pitted. The thing steamed like a teakettle as they forced water into the system under pressure. I made eighty-nine laps like that, pitting for water half a dozen times.

There was more excitement in the first turn. Bill Simpson rashly dove underneath Al Loquasto, who deliberately turned right and spun rather than wreck them both. I was the next driver behind Al. His car was broadside on the track in front of me, moving at well over a hundred miles an hour. Would he slide up the banking and into the wall, or down toward the infield? My answer would determine whether we crashed or didn't. *Down*, I judged, and veered sharp right. The choice was correct. I missed him, and went on.

A decision like that occupies maybe a hundredth of a second, maybe less, and its outcome is clear half a second later. The memory, however, can last a lifetime.

The end of my efforts came at around the halfway point. On the back straight at maybe 180 mph, the blue car bucked as it jumped out of gear. Its bell housing had cracked, gaping almost around the entire circumference. I felt weary to the bone as I climbed out of the car—a weariness that wasn't physical. To struggle that long with a hopeless situation is infinitely more tiring than to run a full race at top speed.

Our tenacity was good for twenty-fourth place. My teammate Dick Simon's second tenth-place finish of the month (the other being at Milwaukee the previous week) was a note of cheer for the Vollstedt team. It was late in the day and most of the hubbub had subsided when a figure appeared at the door.

"Hey, lady."

It was Bill Simpson. The hairs bristled on the back of my neck. What was his problem this time?

"I just wanted to let you know," he said, "you did a good job on the start. I thought you were going to be a problem, and I was wrong."

Our eyes met and held.

"Thank you," I said. I didn't smile. Then he was gone. I felt my muscles uncoil as if you'd put meat tenderizer on them.

One step at a time.

Actually, no one had a bad word to say about my driving after the race. This time, all the heat fell on Rolla. *The New York Times* called the blue car an "antique"; the Trenton *Times* called it "shabby" and "clearly inferior to anything else on the track." When Rolla and I talked about the next scheduled Indy-car race, at Michigan Speedway in July, we were absolutely agreed that without adequate prior test time, we wouldn't go. The only problem was, where was the money going to come from?

As Rolla said to a reporter, "We've had five million dollars in publicity, two million dollars in conversation, but not one actual dime from anyone other than Bryant Heating and Cooling."

Lynda Ferreri had been at Pocono for the weekend to negotiate with Rolla over my NASCAR future. He and Lynda reached an agreement of some sort, and all three of us acknowledged that my primary allegiance was to Rolla's team, that I would drive for Lynda only when it didn't interfere.

Lynda hadn't been idle since the Charlotte race. Our success in the World 600 prompted her to look for more of the same. Our Charlotte sponsor, NAPA/Regal Ride, turned her down on June 15, three days before practice started at Pocono. That very day, the head of STP had called me. Would I care to drive a team car of Richard Petty's in the NASCAR Winston Cup Firecracker 400 at Daytona on July 4? The offer doubled my pulse rate, but it was fraught with peril. Such a car should be first-rate, but would it actually? The ride was the sponsor's idea, not the team's. Richard Petty had continued his vicious sniping at me in the press. This golden apple could be poisoned with no trouble at all.

Meanwhile, a new development was in the works. The president of NAPA/Regal Ride went fishing with the president of Kelly Girl temporary office services, Terry Adderley, and the "old boy network" bore fruit. By the time the fishing trip was over, Adderley was pumped up about NASCAR, and interested in pursuing an arrangement with Lynda and me. Lynda told me they would go for half a dozen races.

So, a possibly topnotch car, possibly not, for a single race with the Petty/STP team; or six races for Kelly Girl with a newly assembled team that had a few problems? In the end, I figured that six Winston Cup races were better than one.

On the day after the Pocono 500, Lynda Ferreri and I drove west toward the Susquehanna, where her aunt lived near Wilkes-Barre. It was a chance to chat under less pressured circumstances, and the more I saw of Lynda, the better I liked her.

Since college, I had had few women friends. I worked and played in men's fields, and most of my friends for the last fifteen years had been men. Now, here was a woman to whom I could relate. She, too, worked in a "man's field," upper-echelon banking, and knew what it meant to confound low expectations based only on gender—knew the pleasure of doing that, as well as the frustration and the obstacles. For the most part, like me, she dealt with traditional limits for women by ignoring them. She was highly intelligent and resourceful, good company, and good to work with. And now, we were to be allied in a great adventure.

Lynda was thirty-two, six years my junior, a strikingly attractive woman with strong, dramatic features. Her manner was engaging, her large brown eyes as warm as her smile. She had a great voice, throaty, a social drawl leavened with the lilt of good humor. Her sentence structure was idiosyncratic, a jumble of phrases glued together with verbal commas and dashes.

As we followed a two-lane route across the Lehigh River, through golden-green fields banked with orange tiger lilies, Lynda told me a bit more about herself. "I grew up in Pennsylvania," Lynda said, when I remarked that she didn't sound Southern. "Ferreri was my ex-husband's name, but it was the name I was already known by in business, so I kept it."

Lynda had worked in New York City until she moved to Charlotte as Vice President for Communications at a large international bank. Both the South and stock car racing were, Lynda said, "a whole new world to me. I mean, when Humpy told me it was a stock car race, I said, '*Stock* car? Could she drive my Mercedes?'"

She was joking, of course, but she had been learning fast. And she wasn't intimidated by anybody, which would prove to be a great good thing.

Later that same day, she got a green light from Kelly Girl to enter the Firecracker 400 Winston Cup race on July 4th. Part of her agreement with Kelly was that Ralph Moody would be team manager. Moody's long-standing reputation had plenty of clout with the Kelly executives.

So, three days after the Pocono 500, I headed for Daytona for my second-ever Winston Cup stock car race. In the little airport terminal, so familiar from those passionate days of the Daytona 24-Hour, the headlines blared "Beware, Gentlemen, Guthrie's in Daytona."[3]

My father called that morning. "It's official," he said. "You've really made it. You're in the funny papers." A "Tank McNamara" series featured me versus stock car driver "Stickshift" and a gang of pot-bellied, beer-swilling cronies.

I drove straight to the track to sign in near the main entrance,

---

[3] Jacksonville (Fla.) *Times-Union*, June 30, 1976

behind the towering backside of the high-banked turns. NASCAR regulars, waiting in line to register, eyed me covertly. Some men spat on the ground.

Inside the huge bowl of the track, Ralph Moody was unloading the race car from an open trailer hitched to a small U-Haul truck. Enormous, gleaming tractor-trailers belonging to the top teams towered over Moody's rig. The race car was no longer red—one of my least favorite colors—but green, Kelly green. Green was a taboo color in stock cars just as it was in Indy cars, but I liked it just fine. Lynda Ferreri's new car owner's No. 68 stood out in bold white with a black outline.

Johnny Rutherford and A. J. Foyt were both entered in the Firecracker, in one of their occasional excursions from USAC. Rutherford, fresh from his Indianapolis 500 victory, spelled out what it took to win. "Not only must you have the right car, the right crew and the right preparation. You must have it all together. It's a team effort."[4]

When practice started on Thursday, we didn't have it all together—not in the least. Once again, the handling was loose and unstable; once again, Ralph Moody's position was "They're all like that." My best lap was a miserable 162.308 mph when the day's activity was cut short by rain. A record sixty-two cars were entered, and only the fastest forty would start.

Qualifying started the next day, but there was no sense putting the car in the qualifying line when we needed ten more miles an hour. I struggled with Moody's employee, Will Cronkrite, who did the actual wrenching. Cronkrite was secretive and kept no written records of changes—much less the effects of those changes. Talking with him was an exercise in futility.

"What's the wedge?" I asked. The car was still loose, and more wedge could help—if it wasn't too great already. (Wedge was the stock-car way of measuring weight distribution at the rear of the car.)

"An inch and an eighth," he said. That was about right for this track, I had heard. But a few minutes later, when he jacked it up, I measured the wedge myself. It was three quarters of an inch. Whether he was deliberately lying to me or just didn't know, the result was the same: bad. Then we hassled over a spring change in the rear to give the car a little more push, and instead of softening the spring as I asked him to, he stiffened it, making the car looser still. I

[4] Daytona *Evening News*, July 2, 1976

nearly wrecked the car on that setting.

Ralph Moody kept in the background, shrugging his shoulders. "You just got to learn to put your foot down," he said.

When the track opened for practice again, the car was squirrelly as hell, spooky, and the speed didn't improve.

I spent a sleepless night. Without some drastic changes, I was going to miss the show.

Early the next morning, I found Moody, and gave it my last shot. "If you don't want to believe what I'm telling you," I said, "if you have any interest in getting this car into the field, find a driver who's been around for a while who's willing to take the car out. See what he says."

Moody indicated it wouldn't make any difference anyway, but he did find another driver who would test the car: Cecil Gordon. Cecil, as I came to know him, was one of the nicest guys in racing. Always an underfunded, independent driver, he was as generous and polite on the track as he was off it.

His test drive made all the difference in the world. Cronkrite did at least some of what Gordon told him, and suddenly I had a drivable car in my hands. Not wonderful, but drivable. I qualified thirty-third out of the fifty-three drivers who made qualifying attempts, at 172.120 mph. It was a monumental relief. Johnny Rutherford was fast for the day at 179.043, starting twenty-first.

Cecil Gordon, who had qualified sixteenth, stopped by after the run, and we hugged. He had saved my life, in a way—my racing life. Moody, however, was just as little disposed to share credit as he was at Charlotte. Someone asked him what changes he'd made, that had enabled the car to go ten miles an hour faster than the day before.

"We changed the driver's mind," Moody said. "We told her that if she didn't run faster, we was going to throw her in the lake."[5] But he tempered it by adding, "Believe me, she's a racer."

On race day, the temperature rose over 90 degrees, with humidity to match. A record July crowd of some 75,000 made its way into Daytona's enormous bowl. I changed into my driver's suit in the public women's room, then walked back through the garage area to our spot. Little groups of crewmen looked at me squinty-eyed. Conversations ceased as I passed. Well, screw 'em. They had no power to affect who I was and what I was going to do.

[5] Sarasota *Herald-Tribune*, July 4, 1976

Then it was time to climb into the car. One minute to go, clear the grid. Then the explosion of sound. The tachometer needle leaped up to prove that my engine ran, its roar drowned in the rest. We rolled down pit road and onto the track.

On the pace laps, I considered my neighbors. On my right was Richard Childress, later to be the highly successful owner of Dale Earnhardt's team. Future star Bill Elliott was five spots behind me. I didn't know any of these men at the time.

The yellow lights on top of the pace car went out and the starter held up a finger. One lap to go. We scrubbed our tires, weaving sharply back and forth. A stocker felt unsettled at low speed, as if it might fall into pieces on the next turn of the steering wheel. That would change at speed, as the great mass of the thing loaded the suspension against the rough banking, squeezing the springs, compressing rubber bushings, distorting all the angles of the suspension geometry into a configuration that somehow worked. On the back straight we snugged up into proper formation, a neat tight pack for the start.

An enormous roar of engines: the race was on, and the immensity of noise told you so before the mass of the cars responded to their open throttles. I ran up through the gears with one eye on the tach, still unable to hear my own engine. Turn 1 would be ticklish, with the pack at full speed and still tightly bunched. The banking of the turns at Daytona was 31 degrees—an inclination so steep that, if you tried to climb it on foot, you found yourself reaching out to touch the pavement. But when you ran at those turns at 180 mph, they looked perfectly flat.

We got through Turns 1 and 2 without incident, and spread out along the back straight. So we were off—thrashing, jostling, feeling out car and track, judging our lines, judging our competitors. Just before tilting into Turn 3, I threw a glance across to Turn 4 and the front straight. Then the car slammed onto the banking, and the line of sight was cut off by the roof of the car. I locked onto the landmarks that showed the line through the turns, the patches on the pavement that gleamed whiter than the rest. Left wheels on the first white patch ... two to three feet above the next patch ... then start hauling it down, at the red-white-and blue sign. "DAYTONA" was lettered onto the wall at the center of the pair of turns, and another key to the line was the Y or T, to start pulling it down. Toward the exit of Turn 4, left wheels on the outside edge of the white patch just before the bump. That was the big bump in the track where the tunnel to the infield ran underneath, and it had been the launching point for many a spectacular accident.

Through the D-shaped bulge on the front, the back end of the car was light and floaty, nervous, just as at Charlotte but for a longer period of time. Actually, the car was nervous and unstable everywhere; the least stable car I had ever driven. But what did I know? Maybe Moody was right: that was just the way stock cars were.

We ran the whole race, four hundred miles in Florida's July heat, with only two yellow flags. Buddy Baker's engine blew in the first half-hour, spewing flames, enveloping Turn 2 and the back straight in thick oil smoke. Buck Baker, Buddy's father, and Cecil Gordon, whose contribution to our setup had been so invaluable, suffered the consequences. David Pearson spun in the oil and Buck Baker, trying to avoid him, crashed heavily into the back of Cecil's car. Buck drove to the pits and passed out. Both drivers were taken to the hospital, then released.

The second yellow came on Lap 133, and the cause of it was my green Kelly Girl Chevrolet. I had been holding my own; Lynda said later that we were in the top ten. Then the handling deteriorated. A tire was going soft. Between Turns 3 and 4, the tire collapsed and the back end whipped out and around. I snapped the wheel left and locked up the brakes. Luckily, I had already slowed enough—to maybe 165 mph—that the car went down the banking instead of up. Nobody hit me. I reached the infield grass and slid to a stop.

The thing still to fear was that another car might have spun in the smoke and be headed my way. The thing to work at was to GET OUT of the infield, back to the pits, change the spin-damaged tires, and get back in the race. The rest of the field was whizzing past, racing toward the yellow flag at start-finish—all those cars I had worked so hard to pass.

The infield was slick and swampy from summer thunderstorms. I rocked the car out of the mud, eased it up onto the track apron, stood on the gas, got fresh tires, and went on.

In a way, the spin was good for me. It loosened me up, blew away the constraints. The irritation and anger I felt over baseless hostilities rose to the surface and found a focus, though my mind still had a steely grip over that emotional force. Now I was hot for just one thing: making up the lost positions. I ran my fastest laps in the last sixty miles.

When the checkered flag fell at half past eleven, we were in fifteenth place. Cale Yarborough won. A.J. Foyt was fourth, one lap down. Bill Elliott was nineteenth and running, six laps behind me. Johnny Rutherford was out with a broken rear axle housing.

Up in the press box, Cale Yarborough came close to passing out.

He sat with his head on his knees for ten minutes before recovering enough to speak. Perhaps it was this brief display of weakness that spurred him to macho commentary. "There's no way a woman could be physically strong enough to drive my race car like I did today. If there is, I don't want to be around her," he said. This was headline material around the country.

The statement had a grain of truth to it. At about five feet six inches, Cale Yarborough *had* to be tougher than anybody. He liked his car set up loose, oversteering, even for a race. A loose setup left no room for error. The back end of the car would keep trying to overtake the front. So Cale had to chase it all the time, sawing at the wheel. That contributed to his ferocious-looking style.

Like many road racing drivers, I had worked hard to develop a smooth style, which was theoretically faster than a rough one. A smooth style was efficient for both car and driver. It wasted nothing, and if you had judged correctly where the edge was, you could stay closer to it. One thing a smooth style wasn't: it wasn't heroic-looking. You weren't always treading on the hem of catastrophe, losing it and saving it. Whether or not I could drive a car like Cale did, I wasn't going to because I didn't believe in it.

Yarborough aside, the post-race commentary from other drivers was reasonably objective. Ricky Rudd expressed the preponderant sentiment: "She was just like another guy out there."[6]

But a backlash still crackled through part of the press, some of it quite imaginative. The drift was that since I hadn't run with the leaders in this, my second Winston Cup race, I never would; and should quit. Fans did their part to stoke the fire. In a letter to *National Speed Sport News*, one woman wrote: "If the Boy Scouts can keep a girl out, why aren't there enough real men in racing to stop this craziness?"[7]

I was starting to lose my sense of humor about this stuff. For most of my life, I had been blissfully ignorant of the depth and strength of cultural convictions that women ought to keep their place. Now, I was getting my nose rubbed in it

The reality was this: by the time I left Daytona in July of 1976, my oval-track racing record consisted of two NASCAR Winston Cup races and two USAC Indy-car races. In the stockers, both finishes were solidly in the top half of the field. In the Championship races, I had run in the top half before the car broke. It was a record that no newcomer of that era needed to be ashamed of.

[6] Jacksonville (Fla.) *Times-Union*, July 5, 1976
[7] July 7, 1976

SETTLING IN,
HOLDING OUR OWN

Two weeks after the Daytona Firecracker 400, USAC hosted a double-header at Michigan International Speedway: a 200-mile race for Indy cars, followed immediately by a 200-mile race for USAC stock cars. Both Rolla Vollstedt and Lynda Ferreri filed entries, for my blue Vollstedt-Offy and my green Kelly Girl Chevrolet. Just four drivers planned to run both events: A. J. Foyt, Roger McCluskey, Tom Sneva, and me.

We would have to adapt quickly, between sessions, to the immense differences in speed and handling between the two kinds of cars. And for me, the track itself required learning. Michigan, a two-mile high-banked oval set into rolling green hills sixty-five miles west of Detroit, was the fastest track on the Indy-car circuit. Back then, steel guard rails formed its outside perimeter. Compared with the concrete walls of Indianapolis and Daytona, the guard rails looked both insecure and deadly. Furthermore, their convergence in perspective created an optical illusion when you came out onto the back straight. It deceived the eye as to the layout of the turn and the direction of the track. Michigan was where Merle Bettenhausen, Gary's brother and Tony's son, had lost his right arm just a few years before.

But it was here at Michigan that Rolla Vollstedt's team redeemed itself. My teammate Dick Simon qualified seventh-fastest, in Rolla's silver car. Tom Bigelow and future Indianapolis 500 winner Tom Sneva formed the row behind Simon. And starting directly behind Sneva would be me, the twelfth-place qualifier, at 186.480 mph. I believe it was the fastest qualifying speed ever posted by the blue car, eight spots higher in the field than Sprint-car champion Bigelow had qualified it at Michigan the previous year.

So here was Rolla's much-maligned blue "junkbox" solidly in the middle of a field of the best drivers in the United States. Among those behind me were three-time USAC Sprint-car champion Larry Dickson; two-time Sprint-car champion Roger McCluskey, who had competed in almost two hundred USAC Championship races and was the

National Champion three years earlier; and Sprint-car legend Jan Opperman.

Gordon Johncock saw Rolla in the pits. "You were right," he said, "she *is* a race driver who just happens to be a woman."

My qualifying speed had made the women's closed-circuit speed record officially ours, and although I couldn't have cared less, Rolla was pleased. All that mattered to me was our gratifying position in the field for the race, and I headed out for stock car practice in high spirits. My eye being tuned to Indy-car speeds, however, I had some thrilling moments in the turns before I adapted to the "taxicab's" capability.

As usual, the green Chevrolet had a few problems. The worst of it was the Chevrolet's unstable rear end, which wobbled about like a giant Slinky toy. This had caused me trouble since the beginning, even with Herb Nab's setup at Charlotte. Darrell Waltrip was one of several drivers who commented publicly[1] that my car appeared to be too loose, unstable. For now, all I could do was grit my teeth and bear with it. I qualified thirteenth out of fifty stock cars entered for the thirty-eight-car field.

As the sun dropped lower, casting a rosy glow on my already rosy world, I met Gordon Johncock near pit road. "Looks like you're doing pretty well," he said. "You might try running higher up on the track. You'll find it's smoother there."

I thanked him, and could hardly wait to tell Rolla that Johncock had spoken to me, offered a tip. Progress might be slow, but progress there was.

Next morning, when the green flag fell on the Championship race, I quickly moved the blue car up to tenth place. Then a tire went soft, cut by some invisible piece of debris. I was forced to pit under the green flag, a setback difficult to overcome. A second pit stop under the green flag put me completely out of serious contention, and I finished thirteenth. Dick Simon was classified nineteenth, after a universal joint broke. But we both had run fast while we were on the track, showing that Rolla's cars could be top-ten contenders, not junk. We needed that—all of us. Gordon Johncock won.

The strength of that showing was still with me as I waited for the start of the stock car race. A solid grip on the lesser capability, the lower cornering speed, of the Chevrolet was essential. I forced my

---

[1] *Car and Driver*, September 1976

mind's eye to make the change.

About an hour into the race, a flat tire sent me backwards into the guard rail. The car suffered relatively little damage, and after a few laps, I was back in action just as a spectacular two-car wreck tore out 150 feet of guard rail. My Chevrolet collected some of the debris. The field was red-flagged to a halt that lasted over an hour. We stood near our cars in a sort of limbo, talking quietly, relieved to learn that the drivers were alive and relatively well. On the green, I pitted for extensive repairs (none were allowed under a red flag) and finished in twenty-first place. Foyt won.

So while the final race standings didn't exactly cover us with glory, I was settling in, holding my own, doing better than a lot of veterans. The USAC drivers, a few of them anyway, were starting to include me in their interplay and backchat. As hostilities diminished, some of the true joy of racing crept back into my life. Little tingles here and there, like the return of sensation to a hand or foot that was asleep, buoyed my spirits. It had been just a year since my winter solstice, the nadir of my fortunes. Surely I ought to feel the return of light.

To fill the break in schedule before the next major race, I accepted some short-track stock-car racing invitations in Wisconsin and Oregon. The money was good, but more to the point, I wanted to build up experience in dense traffic. On road-racing circuits, you drove mostly against the track. On the ovals, you drove mostly against the other drivers. Nowhere was traffic denser than on the bull rings, a quarter to a half mile long.

These races were both colorful and fiercely competitive. Lapping side by side just inches apart, the pack of cars resembled a school of fish: turning, accelerating and braking in perfect unison. Short-track racing indeed taught me about traffic, and it also taught me that I was a fish out of water on anything much shorter than half a mile.

On the sixth of August, Vollstedt's team was testing at Trenton again. Dick Simon sorted out both our cars, as usual. Contrary to the normal precept of only changing one thing at a time, Dick could make a few laps, then change the stagger, the wing angles, the shock absorber stiffness, perhaps a spring, and make a great improvement in the handling. I was only beginning to get a grip on what sort of problem with an Indy car could be cured by what sort of change. Indy cars were subtle, often baffling, and with Simon making so many changes all at once, it was hard for me to analyze which change did what.

In mid-afternoon of our test day at Trenton, Simon was exiting Turn 4 in the blue car when we saw him waver and slow. He veered into the infield, nearly skewering the car on the end of the guard rail. A huge ball of vapor enveloped it as he came to a stop. We grabbed fire extinguishers and took off at a run. By the time we were halfway to him, he was out of the car and writhing on the grass. A water hose had burst, spraying scalding water and steam down his back and buttocks. The guys ran for buckets of cold water, pouring it over him as he struggled to regain his composure. "I couldn't see," he said. "I couldn't see anything. I thought the whole car was going to blow up." Melanie, his wife of three months, thought he should see a doctor, but Simon refused.

It should have been me, I was thinking. *If Dick hadn't been shaking down the car for me...*

How I wished for a chief mechanic with whom I could work on chassis sorting ... but that took money, additional sponsorship. We didn't have it.

Nine days later, I qualified for the Trenton Indy-car race a second slower than I had in May, and was almost too disgusted with myself to climb out of the seat. My performance in the race, while adequate enough to finish fifteenth, was uninspired. I hadn't been able to access the extraordinary state of being necessary to excel at this game.

Was I starting to lose my enthusiasm for heroic efforts with the blue car? Conventional wisdom said that if a rookie drove a mediocre car with better results than would be expected of it, people would notice. But so far there wasn't a hint of the dollars that everyone had been so sure would be forthcoming if we succeeded.

At the end of August, the Vollstedt team was back in California for the Ontario 500, the third and last race in USAC's Triple Crown of 500-mile races for Championship cars. A Santa Ana wind blew relentlessly—hot, gritty, and horribly polluted. Our fortunes were as miserable as the weather. We lost two engines in as many days. By 4 p.m. on Thursday, the last day to qualify, practice time was running out and things were stacking up. I set out to shake down the latest changes. Halfway through Turn 2, my back suddenly felt hotter than it should have.

It's amazing how fast you can kill the engine, get the car out of gear, undo the safety belts, and make ready to depart the premises, while braking hard toward the inside of the track in the direction of the fire trucks. All you need is sufficient motivation. Dick had been scalded by this same engine at Trenton. That's about as motivating as it gets.

I was luckier than Dick: got everything shut down in time to escape injury. The hoses didn't burst. The excess heat dissipated, and a tow truck hauled me in at the end of a rope.

Back in the garage, they found depleted coolant and a leaking hose. I doubted that a hose leak was the root problem. The burst of heat had been too sudden. Sure enough, when I brought it back up to speed, the water temperature gauge pegged almost immediately. I shut it down and coasted into the pits. The crew pushed it into the garage area without a pause. Streams of coolant and vapor and a sizeable crowd trailed behind us. The water pump had seized. Changing the water pump on an Offy was normally a two-hour job. It was now 4:13. Qualifying ended at 6 p.m. The guys tore into the car like demons. I watched every move, anticipating each man's need for a tool, handing them wrenches, stashing pieces of car. They had it running at 4:38, at the cost of multiple blisters and scrapes. Rolla had taken to answering the ever-ringing phone with "Vollstedt's Snake Pit."

They'd done their job, now I had to do mine. Warmed it up, stood on the gas. Everything was working right at last. The very first lap was my fastest yet, easily fast enough to make the field. This wasn't going to be like Trenton; I had gotten my grip back. Two more laps and we would present ourselves to qualify.

Then, on the back straight, the engine sputtered and went soft.

That was the end.

In the Ontario pits and garage area all week long, crews and drivers had offered friendly greetings. The change in atmosphere that had been evident at Trenton was the greatest imaginable relief, as if a ton had been lifted from my shoulders. And I heard many wonderful rumors about my prospects for next year. The most charming rumor was that A. J. Foyt was going to field a second car for me. But you couldn't put rumors in the bank. The bottom line was, I wasn't in the field for the Ontario 500. I had nightmares and bad dreams for a week.

Next up was the NASCAR Winston Cup race in mid-September at Dover, Delaware, a high-banked one-mile track. Lynda and I tried a new tactic: Dick Simon agreed to test and set up the Chevrolet, three days before the race. And indeed, Dick's forcefulness of character and his skill at car sorting resulted in perhaps the best-handling setup yet.

Ralph Moody was well pleased with my sharply higher speeds, his usual dour impassivity replaced by lively good humor. Actually, I liked Ralph Moody—when I wasn't fighting with him over setups. Most people did. Cronkrite, however, sulked. The car wasn't set up his way, therefore it was wrong.

When we lined up to qualify for the Dover race, the setup and handling were still about the same as when Dick Simon left. To this day, it does my heart good to look at that starting lineup for my third ever NASCAR Winston Cup race. Cale Yarborough had the pole at 132.337 mph. Like most of the top drivers, he was running a car built especially for the medium-length tracks—a Chevrolet Monte Carlo for Dover rather than the nose-heavy Chevrolet Laguna model that suited Daytona, which was what we had. The top teams also used a hot qualifying engine that would afterwards be exchanged for a longer-lived race engine. After Cale came Richard Petty, Darrell Waltrip, Buddy Baker, David Pearson, David Marcis, Bobby Allison, Dick Brooks, Benny Parsons, Lennie Pond—Winston Cup winners and champions. The next driver was me, in eleventh place at 129.398 mph. Just four months earlier, many of these drivers had assured the world that I was incapable of driving fast enough to earn a starting spot in a forty-car field. This time, hardly any boos mingled with the cheers from the grandstands.

My intense satisfaction was short-lived. It was the end of the day. The track was closed. Next time out, we'd be starting the race. Coming back to our spot in the garage, I found Cronkrite busily screwing away on the right rear spring perch.

In a rage, I tore up to him. "Goddamn it, put it back like it was!"

"Don't interrupt me."

That topped it. I entered red-mist mode.

Moody interceded. The underside of the car was scraping, he said.

Well, why hadn't it scraped before?

They'd changed the headers.

"So put the old ones back!"

No, they wouldn't do that. Besides, the setup that Dick Simon had come up with wasn't going to work during the race. They wouldn't tell me what else they had changed.

From then on, I never left them alone with the car unless whatever they might change could be checked out on the track.

My head was spinning. As I headed for the race track next morning, all I could do was hope for the best.

It was a catastrophe. Cars went by me as if I were tied to a post. The green Chevrolet was a different animal, and completely intractable. Once the tires heated up, my lap times rose to a full three seconds slower than what I'd qualified at.

In sixteen laps I pitted, livid. Cronkrite fussed with it, making it worse. Thirty-three more laps of humiliation was as much as I could stand. Half an hour after the start, I parked it. Climbed out of the car, threw my helmet over the pit wall, delivered a few baroque remarks, and left.

Lynda and Moody caught up with me in the garage area. It was important to the sponsors that I continue, they said. Grimly, I got back in the car, fishtailed down pit road, and did my best. The green Chevrolet wasn't the slowest car on the track by a long shot, but it sure wasn't eleventh fastest. A hundred and ten laps later, the engine threw a rod out the side of the block. The car went round in its own oil, reaching the grass without mishap. I spent the rest of the race in the infield between Turns 1 and 2, studying the drivers' lines, style, and traffic patterns. The mental discipline was a useful way of transmuting my murderous rage.

The situation was this: while Lynda owned the team and paid the bills, she was a novice. So was I. After three Winston Cup races, we still had a credibility problem, and we were excluded from the good ol' boy network of racing information that might have clarified our path. Will Cronkrite was Ralph Moody's employee, and while Moody showed no inclination to make a change, Lynda had already begun a quiet search for a new crew chief. In the week after Dover, her initiative bore serendipitous fruit. She called me with amazing news.

"I went to Buddy Parrott's shop last night," she began. Parrott had been one of her candidates. "Even though Buddy was already committed to someone else, I thought he might talk to me, share some ideas about your handling issues. And Darrell Waltrip was there. They heard me out, and then Darrell said, 'Janet may have a point, because I don't see much wrong with her driving. I figure Ralph's been around, but frankly, I could *never* drive that car the way you guys have it set up.'"

I felt a sense of relief so strong that tears came to my eyes.

Lynda said, "Darrell says that our car has a narrow rear axle, something like sixty inches, when the legal maximum is sixty-two. He said that a wider rear axle makes all the difference."

I was dumfounded. Two inches! No wonder the thing was unstable!

I flashed back to my first season in my Celica, three years before. The Celica's rear axle was narrower than the legal maximum by half an inch. I was poor as a church mouse, living behind a storefront, helping Ralph Farnham move boats. I spent several hundred 1973 dollars on quarter-inch spacer plates and longer wheel nuts, just to get that last half inch of track.

That's how important it was. And this was two inches!

Lynda had proposed the wider axle to Moody that same night. He said it would make no difference. With her usual first-class diplomacy, she persuaded him to acquire one anyway.

I thanked Lynda profusely. It was a rare bank vice-president who would chase around to race car garages in the middle of the night, seeking an answer to a problem she could barely define.

Our next Winston Cup race, the National 500 at Charlotte, fell on October 10. The green Chevrolet still had its narrow rear axle; Moody said he hadn't been able to locate a wider one. I qualified twenty-sixth, within a hair of the speed I ran in May. Fifty-nine cars attempted to make the field. Nineteen were unsuccessful.

On race day, the green Chevrolet wasn't wonderful. And some defect or other kept me in the pits for two full laps on the first yellow, just eight laps after the start. I eventually finished 22nd. Donnie Allison won. A. J. Foyt parked his car on Lap 59. The handling of his car was evil, A. J. said angrily. "There was no point in endangering myself and everybody else, so I just parked it."[2]

I knew just how A. J. felt.

The last Indy-car race of the 1976 USAC Championship season was scheduled for November 6, at Phoenix. This was to have been the blue car's farewell outing, but our test session used up Rolla's last engine. The only reasonable thing to do was withdraw.

Before the blue car was packed away that night, I sat on the edge of its tub, looked down into its seat, out over its nose, and thought back over the passions of the year. The first Indy car I had ever seen— how quiet it was now, how still, under the Arizona moon.

From now on, I thought, *it will no longer be a race car. It will be for*

[2] Associated Press, Portland *Oregonian*, Oct. 13, 1976

display, shiny, chromed, perfect; without the marks of its passage along the tracks at Trenton, Indianapolis, Michigan; no bugs in its teeth, no sandblasted paint from dirty circuits on its nose. No longer alive.

Saying goodbye to the blue car, however poignant, cleared my mind for what lay ahead: a whole new world. The door was opened by S. D. Murphy, Shirley Murphy, known as Murph. Murph was in his late seventies, tall, with a commanding presence and a long history at the Indianapolis 500. His company, Thompson Industries, had sponsored A. J. Foyt in the 1960s and early '70s. Murph had attended every single Indianapolis 500 since its inception in 1911. Deafness and blindness were creeping up on him, but he disdained making any concession to their approach.

We had met back in April, shortly before my first Indy-car race, just an introduction in the motel dining room on the Speedway grounds in Indianapolis. Murph took an interest, and kept in touch as 1976 wore on. When Foyt announced, on the last day of qualifying in May, that he wouldn't let me make the qualifying attempt in his car, Murph went to see him, tried unsuccessfully to change his mind. Ever since, Murph had been rotating various schemes to get me into better equipment. In October, his work bore fruit.

The day after the Charlotte NASCAR race, Rolla and I joined Murph in the Indianapolis offices of Nick Frenzel, the president of Merchants Bank. Nick's father Otto, the founder of the bank, had been a pillar of Indianapolis' civic structure and Murph's old friend. Murph had negotiated a sponsorship agreement with the bank. Nick was cordial, sharp, and attentive. We shook hands all around, and left the bank in high spirits.

At almost the eleventh hour, Rolla would have the money for more competitive cars. Together with the extra funding offered by Bryant, it meant we wouldn't be behind the eight ball any more.

Not long after that, Lynda Ferreri called. Kelly Girl would sponsor my campaign for Rookie of the Year in the 1977 NASCAR Winston Cup series.

My cup runneth over, I thought.

HAVING FUN AT LAST

The Los Angeles Times 500 in November at Ontario, my fifth NASCAR Winston Cup race, was the last event of 1976. It played out like a microcosm of my inaugural racing season at the top levels of the sport. Our newly-installed wider rear axle represented a great leap forward, and after the usual desperate struggle over the setup, I felt we were in reasonably good shape for the race.

Ontario Motor Speedway was jammed. Dressed and ready, I pressed through the crowds behind pit wall toward my car. Halfway down pit road, I overtook a slight figure that seemed familiar—could it be—"Do I see the world-famous..." I paused half a beat, and saw his shoulders stiffen as he anticipated the word *actor*—"champion race driver?"

Paul Newman, who had just won the SCCA D Production National Championship and the Atlanta runoffs' prestigious President's Cup, turned around.

Well, I *never* expected a bear hug from Paul Newman!

It was the first time I had seen him since the last SCCA National at Bridgehampton a year before. The warmth of his greeting seemed an omen for the day.

We were about an hour into the race. There'd been no yellow flags yet, not a single break in the pace. The green Chevrolet was handling better than ever. With the back end nailed down, not wobbling as it had before, I felt more confident in the vicinity of other cars.

My disinclination to run within inches of the competition had engendered some criticism. There was a reason for it. No way would I risk putting someone else into the wall. An evil handling characteristic in my own machine would not become someone else's problem, not in my hands. The new, wider rear axle was making a huge difference.

Coming out of the pits after my second gas stop, I picked up Bobby Wawak, a Winston Cup veteran. Soon I found I had someone to play with. My biggest pleasure in sports car racing had always been a closely matched race, whether it was for first spot or eighth. Now here was a playmate in NASCAR.

Lap after lap, we went back and forth. He went deeper into the turns, but my line was better and at the exit I'd be ahead. Our engines pulled almost evenly, his with the slightest edge over mine. He went from my rear bumper to my front bumper on the long sides of the track. I looked over every now and then, grinning, as we blasted along side by side. Bobby never looked back. Eventually we encountered slower traffic, and I pulled out enough distance that he lost my draft.

What I didn't know was that up front, at the lead, nothing spectacular was happening and people's attention had drifted back in the field. From the Ontario *Daily Report*, November 22, in a story by its editor, John Jopes: "Besides the display of her unusual courage, spunk and cool, Guthrie provided the best of the day's action in what could have turned out to be a pretty dull race ... She and Bobby Wawak, both driving Chevies, provided the only real dicing of the day ... a happy crowd [was] attracted to this race-within-a-race..."

Then I played in other traffic: caught a clump of cars that were drafting each other, merged into the thick of them, munched them one by one, and left them behind.

Years later, talking about this race, Lynda Ferreri said, "I've never seen you happier."

Shortly after the halfway point, Carl Joiner spun at the exit of Turn 4. Something warned me of it—the first puff of dust, or a yellow light in my peripheral vision and I rounded the turn to see his red-orange Chevrolet smashed nose-first on the outside wall down the straight, scraping sideways along the concrete in a vibrating cloud of dust and smoke. I squeezed harder on the brakes as my car came straight. Between Joiner and me, Frank Warren was easing toward the center of the track. Joiner's smashed car was still moving at a pretty good clip. Would it stay on the wall? I judged that it would, and started bearing left, toward the inside. So did Warren. Then Joiner's car left the wall, backing slowly toward the center of the track, forcing Warren farther left yet.

I was running out of room. Bearing more and more left, none too stable under heavy braking, I found myself aimed at the end of the wall that separated pit road from the track. It looked sharp as a giant spear—a most uninteresting destination.

To the left of that was pit road, full of people. At maybe 150 mph and unstable, I couldn't think of escaping by that route.

I was almost clear of Joiner—but not quite. Through each eternal millisecond since I saw him, the macro principle was this: I was *not* going to T-bone that car. A T-bone, where the nose of an oncoming car thrust into the door of a car that was broadside on the track, was the most fatal of stock car accidents. So there was only one choice left, and the result was predictable.

I turned the green Chevrolet sharp right. Sure enough, around it went. When it quit rotating, I was going backwards at a forty-five degree angle to the inside wall. I braced for the impact, knowing that my head should be back against the head plate, unwilling to add backward momentum to get it there.

BANG!—a lot more noise than force. Somewhere in the spin, I killed the engine. It seemed to take three or four years to get it fired up again. Being parked sideways on the straight in the middle of a cloud of smoke was an even less interesting location than the spear-shaped end of the wall. Finally it ran. In my eagerness to depart, I probably fried the clutch.

Straightened out and rolling, I hustled around the track and into the pits. There was some vibration, but nothing peculiar in the handling. Could we possibly have gotten away with this?

They changed all four tires and I rejoined the pack. As we circulated under the yellow, not much seemed amiss except for the clutch. It was tender as a baby's bottom. The slightest excess throttle, even in third gear, caused slippage. On the green, nearly everyone went past. It took almost a lap to bring it up to speed. Then I started picking them off again. The clutch held. It barely held, but that was enough. After a while, they hung out my pit board: "U R 12TH." What a lovely sight—but still, a long way to go.

We were a little over two and a half hours into the race, and fatigue was creeping up like a lion through tall grass. It must warily be held off, its approach carefully kept track of. (I couldn't confess fatigue to anyone but myself, not even later; not even when other drivers were taking relief, not even when they needed oxygen after getting out of their cars. Such confession would instantly make a weak woman out of me, too weak to be driving race cars.) At each race, with the changes in handling, the car found a different portion of my anatomy to attack. This time, it was my left arm and the area where a scoliosis troubled my back. On the straights I dropped my left hand into my lap, talking to myself.

Easy now, smooth and easy. The smoother, the faster. Give it its head, don't force it.

I kept lapping the same cars: Ed Negre, Frank Warren, Elmo

Langley—and Cecil Gordon, who always looked over and smiled. Our pit board showed that my lap times were as fast as ever. I thought, *we're all tired, all of us who are out here.*

Then, suddenly, there was our number on the pole, in the top ten. What a sweet sight! I indulged in the luxury of admiring it. Number 68 moved from ninth place to eighth, then seventh...

At the exit of Turn 3, the handling went squirrelly.

A flat!

The car made a hard wiggle to the right, toward the wall. I caught it, gingerly pulled left again, testing. It squirmed. Big trouble. Braking hard, I squeezed into the pit entrance, slithered to a halt, gestured feverishly at the corners of the car.

Why weren't they changing it? Why were the NASCAR pit officials waving their hands no, turning away? Why was Moody making a slicing motion across his throat, kill the engine?

Moody said, take it to the garage.

No! It couldn't be over ... I pounded on the steering wheel, slammed the roof with my hands. Then got a grip, fired it up and drove it in; climbed out and looked. The left rear wheel was slanted in at the top by some ten degrees. The axle housing had snapped in two. Axle housings didn't break; but this one had been salvaged from a badly wrecked car. There was absolutely nothing to do but stand there and take it.

Incredibly dirty, sweaty, and frustrated, I peeled off my gloves. People were starting to run up. Strangers. A guy from the *Times*. What happened. I told him. Pulled off my helmet, wiped my face with the back of my gloves. The creamy Nomex turned black. A crewman arrived from the pits. We looked at each other. I half-smiled, shrugged. There was nothing to be said. Chris Economaki hustled up with his ABC-TV crew. Eventually, I noticed that my back hurt like hell.

Finally, Lynda squeezed through the crowd. We looked a long look at each other. Such a difficult goal, such strength we had both put toward it. So close to being achieved.

"It was a *great* ride," she said. "Do you realize we were in sixth place? They put it on the pole just as you pitted. It's terrible that it broke, but fantastic while it lasted."

Hubbub. I was dragged over to the press box, where I learned it was believed that I had tangled with Carl Joiner, had hit him. *Great.* That's what their assumptions about a woman driver did, I thought:

Joiner spins and crashes, I come along two cars later and miss him completely, damaging my own car in order not to hit his, yet even though it happened right under their noses, their perception of it cast a shadow on my conduct.

Suppressing my indignation, I pointed out that I never touched him; that the Kelly green car bore not a trace of red paint; that there wasn't a mark on it anywhere except at the right rear corner where I backed into the wall. (A film of the accident made the actual scenario clear.) But a person named Cory Farley, with the trade paper *Autoweek*, couldn't be bothered to go and look. He wrote that I "lost it at the exit of Turn 4 and looped into the inside wall after nailing Carl Joiner, who was sitting still dead center in the track." More than thirty years later, this falsehood still rankles.

After twenty minutes, the Kelly PR men hauled me off to their suite. My driver's suit still clung to my skin, sweat-soaked, dusted with rubber bits, and saturated with the extraordinary scent of a hard race. Those pheromones aren't like anything else I've ever smelled in my life—not ugly like the smell of fear or helplessness, but powerful stuff.

A big contingent of women from Kelly's San Francisco office was just coming out the door. They bubbled over with enthusiasm, congratulations and commiseration. Into the middle of that, straight through the crowd, burst Paul Newman with a *really* big hug that seemed to last forever. Through a cloud of euphoria, I could hear a lot of squeals. The Kelly guests thought it was even more exciting than I did, and I thought it was pretty darned exciting.

David Pearson won. Bobby Wawak, my sometime competition, finished sixth.

Ralph Moody was as exuberant as I had ever seen him, when he came to the Kelly suite to watch the end of the race.

"What are you doing to that car?" he asked cheerfully. "First you back it into the wall, then you break its leg, and then you sit there pounding on it!"

"It was good while it lasted, "I said.

A friend and I went to see *Rocky,* the first of the series, new that fall. As we walked home in the gray Manhattan dusk, he said, "There *are* certain inescapable similarities..." and I laughed.

Acquainted now with these peak forms of the game, intimate with the intensity of their demands, I knew I was matched with a challenge that would require all I had, and then some. I loved what lay ahead. It filled my heart.

TOP ROOKIE: THE DAYTONA 500 AND RICHMOND

Whether you were bound for hell or someplace closer, you still had to change planes in Atlanta. As I boarded the flight from there to Daytona Beach on February 10, someone tugged my coat: A. J. Foyt, already seated in first class, greeting me with a smile. He too was entered in the Daytona 500. Back in coach, I passed three of his guys. All were easy in their greetings now, no reservations in their eyes.

NASCAR territory wouldn't be as friendly as this.

With each race last year, the flak had diminished, but in the three-month hiatus since Ontario, it had built up again. Kelly's and Bryant's recent press conferences were speckled with it, skeptical questions and hostile quotes—as if what I'd done in 1976 was so far in the past that it could safely be ignored.

The top NASCAR teams had been testing their cars all winter. All I could do was imagine, as I panted around a quarter-mile high school track on foot, that Cale Yarborough and David Pearson were right in front of me. Or right behind.

"Hi, I'm Jim Lindholm."

He materialized out of the darkness, the swirl and jostle of racing people that filled the fragrant night in Daytona's open-air baggage claim area.

"Thanks for meeting me."

We shook hands. He was about my height, I reckoned, if I didn't have high heels on. He looked to be in his early thirties. "I'm sorry to have interrupted your dinner," I said. A Kelly Girl sponsor function was in progress, and Jim had left it to pick me up.

"Not at all. Here, let me take that for you."

He was neatly dressed, broad-shouldered, muscular, with light brown hair and moustache, strong eyebrows that shielded a direct blue gaze; a delicately modeled chin, small hands and feet.

He was my new stock car crew chief.

His experience was on the short tracks of Washington state. He had come to Moody in January, looking for a job in the heart of big-time auto racing. Lynda said that, in spite of being a Northerner, he was fitting in.

So who was he?—this man who was putting my car together, that should run close to 200 miles an hour? Was he thorough, responsible, would the bolts be tight? Did he care? Did he care about racing, did he care about his work? Did it faze him to work for a woman, was he marking time for a better job? Would he believe what I said? What did he know about making one of these beasts handle? Anything? How much of his short-track experience would apply to Daytona's aerodynamics? Could he learn?

As we drove toward the Beach, I queried him on the car, probing gently. His answers were straight but short, unrevealing; didn't convey what I wanted to know.

A pretentious restaurant crowned our oceanfront hotel. Jim and I found seats across from each other at a long, sparkling table where conversation was in full swing. Besides Lynda, the Kelly executives, Ralph and Mitzi Moody, there were people new to our group: driver Salt Walther and his entourage.

Salt, the heir apparent to Dayton/Walther Enterprises in Ohio, was at the heart of 1973's terrible crash at the start of the Indianapolis 500. Some people thought he was responsible for it. Spectators were injured, and Salt lost most of the fingers of his left hand. He wore a black leather glove to cover the deformity.

At Indianapolis this last May, where he qualified twenty-second, he had been a walking commotion. In the pits he wore a tight jumpsuit with red and yellow lightning stripes, zipped open to the navel, exposing masses of gold chains in his chest hair. On each arm he sported a young woman of equally flamboyant mien and dress. He was twenty-nine years old. A good many drivers thought he wasn't playing with a full deck.

Walther had engaged Ralph Moody to field a car for him at Daytona, his fourth NASCAR race. Now he and his personal press agent were dominating the table, telling stories and jokes.

I kept my eyes mostly on Jim. Throughout dinner he said hardly a word, but watched and listened. He seemed to feel my gaze but didn't return it.

I'd just have to wait and see.

Tech inspection and practice started the next day, Friday the 11th of February. I hadn't been wrong about the atmosphere. To make sure we understood our status at Daytona, NASCAR assigned Salt

Walther's car a place in the covered garage, while mine remained outside in the rain. Ralph Moody must have felt the impact of this treatment also, but he suffered in silence.

Jim Lindholm, I saw, worked hard. He moved with confidence. He was thorough and meticulous; he gave his entire attention to what he was doing. He took orders from Moody well, and he asked questions when he needed to. The questions were intelligent, succinctly phrased.

Will Cronkrite, still in Moody's employ if not in Lynda's, was chiefing Walther's car. I could almost find it in myself to feel sorry for Salt. Cronkrite harboured hard feelings over his removal from the Kelly car, and made it clear that he would soon have Salt going a great deal faster than I ever could. This amused Ralph Moody to no end, and he kept me only too well informed.

As soon as tech was completed, Jim Lindholm had my car ready to go. That was wonderfully reassuring. It was great to have someone help me keep track of NASCAR's plans for practice, for a change. I liked Lindholm more and more.

The bad news came out on the track. I reached 177 mph without too much trouble, 5 mph faster than I'd qualified here in July, even though the front end was wobbling about. (February's cooler temperatures helped.) Push it any harder, though, and the wobble turned into gross instability. Lateral control in the turns was horrible: my lane plus or minus a lane. It meant I couldn't run fast when anyone else was near; couldn't take the chance of my car leaping over and into them.

Pole speed was expected to be in the high 180s. A record eighty-two cars were entered for the Daytona 500 this year.[1] Half of them wouldn't make the field. We struggled with the green Chevrolet Laguna through the weekend. Jim didn't know much about high-speed setups; but he knew enough to know he didn't know.

The first phase of qualifying was set for Sunday. The green Laguna was still wandering. I made a banzai run, one of the riskiest things I ever did in my life. In each turn, especially Turn 2, I wasn't sure whether I would exit next to the wall or ten feet outside the track. The engine, however, pulled without a hitch. The result was 180.603 mph, giving me a starting position of twelfth in one of the twin 125-mile qualifying races on Thursday.

Half an hour later, I was headed for London. I was one of six

---

[1] *The New York Times*, Feb. 13, 1977

finalists out of a hundred nominees for the International Award for Valor in Sports, to be presented in the Guild Hall of London the next day. The organizers had exerted tremendous pressure to get me there, but my priorities were crystal-clear. Only the fact that I luckily drew a spot early in the qualifying order enabled me to catch the connecting flight via Miami, still covered with sweat and dust. The shower in the garage-area drivers' lounge was reserved for men.

Twelve and a half hours later, a Daimler limousine stood waiting at Gatwick. There was barely time to clean up and change. At the 800-year-old Guild Hall, the Orchestra of the Scots Guards trumpeted in the Lord Mayor of London, in his medieval robes and chains. Similarly clad dignitaries followed, while waiters proffered champagne.

In truth, I was abashed at the company I was in. The achievements of the five other finalists cast mine into deep shadow. Shun Fujimoto, for example, led his gymnastic team to Olympic victory with a freshly broken kneecap and torn ligament, and no painkillers. Then there was Niki Lauda. Horribly burned in a crash at the Nurburgring in 1975, the World Champion Grand Prix driver was given last rites. Six weeks later, he was back in competition—even though doctors told him that without immediate skin grafts, which would have kept him in the hospital for three months, he would be disfigured for life.

I couldn't really see how I belonged in this company. All I had done in 1976 was pounce gleefully on the chance of a lifetime. The valor part, if any, lay back in those anonymous years in Ralph Farnham's shop, the grim obsessive struggle to make the Celica competitive on the slimmest of shoestrings.

Niki Lauda and I had met before. He had been a man of considerable physical beauty and great personal charm, ingratiating, a flirt. When he walked into Guild Hall, a murmur ran through it. Disfigured was a mild word. But the amazing thing was, his gaze showed little trace of damage, or the agony he had been through.

You forgot what he looked like, because he *made* you forget.

When presented with the International Award for Valor in Sports, Niki said, "I'm no hero ... it's all part of being a racing driver."

Next morning, the limousine and its driver were at my disposal. It had been years since I was in London. I was twenty then, seeing Europe as a hitch-hiker, sleeping in youth hostels, my total budget just under four dollars a day. I remembered limping into Trafalgar Square in British shoes too small for my American feet, my lunch budget squandered on two exquisite British chocolates.

I asked the driver to take me to Trafalgar Square.

We stopped at the great bronze lions on the south side. Passers-by gawked and peered toward the limo's dark windows. I looked out into the fog, and back in time, and thought about the choices and the turns of fortune that had brought me back to this place.

Take the big chance, I thought, *dare it all ... and you end up in a chauffeured Daimler limousine.*

Or damaged.

Am I as damaged psychologically, after those crushing years with the Celica, as Niki Lauda is physically?

At six that evening I was on the plane back to Florida, laden with whole boxes of exquisite British chocolates for Lynda and the crew.

In practice on Wednesday afternoon, the green Chevrolet Laguna was no better. Ralph Moody mentioned that he had sent driver James Hylton out in it for a few laps.

"He was just testing for leaks," Moody said. "He only ran about a hundred forty-five miles an hour."

Heck, a Winston Cup car was hardly idling at that speed.

Next morning, in the garage area, I hid in the U-Haul truck and turned my mind to Athena. She had been here for practice and qualifying, her presence large, quite still. But now she was elusive. Something was wrong.

What is it, a crash, injury? A crash, however caused, would "prove" my incompetence and by extension, that of other women.

Her answer seemed to be, no, that wasn't it. Her ambiguity remained.

Drivers' meeting, roll call, the usual. As we headed for our cars for the 125-mile race, I intercepted James Hylton and asked him whether he could give me an opinion on my car's handling. He was surprisingly frank.

"Yes," he said. "I told them it was darting. I'm not about to tell Ralph Moody how to set up your car for you..." He gave me a searching look, as if asking whether I liked it like that.

"It's scaring the shit out of me," I said.

"I think the steering ratio is wrong." He paused.

"I couldn't drive a car like that," he said. "Be careful."

By the start of the first qualifying race, I had managed to get my head in gear; was determined to make the best of it. It didn't help. As we whistled into the turns, the cars that had qualified at about my speed just packed up and left. There was no way, weaving and wandering about as I was, that I was going to run side by side with anyone. I dropped six positions, finishing eighteenth. That wasn't good enough to get us into the top thirty starting positions for the Daytona 500 that were established by the qualifying races. We were at great risk of missing the field.

I had been sweating bullets on every lap.

I drove it in and parked it, feeling half asphyxiated and totally wiped out. Through the interviews and TV stuff, I held on to my self-control by the slenderest of margins. Finally they let me go. As I headed back through the garage, Jim Lindholm caught up with me, an air hose coiled across his shoulder.

"You had a tough time out there, didn't you?" he said.

How could I crack, burst into tears, in the middle of this post-race hubbub, the drivers and crews? How could I not? I scratched my forehead for a second, hiding my face with a glove-covered hand, until I mustered a semblance of composure.

"One feels like such a damned fool," I said.

We walked a bit in silence. "Give me half an hour to get the pits packed up," Jim said. "I'll meet you at the truck."

He had seen enough. He had gotten an eyeful of the wobble. He opened his notebook and showed me every component that was in the car, from the moment we arrived. It was a statement of trust, and I was gratified and immensely relieved. This was a solid guy, who wanted to run up front just as badly as I did.

We sat in the U-Haul's cab and talked for a long time: the problems communicating with Ralph Moody; Hylton's input. But how should we proceed? Jim was a stranger to NASCAR, and I was barely more than that. Cronkrite had kept me in the dark, or lied; I had no baseline. What I did have, at long last, was an ally. We set out to see what we could learn about setups for the Daytona 500.

USAC's old hero Jim Hurtubise, the man of the burned hands, drove NASCAR now and then. From the moment we met in the dark bar of the Speedway Motel, he had been friendly and open. Now he was generous, even though he had qualified slower than I. He thought both front springs were too soft.

Later I reached Ted Wenz in New York, one of the best chassis sorters in SCCA open-wheel racing. He pointed out that, now that the back was fixed, any previously existing front-end problems would be unmasked and, since the front was being made to work harder, aggravated.

Within the hour, Lynda had a copy of the starting field for Sunday's race, the Daytona 500. We had made it. The rules assigned the last ten spots, on the basis of qualifying speed, to those whose finishing positions in the 125-mile races weren't high enough. My banzai qualifying run had put us in the last, fortieth spot. Johnny Rutherford and Bill Elliott missed the show. Johnny had finished nineteenth in the second 125-miler; he too suffered handling problems. "If it's loose and spooky," he told the Daytona paper, "I can't run in the traffic."

I rode back to the hotel with Ralph Moody, hoping to persuade him that action was required. Again, he sang his long song about how "they're all doing that."

Jim called my room, and we compared notes. Without Ralph's cooperation, we might not be able to do much.

I wrote in my journal: What I think is, there's no hope of working with Ralph Moody. He won't believe anything I tell him about a race car, and I don't believe he can set up a race car. How can that be possible? His reputation is huge. Yet I can't ignore the evidence. Either I can't believe in myself as a driver, can't believe what my senses tell me, or he's wrong.

Not long after the 125-mile race, I had run into Joe Frasson, whose car I had driven for a few laps at Charlotte in May of '76. Before the race he had said, "Be careful out there" when the more customary salutation was "Have a good day." Now he stopped me for a moment.

"That was a nice save," he said.

I didn't know what he was talking about.

"Turn Three—my transmission went. I swear to God, I didn't know how you were going to miss me. When you got by, you were so sideways I was sure you'd lost it. Anyway, thanks."

I was glad; but thought to myself, *that took no more than anything else I did out there. That's why I don't remember it.*

On Friday, we made no progress. Jim and I proposed various changes; Moody turned them down.

Just one practice session remained. I rode out to the track Saturday morning with Lynda, who urged me to make one more attempt to persuade Moody that something had to be done.

I found Moody and told him we had to talk. We sat in his van. I didn't bring Herk's or the others' names into it, but said that stiffening the front would seem to make sense; made a trapezoid with my hands, to show how the leverage would be, with the wider rear axle installed.

We went through two rounds of "they all do that." I didn't seem to be making a dent.

"You can't expect to run with these other guys right away," he said, "they've been around a long time. You gotta learn to drive it down in the turns or it's *gonna* feel bad."

I was at the end of my rope. I said, "I can brave it out by myself. I can run a couple of laps qualifying not really knowing whether I'm going to put it in the wall coming out. But I can't run next to other drivers that way, because that's *their* life."

It's possible that he noticed my voice starting to shake.

He said, "I'll see what I can find out."

It was out of my hands now, the die was cast, whether he found something that worked or didn't. This was our last chance.

Later I learned that he talked with Donnie Allison and with A. J. Foyt. I don't know who persuaded him to change the setup in the green Chevrolet. Jim flew into action.

Just before the last practice session, Jim told me what some of the changes were. A stiffer right front spring, a front sway bar nearly three times as stiff. More than three times as much caster on the right, twice as much on the left. Huge changes.

I warmed it up, stood on the gas. Soon I was flying through the turns.

It's fixed! Sonofabitch, it's fixed!

After four laps I brought it in for tire temperatures, then out again. I was running four miles an hour faster than the day before, and it was *easy*.

I can run next to the wall, I can put it where I want it, I can do anything, it's fixed!

In my exuberance I failed to pay sufficient attention to the rapid loosening of the rear. The car was losing its wedge, probably as the rear springs settled; that heated the rear tires to the point where they lost their grip. In the middle of Turn 2, the back end slipped out. I was too close to the wall to catch it, didn't have room to turn right.

Uh-oh. The hundredths of a second stretched out, infinitely elastic, like time at the speed of light.

Well, better hit it flat.

I twitched right just enough to broadside the wall, rather than take all the force on the rear corner; held it there for an instant, eased off and down to the bottom of the track as carefully as porcupines procreate. It had made quite a racket, but nothing seemed terrifically wrong. At a less-than-aerodynamic speed, I taxied back to the pits.

I was so happy I could hardly stand it. Jim and Ralph were understandably confused by this. They pried out the fenders and re-set the toe, readjusted the wedge, changed the outside tires. I was wildly impatient to fix whatever trivia might have been affected, hot to go out again. In two laps it was clear that the handling had changed—the camber was knocked way off—but we were still in the ballpark. I came in for a full set of new tires, and scuffed them two laps for the race. Then the checkered flag waved, the track closed.

If ever there was a hair's-breadth save, that was it.

At driver introductions, I took Ralph Moody to collect the kiss from the beauty queen. After all, at the end, he had indeed sought out the right advice, and agreed to change.

At the start of the Daytona 500, it took me a dozen or so laps to figure out how, with its new setup, the car really wanted to be driven. The big difference was on the entrance to the turns. At the instant you hit the banking, while the car was still light and floaty and the steering neutral, you needed to crank the steering wheel all the way over, about ninety degrees. When the banking took hold and the mass of the car bore down on the outside tires, you needed to be aimed about as far left as you were likely to get; otherwise the car would try to squirm up the track. Had I driven it like that before, I'd have backed into the wall fast enough to go all the way through it.

On the fourth lap of the race, the car of my Ontario playmate, Bobby Wawak, caught fire. At close to 180 mph, the airstream fed flame toward the driver with the force of a blowtorch. He braked hard toward the infield, leaped out while the car was still moving, ran toward the track hospital.

The second yellow, for a stalled car, was well-timed for me to refuel and get fresh tires. But when I pitted, the crew looked like the Keystone Kops. What the hell was going on? Confusion reigned. The pack, slowly circling the huge track behind the pace car, came abreast of our pit and went on by. Steam came out my ears. We had just gone a lap down. It was bad enough to break my concentration for the next lap or two.

A set of wrong-size lug nuts had somehow been affixed to one of the wheels, and the air supply to one of the wheel wrenches was disconnected. Thinking about it recently, I wondered whether it was sabotage. Back then, I wasn't that paranoid. The radios were barely functioning, and the next yellow was a short one. By the time they brought me in, the track was green. It cost us another lap. The good news was that out on the track, the green Laguna was handling better than ever. It was so stable that even the day's high winds, gusting to 30 mph, didn't upset it much. I had a wonderful time, feeling delectably ferocious as I passed cars right and left.

Johnny Rutherford and I had quickly worked our way up from the back of the field. (NASCAR predictably found a way to include him in the race, by disqualifying one of Bobby Wawak's cars. That moved me up to thirty-ninth, and Johnny started fortieth.) He worked wonders in traffic, using the draft for all it was worth. It was great fun to be running so close, and watch his moves. Unfortunately, he was forced out on the twenty-ninth lap.

Mostly, I had clear sailing. The big attention-getter was Salt Walther. Lynda and the guys told me afterwards that every time I lapped him, he pulled into the pits, yelling at the top of his voice for Cronkrite to do something. Out on the track, Walther was a loose cannon. At one point I overtook him in the D, the long tricky curve in front of the main grandstands. No other cars were near. I was almost committed to the pass when he moved over, suddenly and hard. Good thing I was suspicious, ready for trouble, or he'd have put me in the wall. I hit the brakes—a touchy thing to do on that part of the track—and he missed. Two turns later I got safely past him, and went on.

Later I lapped him yet again, but this time a complication lay ahead: traffic, an unstable clump of three cars, one of them right on the ragged edge. Its driver, normally a more sensible fellow, was trying to keep up with competition that outclassed his car. For the last lap or two, I had been looking for a clean shot past the lot of them. They were holding me up, and Walther was able to catch my draft. He tucked up close, bobbing and weaving. Now I was a sandwich: one squirrel ahead, and another on my rear bumper. It couldn't last.

When this knot comes undone, I thought, I want enough room between me and it to thread my way through the wreckage.

I eased off the gas, dropped back. It didn't take long. Salt later claimed that a car had nudged him from behind. He veered up three lanes and took out Buddy Baker, who was contending for the lead, and Dave Marcis as well. Most of the debris had come to rest by the time I reached it, and my car was unharmed. Baker's car was crunched and the handling spoiled, though he soldiered on to the end of the race. Salt was unhurt. His car was firmly stuck into the wall.

When the green came out, I picked up the pace again.

On the yellow after that, the double line that formed for the restart put me abreast of A. J. Foyt. When the cars were steadied, I looked over. The cool cosmic cowboy was chewing gum; looked back with an easy, happy smile and a wave.

Toward the end of the race, I was running 179 mph—almost as fast as my qualifying speed—at a time when race leader Cale Yarborough, who qualified at 188, was running 182. Lynda, keeping lap times in the pits, showed the lap sheet to Jim. "Not too shabby," she said.

Ten laps from the finish, I was in eighth place.

Then the engine went sickeningly soft. I smelled the escaping oil, saw black smoke behind, pitted. Moody looked under the hood, and waved me out again. Hugging the bottom of the track, I was shown in ninth place at the checkered flag.[2] A subsequent official recount dropped me to twelfth—but nevertheless, Top Rookie of the Daytona 500.

It was a good race. Cale Yarborough's victory put him on the cover of *Sports Illustrated* that week. Benny Parsons was the only other driver on the lead lap. A. J. Foyt, finishing sixth, was three laps down. The spread was typical of races of that era.

Later, at the hotel, I dropped off the prize money checks to Lynda at her room. "We got away with it this time," I said, "we lucked out, but it can't go on. If Ralph won't believe what I tell him about the car, we have to find someone who will."

Lynda said, "Part of the problem is, the sponsors, the top guy at Kelly has perfect confidence in Ralph, it's a big part of why he bought the program this year."

"I don't care if he *is* Ralph Moody," I said. "It can't come down to the eleventh hour before we make a dent in him."

"I hear you," Lynda said.

Moody was hosting a party in his room. The sponsors were there, and some of the crew, everyone pleased as punch. So we celebrated along with them. Why not?

By the end of that week, we were in Richmond, Virginia. Ahead lay a new hurdle, something completely different. Richmond Fairgrounds Raceway was a short track, a flat half-mile. With its laps in the 21-second range, there'd hardly be time to take a deep breath between turns. Besides, short tracks were notoriously the last holdout of the infamous NASCAR crashing and banging, pushing and shoving style.

[2] Des Moines *Register*, April 10, 1977

Most of the hot teams had short-track cars built especially for the five half-mile tracks on the Winston Cup Circuit. We, of course, had only the Laguna, a superspeedway car, but that wasn't my main concern. My adventures in Wisconsin taught me how little I knew about short-tracking. I was blunt about this at the press conference arranged by Kenneth Campbell, the genial, gentlemanly track promoter. He'd given me a copy of Wednesday's Richmond *News Leader*, which noted:

"Last weekend at Daytona, the word went up and down the pits that Janet was entered in the rough-and-tumble Richmond race. Some of the drivers simply chuckled. One smiled and said, 'Let's put it this way. She'll get lots of experience.'"

"They've laughed before," I said, "beginning at Charlotte. But they may be right about the experience. I'm a damn good race driver, but I'm not Wonder Woman."

Campbell had arranged an introduction before the Virginia House of Delegates in Thomas Jefferson's exquisitely beautiful Capitol, its home since 1788. As the members stood to applaud, I was swept back in memory to the year before: the grim desperate labor, the borrowed garage I might be thrown out of at any moment, the scuttling of furtive creatures in dark corners.

Richmond marked the team's first outing with a truck of our very own. Lynda had bought a handsome GMC. It wasn't a huge chrome-laden eighteen-wheel tractor-trailer like Petty's or some of the others, but a neat, compact unit that swallowed the race car, the tires, a couple of spare engines, and all the rest of the support equipment. The truck also served me as a changing room (it came in the nick of time, since the public women's rooms at Richmond were outside the race track, inaccessible).

Ralph Moody's position on chassis-sorting had softened a little, but not much. Practice was sharply limited. The track opened Friday morning, with the first round of qualifying set for the afternoon. My qualifying attempt was dead slow. We would have one more chance, the next day. I went running with Jim that evening after the track closed, pounding my frustrations into the soft red shoulders of the road that led toward the airport; hashing over possible setup changes with him as we settled into a jog. We paused a moment before turning back.

He said, "I'm convinced that, if the car is right, you'll push the button. You have the capability and ... you have the courage."

Funny word, courage, it just sits there, it's a word not much used, people get embarrassed about it. Jim looked me right in the eye while he said it.

In the morning, there was the usual frenzy of photographers. Lynda watched with amusement. "Ringling Brothers just called," she announced after a while. "They've got this elephant you'd look great on."

"Thanks, pal."

Escaping for a moment, I asked Ralph Moody to join me inside the truck, where we were sheltered from prying eyes and ears. I spoke in deadly earnest, and our tough conversation ended in a meeting of the minds. The day went well. We qualified third fastest of the twenty cars that made the field that day, putting me thirteenth in the field at 90.505 mph, and fastest rookie. Ricky Rudd, one of my major competitors for Rookie of the Year, was five spots behind. Then we changed a few more things, and went faster yet. Jim could apply his short-track experience here. The car still pushed heavily, but we were in the ballpark.

On race day, the pace was furious from the start. It wasn't long before my inexperience combined with the car's heavy push to trip me up. I went into Turn 1 too deep. My car plowed toward the wall, refusing to answer the wheel. The driver behind seized his opportunity to dart inside, and that was all it took. I was trapped on the outside lane while a train of seven cars went by underneath. All I could do was grit my teeth.

Darrell Waltrip brought out the first yellow by spinning at about the twentieth lap, which gave me a chance to organize my thinking. With thirty cars fitted into half a mile, the track was busier than a hornet's nest. I couldn't afford another mistake like that. How to deal with the push?

Once again, I drew on my Jaguar days. When the green came out, I dived into the first turn faster than before, then whipped my foot suddenly off the gas. The back end of the car snapped toward the outside. When the nose was aimed where I wanted it, I got back on the gas again. Problem solved—for the most part.

Just as advertised, there was plenty of pushing and shoving in this race. It wasn't that anyone was picking on me; they did it to each other just as freely. Now I started pushing back. I kept lapping a red and black car that moved over for everyone else but me. When he shut the door on me for about the third time, I gently nudged him out of the way.

This was fun!

Ahead of me now was Ed Negre, a short-track veteran, and he was unwilling to be passed. He leaned on me when I tried the outside, using my adhesion to help him get through the turns. He also leaned on everyone else. This was entertaining to watch, but dirtier than I was willing to copy. So I tucked in behind, and let him push people out of the way for both of us. After a while I got past him, and went on.

I was starting to get the hang of this. Directly ahead lay my next prey. Trouble was, Cale Yarborough was coming up from behind. Could I get past the slower car before Cale arrived on my bumper? I thought so.

I was wrong.

Whump! My car swayed as Cale nudged me aside.

Oh, shit.

I've caught enough flak from Cale without even doing anything to him. Now he's hit me, and I deserved it.

Well, I couldn't worry about it now. The fray continued. Every now and then, the bumping escalated into major wrecks. I wriggled through them all scot-free. My tail-out cornering technique gave drivers a tempting target, and the tail got smacked quite a bit. It didn't cause any problems.

Meanwhile, I was slowly realizing I'd made one huge and irremediable mistake. With Bobby Wawak's burns at Daytona in vivid memory, I had chosen to wear full Indy-car Nomex underwear and a head sock, as well as the double-layer suit. It was like wearing a ski suit to do aerobics in a sauna. I was grossly overheated, and would soon need relief. But we were past the halfway point, and if something stopped the race now—rain, say, like what was developing in the northwest—the race would be declared complete. How long could I keep this up?

Every twenty-two seconds, that darkened quadrant of sky came into view. *Athena,* I prayed, *those dark colors are yours. Athena, send the rain.*

Deep purple-gray-blue clouds loomed overhead. My lap times had fallen off by half a second. I was still holding my own among drivers I had run with at the start, but it couldn't last.

Finally, the rain came. Huge blots spattered the windshield, while the sky turned to ink.

Why don't they throw the yellow?

I was hanging on with my eye teeth. Track action was spectacular as cars skidded about the increasingly slippery surface. At last, the yellow lights winked on.

They ran us around under the yellow for what seemed an eternity, while the heavens opened and lightning flared. Paradoxically, now that the requirement for performance was gone, I felt even worse than before.

Red ... please, please throw the red ... what's the point of circulating in a downpour? I had seen traffic on freeways come to a standstill for less than this.

Finally, they red-flagged us to a stop on the front straight. It would be a cold day in hell—or on a short track, rather—before I wore long johns and a head sock again.

Slowly, the drivers climbed out of their cars. I undid the belts, pulled off my helmet. The cold air felt wonderful. I hitched myself out the window, stood ... and everything went black.

Quickly I leaned forward and down, braced my hands on my knees, braced my weight against the warm flank of the car. The track swam back into view. No one seemed to have noticed.

I can't pass out. Other drivers can pass out, I've seen it happen, once they're out of their cars. Richard Petty can pass out.[3] *But I mustn't do it.*

Jim Lindholm came hustling up with an umbrella and the car cover. "Come on," he yelled as he threw the cover over the roof.

"Not yet," I said.

Could I actually get away with pretending I thought this torrential downpour was going to end in moments, and I wouldn't leave the car because I was just unbearably eager to get back in the race?

Maybe to everyone else; but not to Jim, I couldn't. I told him.

So he stayed with me, maintaining the fiction, holding the edge of the car cover over our heads. Every now and then, I straightened up a little to see if things were still turning black. A color picture of us like that ended up on the cover of *Panorama*, a Virginia Sunday news magazine. I was smiling to beat the band, and the pose looked almost credible.

It must have been ten minutes before I figured I could walk to our truck, where Lynda and the guys were keeping some reporters entertained. "More, gimme more," I grinned. "All that crashing and banging, whoo-eee! I like that."

Near dark, the race was called. We were twelfth, and Top Rookie for the second time in a row.

[3] "I've passed out when I've gotten out of the car ... It just seems when you turn the motor off, you turn yourself off too." Richard Petty, quoted in *Stock Car Racing Magazine*, March 1978.

Recovered, I picked up champagne for everyone on the way back to the motel. We gathered in Ralph Moody's room. He was as happy as I had ever seen him, and called a friend with the news.

"She's meaner'n Cale Yarborough," he said, "beatin' on people's tails, whammin' 'em. She thought it was fun."

Moody had warmed toward Lynda and me, and we were rewarded with a few of his classic tales. It would be hopeless to reproduce them without gesture and sound effects; but a sample of their substance was the time he won a race while unconscious, taking the checkered flag after his windshield blew in and knocked him out cold after the final turn.

A reporter arrived, a woman who had been with us all weekend. She had just come from the winner's press conference, where Cale was queried closely about our encounter.

"He said, 'Why are you singling her out? We just went for the same spot at the same time. It happened with about ten other drivers today, too. She drives as well as any rookie I've seen.'"

Lynda and the guys and I whooped with laughter and delight. This was progress indeed.

The Richmond *Times Dispatch* commented next day, "Janet Guthrie insists she is not Wonder Woman. She is wrong."

LOADED FOR BEAR

Everywhere we went that fertile spring, progress was the word. Ahead lay the NASCAR races at Atlanta, Bristol and Talladega, each bursting with luscious promise. The path back to Indianapolis, the Everest of racing, lay entwined with and reinforced by the stock car events. Fueled with joyous anticipation, I leaped toward the next upward steps.

Based on the addition of Merchants Bank funding (which Bryant later bought out) to his basic Bryant sponsorship, Rolla Vollstedt purchased a prototype Lightning driven by Roger McCluskey the previous season. Our sponsor contracts specified a "proven car" for me, and the Lightning was said to have exceeded 198 mph in a private testing session on the newly repaved Indianapolis Motor Speedway. That speed might or might not have been achieved with the legal maximum turbocharger boost; but the car had qualified well in 1976. McCluskey put it sixth fastest in the field for the Indianapolis 500, at 186.500 mph,[1] then second fastest in September at Ontario, a faster track, at 189.235.[2] Rolla took its design as the point of departure to start building a new car for Dick Simon.

My debut in the Lightning was planned for the first USAC Championship race of the year, a 200-miler at Ontario in March, one week after the Richmond NASCAR race. My hot new race car was beautiful: sleek and elegant, white with lime-green trim. But when practice opened, the hot new race car's engine wouldn't start. Not for a whole morning. Around 1 p.m. they got it running, and I warmed it up. Even at such low speeds, the Lightning was wildly different from last year's car. It had a creamy-smooth feel to it, like the fast-caterpillar feeling of A. J. Foyt's Coyote. I brought it in for a plug check, then out and stood on the gas.

Wow.

Except for a handful of laps at Phoenix in November, it had been

[1] Indianapolis 500 Yearbook, 1976 and 1977
[2] Los Angeles *Times*, Sept. 3, 1976

six months since I last drove a Champ car. What a rocket the thing was—even with a malfunctioning engine, which resisted cure. When practice came to an end, I dived headlong into my frustration consolation: pork rinds, M&M's, and beer.

Dick Simon lost an engine in the silver Vollstedt car on his third lap, a broken piston. Rolla had brought two spare engines, and the guys spent the night replacing it.

Next morning a high wind swept the valley, gusting to 40 mph. It buffeted the garage-area buildings, turbulent and wild. When it stopped, it came back even harder from the other direction. Dust and grit flew from the valley floor, stung the face, burned the eyes. A wind like this could toss our cars around like paper airplanes, and the track stayed closed most of the day. It opened long enough for Dick Simon to lose his second engine. There was one spare left. In principle, it was the spare for my car.

Rolla took me aside. "We're down to our last spare engine," he began. As always, he was being scrupulously fair. Before he started his next sentence, I interrupted.

"Of course," I said.

The engine went into Dick's car. The wind howled. There was no more Champ car practice that day. The next morning, Saturday, I lost an engine on the second lap. It was a burned piston this time.

Rolla immediately set out to find another engine to purchase or rent. I found a quiet corner and thought about it. With only six hot laps in the new car, I was still slow, and not at all comfortable. Qualifying was imminent. There'd be no more practice, by the time the engine was changed.

If I got super-tweaked, I thought, I might add ten miles an hour on the qualifying run—and I still wouldn't be at the car's potential. We'd all look bad.

Rolla returned from his engine hunt, discouraged.

In the end, economics tilted the balance. Rolla withdrew my car from the race. I agreed it was for the best; and ate more pork rinds.

The *Today* show had sent Barbara Hunter to Ontario for an interview. We did it in one of the trackside suites.

"Someone asked me," she said, "if I could be anyone else, who would I most like to be? And I said, Janet Guthrie. Now, if you had to be someone else, who would you choose to be?"

"Uhh—ahh—a social butterfly!"

I don't know which surprised me most, the question or my answer to it. Where the heck did that come from? Could it be that my tingling sensation of returning life, in this glorious, hopeful springtime, had liberated my long-suppressed desire for a normal social life?

Back in NASCARland, practice opened on Thursday, St. Patrick's Day, for the Winston Cup 500-mile race at Atlanta. The Kelly green color of my Kelly Chevrolet failed to bring us the day's good luck. The handling was awful. On Friday things were worse. Our qualifying attempts weren't even close.

Saturday offered our last chance to qualify. I was awake at five that morning, replaying practice laps in my mind. The car wasn't right, that was clear enough. If I tried to run the conventional line, follow the other drivers through the turns, it was hopeless. What could I try that was different—different enough to turn a failing into an advantage?

Atlanta was a high-banked track. The fastest line was normally up at the top, near the wall. When practice opened Saturday morning, I tried out my new idea. Just before the entrance to Turn 1, I peeled away from the wall and dived for the bottom of the track. As I clipped the flat part between Turns 1 and 2, I snapped my foot off the throttle completely. Just as at Richmond, this sudden change broke the back end loose, and I came back hard on the gas. As the car drifted up the banking, it stabilized, so that I could keep full throttle from the bottom all the way up to the top of the banking and, of course, from there on down the straight. The car took to this treatment like a duck to water. My heart soared. Turns 3 and 4 required a slight variation, and traffic could complicate matters, but it looked like I'd found the answer.

Then, WHUMP! Bits of engine—smoke—oil—Turn 3 a heartbeat away.

I wrestled it down out of the groove and onto the flat part while killing the ignition, accessories, differential cooler; whistled into pit road still trailing oil and smoke. Balancing momentum against maneuverability, I made the U-turn into the garage area and coasted to a stop in our spot while the guys were still running to catch up. The last round of qualifying would begin in less than three hours.

There's nothing like a crisis engine change to draw a crowd in the garage area. The crews of thirty cars that had made the field had little to do. We worked within an attentive circle of expert onlookers. For the first time in this venue of competition—really, the first time it had been necessary—I picked up the wrenches and dove in with the rest of the crew.

Ten spots remained open in the field for tomorrow's race. Twenty-seven drivers would soon try to fill those spots—among them Cecil Gordon. If we didn't finish our engine change in time, I would be one less driver for Cecil to try to beat. Money and points were at stake.

"I'll get my auxiliary pump," Cecil said. "You'll never get the engine pieces out of the oil system without one." And he did. One of his guys worked like a bear to flush the system, scooping up the deadly shards of metal. At the very last minute, we found the oil pump itself was jammed. Donnie Allison pulled a pump off his spare engine for us. We were in business.

Trouble was, we had yet to post a lap anywhere near fast enough to qualify. My newly discovered technique wasn't fully developed; there hadn't been time. Practice was over. Our next laps would comprise the qualifying run. In case we needed a little more pressure, we could think of the busloads of Kelly Girl employees filling the sponsor's expensively rented, catered suite overlooking the track.

I walked along with the car as the guys pushed it toward the front of the qualifying line. I felt it and smelled it, making the car part of myself.

How to describe the strange space you inhabit, the place you go to, when getting ready to attempt the improbable if not the impossible? Athletes and opera singers know about this place. It's where I found the extra miles an hour.

We posted the fourth fastest time of day, putting us thirty-fourth on the grid. Once again, I qualified faster than Johnny Rutherford (who would start twenty-third, since he qualified on Friday.)

And Cecil Gordon made it, on the last row.

After three days of stress, we were one happy team that night. Lynda Ferreri, Ralph Moody, and all the crew came to celebrate in my suite with delectable Southern barbecue.

Dinner was over and the guys were drifting out the door when the man I'm calling Alex appeared. We had met earlier in the year, and sparks flew almost instantaneously.

"Congratulations," he said. "That was a nice run today."

Lynda, Jim, Alex and I talked for a while. Alex was the last to leave. For a while I thought he was going to make a move. It didn't happen.

Pale pink flowering cherries filled the courtyard. I watched Alex walk out into the fragrant night and vanish into the darkness under the cherry trees.

Next morning, race day, was sunny and cool. A heavy rain in the night left drifts and rivulets of pink petals on the lawn around the pool. I woke early, as usual before a race, and let my conscious mind play over the night's deep dreaming.

Should we tighten up the car, add a couple of rounds of bite? "Bite" was another word for wedge, the different amount of weight carried by each rear wheel, except that wedge was measured in inches while bite was measured in turns or rounds of the threaded upper spring perches. Less wedge or bite made the car looser (oversteering); more bite, the reverse. Musing over the way a track changed in the first hour of a race as rubber and oil were laid down on it, I concluded that we should add bite.

I was too late. The crew had been especially industrious this morning. By the time I reached the track, the car was already through technical inspection and out on the line—earlier than required. It was no longer legal to lay a wrench on it, until after the green flag. I was to regret that a very great deal before the race was half an hour old.

The NASCAR driver-introduction ceremonies were the usual ordeal. Again, I took Ralph Moody to collect the kiss from the beauty queen. (I had mixed feelings about this: it meant I, too, was treating the beauty queen as a sex object, the spoils of battle. But heck, nobody forced her to be a beauty queen, and it sure got me off the hook.) Then I was called back. A representative of First National City Bank had a pair of $500 checks to present, for my top-rookie finishes at the Daytona 500 and at Richmond. The poor fellow looked like he enjoyed handing those prizes to the female rookie about as much as I liked dealing with the beauty queen.

The clock wound down toward race time. I hated this stretch of time, when the butterflies arrived to do their work. Then *The Star Spangled Banner*, perhaps the worst moment of all; it felt like "we who are about to die salute you." We climbed into our cars. Three pace laps, then the green. Stand on the gas.

Starting as far back as I was, but with the car now capable of running faster, the pack ahead looked to me like the Long Island Expressway on Sunday afternoon. It gave the impression of crawling, though clouds of dust proved otherwise. I bobbed and weaved, looking for a way through traffic. By the time the pack got strung out, I had already passed a lot of the Friday qualifiers and was having a ding-dong battle with Tighe Scott, the driver whom Salt Walther had accused of causing his multi-car crash at Daytona. Tighe made his orange Chevrolet exceptionally difficult to pass. Meanwhile, sure enough, the car was getting loose, and looser still.

Damn! Sure wish I'd gotten those two rounds of bite before the start. I'll get it when we stop for the first yellow.

But there wasn't any yellow! We ran straight through to the fuel stop, a hundred and thirty miles, with nary an incident. The radio ceased to function on the first lap. No one could hear my transmissions, my urgent request for bite as soon as I reached the pits. Nor could I hear any message to pit for fuel, but had to locate and read it on my pit board.

The leading handful of cars crept up behind. It had taken them this long to put a lap on me, and they gained ground at a snail's pace. That was exciting! At exactly the wrong moment, I lost my grip on one of the most important maxims in racing, one I thought I had internalized years ago: you can *never* afford to get excited on the race track. It caused a bad mistake. On the pit stop, I didn't tell them I needed bite until too late. By the time I got the message across, the car was off the jacks, and they waved me out. I cussed my lapse all the way down pit road, then got a grip. There'd be no more excitement today.

Once again, incredibly, there were no yellows for the whole tankful of gas. My car got looser and looser, the back end trying to overtake the front at every move of the steering wheel.

So how many rounds of bite do I need now? Four? Six? Is it remotely possible that two would do it?

As the laps on the scoreboard approached 130 and my pit board finally appeared, I settled on four. Crewman Sid Slimp twisted the wrench on the right rear spring perch while they changed left-side tires, and I smoked back out onto the track in record time.

Oh, wow, does that feel good!

It took a few laps to figure out how very much faster I could go. I made sure the new tires had reached their operating temperature and stabilized, then tried out the high line and found I still couldn't hold it. But on my idiosyncratic low line, the handling was all I could ask for. Just at that point, the leaders drew up behind. David Pearson was leading the race. Donnie Allison, second, was a few car lengths back.

Sonofabitch, I can run with them!

This time I kept the pleasure very well controlled.

I let Pearson by, then tucked in behind him on the front straight. We entered Turn 1. I peeled away from the wall, swooped for the bottom, and rose up at the exit of Turn 2 side by side with his white and red car. The big gold letters of David's famous Woods Brothers machine gleamed in the sunlight, two feet away. We ran side by side down the back straight, so that I entered Turn 3 from the lower lane. With this slight disadvantage, I exited Turn 4 a few inches behind him, drifting up to the wall in David's draft.

This went on lap after lap.

Sid Slimp said afterwards, "He thought he had a green car pasted on his mirror! He couldn't believe it, he thought someone cut out a picture and stuck it there!"

Traffic confused the issue a couple of times. Donnie Allison pitted. Finally, I got a good clear shot at Turns 1 and 2, and made the most of it. At the exit of Turn 2, I had half my car's length ahead of David Pearson. With a faster exit speed than his, I held the lead all the way down the back straight.

Lynda Ferreri said afterwards, "Fifty thousand people stood up and *screamed!*"

On the next lap, Pearson pitted.

My car's handling remained right on target. At various times on this tankful, I flew by Elliott Forbes-Robinson as if he were tied to a stump. Tighe Scott moved down for me now, as I had for him. Sam Sommers, one of my main competitors for Rookie of the Year, had vanished out front at the beginning of the race. Now, I must have been ten miles an hour faster. It was luscious.

But where was the pit board? I'd been looking for it for several laps. The engine coughed, then quit. They had miscounted the laps, run me out of gas.

It happened just a bit too deep in Turn 4 to reach the pit entrance. I coasted two miles around the track, hugging the bottom, praying I'd make it back to the pits without a wrecker. Slowly I rolled in, they filled it up, and off I went.

The engine, however, had been dealt a mortal blow. Most likely, the insufficiency of fuel created a lean condition that burned a hole in a piston. Trailing smoke, feeling as if my heart would break, I packed it in. We were through.

In the pits, Lynda Ferreri looked as if she would burst into tears. I put my arm around her shoulder. "Next time," I said.

Later, I thought about the meaning of that spontaneous gesture of solace and support, not a hug but a form of embrace used more often by men than by women, to transfuse strength and confidence, as if they were blood. The gesture seemed to characterize the relationship between Lynda and me: more typical of male bonding than of female friendship. We worked in pursuit of a shared goal, the highest possible racing finishes, which was serious business to us both. Lynda was totally confident of my ability on the track, and I was totally confident of her support and her strengths. Above all, we were women allies in a man's world, a good part of which still bristled against us. Sometimes I felt as if we were the Two Musketeers, fending off the evil Cardinal's hordes.

In any event, the race at Atlanta was our best performance yet; and bore the promise that better still would come. Lynda had remarked, early on, that the sexism inherent in NASCAR racing was an astonishment to her. Now, she said, "I feel like we're standing outside the walls of Jericho blowing our trumpets—and the walls are falling down!"

The alarm rang long before dawn. I had an early-morning flight from Atlanta to Indianapolis for a day's worth of meetings with Rolla Vollstedt and our Indy-car sponsors. I was stiff and sore, as usual after a stock car race—as if I had spent the day inside the tumbler of a concrete mixer—but my heart was singing.

It wasn't just that I had run with David Pearson, who was leading the Atlanta 500, and had even passed him for half a lap. It wasn't just the cherry blossoms, and Alex. There was one thing more, something that made me feel like a kid before Christmas: something Johnny Rutherford said.

Not long before the start of the race, our paths crossed in pit road, and we paused.

"You know, Janet," he said, "A. J. hasn't given me a moment's rest since you outqualified me again. I told him, 'A. J., your turn will come.'"

After Atlanta, in the month before Indianapolis, Rolla Vollstedt brought the Lightning to Ontario for three days of testing and development. Instead of being a day late and a dollar short when we arrived at the Indianapolis Speedway, we'd be prepared, loaded for bear, ready to show what we could do.

But Ontario was also where I discovered how elusive the edge was, in the Lightning. While my lap speeds rose ever higher, the car told me nothing about its ultimate grip. The feeling of the chassis changed not a whit. I was baffled by this.

A couple of years later, I mentioned my inability to sense the Lightning's edge to driver Jerry Grant. "Didn't you know?" Jerry said.

"*Nobody* could find the edge with a rising-rate rear suspension. What good is a faster suspension design if the driver can't tell what's going on? That's why everyone who ever owned one of those cars got rid of the rising-rate rear."

Jerry's remarks felt like sunrise. My season in the Lightning, however, was spent in the dark on this.

Nevertheless, I carried away from Ontario a delicious, full-bodied sense of readiness for the opening of Indianapolis Motor Speedway. For the first time, I felt we'd be on an even footing with much of the competition. The car might be a year old, but it was a good fast car. Other teams might have done more extensive testing, but at least we had gotten a grip.

Our last night in Ontario, we celebrated at dinner. Dick and Melanie Simon chose a restaurant where the artichokes were superb and the waiters wore short shorts. They were good looking young guys, and as Dick and I talked about race car setups, I amused myself by ogling their muscular legs. This pleasant diversion might almost have been a metaphor for the revolution in women's lives in 1977. I, a woman, had just lapped Ontario Motor Speedway at the highly satisfactory speed of 180-odd mph, and now might boldly eye the attractions of the opposite sex.

It's about time, I thought gleefully, that the tables were turned.

Next morning, Thursday, I was on an eastbound plane. Practice would open Friday for the NASCAR race at Bristol, a high-banked half-mile track deep in the Appalachian mountains. This was Daniel Boone territory, where the corners of Tennessee, eastern Kentucky, and West Virginia met. Elizabethan English was still spoken in some of the more remote hollows, and the start of a race at Bristol was traditionally hailed with a full chorus of that blood-curdling cacophony known as the Rebel Yell.

The promoter had scheduled a press conference for Thursday evening, complete with local and state dignitaries. But my flight had a fire onboard, and I drove into Bristol two hours late. The promoter had held on to his crowd by plying them liberally with booze. The roomful of men was boisterous, irritated, unruly, just on the edge of getting out of control. One could well imagine what sort of humor they had been passing around as they waited. The track rep looked acutely uneasy, and so did a couple of women near the walls.

It didn't take five seconds to get the picture, especially when the first question asked was the same old thing about how could I possibly imagine I'd have the strength to drive a 3,700-pound stocker at Bristol.

What happened then was very odd. It was intuitive, quicker than thought, metaphysical. I had been tired by the trip, and was mostly thinking about tomorrow's practice. Suddenly and strangely, I felt the anxiety induced by the situation drain from me; I became powerful, peaceable, and assured, and I directed this deep calm to each person who spoke. (Even at the moment, I was thinking, *Where the heck did this come from?* Later, I recognized similarities in the process called "centering.") In any case, the rowdy hubbub subsided and the potential for chaos was defused.

One of next day's papers said that I addressed the group "like Pete Rose scooping up a routine grounder."[3]

Bristol racetrack called to mind a teacup—a teacup for a Titan. Things were more relaxed than at the longer tracks. Even the NASCAR officials seemed less officious. Astoundingly enough, for the first time ever, they put our car through technical inspection in its proper order. This might not sound like much, but in fact it was a very big deal.

Until your car had passed tech inspection, you were not allowed out onto the race track for practice. And every moment of practice— the time for shaking down your suspension, and making changes to it—was precious.

Everyone knew that if a driver or crew chief offended NASCAR in some way, one of the punishments was likely to be an unexplained delay in tech inspection. According to the stated rules of the game, the order of tech inspection was determined by the order in which competitors signed in at the race track. In actual fact, the hot dogs, the big names, got inspected first. All the rest of us sat around and waited—car up on jacks, hood up, air cleaner off—until our turn came.

Among the many ways in which NASCAR made it clear that they were not truly, deeply thrilled to have a woman driver in their ranks was that, no matter how early we arrived at the race track, we were always inspected last. The lowliest and slowest of the independent drivers, who might have pulled his truck into the garage area while we were hood-up and ready, was roaring around the race track long before the inspectors "remembered" our presence. At the Daytona 500, Salt Walther was out in practice a good two hours before we were

[3] Kingsport (Tenn.) *News*, April 15, 1977

cleared. Even Ralph Moody was powerless to put a stop to this treatment. At the previous race, Atlanta, we had been badly hurt by it.

Lynda Ferreri then made an audacious move. She went to see NASCAR's Director of Competition and pointed out that we were putting a hell of a lot of money in NASCAR's pockets—everywhere we went, track attendance records were set. She doubtless made a few other points as well. Whatever the reason, at Bristol we sailed through tech inspection as slick as a whistle.

That wasn't the only surprise. It was at Bristol that the glacial hostility of some of the upper-level teams first showed signs of a major thaw.

Within the first three sessions of Friday's practice, I was fast enough to make the middle of the field, just short of the top ten. The faster I went, the higher crept the engine speed—too high for its health. We fixed that by installing a differential with a more appropriate ratio, but it was open instead of locked and the car's handling changed dramatically. The lap times deteriorated, and no amount of fooling around with the suspension seemed to help.

Meanwhile, I had seen that the engine was possessed of a mortal defect. From the exit of each turn, as I stood on the gas, the water temperature rose dramatically down the length of the straight: the mark of a cracked cylinder head or gasket leak. At each combustion stroke of some particular piston, fiery expanding gases were forcing fluid out of the cooling system. I pitted, we filled the radiator, made some suspension changes, and went out again. We would have to live with it, in order to get our practice laps today.

One of the setups we tried was unusually loose, and I spun in Turn 3, bringing out the yellow amid clouds of tire smoke. As I pitted, I saw Buddy Baker at Ralph Moody's side. Baker seemed to be offering advice. I climbed out of the car and joined them.

"A little loose?" Buddy said.

"A little."

"One thing you might try, don't go in so deep."

"I've been using the point on the wall where the red paint begins." I didn't mention that I was trying to get as deep into the turn as Cale Yarborough did before I got off the gas.

"Well, try backing out of it just a hair early, where those two stripes are." He pointed. "I found I could get on it two car lengths sooner if I didn't go in quite so deep."

A top Southern NASCAR driver was giving me a tip!

It took a locking differential to cure the looseness; but Buddy's help was both astonishing and accurate.

Then there was Cale.

It was afternoon. I was stretched out on one of the truck ramps, eyes closed, running laps in my mind. What clues could I pluck out of all that sensory input, that might make a difference?

A shadow fell. I looked up to see Cale Yarborough regarding me with thoughtful amusement.

This was unheard of. Cale Yarborough had never so much as nodded in our direction, not since the assistance Rolla Vollstedt extracted from him at our NASCAR debut. His pit was all the way on the other side of the track, in front of the grandstands with Buddy and the rest of the stars. What was he doing here? I scrambled to my feet. To this day, I have no idea what we talked about.

That afternoon, we lined up for the first qualifying session. On the second lap, the offended piston gave way. None of the regular crew were yet at Bristol, so Jim, Ralph and I pulled the engine. It was rather fun to be twisting wrenches again, bantering with Ralph—who normally didn't lay hands on the car himself—and with Jim. We worked with the easy efficiency of long experience, and had the engine out and stripped of its accessories by the time NASCAR's white-garbed elder strode through the pits, chanting vespers.

"The infield is closed for the day. Put down yo' tools and go home. The infield is closed for the day..."

Next morning, the new engine went in, but the differential situation remained hopeless. I qualified just two one-hundredths of a second faster than my very first laps of the track on Friday. We would start twenty-first in the field.

It certainly wasn't what we had hoped for. Jim Lindholm went out looking for a cure: a locking differential of the correct ratio. He found it, and Lynda bought it. We barely had time to check it out before practice came to an end.

Sunday, race day, dawned hot. Five hundred laps of Bristol made for a notoriously brutal undertaking, and several drivers had already lined up relief. "Gettin' outta your car" was no disgrace at Bristol. Ralph, Lynda and I discussed a few candidates as Jim and the rest of the guys laid out the pit equipment. Presently, it was time.

The high banks and abbreviated straights of Bristol's half-mile engendered close combat. Unlike Richmond, however, there wasn't much pushing and shoving. The Bristol banking was as steep as Daytona, with the same resultant heavy downforce and high side loads. But instead of Daytona's long straightaways, where you had a few seconds to take it easy, at Bristol's half-mile track you were barely out of one turn before you entered the next. Bristol was a hell of a mean, tough race track. I loved it.

I loved it because we had hit it right. The setup was perfect. Our Laguna may have been the only superspeedway car at the track, carrying 500 more pounds on the nose than Cale's Monte Carlo, but it handled better than we had any right to expect. By the time the field sorted itself out, I was running in ninth place, and I held that position for a long, long time.

At 170 laps, though, our luck broke. When I pitted for fuel, still in ninth place, one of my signals was misinterpreted as a request for more bite. When I brought the car up to speed, it pushed a ton. Getting into the turns was like wrestling with Godzilla. A hundred laps later, the struggle took its toll, and I signaled for relief.

Crewman Jack Bryant said later, "We knew it was coming. Your face was as red as that wall there!" They fixed the bite and put a young unknown, Rick Newsome, in the car. Rick did a good job with it while the guys poured cold water over my head and down my back.

At the second fuel stop, I climbed back in again.

Somewhere along the way, the engine went sour. I ran on seven cylinders to finish eleventh. Still, our team was showing its mettle. Our announced objective of top-ten finishes in this, my rookie year, had been treated as a joke. To run ninth at Bristol, as early and as long as I had, was no joke.

When the green flag drops, the bullshit stops.

A horde of spectators poured into the infield. I was weary and only partly resigned to the engine malfunction as I signed autographs, still soaked with sweat and covered with rubber dust. In that sea of faces, suddenly there was Alex.

"Dinner tonight?"

"Great." Most everyone else would be leaving, but I had a couple of days off and planned to look around this lovely, obscure part of the world.

Our conversation that evening was mostly about racing. The unspoken language was about something else. Its outcome was inevitable and sweet.

Next morning, Alex and I set out in search of a cave behind a waterfall where Daniel Boone hid from hostile Indians. I had brought from New York an old WPA guide to Tennessee, one of those marvelous depression-era books that are America's closest equivalent to the Blue Guides, and we followed its directions through a fragrant pale-green landscape frosted with dogwood. The cave was gone, though, washed away since WPA days.

When I reached my apartment in Manhattan on Tuesday, I found a dozen long-stemmed red roses and a card signed, *Love, Alex.*

The last NASCAR Winston Cup race before the opening of practice for the 1977 Indianapolis 500 was set for May 1, at Talladega, Alabama. The 2.66-mile high-banked track, seventy-five miles east of Birmingham, had plenty of mystique. Most of the mystique was sinister. An Indian curse was said to lie on the land. Drivers and crew members had lost their lives in strange and unusual accidents. Nineteen race cars, almost half the field, were once demolished in a single crash. The most recent fatality at Talladega was NASCAR hero Tiny Lund, killed in a T-bone crash two years before.

So Rolla Vollstedt had plenty of reason not to want me running in the Talladega 500 just one week before the opening of practice for his best-ever shot at success in the Indianapolis 500. An injury serious enough to keep me out of a race car for the rest of May would cost Rolla dearly. He let me know his feelings, in no uncertain terms.

Contractually, I had the right to run there if I pleased, but it was hard to argue with his position. If it weren't for Rolla, I'd be a very fast pedestrian at that moment, instead of a serious contender for NASCAR Rookie of the Year.

On the other hand, Talladega offered one of Lynda's and my best chances to regain the lead in the Rookie standings that we held early in the year. (Ricky Rudd had taken over the points lead after USAC Championship licensing rules kept me out of the NASCAR races at Darlington, North Wilkesboro, Rockingham, and Martinsville.) Talladega was the kind of track for which our Laguna was designed and built. Its setup there would be close to what had worked so well at Daytona. The prospect was succulent and tantalizing. I agonized over the quandary at great length.

An idea for a compromise arose from a loophole in NASCAR's rules. The rules permitted a substitute driver to take over a car for all but the first lap of a race; and NASCAR history brimmed with interesting applications and manipulations of this rule.

We needed this race at Talladega. I called Rolla. He grumbled, but gave his consent.

Ralph Moody proposed Lennie Pond as our substitute. Pond had yet to win a Winston Cup race, but was Rookie of the Year four seasons previously. Lynda and I could both see trouble if a NASCAR veteran drove for us. Moody rejected our other suggestions. Finally Lynda said, "I'll check it out with NASCAR in advance." And she did, returning with the news that we were simply obliged to follow the written rules.

We made no secret of our plans, which reached the newspapers by the time we arrived in Talladega.

Practice and qualifying went nearly as well as we could have hoped. Talladega was so huge and so steeply banked that if the car was properly set up, you never had to lift your foot off the gas. We reached that point almost immediately. Additional speed then became a question of tiny changes in the trim—lowering the rear spoiler just a shade, or reducing the rake (the extent to which the back end was higher than the front). Some of these changes destabilized the car to the point where my heart was in my mouth, but in the end, we had what we wanted.

We made the field on the first day's qualifying (for the top fifteen spots), thirteenth fastest at 186.387 mph. Maybe it was the qualifying run that did it. Maybe it was our performance at Bristol, that obscure and brutal track. Whatever it was, I will always remember Talladega as the watershed of our acceptance in the Deep South. No longer did little groups of crewmen look at me squinty-eyed, and stop talking as I passed. No longer did I have to take a deep breath and brace myself before walking through the garage area. The change in atmosphere was a huge relief.

The reporters who covered NASCAR noticed it too, and queried several top drivers. Buddy Baker: "Look what she did at Atlanta. She got right up there and ran with Pearson. I think now instead of making smart cracks about her they're looking at her as a race driver."[4]

Not that NASCAR had turned into some kind of a love fest. We were a long way from that. Richard Petty remained sour as always, with one grudging addition: "I really can't say she can't drive as good as some of the others out there."[5]

Big of him, I thought.

Qualifying on the first day gave us the precious leisure in which to make the car go faster yet. I drafted with a couple of guys, making sure that the car remained stable when hooked up (running in a train of cars). Altogether, we were better prepared than for any race yet. Come race day, I was sure going to hate to get out of that car.

[4] The Anniston (Ala.) *Star*, April 28, 1977
[5] ibid

On Saturday night, the night before the race, the roof caved in. NASCAR announced that they wouldn't permit our relief-driver plan after all. If any driver relieved for me, our finishing position would be disallowed, would not count toward the year's points.

Somewhere in the hours that followed, the auto racing reporters decided that we were being screwed. They also decided that they were going to do something about it.

Exactly how they moved, in those dark Southern corridors of power, would always remain a mystery. When it was over with, NASCAR had backed down.

I suppose that, had the car run to the end of the race, and had the finishing position been high, there might have been further adverse fallout. But it didn't happen that way. On the start I moved up, and was in ninth place after the first eleven laps. Bobby Allison then brought out the yellow with a blown engine, and I turned the car over to Lennie. His lap times were neither faster nor slower than mine. (The basis for the uproar, of course, had been the presumption that Lennie could drive my car faster than I could.) About midpoint of the race, the engine went, and that was the end of the story.

Indianapolis was next.

SEISMIC CHANGES

Two historical milestones marked the Indianapolis 500 of 1977: A. J. Foyt became the first driver ever to win four times, and I became the first woman driver to earn a starting spot in the field. Rolla Vollstedt's Bryant Lightning/Offenhauser and I appeared on the front page of major newspapers across the country, and countless editorials pontificated on the symbolism of the event. My own position was that *of course* women could do these things, and why in the world did anyone ever think otherwise? But many people seemed to perceive it as a defining moment in the evolution of women's cultural role.

Although a flawed intake valve brought my race day to an early end, our month of May '77 had major high points as well as lows. When I set the fastest time of day on opening day of practice, we served notice that our competitive position had been sharply honed. When I spun and hit the wall on the fourth day of practice, we were still among the ten fastest cars on the track. (Entries had been filed for eighty-five cars that year.) Then came excruciating, endless days of repair and struggle with an unpredictable, mysteriously malfunctioning machine; and finally, the joy of putting the car securely in the field. Not only did I again set fastest time of day, I posted the fastest qualifying time the entire second weekend of qualifying, on a track that by then had been made slippery and slow after a week of hot days without rain. Rolla Vollstedt's team had indeed accomplished a great deal. And my name would forever after be followed by a comma.

In the week after the 1977 Indianapolis 500, I was besieged by would-be agents, authors and movie producers. The Hollywood business especially was way over my head, and I sought advice from Paul Newman. He was thoughtful and kind. I signed up with the agency that was his second choice, which had courted me most assiduously.

But as always, the most important thing to me was simply the next race. That would be the Michigan 400 Winston Cup race on

June 19, where I continued my pursuit of Top Rookie honors. Crew chief Jim Lindholm based the Chevrolet's setup on what we learned at Daytona, and it worked well. I qualified twelfth, one spot ahead of my rookie rival, Ricky Rudd. In last place, making the field for the first time, was a car belonging to Rod Osterlund, whose team was eventually to become one of NASCAR's most successful. His enormous, glittering tractor-trailer full of the most expensive machinery had been showing up since early in the year, but until now his car hadn't gone fast enough to qualify.

On race day, June 19, our quirky radio selected a new and different failure mode. The moment I fired up the engine, all communication ceased. What remained was an intermittent POPP! POPP! of tremendous volume, at frequent but random intervals. It was inescapable, blown into my ears by the speakers embedded in my helmet. I tried to pull the wiring apart, but the coaxial cable was too tough.

One always needs a degree of stoicism in racing, but one needs the stoicism of Marcus Aurelius to ignore sensory input of that sort. Worse, I had wanted a few laps of practice to test the radios, but Moody insisted it was unnecessary.

Since communication was perforce by pit board, I made my first pit stop under yellow one lap later than the cars with functioning radios, which put me far back in the pack. On the track, however, I was faster than ever. I had worked my way up through traffic to regain my starting position before Darrell Waltrip, leading, appeared in my mirrors. He overtook me in snail-like increments. Cale Yarborough was drafting him, in second place. When the moment came, I pulled down and let them by, then caught their draft.

Cale passed Darrell.

I passed Darrell!

I stayed on Cale's bumper for a good many laps.

After passing Darrell, I was thinking, *Cale, you're next. I'm going to pass you, the leader, and get my lap back.*

Oh, I was hot that day.

Then the engine quit dead. I reached my pit on momentum.

It was excruciating. It was unbearable.

An eternity later, I was back on the track with a new distributor, more than twenty laps down. It had given me time to disconnect the radio cable.

Soon after, I had a close encounter with Marty Robbins, the

country-western singer. Although Robbins ran just an occasional NASCAR race, his track manners were excellent and he knew what he was doing. I had lapped him often enough to feel secure about it as I overtook him near Turn 3. Then a flat tire sent him sharply into my path, but with some artful dodging, I veered clear. It was quite a way to make his acquaintance; he was a lovely man.

The most spectacular moment came when Ricky Rudd's engine blew. Terry Ryan's car, covered with Ricky's oil, shot up across the track, aimed straight at my door. I stood on the gas and turned right as hard as I dared. Turning hard right in a stocker that's set up to turn left is always a dicey proposition, and I couldn't believe I'd gotten away with it. He missed me by inches. Terry escaped unhurt, after hitting the wall.

At around 350 miles, a cylinder head cracked. I coddled the engine to the checkered flag. Cale Yarborough won. I coasted to a stop on pit road. Climbed out, walked up toward our pit. I was disgusted to the point of nausea.

Lynda Ferreri had jumped down from the biggest toolbox, where she perched during every race with her lap sheets and stopwatch. She met me at the garage gate. Even in this heat, she looked every inch the banker: blue blazer, gold jewelry, crisp white collar, stylish and functional hat. But the expression on her face looked as sick as I felt. We walked together to the truck, the big green and white transporter, talking. My language was terrible. The radios, the cylinder head. "What the #@&* is going on with these engines?" I said. My profane rant over the day's mechanical failures went on at some length. "Why the #@&* should a distributor break? Distributors don't break. #@&* cylinder heads don't crack unless they've been used too #@&* long. And if that #@&* Moody had let me test the radios like I wanted to, we'd have had a #@&* radio that worked, instead of being behind the eight-ball with the #@&* blackboard."

"I know," Lynda said. Her chin quivered, a rare departure from her engaging smile. "I know. Except for Richmond, the engines have failed in every race so far this year. It's awful. But everything Ralph Moody has ever said we needed, I've bought."

She didn't need to tell me that; I had total confidence in her. "This makes three races in a row where we've run spectacularly well before the engine went," I said. "I don't know why the engines are popping, but it isn't me. I've never over-revved one, the telltale needle on the tach shows that."

Ever since Jim had joined the team, with his aggressiveness in acquiring information and his ferocious desire to make the car go faster, our handling problems had dwindled almost to trivia. Now it was the engines.

Lynda smiled faintly. "You should have heard the crowd when you passed Darrell Waltrip. They went wild."

"I was hot today," I said. But my voice was somber.

"Do you know about the little optimist and the little pessimist who both wanted a pony?" she asked as we reached the shade of the truck. "Their father wanted to teach them a lesson, so he filled up a room with horseshit. The little pessimist walked into the room and started crying. The little optimist was laughing and shouting, 'There has to be a pony here somewhere!'"

At last, we could smile. Sort of. It wouldn't be the last time that we quoted that punch line to each other.

I changed out of my reeking driver's suit and headed for the sponsor's big tent. There I signed autographs for the next two hours, smiling cheerfully and fraudulently. I rode back to the hotel with my pit crew guys—Toby, Jack and Ed—making jokes and cracking wise. We all unwound in Lynda's room, drinking some beer, casting a veneer of merriment over the depressing outcome of the day. Presently, I found myself alone with Jim Lindholm.

Lindholm said if it wasn't for me, he would quit the team. He, too, was unhappy with Moody's operation and its results. His words struck fear into my heart; he was the best thing the team had going for it. Something would have to be done—and soon.

Next day, I flew to Pennsylvania for the Pocono 500 Indy-car race, the second of the year's Triple Crown 500-mile events. It was a traumatic week, and a watershed. The alliance that had seen Rolla Vollstedt's team put the first woman in the field for the Indianapolis 500 was coming undone.

Phil Casey, the chief mechanic whom Rolla Vollstedt had hired for my car at Indianapolis, had quit. This was terribly bad news, at a terribly bad time. The last thing in the world I wanted was ever again to ask Dick Simon to shake down a car for me. Dick's wife Melanie seemed to believe that if it weren't for me, Dick would be winning races. Never mind that it was I who had brought in the money on which Dick's car was built and on which the team was run; nor that I had twice given up a race in favor of Dick when the team ran short of engines. She had persuaded two of Dick's crew members of his disadvantage, and hostility was rampant.

Pocono was a tri-oval, and no two corners were the same. If a car handled properly through one of its turns, it was a good bet to be bollixed up in the others. Compromises had to be found, despite the tension within the crew. With the help of three volunteers whom I had enticed to the race, we got it done.

When time came to qualify, I was primed and hot. Bobby Unser had qualified at 184.729. I thought I could better that. Flames came out my nostrils at the very thought. A handful of drivers could get through Pocono's infamous Turn 2, where the pavement rolled and buckled, with the accelerator pedal pressed firmly to the floor. I had it in mind to be among them.

Talk to me, little car ... steady hands...

Green.

Crews and drivers in the pits couldn't see a car in Turn 2, but they listened to the pitch of the engine during qualifying attempts. The sound came clearly across the huge flat infield. If the pitch didn't change—if the driver didn't lift in that most treacherous turn—people would look at each other with traces of a smile.

As the sound of my passage through Turn 2 reached the pits, Ted Wenz said, "I don't think she lifted." And I hadn't. I didn't make it all the way through the turn, either. As the car came down on its suspension after the last bump, the back end came out and around.

Left left left! Turn the wheel left, lock up the brakes.

Look at your hands.

Just as at Indianapolis, instinct told me I had already turned left; but my eyes saw that the wheel was still turned right—the deeply instilled reaction that might prevent the car from going all the way around. I corrected, and the car spun harmlessly into the infield, missing the wall by a foot or so. Later, I qualified twenty-second at 176.074 mph. *No heroics,* I was thinking. *Just put it safely in the field.*

By race day, nothing had improved in Vollstedt's team's internal workings. I resolved to have a serious talk with Dick Simon at the first opportunity.

At the green flag, I gained a few positions before the Lightning's engine soured. An oil leak was saturating the magneto. I retired the car on Lap 77, and was classified in seventeenth place. Dick Simon lost his transmission. Tom Sneva won.

The next day, I asked Dick to join me in one of the vacant offices. I told him how much I appreciated his help and support over the last year. I told him that the deteriorating situation, the effects of

Melanie's hostility and resultant fragmentation of the team could be expected to harm both our efforts. Rolla Vollstedt deserved better than that.

For the rest of the season, I said, I would focus on NASCAR, and run only such Indy-car races as Bryant Heating and Cooling required. I also said I hoped we would be able to work together at whatever those obligatory races might be, that we owed it to Rolla to do so.

Finally, I told him that an option for a movie of my life story was about to become a signed contract, and that I was going to split the money three ways with Rolla and with him. This, he was certainly happy to have. The checks for the option were distributed within the next few days.

I left the lush summer greens of the Poconos feeling the full emotional effects of these seismic changes. It was helpful that Alex agreed I had done the right thing.

Four days later, on Friday July 1, practice started in Daytona for the NASCAR Winston Cup Firecracker 400. Something curious was in the works. Italy's Lella Lombardi and Belgium's Christine Beckers, the two most successful and prominent women road-racing drivers in the world, were coming from Europe to drive in this race, courtesy of NASCAR. The Miami *Herald* reported "speculation that [Bill] France spent up to $25,000 in expenses and guarantees"[1] to bring them in. From what we learned around the garage area, that number seemed extremely conservative.

The Daytona/NASCAR press releases, which had been issuing forth since mid-June, described the event as a "showdown" among the three of us. Not a few reporters had taken the bait and were practically licking their chops over the anticipated catfight. They had been calling me for days.

"What do you think of running against the world's two best women drivers?"

"I'm delighted," I said. "It indicates NASCAR is coming to understand that what I've always said is true: on the track, being a woman doesn't make a bit of difference. And we won't be running against each other, but against the sixty-plus other drivers who are entered for this event."

But what *was* NASCAR's motivation? Lynda Ferreri and I had talked about the oddity of the situation.

[1] July 3, 1977

NASCAR's attempts to hamstring our operation had been relatively subtle, so far. The worst they had done—at least, as far as we knew—was delay our tech inspections at most events as long as possible, cutting our practice short. As an annoyance, they usually left us out in the rain without a garage until we had qualified for a race and the non-qualifiers who'd had a roof over their heads had gone home. (And we had never failed to qualify.) So why was Bill France, the man who yelled at Humpy Wheeler for inviting me to Charlotte for my first NASCAR race, suddenly in love with women drivers, smitten enough to spend this much money on them?

Lynda said, laughing, "That's easy. If they can discredit us in the eyes of our sponsor, they'll have taken a big step toward purging their fields of women altogether." With two top European road racers who were unlikely ever to return to Winston Cup racing—it wasn't their game, after all—driving the best equipment that NASCAR's wealth and power could command, and their "showdown" press releases, NASCAR was stepping up the heat.

"Why?" I asked.

"Haven't you read all those letters to *National Speed Sport News*," Lynda said, "about how if a woman can qualify at Indianapolis like you just did, that proves Championship racing is a pantywaist sport, and real race fans should go back to Sprint car races where the real men are?" Indeed, I had read those letters. "So," Lynda went on, "NASCAR isn't stupid. They don't want the status of their sport to be downgraded, as professions often are when women enter them."

Both Lombardi and Beckers were exceptionally accomplished drivers. Lombardi had finished as high as sixth in a Grand Prix Formula 1 World Championship race. Beckers was her co-driver in the 24-Hour race at Le Mans and in the Daytona 24-Hour, where they had qualified fourth fastest in the field. Ralph Moody told us that Chevrolet had been induced to supply their hottest engine for Lombardi in this race. Jim Lindholm learned that her car had been gone over by Hutcherson-Pagan, a highly regarded race shop. He figured that this alone must have cost NASCAR at least $10,000. The Orlando *Sentinel Star* noted that NASCAR had given the newcomers choice garage assignments: Lombardi next to A. J. Foyt, Beckers next to David Pearson. The *Star* also commented that our team remained, as usual, billeted with the backmarkers.[2] The question of garage assignments was not as trivial as it might seem. Much could be

[2] July 2, 1977

learned through proximity—or not learned, through separation. NASCAR had always made sure we were widely separated from the top teams.

I credited Kelly Girl, our sponsor, for putting money on the line for a full year of racing. "Particularly," I said, "when the whole world was shouting 'publicity stunt' a year ago. This is a serious racing operation and always has been."

Lombardi and Beckers could both be expected to make a good showing. But it seemed unlikely that anyone, however good a driver, in however good a car, was going to do better than a team that had run the track before and had half a season of regular competition in this league under its belt. We met in the garage area. Lombardi spoke no English, and Beckers' English was only a little better than my rusty French, but I told them I'd be glad to help in any way I could. Reporters had clustered around, notebooks in hand, to watch us scratch each others' eyes out.

Christine said, "When I first took it out on the track, I thought, *what* am I doing here?" Lombardi had been quoted as saying it was "like riding a buffalo."

"These cars feel a lot different," I told them, "but you'll get used to it. When you get up to speed, they feel a lot more solid and stable. Once you get going, if you want to draft together, just let me know." Out of the corner of my eye, I could see some mouths hanging open.

Altogether, those four days at Daytona in the fierce heat of July were like walking through a minefield. Richard Petty was badmouthing me again, and my slow burn was coming to the boiling point. Then there was the Moody situation. July's blistering temperatures and slower speeds called for major revisions in the setup. At the last moment before qualifying, Jim and I got it done. Someone asked Moody what the changes were, and printed his favorite answer in the Speedway's *Pit Notes*. "We changed the driver's mind. We told her that if she didn't run faster we were going to throw her in the lake." The humor of this escaped me completely.

Early on Friday, Moody had been over to see Junie Donleavy, who was fielding Lella Lombardi's car, to give him a hard time about it. He was in a fine mood when he returned. "I told him, 'Now you're down to my level,'" he said to us cheerfully.

He really didn't have a clue. "Down to my level." With an underlying attitude like that, how could we not have trouble?

In hindsight, I have to give Moody credit for all the heat he must have taken—of the kind he handed out, in turn, to Donleavy. Crewing for a woman in NASCAR had to be twice as rough on the guys as in USAC. As recently as our Atlanta race that March, crewman Jack Bryant had turned up on race morning with a black eye, refusing to tell me how he acquired it. A few half-overheard phrases, though, indicated he had probably been defending the team's honor.

However, the subsequent change in atmosphere around the garage area that was so apparent at Talladega continued to be a huge relief.

The first round of qualifying was Saturday afternoon, and the fastest twenty cars would constitute the top half of the field. Thanks to our chassis adjustments, I could run the track without lifting. Trying to push the accelerator pedal right through the firewall, I guided the green Laguna delicately over the smoothest and most efficient parts of the track. We made it, at 181.755 mph. Lella and Christine didn't.

Jack Bryant, he of the black eye, looked like the cat that swallowed the canary. "They're spending fifty thousand dollars to blow us into the weeds," he chortled, "and they cain't do it!"

On Sunday the Europeans made the field without trouble— Lombardi in twenty-ninth spot, Beckers in thirty-seventh. Meanwhile, Lynda and I had other fish to fry. Jim Lindholm had proposed a plan. Space was available, he said, in a long row of garages at Hutcherson-Pagan. Engines (and rebuilds for engines) could be purchased from Parky Nall, who supplied a few other independents. Jim could work out an agreement with Dick Hutcherson for the use of whatever equipment we might lack.

Lindholm was willing to take over the operation of the team. In my opinion, he was able. Much as Lynda Ferreri and I liked Ralph Moody personally, away from the race track, and much as I respected his illustrious history, she agreed that a professional change was needed. First, however, we had to convince the sponsors. They had been persuaded to spend their money in part by the weight of Moody's reputation.

What happened on race day shifted the balance. The engine blew itself to shreds in just eleven laps.

KA-BOOM!

The car filled with smoke. I shut it down, coasted into the garage and climbed out, feeling as if my limbs were made of lead. A broken crankshaft had made mincemeat of nearly everything.

It's almost impossible to describe the frustration of such a moment. You have entered the space necessary to launch a 3,700-

pound race car toward four hundred miles of competition with some forty others, dancing through the turns at speeds greater than a Boeing 737's on takeoff. Then you are cut off, ousted, and there is nothing you can do with all the force you have marshalled. I hadn't even worked up a sweat yet.

I walked outside. Rain moved across the sky to drench the track, and the race was stopped. Meanwhile, Jim Lindholm and Ralph Moody were back in the garage. Jim told me later that Kelly Girl president Terry Adderley stalked over to the garage from the grandstands. He was furious. "What's wrong with these #@&* motors?" he said. "They won't even go ten laps!" Moody walked away without a word.

That night, Lynda, Jim and I met with the Kelly executives. I recommended the transfer of the team to Jim, under the Hutcherson-Pagan umbrella. "If we make this commitment," I said, "I will give up my USAC Championship license in order to run the NASCAR races that conflict with USAC's schedule." USAC's rules and races had so far kept me out of eight NASCAR races, a major handicap in a rookie contest that had been described as the most competitive in years. My remaining obligations to Rolla Vollstedt could be kept by driving on my FIA (international) license, which USAC would accept. The Kelly executives were persuaded, and the die was cast.

Ralph Moody caught up with me later that night, upset. "I think it's time you knew what's going on around here," he said. "That crankshaft has been run since the beginning."

Lynda and Terry had said it was supposed to be an all-new engine.

It was doubtless unfair to Moody for the rupture to come over a tired crankshaft; but at this point I didn't care.

Lynda and I and the Kelly executives agreed on a statement that we parted with Moody by mutual consent. Much of the press, however, reported that he had quit, and that our team would suffer in consequence. Eventually, our successes on the track smoothed over the issue and it died a natural death.

Richard Petty won the Firecracker 400. Christine Beckers and Lella Lombardi dropped out with mechanical problems. They never ran a stock car race again. Not until eleven years later did another determined woman, Patty Moise, compete in that race.

The effects of fundamental changes in both my Indy-car and NASCAR teams would soon be felt. I was cautiously optimistic. But first came something completely different: the Six-Hour World

Championship of Makes race on the Grand Prix circuit at Watkins Glen, among a galaxy of international star drivers. It was my first sports car race in nearly two years, a return to my racing roots. We finished tenth overall in a single-turbo Porsche 934, and I had good cause to be satisfied with my part of it. And best of all, in a week's time there would be another race.

The Kelly executives at Daytona had expressed concern over all the racing I was doing, thinking it might be too much, might take away from their NASCAR team.

"Look," I said, "I used to hold a full-time job that kept the rent paid *and* do all my own mechanical work *and* race every weekend. This is a piece of cake!" And a luscious piece of cake it was, too.

How can I possibly explain how much I loved this sport? Or why? Like the old line about sex, even when it wasn't very good, it was good, and when it was good it was fantastic. On the track, you accessed a state far beyond anything in ordinary life, and afterwards, euphoria naturally followed. Everything looked better, smelled better, tasted better, felt better, when you had extended yourself that far. The sport's multiple complexities included the satisfaction of bettering your competitors in an environment that posed certain hazards, while at the same time you were responsible for their well-being.

Nothing that I know of is anything like it.

The morning after the Six-Hour, I made a pilgrimage to the wild and scenic chasm that gave Watkins Glen its name. Since 1963 and for as long as I raced there, its extraordinary beauty had served as solace and counterpoint to my racing triumphs or misadventures. An ancient trail wound two miles up the labyrinthine gorge, behind waterfalls, across footbridges, through dark fern-filled grottoes and past white-water cascades that danced in the sun. Far overhead, trees fringed a narrow swath of blue sky.

Somewhere in the depths of the chasm I paused, looking upstream across a quiet pool and into the light. A towering cliff face glittered with water that caught and refracted shards of light, a dazzle thrown over the dark grey stone ... grey, the color that belonged to Athena. And the cliff became her shield, and the silence her words.

You did well.

The benediction was not of this race, but of the month of May, and the other formidably difficult times she had been with me. It brings tears to my eyes now, as it did then.

How can I put this in a book? It sounds foolish. But that was how it was. I had asked nothing of her, she came from beyond thought.

There followed a sense that, from now on, I would be on my own ... mostly. That she had seen me through the impossible parts, and that the rest could be handled without her help.

That was all.

I am reminded, as I write this, how throwing the net of words around the really important stuff was something I often had neither time nor strength to do, because I needed both for the next event.

Nashville was next.

ONWARD AND UPWARD IN THE DEEP SOUTH

Jim Lindholm was tense as a drawn crossbow. The Nashville Winston Cup race on July 20, 1977 was his first event as crew chief, and he took his responsibilities as seriously as a heart attack. He and I and Sidney Slimp, the dark-eyed young Alabama farmer who handled fueling, were having lunch: collards, cornbread, and ham, with glasses of sweet iced tea. No one else on our team was yet in town.

Outside the little diner, Tennessee baked in temperatures several degrees beyond the century point. A gleaming black stretch limousine, lent for our use by a local enthusiast, stood incongruously at the diner's door. The team truck was parked out at the race track. Jim had been first crew chief to sign in, which in theory established us as first in line for tech inspection, and to emphasize the point he had left the truck parked with its nose to the locked gate. By now a dozen or more tractor-trailer rigs would have lined up behind, waiting for the track to open at two this afternoon.

"Okay," I said, "here's what we're going to do. I'm going to drive that limo, and you two are going to sit in the back, and we're going to drive right past all those guys lined up beside their rigs, with our windows rolled up and the air conditioning on. Show those rich teams how to treat their crew members right!"

And so we did, even though the air conditioning failed and we nearly perished of the heat. Jim cheered up a bit. He had a vestigial laugh that sounded something like the grunt of a panther, and I heard it once or twice as we proceeded majestically to the front of the line.

My confidence in Jim proved justified. We had a few little problems in practice, qualifying smack in the middle of the field; but it was done without trauma and hassle, and we went faster after that.

This was to be a night race, the only one on the Winston Cup circuit. Late in the afternoon, I called a crew meeting in the truck. I asked each man for input: what problems had he seen in the past, what problems could he anticipate given the particular circumstances of this race? What ideas did he have that might improve our chances of success? The time was well spent, and our "prayer meetings" became a fixture at each subsequent event.

Night fell, and the temperature dropped a bit from its afternoon peak of 115° F. With a length of 420 laps, the race would last over three hours. We took the green at 8 p.m., in the lurid glare of sodium-vapor lights. The first yellow came before we completed a single lap. Dante's Inferno had nothing on Nashville that night. The orange-lit, murky air was filled with tire smoke and exhaust and the effluvia of crashed cars.

Nashville was a flat half-mile track, and just as at Bristol, the pits were divided. Don Wall, a gruff ex-Marine sergeant who always treated me with scrupulous fairness, ran the front pits to which the favorite drivers were assigned. The backside was handled by a round-faced young Southerner who was studying up to be a bully, and found NASCAR a great place to polish his style. I'll call him Curly. Both sides were badly cramped, and in the darkness and jumble it was ticklish business to get in and out of the pits.

A low wall stood between the track and the pits, and NASCAR's rules were that if a competitor exiting the pits under the yellow reached the end of the wall before the pace car did, the driver would get a "Go" sign from the official stationed there, and could continue on out and around to catch up with the pack. Once the pace car reached the end of the pit wall, the sign would be reversed to "Stop," and the driver must wait for the whole pack to go by before proceeding, thus going a lap down. Speedy pit stops were therefore of the essence, and the guys were doing a great job. I was full of fire.

Somewhere after the first hour, as I tore out of pit lane a good two car lengths ahead of the pace car, Curly twirled his sign to the octagonal red Stop. Grinning hideously, he held me at the end of pit road while the pace car and the field went on by. We were close enough that he could see into the car, and could lip-read what I was calling him, and grinned even more, with loathsome satisfaction.

The move was so blatant that I got mail about it from fans.

Curly held the red while the very last stragglers, half a lap behind, caught up to the pack, before he finally let me go.

I set the rage aside and got on with the job.

Like a good many drivers that torrid night, I took relief. Richard Childress' car had been wrecked on the thirty-second lap, and sometime during the second hour, he took over my car.

It was dark in the pits; Richard and I wore similar goggles. How could Curly tell that one of the good ol' boys was now behind the wheel of the green Laguna rushing toward him? Curly flipped the red to Richard as he had to me.

Childress ran the stop sign without a moment's hesitation. He got black-flagged for his trouble. If you didn't answer the black flag, after three laps they quit scoring you, so there was really no choice. They held him in the pits for a lap at least, I think it was more.

The guys on the crew were grimly amused. "Guess ol' Richard is findin' out what it's like," Sidney said.

At the next fuel stop I got back in the car, and though there was no more trouble with Curly (who must have recognized Richard when he held him up at the black-flag stop), the race went downhill for us after that. The brakes were in poor shape when I gave the car to Richard, and when I took over again they were all gone. Pit stops became tricky. It took nearly a lap to slow the car, going down through the gears. On pit road I killed the engine with the car in first gear, modulating the speed with the clutch to bring it to a halt. Then I prayed that it would start again. Later, I got tangled in somebody else's crash, and while it didn't damage our car badly enough to put us out of the race, it held us back. I finished fifteenth. Darrell Waltrip won. Ricky Rudd, who had started two spots behind me, finished tenth with relief from David Sisco.

"I couldn't believe it," Childress said afterwards, his eyes widening at the recollection of what Curly had done. He also felt that drivers whom he was lapping wouldn't move over for the green Chevrolet—something I was used to, and hardly noticed any more. "It was an educational experience," he allowed.

Lynda and I talked about it that week: was there *anything* we could do to get a level playing field from NASCAR officialdom? I thought there might be a possibility with John Cooper, a Northerner with a strong racing background who had recently joined NASCAR in an upper-level management position. He and I were slightly acquainted, and I arranged to meet with him in Daytona four days after the Nashville race. Our new commitment to NASCAR was not yet public, and Lynda and I thought we might gain some ground by bargaining to do what we were going to do anyway.

We didn't gain a thing. Cooper stonewalled; maintained we were being treated just like everyone else. Perhaps he even believed it.

The 500-mile NASCAR Winston Cup race at Pocono followed Nashville by two weeks. My USAC resignation was a front-page headline in *National Speed Sport News* at the track the day after we arrived.

As usual, Jim Lindholm signed in among the very earliest teams at the track. By 9 a.m. on Friday July 29, our car's technical inspection was completed—except for the very last step. Competition Director Bill Gazaway's brother Joe had yet to examine the underside of the car.

We waited. And waited.

By noon, the track had long since opened for practice. The hot dogs were blasting around. So were our main competitors for rookie of the year, Ricky Rudd and Sam Sommers. So were the good ol' boys who formed the back of the pack, the ones I regularly lapped: Baxter Price, Frank Warren, Elmo Langley. All of them had signed in after we did. Even Tighe Scott, a Northerner who was often rebuked at drivers' meeting for erratic driving, was out on the track.

At noon, the tech inspectors went to lunch.

At 1 p.m., they ambled over to our car. In four minutes they were done.

This was a hell of a note.

Jaw set, Lindholm dropped the car down off its jackstands while I strapped myself in. We hadn't a moment to waste. I tore out onto the track while Lindholm ran for the pit wall. For the rest of the afternoon, we sought the compromise setup required by Pocono's three dissimilar turns. We changed caster, camber, rake, wedge, the sway bar, and most of all the springs, which flew like popcorn as we made up for lost time.

When Saturday came, we qualified tenth fastest in the field. It was our first top-ten start. It seemed only natural, as if *of course* we were going to do that—now that Jim was running things.

Ricky Rudd qualified twelfth, Skip Manning (the previous year's top rookie) eleventh. Ricky, Skip and I ran together for most of the race, until I spun on a tire that was going flat and we had to change all four tires under the green. That hurt us. We finished eleventh, with cracked headers and no brakes. Ricky was seventh. Benny Parsons won.

We would meet again at Talladega, Alabama, where practice opened in just three days.

Was it the drums of those ancient Indians that thumped in my ears, or was it really just my heart? You didn't have to be particularly sensitive to pick up bad vibrations at Talladega. The vanquished Creek Nation had good reason to populate this shallow valley with hostile ghosts, as legend claimed.

Stepping gingerly over the tools and parts that made a tangled snare in the pitch-dark interior of the race transporter, I turned the handle of the big rear door and rolled it up onto its overhead tracks. The dazzling white infield of Talladega Motor Speedway filled the truck with light. I zipped the front of my driver's suit the rest of the way up, and jumped down onto some discouraged wisps of grass.

The green Kelly Chevrolet had been ready for the final phase of tech inspection since 10 a.m. Now it was 1 p.m., and Jim Lindholm said the inspectors were getting close.

A tingling reluctance to head for the track crept up the back of my skull. I took a deep breath; walked around to the front of the truck and looked across the infield, which shimmered in the August heat. Far out on the high banking of the turns, competitors circulated. From this distance they looked tiny, and the faint drone of the engines belied their mid-180s speeds. The outer edge of the banking at Talladega was as high as a five-story building. Race cars caught up in the frequent mishaps here could bounce considerably higher than that.

The atmosphere of menace that hovered over the place was clearly having an effect. That wouldn't do. Feeling spooked could lead you to make little mistakes. Little mistakes at Talladega could turn into unseemly spectacles. Sometimes the boundary between the butterflies (useful) and fear (counterproductive) could get blurred.

Standing there at the front of the truck, I worked on my state of mind until I was in the useful space.

When I reached the garage area, the inspectors were just finishing, though the big green Chevrolet Laguna was still up on jackstands. When Jim set the car on the ground, I was already strapped in and ready to go.

As always, the car felt like utter junk on the way out to pit road. The messages it sent through the steering wheel and at the seat of my pants reminded me of my old tow cars, the $25 refugees from a wrecking yard that I hauled my Jaguar to the sports car races with, ten years before. It was always an amazement to feel the Chevrolet stabilize and settle down once it reached aerodynamic speed, out on the track.

In a couple of laps, just long enough to get the tires warmed up, I could run through all the turns flat out. I pitted. The lap was 182 mph. From now on, as long as I didn't get the car "bound up" by jerking it around, or trying to force it to go where it didn't want to, increases in speed would come from changes in its trim, as the sails of a boat might be trimmed.

Neither Jim nor I acknowledged our excitement with anything more than the exchange of a glance. Our Laguna was built for this kind of track. Our new engines, from builder Parky Nall, seemed to have more power. How much faster could we go?

Over the course of the afternoon, as we varied the setup, we found out. Donnie Allison gave us good tips about toe-in and tire temperatures. Jim Lindholm's eagerness to try out the next thing that might help made the work a joy. Each minuscule change brought us just a little more speed. It was exhilarating, delicious. I would roar down pit road, circulate just long enough to get a meaningful lap time (one with no traffic problems and conversely, no assistance from the draft of other cars), and zoom back into the pits.

"One eighty-six? All *right*! What can we try next?"

Meanwhile, the tech inspectors were preoccupied elsewhere. Cheating rumors were rampant that day, and the inspectors found expandable, oversize fuel tanks in five cars, including that of our rookie competitor Sam Sommers. Legal tank size was twenty-two gallons; the innovation was a tank that held its legal size during tech inspection, but could subsequently be expanded by almost six more gallons. It was typical of the stock car racing ethos that Sommers' crew chief told *Sports Illustrated* that "if I'm going to get caught cheating, I want to get credit for it!"

Our car, as far as I know, was completely legal; and I also believe that had there been anything illegal about it, I would have known. Cheating of any sort never appealed to me. I figured a fraudulent victory was no victory at all.

By the time vespers sounded ("Put down yo' tools and go home. Put down yo' tools..."), we knew of only a few cars faster than ours. The catfish and coleslaw at dinner that night were incredibly delicious, seasoned with the world's greatest flavor enhancer: eager, well-founded anticipation.

For qualifying, Jim removed the fan and blocked off the radiator. Sid and Toby polished every inch of the car, including the sidewalls of the tires, inside and out. All was ready when the time came. Don Wall waved me onto the track. I let the car fly through the turns as lightly as if guided by thought alone.

When it was done, I had nailed down ninth starting position in the field, at 189.391 mph. Among those who would start the Talladega 500 behind me were David Pearson, Bobby Allison, Ricky Rudd, Bill Elliott, Johnny Rutherford (in A. J. Foyt's car!), Neil Bonnett, Buddy Baker—and Richard Petty, eleventh in the field. Petty would line up on Sunday with my green Kelly car in his face. Reporters clustered around the green Kelly car after qualifying, of course. "The grandstands went wild," one said.

Petty's first comment was, "The doll out-qualified me, didn't she?

I guess she out-drove me, too."[1] Then he thought better of it. "It just goes to show what I been saying all the time, on a track like this it doesn't matter who's in the car."[2]

Johnny Rutherford, who had more victories in Indy-car racing than anyone except Foyt, had a different perspective. He had qualified twelfth and was asked if he thought he could win. "This racing down here is another world ... just look around," he said. "It would take me two or three years here to really be a winner."

The biggest surprises came in a couple of quiet conversations later on. A major NASCAR star, whom I will not name, was leaning against a bench as I walked past.

"Good run," he said.

"Thank you." I stopped. He had rarely spoken with me before, but seemed to want to say more. I took my sunglasses off. A couple of months earlier, I would have stayed in hiding behind them.

"We was talkin' about you and Moody splittin' up," he went on, "and I said, 'You know, that might be the best thing that ever happened to that girl.'"

The driver had been familiar with Holman-Moody during their glory days. When I managed to get my mouth closed, I said, "I can't comment. We wanted to part friends, and I think we did."

Not long after that, I ran into several of Neil Bonnett's crew. Neil's positive opinion of my driving had been in the local paper that day. One of his guys now said to me, in that wonderful deep-South accent, "I didn't want to mess in nobody's business, but it's good you got out of all that."

To say that I was astonished by these remarks would be a great understatement. After more than a year of struggling with "those cars are all like that, you just have to learn how to drive it down in the turns," to hear from these men at the heart of the business that I wasn't alone in my perception of the problem—it was overwhelming.

Is it any wonder I feel such great affection for Alabama? Red clay blanketed with thick green kudzu vines, succulent barbecue and golden deep-fried catfish, coleslaw served in the celadon curl of a crisp cabbage leaf ... and the tanned, weathered faces that had opened up at last.

A high starting position required a headlong rush, after driver introductions, to get into the car and get set. My pre-race butterflies

[1] Birmingham (Ala.) *Post-Herald*, Aug. 5, 1977
[2] Anniston (Ala.) *Star*, Aug. 5, 1977

were supercharged. For the first time, I would be running in the lead pack on a superspeedway, in the tight draft that formed at the front. What would the car do in the middle of such a draft, how would it handle, what would it feel like? I could expect to turn laps at least five miles an hour faster than in qualifying. This was unknown territory.

Jim Lindholm had draped a fender cover over my windshield to block the sun, blinding me to the countdown. A hooded falcon must feel like that before it is launched. The red and blue of Petty's Dodge in my mirror, however, was all too clear.

It's just another race car, I told myself.

"Lady and gentlemen ... start ... your engines!"

Jim ripped the fender cover away, squeezed my shoulder, then ran for the pits as we lumbered down pit road and out onto the track. On the long slow pace laps, all the tension turned to readiness, that mysterious transformation I had experienced for so long. Talladega's turns were banked at thirty-three degrees, and while the pace car strained to run its fastest, we nearly fell down out of our seats. It was amazing how those turns looked flat as a pancake when you ran at them twice as fast.

Cued by each other's engine sound, forty drivers simultaneously stood on the gas. The green flag fell, and the Talladega 500 began. Coo Coo Marlin, a driver of long experience, was starting on my right. Comfortable with him from running together before, I tucked tightly in behind him as the pack blasted into the first turn.

Halfway through Turn 1, Marlin's driveshaft came apart. The biggest piece of it, some six feet long, bounced over the top of my car. Most of the rest came through my windshield. Big chunks of universal joint shattered the glass. Marlin's engine disintegrated immediately, and his oil joined the flying glass that circulated in the roaring turbulence around my head. But all that was minor, compared with what I expected next.

With no power at his rear wheels, there was no way, simply no way at all, that Marlin could keep his car under control. He would be sideways in front of me, in front of the whole pack. Some thirty cars, fifty-five tons of steel and fuel, were bunched up right behind us. This was going to be a hell of a big mess.

It wasn't possible—but Marlin did it. Just slightly sideways, he carried it up to the wall as he lost speed, and I slipped by underneath him. We all got away clean, thanks to his amazing feat.

I hurried toward the pits as fast as I dared, peering through the oil and what remained of the crazed, broken glass, calling on the radio for the guys to fetch a new windshield from the truck, hoping they could hear me. They did. The windshield was there almost as soon as I pulled in. But it took a long time to replace it—the steel safety straps across it, the gasket holding it in place, the molding— and the green flag had long since been out, the debris on the track cleaned up, by the time we were running again.

This was a day for stoicism if ever there was one. Before too long, my engine blew. Earlier in the year, Junior Johnson's team had changed an engine for Cale Yarborough in mid-race, and Jim Lindholm was ready to do the same. (It was NASCAR's system of awarding points that made this worth while.) I coasted down pit road rather faster than prudence demanded, defied a one-way sign at the closest gate into the garage area, and made it nearly to our spot as the guys ran in from pit road.

They worked like a house afire, changing the engine in less than an hour, incredible as that may seem. Out I went, and turned my fastest laps of the race, hot to run to the end. That didn't happen either; we lost the second engine, probably due to engine bits in the oil lines left over from the first one. What a day.

When the checkered flag fell, Donnie Allison had won, with relief from Darrell Waltrip. Ricky Rudd finished fourth. Ricky had blown his engine after qualifying, and Darrell Waltrip lent him one. Some engines were more equal than others, for sure, and Ricky made the most of his new found power.

I left Talladega feeling much less downcast than you might think. The fantastic job the crew had done, the fury with which they had attacked and accomplished the engine change, made me feel full of heart. A team effort! Enthusiasm, a refusal to quit—this was what we had needed so badly, what had been lacking before. Eleven races remained in the NASCAR season. The Rookie of the Year prize could still be within our reach.

The next NASCAR race was set for August 21, at Michigan International Speedway. Practice was to start on Friday morning. It started without me. A restaurant in Detroit was the probable culprit; I was astonishingly, violently ill. After a sleepless night, I struggled out to the track around noon, weak as a wet dishrag. I qualified fifteenth, which was dandy under the circumstances. Bobby Allison and Bill Elliott formed the row behind me. On Sunday it rained, giving me one more day to recuperate.

On Monday, we notched our first actual finish in the top ten.

NASCAR had me in ninth place at the end, but then credited Terry Ryan with an additional lap and moved me back to tenth. The finish could have been better—we had some trouble with the transmission—but we had run in the top ten so often for so long, only to see the finish elude us, that to finally make it was simply a relief. Darrell Waltrip won.

By Thursday night we were back in Tennessee, at Bristol again. It was an incredible weekend. Friday morning I took the car out for a just a few laps.

"How does it feel?" Jim asked.

"Feels pretty good to me."

So we didn't change a thing. That afternoon, we qualified ninth. Ninth! In a superspeedway Laguna theoretically unsuited to this high-banked half-mile track. All the Chevrolet hot dogs brought Monte Carlos to Bristol—Cale Yarborough, for instance, who took the pole and was eventually to win the race. For the second time in a month, Cale was caught at tech inspection with an oversize fuel tank, incurring double the previous fine.

Jim put the race setup in the car, just a couple of minor changes, and I took it out for a few laps.

"How does it feel?"

"Feels pretty good to me."

So we didn't change a thing! We packed it up and went back to the motel. It was so unbelievable to be right on the money with the setup, we hardly knew what to do with ourselves and our light hearts. (As superstitious as farmers, though, we said not a word to each other about how well things were going.) The afternoon was scorching. We sat around the swimming pool and drank a little ice-cold beer and the guys threw their team owner Lynda Ferreri into the pool—chic clothes, chair and all.

On Sunday, we ran our first race ever where our only problems were minor ones. The engine didn't blow. The tires didn't go flat. Nobody crashed where I couldn't avoid them. The handling remained right on target. It was a blistering day, and I took relief for a while (as did other drivers) but it didn't cost us much time.

We finished sixth.

Oh, it felt good. It felt so good. It was like, *of course* this is what we can do. Hadn't you noticed?

A TALE OF TWO CITIES

Wonder Woman, of course, is make-believe, a TV character. However, Janet Guthrie is going to attempt a feat this weekend worthy of the fabulous female ... She will try driving in two tough 500 milers on opposite ends of the continent within 24 hours...
—Tom Higgins, Charlotte *Observer*, August 31, 1977

Tom Higgins wasn't exaggerating by an awful lot. The Ontario 500 USAC Championship race, which was my firm obligation to Rolla Vollstedt's Indy-car team, fell on Sunday September 4, in California. The Southern 500 NASCAR race ran the next day, Labor Day, in Darlington, South Carolina. The races themselves were just part of it. Practice, qualifying, and the Darlington rookie test would have to dovetail as well. It meant crossing the continent four times that week.

The Southern 500 was the granddaddy of all the deep-South superspeedway races, a classic event on a track so tough that the only rookie test anywhere in NASCAR was required. My commitment to Ontario seemed to preclude Darlington; but the thought of missing the Southern 500 was agonizing. Lynda and I pored over airline schedules. The post-race trip from Ontario to Darlington looked impossible, the rest merely difficult. Then Bobby Allison gave us an idea. He was racing at Darlington, of course.

"You're driving at Ontario?" he asked. "I'll be watching. I'm flying out and back with Warner Hodgdon in his private jet."

The wave of adrenaline nearly knocked me over. "There wouldn't be an extra seat coming back, would there?"

Bobby said he would ask. There wasn't. Lynda then approached Bruton Smith of Charlotte about his Jet Commander. We could use his jet, but we would have to come up with pilots and fuel, which didn't seem impossible. Lynda filed our entry for the Southern 500.

Practice opened at Ontario on Sunday the 28th of August, the same day we finished sixth and Top Rookie in the Bristol NASCAR race. After a long night of connecting flights to Los Angeles, I arrived at Ontario in the morning to find my white and green Lightning under repair. Dick Simon had been at the wheel when the radiator split. Ontario suffocated in thick yellow pea-soup pollution as usual, and the temperature was solidly into the 90s. The car was ready shortly before lunch break. Simon took it out. He turned a slow 177 mph. The engine was running suspiciously hot, he said. While the crew changed chassis settings, they muttered about its water pump.

Water pump seizure was what scarred Dick at Trenton. The concept of a failing water pump gave my butterflies something to focus on, anyway. I took the car out for a couple of highly tentative laps, barely taking my eyes off the water temperature gauge, when the track shut down for lunch.

I've got to get my head in gear for this, I thought. More than two months had elapsed since I last drove the Lightning. I had a precious hideaway, a private back room at Champion Spark Plugs. There I buried myself in an overstuffed chair and did laps in my mind, dredging the feeling of the Lightning out of its storage place deep in memory.

The technique was effective. More than twenty years later, with the aid of PET scans and MRI's of brain activity, scientists have learned that when piano students rehearse a piece in their minds, their cortical map changes in exactly the same way as when they practice on the keyboard.[1] Mental rehearsal was a process I used throughout my racing career.

Toward the end of lunch hour I went back to the garage. The radiator had split again. The water pump leaked, and a right front wheel bearing was shot. We were through for the day. I took my driver's suit off. The harsh yellow wind grated my nerves. Ontario was too damned hot.

In spite of Rolla's best efforts, the team atmosphere was palpably strained. Rolla was financially harder-pinched than ever, which must have contributed to the disarray. "I've got too much year left at the end of my money," he said, making a jest in adversity as usual, but his resilience was stretched taut. The two young guys assigned to crew my car were new volunteers. Rolla overheard his chief mechanic, Harold Sperb, make a contemptuous joke over their inability to use a clutch-centering tool, and his customary good humor vanished in a cloud of steam. "That's what I raised his salary for," he fumed. "It's *his responsibility* to supervise those guys and if they don't know how to do something, to make sure they *do*."

[1] *Newsweek*, July 24, 2000

It seemed more and more clear that I couldn't go on like this. The close cooperation that had seen Vollstedt's team through the trials-by-fire of 1976 was irremediably broken. You could easily cast Rolla in the operatic role of Wotan, fate-buffeted chief of the Norse gods, and this race as twilight for all that we had done.

Sadly, I resolved to seek another ride.

Might as well start at the top, I thought, and set off to find A. J. Foyt. He wasn't here yet, his crew said.

On Tuesday, an engine change kept the Lightning in the garage until 3 p.m. Out on the track, I was super-tense, straining to master the car. Try as I might, I couldn't find the key to working *with* it. My fastest lap was just shy of 177 mph. That left a lot of speed to be made up the next day.

I talked at length with Pete Gross, who had been on the crew at Indianapolis. He urged me to leave the team, for the sake of my life. Things don't get done on your car, he said; things don't get inspected.

I thought, *the oil temperature gauge in the Lightning broke at Indianapolis in May. It's still broken, hasn't been replaced.*

On Wednesday, I woke in the grip of fear, which wasn't entirely irrational. As I warmed the car up, in the low gears, I thought: how can I possibly get out of this?

Reluctantly, I stood on the gas. Soon I had a pair of laps in the 180s. I was talking to myself, struggling to relax, to lean on the car, to stretch my nerve endings out where they didn't want to go. Surprising myself a little, I got a grip. It didn't take anything to keep my foot down on the straights, of course; but in the turns, my right foot actually developed a cramp from the struggle between muscles that instinctively sought to lift and my will, which forced it farther down.

When practice came to an end, we put the car in line to qualify. If all went well, I might make the last flight out of Ontario, and reach Darlington around noon next day. Salt Walther was eighth in line, I was ninth. In the middle of his attempt, Walther's engine blew up. My airline connections to Darlington blew to smithereens right along with his engine. It took a long time to pick up the pieces and spread oil-absorbing material.

It's tricky to be the first to make a qualifying attempt after someone has scattered an engine. You never know just how slick the track is going to be. I took the maximum of two warmup laps, the second one at high speed, to check it out.

Green.

The first qualifying lap was 182.8 mph.

Good, if I can keep that up for four laps, we'll be fine.

On the second lap, right over the crash site in Turn 2 where the Santa Ana wind caught the car in its teeth, my engine let go. I kept the Lightning out of the wall, though it got a little sideways; flipped it out of gear and shut it down. The tow truck hustled up and threw me a line, towed me up pit road.

Rolla was standing at the back of the qualifying line. He motioned me to a stop there, as if to put the car in line for qualifying again. It was heartbreaking. I knew he couldn't afford this loss.

"No use putting it here," I said. "It's bad." I climbed out, feeling weary. "I think it's the cam gears."

Rolla had one engine left. We would use it to try again, tomorrow. Johnny Rutherford took the pole at 195.111 mph. Mario Andretti was second.

I worked my way past the autograph-seekers to our garage. Just across the way, at the facing garage, A. J. Foyt was leaning on a piece of equipment. He called to me, quizzical.

We talked first about Talladega, where Johnny Rutherford had qualified Foyt's Chevrolet three spots behind me.

Then I said, "I'm looking for another Indy-car ride next year."

There, I'd said it.

A. J. often fielded a second car. We looked at each other.

"I've got to build two new cars for next year," he said. He made a few more noncommittal remarks.

On Thursday September 1, after a fitful night, I woke in a better frame of mind. The Lightning was ready shortly after I reached the track. An hour of practice remained.

"Just two hot laps," Rolla said, "that's all." If we got the car into the field, the prize money would at least cover an engine rebuild. However many laps this tired engine had left in it, we didn't want to use them up before qualifying.

My two practice laps were a shade faster than my qualifying lap yesterday, which was unusual. We put the car in line, and I stayed with it as the guys pushed it along. I wasn't looking forward to these four laps, but I wasn't afraid of them, either.

Never has a qualifying run semed so interminable. I counted off each lap.

One. Rolla showed me the board, 182.

Two. It was 183.

Three. A 182 again. That was the pattern of qualifying here, the second lap the fastest. Just one more.

First corner. Second corner. Just two more corners.

Three. Four. Done.

We were in the field at 182.251, twenty-fourth in a field of thirty-three. I was just behind Gary Bettenhausen, just ahead of Billy Vukovich. I pulled in where the obligatory microphones were; thanked the sponsors and the guys who stayed up all night changing engines; answered the inevitable "how does it feel to be the first woman to qualify for the Ontario 500?" In fifteen minutes, my ticketed flight for Darlington would depart from the Ontario airport. As I ran for the garage, I found a policeman running along with me.

"I'll give you a ride," he gasped.

I shed my Bryant driver's suit, threw on some clothes, leaped into the patrol car.

"Where are your shoes?" Rolla yelled. I didn't know I was barefoot. Leaped out, ran for shoes. We screeched toward the airport with siren wailing, lights flashing.

"We're all frustrated race drivers," the officer said.

I made the plane. The wild ride to the airport was the most fun I'd had all day.

Darlington, South Carolina, lay deep in redneck country, close by the Pee Dee River, in a land of scrub pine and sand. When the track was constructed in 1950 at a length of a mile and a quarter, paved with asphalt, it was unique in the South. The Labor Day race there, the Southern 500, became an instant classic. Later lengthened to 1.366 miles, Darlington's banked turns were of a radius and width completely inappropriate for the speeds of the late 1970s. Many tens of thousands of dollars' worth of machinery was torn up in every race at Darlington. Journalists never failed to remind their readers that the track was known as the Lady in Black.

On this Friday before Labor Day, the infield was already jammed with pickup trucks and motor homes. I followed the chain-link fence around the garage area, looking for the way in. At all their other superspeedways, NASCAR had a stand, booth, or trailer just outside the garage area entrance, where participants got their garage-area credentials. Not here. Finally, I asked directions of a man wearing whites, the white cotton pants and shirt that were the universal identifier of an official connection with a stock car racing event.

"How do you get into the garage area?"

He looked at me with barely concealed contempt. "You cain't," he said.

I identified myself. "So you see, I need to get to my race car. Where is the entrance?"

He looked away, making it clear that I was wasting his time. "Through the cafeteria."

"Where's that?"

"Over yonder." He gestured vaguely while looking in the opposite direction, and I followed my nose. The cafeteria smelled wonderful, the homestyle cooking of the deep South. It was bustling with men in whites. They weren't NASCAR regulars; they were unknown to me, and I to them. A screen door at the back, sure enough, opened onto the other side of the chain-link fence. I walked up to it. A large man in whites barred my path.

"Sorry, ma'am, you'll have to go out the other way."

Again, I identified myself. The official team credential I signed for at registration was pinned to my shirt. The guard pointed to the small print at the bottom.

"No women or anyone under twenty-one allowed in pits," it read.

The infield was loud with the roar of practicing race cars. I needed to be among them. I said so.

"Well, I'm sorry, ma'am, I'm just here to enforce th' rules, an' the rules are, we don't let no women in the garage ayrea. You say you're supposed to be in the garage ayrea, you'll have to get permission from Bill Gazaway."

"Okay, where's Gazaway?"

"He's in the garage ayrea."

We were still at stalemate when a member of someone else's crew came along. His positive identification of me cut no mustard whatsoever, but he volunteered to carry a message to Gazaway, wherever Gazaway might be. Gazaway was running the Darlington rookie meeting, as it turned out. When I finally got there, Darrell Waltrip was speaking.

"There's only one way through Three and Four. If you try to put two cars through there, you will crash. Both of you. Particularly if you're the slower car and, trying to let someone by, you put a wheel on the flat. It'll shoot you right up to the wall and put both of you out of the race."

Darrell had put his Monte Carlo on the pole in qualifying the previous day.

Gazaway said, "We've had pileups here take fifteen cars out of the race."

G. C. Spencer spoke next. At the age of fifty-two, G. C. would soon retire. This was to be his last race at Darlington, where he had put a car in the field every year but two since 1957. Bent and worn, he looked beaten, more like seventy than fifty. The contrast between Spencer and Waltrip, the articulate young lion, could not have been greater. G. C. had a hard time articulating anything. Painfully, he squeezed out a few words: how narrow the track was, how unforgiving of the slightest error.

That afternoon, the second day of qualifying, G. C. set not only the fastest time of day but fourth fastest in the field, at 152.219 mph to Waltrip's 153.493 mph.

Most of our practice time that day was lost to an oddball array of mechanical problems, but at the end, I finally got my first few laps. What a very narrow, lumpy, idiosyncratic track it was. The entrance to Turn 3, particularly, was a mystery. Turn 3 was the one that everyone talked about, and with good reason. When the track closed, I hadn't even begun to understand it.

Alex was there, the warmth at the center of my heart. We drove slowly toward the motel, talking racing, catching up. We were tired, sticky with South Carolina humidity, gritty with track dirt. The motel was awful, stale-smelling, with sagging beds, falling plaster in the bath. The nearby restaurant had pretensions a lot more *haute* than its cuisine. None of that mattered. What mattered was Alex. I slept well, for the first time in days.

The next morning, Lynda Ferreri greeted me with bad news. Bruton Smith's private jet was financially impossible. She had, however, found a complex set of airline connections to Florence, S.C., after the Ontario race. The night between races would be spent on planes and in terminals. My heart sank. Would this tough a schedule impair my performance? The disappointment cast a pall on the day.

I went back to work, learning the track. Someone, another driver, tossed me a red herring. He said that the veteran drivers who were passing judgment on rookie tests wanted the rookie to use only the bottom lane of the track. I tried that. It was amazingly difficult, and the lap times in that lane weren't nearly fast enough to pass the test. Time was running out. This was the last day of qualifying.

Jim said, "The other rookies have used the whole track."

Oh.

Just to make sure, I stopped to speak with Don Wall, who was officiating at the exit of pit road. As always, he was straightforward and fair.

"You can use the whole track," he said.

We had hardly any time left. I turned two laps, came in to check the times. They were still too slow. I tossed the components of our situation around in my mind. The conclusion was clear. I gritted my teeth, drove down to Don Wall and formally requested the rookie test.

"Wait here," he said. "We'll get the observers out."

I did laps in my mind.

A year ago here, only four out of seven rookie candidates passed the test. The rest were sent home. Bobby Allison, three-time winner of the Southern 500 here, had failed his rookie test the first time.

Don Wall spoke into his radio, then turned to me.

"If you see a black flag, it means come in for consultation. We'll tell you what you're doing wrong.

"Okay," he said. "Go ahead."

The rookie test here, unlike Indianapolis, had no fixed duration. It seemed to last forever. Each time past start-finish, I watched the official up in the flag stand. He looked bored. I sure wasn't. I was putting everything I had into getting the speed up to snuff, while staying clean in traffic.

When will this end?

Finally, I saw that he had a furled flag in his hand.

What is it? What *is* it? Is it black?

Slowly he unrolled it; waved it just as I flashed by. It was the checker. In the pits, Jim showed me the lap times. I had found the necessary speed. But the judges were unknown. Richard Petty was likely to have been among them.

Twenty minutes later, I was walking through the garage area when the PA system crackled to life. "Attention in the garage area. Janet Guthrie, attention Janet Guthrie."

At the top of the infield observation tower, men waved.

"You did a fine job on the rookie test," the loudspeaker blared. "Congratulations." Darrell Waltrip, in the tower, made a thumb-to-forefinger sign.

I waved back, took a deep breath, and continued toward my car. A lot of work remained to be done.

Time to qualify. Trouble. The engine skipped and missed. Instead of picking up speed as usual, I ran a tenth of a second slower than in practice. Nevertheless, we were second fastest of the day's sixteen qualifiers. Once again, I was the first woman, etc., etc. Parky Nall had his plane waiting at a little grass strip next to the track. He took me to Charlotte, where I connected through Birmingham, Dallas, and Los Angeles to Ontario. Rolla Vollstedt met the plane.

Lynda had paged me in the Charlotte terminal. "Great news!" she said. "There's a seat on Warner Hodgdon's jet after all. I talked with Roger Penske in the pits at Ontario, and his wife decided not to come to Darlington."

So I slept well that night.

On race day, at breakfast, Kay and George Bignotti asked me to join them. Kay's father Louis Meyer, three-time winner of the Indianapolis 500, was there.

Meyer said, "I feel sorry for you."

I said, "I have enormous respect for Rolla, but he has a complex situation on his hands." I didn't go into details.

Later I studied the mountains, my mind turning to thoughts of mortality. Cucamonga Peak, ten miles distant, was veiled in yellowish-brown smog. Nothing felt right. The Lightning almost certainly had more speed in it, maybe two or three miles an hour, than I had been able to extract so far. Above all else, I was in racing for the internal reward: the knowledge that no one, *no one*, could have gotten more out of a car than I had. I was in racing to find the edge. Without that, nothing was well with the world.

In the paddock area, I tracked down Roger Penske. "Yes," he said, "everything is set." He gave me details of the flight back to Darlington. I wasn't acquainted with Warner Hodgdon, an immensely wealthy man who was newly arrived on the racing scene. From what little I knew, he seemed to enjoy flaunting his wealth and most particularly, his power.

Mysteriously, race day felt open to me. I was ready to give it a good shot. Just as mysteriously, I felt tense. Maybe I was picking up vibes from Hodgdon. I was already suited up when Rolla told me Roger Penske had been looking for me. He had found Rolla instead.

"Jan, he says the seat on the plane is gone."

What??

I ran out the door. With my driver's suit on, I was fair game for the fans, no protective coloration left. Running was the only defense. Through the tunnel, the gauntlet of autograph seekers, to the pits. Penske was on the grid near our car.

"Hodgdon gave the seat to a guy on his crew," he said. He apologized. There was nothing to be done. Certainly, Hodgdon had made his opinion of women racing drivers quite clear.

Ran back to the garage.

Worked with grim determination to get my head in gear.

Time wound down. I taped the protective tear-off cellophanes onto my helmet visor, a seemingly trivial task that tweaked my anxieties right up to the snapping point.

A crowd of 75,000 had assembled in the stands.

The Star Spangled Banner, the pace laps, the green flag. We settled into the race, but not for long. Dick Simon's engine let go after five laps, and the yellow came out.

Back under green, I started moving up in the field. I had found my way into the right mental space. The temperature was in the 90s, with strong unpredictable gusts of wind to keep us entertained. About a quarter of the way into the race, I was in eighth place.[2] Then the water temperature rose. I called in the numbers on the radio. The needle swept back and forth. When it pegged at 110˚C, on Lap 64, I pitted.

Chief mechanic Harold Sperb yelled at me to continue, keep running as it was. "No," I said. This wasn't negotiable. I knew engines too well. And I had no desire to get scalded. I climbed out, so that they could pull the cowling and access the cooling system. They found and replaced a broken hose clamp. Someone ran for more coolant.

Meanwhile, Dick Simon was standing there. He wanted the car; I could see it as clearly as if he were speaking the words.

"Do you want it?" I said. "You can have it if you want it." That was written into the contract, after all, that he had the right to take over the car.

"I'd love it," Simon said, "but I don't want to hurt you."

"Take it," I said.

He did.

I watched, feeling bereft. My power, the power that had propelled me into eighth place, was severed from its application. Just like a car with a burned-out clutch, my interior engine could no longer drive me forward. I felt almost as if my neck were broken and my body paralyzed—the one hazard of racing that I always truly feared.

On Lap 112, as Simon bent the car down into Turn 1, a ball of fire came out the back of the engine. I jumped to Sperb.

[2] Associated Press, e.g. Miami *Herald*, Sept. 5, 1977

"Did you see that?"

"What?"

"That fire out the back of the car."

"Sometimes they do that." He turned away.

Whatever the team problems had been, there was no reason for Sperb to discount my technical sense. *Idiot*, I muttered. Already the yellow light was on. Simon had spun between One and Two, possibly in the Lightning's own oil as the USAC official with the radio told us. He wasn't hurt. The tow trucks went out. I walked back to the garage and changed.

Rolla took me to the airport. In the pits, while Simon was driving the car, Rolla's temper had flared.

"I hope you're not mad because I gave Dick the car," I said.

"No, I was mad because I didn't know the hose clamp had broken. I thought it was just loose."

Dick had been scalded at Indianapolis because of a loose hose clamp.

I asked Rolla to call Lynda or Jim in South Carolina and let them know I would reach Atlanta at midnight.

The mood was somber as we said goodbye

Lynda Ferreri was waiting in Atlanta with a chartered airplane, a light twin. She needn't have come with it; she could have stayed in bed in Darlington, but as always she threw her full force into the success of her team. We reached Darlington at 3 a.m.

I drew on the previous night's reserves, and when the green flag came down to start the Southern 500, I felt ready for it.

I got my doors blown off. Instead of working my way into the top ten, I remained mired halfway down the field. I got passed by guys that I had been lapping for nearly a year. It was miserable, horrid. What was going on?

Meanwhile, Darlington was living up to its reputation. Seven drivers had smashed into each other and/or the wall by the time rain halted the race on Lap 208. It could have rained the rest of the day as far as I was concerned, but no such luck. We resumed an hour and a half later. The Laguna's starter refused its duty, as it had in practice, and the guys pushed it to a start. But I had finally put two and two together. Our problem wasn't just the starter motor. The whole electrical system was involved, including ignition. The gremlins that plagued my qualifying laps hadn't gone away, they had just hidden. I was getting my doors blown off because we were down on power.

It was a relief to figure this out. On the green, I set out with renewed vigor. The race wasn't always to the swift, and the rookie standings were at stake. Sure enough, three laps later rookie Sam Sommers hit the wall and was out of the race. But ten minutes later, it was my turn to be bitten by Darlington.

Darrell Waltrip, leading the race, was some five car lengths ahead as I came out of Turn 2. Cale Yarborough, running second, was tucked up to Darrell's bumper. Part way along the back straight, D. K. Ulrich lay in front of them, in the outside lane. Etiquette required him to move down. D. K. was a good reliable driver, so Waltrip assumed that he would drop into a lower lane by the time he was overtaken. Waltrip was wrong. For whatever reason, D. K. didn't move. Cale saw his chance, and pounced, whipping to the inside to pull alongside Waltrip as they reached the slower car. Boxed in, and reacting too late, Waltrip nudged the back of Ulrich's car.

I saw the nudge, and the result. The back end of D. K.'s car jumped out, and I hit the brakes. D. K.'s car continued to rotate, turning broadside in front of Waltrip and striking Cale's car, which sent Cale spinning. The three cars bounced around, scattering and splatting against the walls here and there, but I had my path picked out, and was sure I would get away clean.

Then I was struck from behind—struck hard. The impact knocked me around clockwise.

My first thought was, *How remarkably stupid. Did he have his eyes closed, or what?*

Later I found out it was Terry Bivens, and that he had drum brakes on his car. I had discs now, that Jim had installed earlier in the year, which probably made the difference.

Bivens then clobbered the right-hand side of my car. I hit the wall once or twice, spun down the straight, and hit the wall again. I may have glanced off some of the other four cars along the way. The engine quit. Crosswise to the track, I peered back upstream. Hordes of cars were bearing down on me, still racing toward start-finish. And me with no starter, dead in the water!

I held the clutch depressed. Slowly, infinitely slowly, the Laguna rolled backward to the safety of the inside apron. Nobody else hit me. With the last of the Laguna's momentum, I cranked the wheel clockwise and aimed it at Turn 3. Our back-straight pits were behind me, and Jim and the guys were running toward the car. They pushed it to a start. I roared around the track toward the pit entrance, feeling it out. The steering was knocked out of kilter. They made repairs, and we went on.

Ten laps later, an appalling wreck on the front straight took out the inside guard rail and seven feet of concrete wall. The drivers weren't seriously hurt. We crawled around under the yellow for thirty-three laps while the guard rail was rebuilt. After that, we ran under green until the end. It had been six hours seventeen minutes since the start of the Southern 500.

It was a measure of the distance we had come that no one, not the press or anyone else, tried to pin the five-car wreck on me. A year earlier, Lynda and I had joked that if a wreck happened within half a lap of me—in either direction—it would be my fault. David Pearson won. We were classified sixteenth, out of twenty-four cars still running at the end.

NASCAR FLEXES
ITS MUSCLE

Between June and October of 1977, I drove one or more races each weekend for seventeen consecutive weeks. It was passionate, grueling, and wonderful; every racer's dream. Reporters kept asking if I expected to win the next race. The drivers at the top of the heap in Winston Cup had averaged five years on the circuit before their first win. By September of my official rookie year, it seemed clear to me that I was going to beat the averages. "We might win this Sunday or we might not," I said. "But we are going to win one day. There is no doubt about that."

The Dover race on September 18, where we finished eleventh, was our fifteenth Winston Cup race of the year. According to the rookie points rules, the best fifteen finishes were counted. From now on, we would be dropping the race with the worst result and adding any that were better, as my two main competitors, Sam Sommers and Ricky Rudd, had been doing for some time.

Mathematically, we still had a shot at the title; but we were going to miss the next NASCAR event, on the half-mile track at Martinsville, West Virginia. The final race that I was committed to drive for Rolla Vollstedt, the USAC Championship race at Trenton on September 25, posed a conflict that could not be resolved. Our sacrifice of Martinsville proved to be in vain. The Trenton race weekend was rained out, and the race was never held.

Our next opportunity was the NAPA National 500 NASCAR Winston Cup race at Charlotte on October 9, the only event for which we ever had a special engine built just for qualifying. When we put the car in line to qualify, we knew of only five cars with faster practice times. Unhappily, I made an error of judgment and spun out. Nothing was bent or damaged except the tires, and my pride. I felt even worse for Lynda Ferreri and Jim Lindholm than I did for myself.

The next day, I was mystified when my qualifying run was some four miles an hour slower than we had expected—an appalling loss of speed. The brand-new tires were certainly suspect, but there was nothing we could do about it now. NASCAR's rules obliged you to start the race on the same tires you qualified with.

On Sunday when the race began, I ran no better than in qualifying. It was mortifying. The car seemed to be balanced well enough—it just wouldn't go through the turns. We changed the right-side tires, the most important ones, on the first yellow, and then changed them again. It didn't help.

After 323 of the 500 miles, we changed left-side tires. Suddenly, I started passing everything in sight.

Charlotte was a physically taxing track, and when the hellacious psychological strain of running uncompetitively was added, the first two hours of the race had drained me of a certain amount of strength. I inventoried what was left. It's toward this part of a race that you start to run on reserves that are never tapped in everyday life. You become distanced from your physical self: the body will do what the mind instructs it, and complaints on the part of the body are irrelevant, to be noted for future remedy and ignored. I felt grim that we had dropped so far behind, but determined to use everything the car could now offer.

How much harder could the green Laguna be pushed? I probed for the edge. As the speed soared, it was good to feel the depth of my reserves. It was even better to see that I was gaining on Cale Yarborough, who was running second, and in the part of the self that stores up emotional material for future savoring, it was fiercely satisfying that I could gain on him in the turns.

I'm not quite sure how I caught him; maybe he had just come out of the pits. But catch him I did, and it was immediately clear that indeed he had more power. (A year later, Buddy Baker told me the engines we were using were fifty or more horsepower down from those of the top-running, Detroit-connected teams.) I tucked into Cale's draft. With this nice tow down the straights, I could stay right on his heels, so I started feeling things out for a pass.

Turn 2, I calculated, was the best place to make a move, and inside of Cale was the place to do it. The first time I tried it, I came even with his rear fender before the blast of straightaway air forced me back into his draft. The next time around, I reached his door. Two shots at it was a good education, and I figured on the third try I could make it stick: pass him, and let him push me down the straight instead of pull. The interesting thing was, Cale's manners were impeccable. A little dirty driving on his part could have shaken me loose. He didn't do it.

NASCAR did it.

They threw me the black flag.

I called Lynda on the radio. "What the #@&* is this black flag?" (In those days before scanners, no one but Lynda could hear me.)

Lynda said, "It's for the chrome trim."[1]

I knew about the chrome trim. The uppermost of several screws that held a thin strip of chrome to the left-hand side of the windshield had come undone. Six or eight inches of it, perhaps the top third, had bent back and was visible outside the window net. The trim had nothing to do with securing the windshield, which was held in place by pieces of steel.

Lynda said, "They say it's a hazard and you'll have to come into the pits and have it removed."

I pressed the transmit button and described to Lynda the ancestry of the NASCAR officials, their sexual preferences, and exactly where they could put the chrome trim when they got it.

By now I was on the back straight. I had three laps in which to answer the black flag before they quit scoring my car.

I reached out the window, straining against my shoulder harness. The rush of air at a 150-some mph made it like arm-wrestling a giant. I seized the loose end and yanked with all my strength. The molding yielded, and I flung it away.

On the front straight, the officials could see that it was gone, and it would be the second of my three laps. On the third, I saw that they had withdrawn the black flag.

Meanwhile, Cale was gone. The aerodynamic drag of my arm out the window, the diversion of focus, and the slight upset of the car's balance had enabled him to pull out a few car lengths, so that I lost his draft. I stayed far out on the ragged edge for a few laps, trying to catch up, but it was futile.

If ever there was a time when emotional detachment, long since an acquired skill, was crucial, it was then. I took my white fury over losing Cale and stored it somewhere. In the last fifty laps of the race, I moved into the top ten; then passed Bill Elliott, the future Ford star, to take ninth. The best was yet to come.

Benny Parsons led most of the race. Toward the end of it, Benny and A.J. Foyt came drafting along behind me, creeping slowly closer in my rear-view mirror. When the time came, I gave them the pass, then tucked into their draft at the exit of the turn. As we blasted

[1] This episode was reported in e.g. Richmond (Virg.) *News Leader*, Oct. 12, 1977

along the back straight, the nose of my car was no more than a yard from A. J.'s rear bumper. Our eyes met as he glanced in his mirror. I knew how this would play out, and loved it so much that an involuntary smile crinkled the grit on my face. A. J. didn't know yet that the draft would supply all I was lacking. But I did.

We bore down into Turns 3 and 4. Earlier on, I had found that a most unusual tactic worked wonderfully there, the way my car was set up. I was deliberately putting my left side tires actually down onto the flat part. We tilted onto the banking at the entrance of Turn 3, and I edged partly down on the flat as I had been doing. When we came out onto the front straight, A. J.'s eyes moved to his mirror again, and I was still there.

Our three cars wriggled and squirmed through the D-shaped part of the track in front of the pits, and soared over the bump into Turn 1. The vertical and lateral Gs gripped us as the cars rolled onto their right-hand suspension, then released us as we skated out onto the back straight. A. J. looked in his mirror again, and I was still there. Since I was the third car in this draft, on the straights my accelerator foot was a hair off the floor. I was tempted to press it down, inch up and touch him.

Now, here is what that clever sonofagun did, after observing *just once* the success of my odd line in Turns 3 and 4: he tried it himself. He nearly wrecked. Whatever the differences were in the setups of our cars, what worked for me was nearly a disaster for him. He didn't try it again. The three of us continued our little parade. I was sorely tempted to slingshot him, but with Benny leading the race and just a few laps to go, discretion seemed the better part of valor. The risk of interfering with their balance was too great.

We took the checkered flag that way: Benny's white car, A. J.'s red car and then my green one.

Terry Adderley, the president of Kelly Girl, had rented a big suite overlooking the track. He said, "The first part of the race I couldn't wait for it to be over, and the second part I wanted it never to end. What happened?"

"Left side tires," I said.

We finished ninth, and Top Rookie for the fourth time.

Sometimes I watch the old video of the finish of this race, taped off ABC's broadcast. The colors are faded now, but the memory is as vivid as on that day.

The NASCAR Winston Cup race in Rockingham on October 23

was about the most grueling race I ever drove, a notoriously brutal event lasting some four and a half hours. We finished ninth, after some gearbox trouble, and won our fifth Top Rookie spot. At the time it seemed like, *well, ninth, that's okay but no more than okay, we are better than that.*

Donnie Allison dominated the race, and won.

Mail had been piling up in my New York apartment for nearly a month. It held bad news. My best chance for an Indy-car ride next year was gone. STP had seemed extremely promising, but a letter from the CEO said their racing budget was to be cut. News from the man who held the option for a movie about me was no better. There had been nibbles from the major Hollywood studios, he said, but no bites. Funding for Indianapolis from that source seemed too far distant to help.

Despite our recent top-ten NASCAR finishes, Kelly executives had been noncommittal so far about their racing plans for next year, and it was making me acutely uneasy. In public, I made the usual cheerful and optimistic noises. I was doing Kelly PR in Atlanta when the Kelly Girl doll fracas burst into the news. Thirty-five *thousand* big rag dolls had been sent to Kelly's customers, the (mostly male) employers of their (mostly female) temporary secretarial help. "Kelly Girl" was stitched onto the dolls' Kelly green dresses. An accompanying letter from Kelly's president told his customers "these dolls have always been favorites and always will be."

The promotion backfired like an exploding cigar. Businesswomen and secretaries across the country expressed their ire. Kelly's public relations director immediately claimed that no one who worked for Kelly Services was called a "Kelly Girl." "Kelly Girl," of course, was the name that was painted on my car. I had figured that sooner or later, this would become an embarrassment to the company. The use of the word "girl" to describe a grown woman was one of the earliest symbolic issues taken up by the women's movement, and had long since become a sore spot among working women. I had entreated the Kelly executives to use the corporate name, Kelly Services, on the car instead, but couldn't persuade them. The doll promotion offered distressing insight into the corporate ethos. Lynda estimated that its cost was about the same as a year's racing program.

I urged Kelly's PR people to counter the news reports of the doll fiasco with news of the Kelly Girl racing team. By now, Kelly's clipping service had filled many enormous scrapbooks with local and wire-service stories and glossy magazine pieces about the NASCAR events. There was also a Kelly advertisement that I liked a lot, showing a pit stop. The crew were leaping, the air hoses flying, and the copy read "Good temporary help is hard to find." A woman team owner, a woman racing driver finishing in the top ten in the country's most competitive series, in a Kelly car—couldn't they capitalize on this to help set right the Kelly Girl doll misstep? But no such move was made.

Rain fell on Atlanta International Raceway on the scheduled first day of practice for the Dixie 500, and not a wheel turned. The garage area was on fire with news of NASCAR's 1978 rules. Chevrolet Lagunas like ours, as well as Monte Carlos, were about to be legislated out of competition. Chevrolet had been winning too many races.

Rain continued all day Friday, leaving the entirety of practice and qualifying to be conducted in a single day. I mused over the rookie situation. It was still mathematically possible for us to win the title, but we would have to do very well while the other two contenders did poorly, both here and at Ontario in November.

What was it about the rain, anyway? Everything bad seemed to happen in the rain. The gloomy drizzle resumed after qualifying, and Jim Lindholm told me he intended to quit the team after Ontario, the next and last race of the year.

There had been friction between Jim and Lynda Ferreri for some time now. Neither had the background to fully appreciate the strengths of the other. Lynda, whose profession was in marketing, was sensational at interacting with the sponsors. But her mechanical knowledge was only slightly greater than zero, which Jim seemed to resent.

Jim was a strong and aggressive crew chief, who would do whatever it took to have the race car ready to go. Unfortunately, Jim was temperamental and often abrasive. He kept laying down ultimatums to Lynda on one subject or another. Lynda had expressed her view of Jim's temperament more than once. "If anyone's going to be a prima donna," she told me, "it's supposed to be the driver. But instead, we have a crew chief who's a prima donna."

I worked hard to convey to each of them the invaluable strong points of the other. Lynda listened more attentively than Jim did, but I don't think either was ever really convinced.

Rain continued into the night. Alex was distant that evening, almost hostile, for no reason that I could understand. A planned vacation together went up in smoke. It kept on raining.

On race day, CBS-TV's live broadcast constraints prompted an unorthodox start on a wet track, under the yellow flag. At the green I was on the move, gaining eleven positions, and ran eighth for a long time.[2] Then a torrent of rain brought us to a red-flag halt for over an hour.

What was it about the rain? Everything bad ... when we resumed, our pit stops were catastrophes. *Each time*, they put me a lap down. The worst of it was a badly bungled stop under the last, long yellow, in the rain. I came out two more laps down, at the tail end of the pack. They threw the green flag on a damp track in an ominous charcoal twilight, with ten laps to go.

On the final lap, a violent crash among the three leaders filled Turn 4 with smoke and flames. I dodged through the bits and pieces, a moving minefield. The drivers weren't hurt. We finished sixteenth out of thirty-three cars still running at the end. Ricky Rudd finished ninth. Our last hope of winning Rookie of the Year had dissolved in the baleful rain.

Not long after the Atlanta race, I was invited to speak at Purdue University, which had been the academic home of Amelia Earhart. A reception followed. One recent graduate was an officer in the U.S. Navy. Pinned to her uniform were aviator's wings. Quietly self-assured, she conveyed what would later be called a sense of entitlement: as if it were inconceivable that anyone could question the ability of a woman to fill the position she held. Another recent graduate, with a master's degree from MIT, was aiming at the scientist-astronaut program. She, too, acted as if the notion of gender-based barriers had never crossed her mind.

Nearby was a woman who had known Amelia Earhart at Purdue in 1935-36. The sense of continuity was strong. So was the sense of re-inventing the wheel, of endlessly demonstrating that women were as capable of significant accomplishment as men, and having this news forgotten once again.

From Lafayette I flew to Detroit for a meeting with the Kelly top brass. My apprehension about their commitment proved to be justified. They informed me that Kelly Girl would fund only five races in the next year. They said that the geographic distribution of the races didn't suit their network of offices, and that they needed money

---

[2] *National Speed Sport News*, Nov. 9, 1977; also CBS-TV race broadcast, in my possession

for capital investment.

I didn't sleep that night. Five races wouldn't hold the crew together. The guys would surely disperse to teams that could engage them for a full racing year. Five races wouldn't cover the cost of a new car, a competitive replacement for the hamstrung Laguna. Our hard-earned progress into the top ten, the chance to win races, would be blasted to smithereens. Racing at the top levels couldn't end like this, not now. It was too soon, there hadn't been enough of it, there was so much more to do. Around dawn, I called Lynda Ferreri with the bad news. By then, I had some ideas. Lynda had some ideas too. We would talk about them in a couple of days, at the Ontario race.

Like the last brief brilliant flare of an incandescent light before it goes dark...

I started the Times 500 at Ontario on November 20 in fifteenth place, but soon moved up to eighth. This huge, smooth track with its fast flat turns, the first big oval I ever drove on, was my favorite place; and I was having a wonderful time. I had run with the leaders before, but not from the very start of the race, on the lead lap.

At a hundred miles I was tenth, within a stone's throw of the leaders, watching Benny Parsons and Darrell Waltrip swap the lead with Richard Petty. Then oil on the track brought out another yellow flag. All nine cars ahead of me dived for the pits. In front of the green Laguna lay nothing but that enormous straightaway, empty. We were in first place.

Holeee...

Calm and collected as always on the radio, Lynda said, "Stay out." She was the keeper of the lap sheets, the record that told us when to pit for fuel. She was telling me to continue to lead, under the yellow flag.

As we idled around the track behind the pace car, I gave careful thought to the restart some laps hence. When the pace car turned off its lights and pulled down into the bottom warmup lane toward pit road, the pack would be under my control. The moment to stand on the gas, and the speed at which we did it, would be of my choice. Restarts were a serious responsibility; they were tricky and could be screwed up. I wasn't going to do that.

My car number flashed to the top of the infield pylon, and I allowed myself the luxury of a brief moment to relish it. Could I hold onto the lead once they threw the green?

I had every reason to believe that, indeed, I could.

If I initiated the restart in second gear, at a speed and rpm such that the engine was just below the peak of its torque curve, I would be as fast as anyone on the track down the front straight and into Turn 1. The way I had been getting through the turns, I could easily stay in front until somewhere along the back straight. Depending on how the drivers behind me reacted to this, unless two or three of them hooked up for a pass, I might hold onto the lead for a couple of laps. Maybe even longer.

My lust for this burned like white fire.

At the start-finish line, the official held up his forefinger: one lap to go. The yellow light on top of the pace car went out. The pack rearranged itself into a double row, lapped cars to the inside. We circled onto the backstretch. I slowed the pack to the pace I wanted, letting the pace car pull out a safe distance. I intended to stand on the gas as soon as the pace car was below the white line in Turn 4, launched toward the pit entrance. If they threw the green flag early, as they sometimes did, while we were still in the turn, the pace car needed to be out of our way. Otherwise, I could anticipate the green at whatever point I chose.

Ready.

In the middle of Turn 3, James Hylton appeared out of nowhere, moving fast, out to my right. What in the world was he doing?

He pulled ahead, accelerating hard. He was passing the leader, under the yellow flag.

The SOB was jumping the start!

But I was *not* going to let Hylton crowd me into making a start that I didn't want to make. I had to get that pace car out of the way, for one thing.

Hylton kept moving. By the time we reached Turn 4 he had passed the pace car, under the yellow flag.

God damn son of a bitch!

When we came out onto the straight, Hylton was four car lengths in front of the pace car, and a hell of a long way in front of the pack.

Everyone else held his position. Surely NASCAR wouldn't throw the green on this grossly irregular situation. They would send us around under the yellow again, and make Hylton go back where he ought to be.

NASCAR threw the green.

I held my lead over the pack, as I knew my engine could, while we thundered toward Turn 1. I would be on Hylton's heels when we got there. He would be in my way. I had lapped him dozens of times this year. He never moved over for me. If I mixed it up with him in Turn 1, what would the regular front-runners do—the drivers who were right on my heels? Always before, when I was running with the leaders, I had been a lap down from them. They would expect me to move over, as I always had. If I surprised them, the result could be a hell of a mess.

When we reached the turns, I stayed in line behind Hylton, and the leaders went by.

Hylton continued to make my life difficult. When I got by him, the leaders were too far ahead to catch their draft.

Bastard.

File it, set it aside. Anger will slow you down.

The Laguna's handling remained all that could be asked. The car worked perfectly in the turns. On the long straights, as usual, the engine lacked a bit at the top end, but a front-runner's draft could haul me along. Some of the top drivers must have expected me to back off if they tried to pass. But I was on the lead lap, running for position, as fast as anyone through the turns. Back off? Not a chance. The middle-of-the-field guys knew that already. The front-runners like A. J. Foyt were just learning it, this day.

Presently I started drafting Bobby Allison. Within a couple of laps, I tried a pass. He nosed in front of me. I tried again. After a few laps of this, Bobby motioned to me, making straight-ahead gestures with his right hand. He meant that I should quit trying to pass him and that we should use our two-car draft to catch up with the next bunch. I did that, briefly.

Bobby Allison kept looking in his mirror. I think all he saw was teeth. I was grinning from ear to ear. Up ahead, the front runners were gaining no ground.

My Laguna's slope nose was its advantage. The pair of us ought to go faster if I ran in front. I tried again to get there. Our cars were evenly matched, equal as to power, and equivalent in handling as well. I could hear when he stood on the gas, and when he eased off, as clearly as if the engine were my own. But Bobby did *not* want to be passed, and did his absolute best to prevent it.

The slingshot was what could get me into Turn 1 (or 3) ahead of him. I dropped back from his bumper, then floored it; ran up in his draft, popped out from behind him at the last minute, and led into the turn. In the short chute, he crossed behind me, nosing into Turn 2 on the inside. At 150 mph, it was a high-stakes game. I kept at it. If my slingshot timing was late and we arrived at the turn nose to nose, he chopped me off. If I was early, he would slingshot me right back, and dive inside. We went back and forth for a long time. About the only difference in our style was, I wouldn't chop across his nose in the turns as he did mine. I gave him running room instead. It was a good match. I loved every minute, more than I could ever tell.

At the halfway point, 250 miles, Bobby and I were still playing together. High up in the starter's stand, the official held out crossed flags. In the back of my mind I noted the halfway signal; but I was preoccupied with something else.

Two laps earlier, the needle of the water temperature gauge had started to swing. At the exit of Turn 2, it read 190 degrees—about right—but with the accelerator pedal pressed hard to the floor on the straight, the needle moved steadily upward, until at the entrance to Turn 3 it read 240 degrees.

No, this can't be happening. If I denied the truth, it had to go away. A cylinder head hadn't cracked. NO!

Maybe I've been running too long in the draft?

The blockage of air to your radiator in a draft could cause overheating. That was why a pair of drivers drafting together generally allowed each other to swap the lead. I eased off a bit and let Bobby pull out some space. The needle continued to swing. With a terrible sinking sensation, I knew that the engine was doomed.

Then an exhaust manifold cracked. The engine changed pitch, and puffs of carbon monoxide-laden gases swirled through the car. The toes of my left foot curled back from the heat that burned on the other side of the firewall.

Ed Negre's car caught fire. I was coming up to lap him at the time. Flames billowed underneath and out the sides of his Dodge. Ed wrestled it down to the inside, squirmed out the window while the car still slithered across the grass.

I pulled the safety pin of the Laguna's fire system. Sooner or later, my engine would let go. It might quietly melt and seize. Or, it might throw a rod out the side of the block, loosing a torrent of hot oil. If it scattered like that, the red-hot edges and flaming exhaust from the cracked header would set the oil on fire. Like Negre.

I was still on the lead lap when my engine finally succumbed on Lap 177, less than sixty miles from the end. It went quietly. There was no fire.

The bitter with the sweet ... this day had offered a surfeit of both. Neil Bonnett won. My playmate Bobby Allison finished seventh. Ricky

Rudd was eighth, becoming Rookie of the Year. NASCAR's complex scoring system gave him 349 points after 25 races, Sam Sommers 335 points after 23 races, and us 306 points after 19 races.

James Hylton's action was without precedent. Once I was out of the race, rage over it boiled through my veins like nitrogen bubbles in the blood of a surfacing diver. The mystery was, why hadn't NASCAR sent the pack around for an orderly start? Reporters asked that question. NASCAR stated blandly that Hylton had been reprimanded. A reprimand carried no penalty or fine. Much later, it occurred to me that maybe, just maybe, the move hadn't been Hylton's very own original idea. It wasn't unknown for a NASCAR official to transmit instructions to a driver, via his crew chief's radio.

Lynda and I talked briefly about filing a protest, but what good would it do? The moment was gone, and nothing in the world could ever bring it back.

Some yellowed clippings from this race lie among my souvenirs. Chris Economaki wrote in *National Speed Sport News*, "The entire crowd [was] on its feet as she dueled Bobby Allison ... later she took on champion Cale Yarborough in similar fashion."[3] *Stock Car Racing Magazine*: "One of the best races of the afternoon was between Bobby Allison and Janet Guthrie. They swapped positions back and forth and ran side by side trying to outbrave each other in action that had the veterans shaking their heads. It was some fine show."[4]

It was the most fun I ever had in Winston Cup racing. At long last, I had found again "that first fine careless rapture" of my sport-car racing years.

[3] Nov. 23, 1977
[4] Issue dated March 1978

CLIFFHANGER

The winter of 1977-78, after the Ontario NASCAR Winston Cup race, was as bleak as anything I had endured since the year I built the Celica. It seemed inconceivable that I wouldn't find a ride, wouldn't be able to build on the momentum and experience of the previous season; yet that was how it was.

Each hour of each day, I sought a way to continue. I hounded team owners. I pitched every corporate executive I met, or could think of, or heard about. I searched *Thomas Register* for names. I pitched executives I met on flights from one wintertime sports banquet to another. I ransacked books on salesmanship, and picked up the phone again.

Experienced and successful marketing agents approached me, offering assistance. I leaped at it. "With the exposure you bring to a company, and your record," they said, "making a deal for you will be as easy as picking money up off the sidewalk."

The rejections piled up in scores, which grew to hundreds. The short dark days and long black nights of winter closed in.

During racing season I slept soundly. As long as I had a car to drive, as long as the savory prospect of the next race lay ahead, I was at peace. But over this awful winter, the hour of the wolf held me nightly in its teeth. At three in the morning, every morning, hairy little monsters breathed in my face. They sneered, "You don't have a ride at Indianapolis. Your Winston Cup rides are too few and your car is uncompetitive."

Then one day, my answering machine held a message that made my heart leap. Seymour Seitz and BBS Productions were unknown to me. They had an offer, they said. Could this be it, at last? My hands were shaking as I dialed the number.

It was an offer, all right. Mr. Seitz wanted to know if I would judge the Miss Universe beauty contest. When I stopped laughing, I said that there was a basic philosophical, ah, *chasm* between us; and thanked him for thinking of me.

The only solace or respite that winter came from looking

backwards, which is never much solace at all. Not long after the Ontario race, sportswriter Craig Stolze asked several NASCAR drivers to comment on my rookie season. Cale Yarborough's answer epitomized the rest: "There is no question about her ability to race with us. More power to her. She has 'made it' in what I think is the most competitive racing circuit in the world."[1]

In a year's time, what a world of change there had been.

Certainly the wintertime came bedecked in honors. *The Ladies' Home Journal* nominated me among its Sportswomen of the Year. There were standing ovations at the sports banquets. Yet all of it felt hollow. I had never wanted to be famous. What I wanted was to race.

In the third week of January, Rolla Vollstedt put my green and white Lightning up for sale. Then Lynda Ferreri broke the news that she would move to a new job in San Francisco in June. Jim Lindholm never got a chance to quit. Lynda fired him in December. The great bundle of brightly-colored balloons that was my racing world in 1977 had floated into a nest of needles and pins.

On January 11, *National Speed Sport News* reported that M. C. Anderson, the team owner for whom my Rookie of the Year competitor Sam Sommers drove, had spent $1,500,000 on his campaign. Later, *National Speed Sport News* reported on a new team effort in NASCAR. Harry Gant would have $200,000 to drive in five races in 1978, in *preparation* for a Rookie of the Year effort in 1979. That was about what Lynda Ferreri had received for our entire nineteen-race rookie season.

A reporter called. The third car on George Bignotti's Indy team was to be assigned to me, and what was my comment?

Bignotti! That would be the ride of my dreams. I called George. It wasn't true. One last brilliant balloon burst into dismal shreds.

The Daytona 500 in February was our first Winston Cup race of the 1978 season. Lynda hired a new chief mechanic, Darrell Bryant, who was capable and businesslike. The top teams had installed Buick or Oldsmobile body styles on their cars to take advantage of NASCAR's new rules. Our restricted budget didn't permit that. We converted our Chevrolet Laguna to a Malibu by hanging a blunt nose clip on it. The result was as aerodynamic as a barn door. We qualified twenty-second fastest out of fifty-eight cars, at 179.734 mph. "I could have read a newspaper at that speed," I growled.

[1] Rochester (NY) *Times-Union*, Dec. 2, 1977

A good finish in the preliminary qualifying race would definitely secure us a spot in the forty-one-car field. This was no time for a conservative start, and I drafted past eight cars on the first lap alone. Then the differential came apart. When the complexities of qualifying were over and the field moved out for the start of the Daytona 500 on Sunday, I wasn't in it. A photographer had been following me around taking pictures for a book, and the look on my face in those pictures—even though I was smiling—makes me feel sick, just remembering.

I couldn't bear to watch. Pointing my old Barracuda's nose toward my parents' home in Miami, I listened to the race on the radio. Bobby Allison won, in his new ride in Bud Moore's Ford. It was his first Daytona 500 victory. I droned on south. My mind's eye wouldn't let up. Relentlessly, insufferably, enviously, it replayed scenes from my long, joyful battle with Bobby Allison at Ontario three months before.

With two and a half months to go, things looked grimmer than ever for Indianapolis. Most of the good rides were gone. Those that remained were uncompetitive. Slowly an idea formed: could I field a team myself?

I had prepared and campaigned my own sports cars for thirteen years, hadn't I? Was it such a big jump?

Yes, it was. The leap was way beyond scary.

If you can keep your head when all about you
Are losing theirs...
You just don't understand the situation.

Fielding a car at Indianapolis was a challenge I understood well enough to be terrified. Nevertheless, I started assembling a structure to do exactly that. Rolla Vollstedt hadn't yet sold the Lightning. His asking price was $32,000 without engine. He shared some numbers with me, for wheels, tires, spares, crew costs, and so on and on. George Bignotti quoted me $27,000 for a new engine and $21,000 for a used one. Bignotti's numbers alone added up to more than my net worth. A lot more.

If I were to field a car myself, the key individual would be a chief mechanic. After talking it over with Rolla, I called Dick Oeffinger, a former chief mechanic at the Speedway who had been around our garage a lot last May.

Oeffinger was a reticent, thin man who closely concealed his thoughts and feelings. He had no formal position on Rolla's crew, but he didn't miss a thing. When problems arose, his eyes gave him away. He didn't interfere, but put a quiet question if a piece was missing in his puzzle-solving process, all the while effacing his physical self, as quietly inconspicuous as a brown hawk in a brown tree. When he made a contribution, it was valuable. Our conversations had been easy. He made absolutely zero allowance for the woman part. No condescension, no uneasiness, nothing. It was clear and straight racing talk, often in shorthand, with silences when we were thinking but didn't need words.

Oeffinger was now leading a more settled life than in the past. He had an auto repair business in New Albany, Indiana, with one assistant. But the love of racing dies hard, and when I called him, he said yes. He missed the sport, he said. He would be willing to prepare and chief a car, but only for Indianapolis. He figured I would have to count on spending $150,000, including the car and the rest of it. Oeffinger had one firm requirement: the Lightning must be in his hands two full months before race day. That meant the end of March. He would take the Lightning apart, examine everything, and put it all back together again with new bolts and bits and all pointed in the right direction. If there wasn't time for that, Dick wasn't having any part of it.

That sort of preparation was half my problem in assembling a worthwhile effort. The other half was the crucial area of chassis setting, debugging the mysterious handling problems that these complex machines never failed to develop. Oeffinger would be out of date in that area, but he was well-connected with current chiefs.

My experience with Jim Lindholm in NASCAR had given me confidence that with an aggressive chief who believed what I told him, we could accomplish through persistence and experimentation a good part of what was necessary. It wouldn't put us on a par with the top teams, with all their background and experience and thousands of miles of testing; but it would get us into the ballpark.

I asked Rolla Vollstedt if he would serve as consultant, offering ten percent of the purse, and he agreed.

The choice for a pit crew for the race was clear: my NASCAR guys. They had said it at Daytona: "If you get somp'n together at Indy, you're not going to forget about us, are you?"

You bet your life I wouldn't. I had been delighted and deeply touched that they were still with us, even with our sharply reduced program; that they hadn't scattered to some other, more active team.

So early in March, I had a structure lined up. I had commitments for a chassis, engines, a chief, a crew: good men who were willing to join me. What I didn't have was money. Without the money, it was all ashes in the wind.

On March 13, the name Jerry Pillersdorf appears in my phone logs for the first time. My old friend Bruce Wennerstrom, who in his spare time presided over the Madison Avenue Sports Car Driving and Chowder Society, had suggested I call him, and I did. Jerry had raised funds for United Jewish Appeal, Bruce said. Perhaps he could do the same for me.

Jerry's initial reaction was along the lines of, you can't get sponsorship?—you're kidding. He seemed intrigued. "I have some ideas," he said. "This shouldn't be too hard."

I redoubled my own efforts. On March 14 the log reads, *Borax—no. Simonize—no. Texize—no. Green Giant—no. Tropicana—no. Bill Smythe, Mecom—no.* And each of these calls represented research, a name, a contact, getting past a secretary, and summoning again the enthusiasm, the positive attitude. Between calls I walked around in circles, talking to myself, beating back dread of the next attempt.

On March 19, I finished tenth in the Winston Cup race at Atlanta. It made no difference.

Monday March 20. I could almost smell the month of May. Manhattan's gray canyons had donned a wispy shawl of green lace. The earth was moist and fragrant. And Dick Oeffinger's deadline was eleven days away.

Tuesday March 21. S.D. Murphy, Murph, A.J. Foyt's elderly former sponsor who had sought support for my efforts, called. "I've just talked with George Bignotti," Murph said. "He has a car he wants to sell that I think you should be interested in. I can't cover the whole thing, but if you have anything else going, I'm willing to put up fifty thousand."

I was overwhelmed. Still, fifty thousand dollars wasn't even half of what I would need.

"I'll get together with George at the end of the week," Murph went on, "and hammer out the details."

Late that afternoon, Jerry Pillersdorf (who had said, "This shouldn't be too hard") and I met in person for the first time. His grey pinstripe suit was tailored to utter perfection, his cuff links and collar pin were quietly expensive, and his white broadcloth shirt of pure cotton wouldn't have dared develop a wrinkle. His manner had the edgy vigor characteristic of many New Yorkers.

Unfortunately, he didn't have good news.

"It's starting to make me mad," he said. His tone implied that a full-court press was in the offing. Jerry had declined the finder's fee that I offered when we first talked, the ten percent that was standard in the sponsorship game. "It's a matter of principle," he said. "You shouldn't be in this situation."

Wednesday March 22. A flurry of day-long activities brought me no closer to my goal. Invited to lunch by Rolex (watches) at the University Club, I declined—until they named some other corporate attendees. Prospects. I went. I saw. I didn't conquer.

Thursday March 23. The sports management company that I had signed with called. I hadn't heard from them in a long time. They had been contacted by Benton & Bowles, the advertising agency for Texaco. B&B wanted to see a proposal for sponsorship! Immediately after the agency hung up, my attorney called with the same news.

Years passed before I pieced the story together. B&B had been considering me for Texaco's ads, I learned. An article about my situation in that week's *Newsweek* magazine had landed on someone's desk at Texaco. They asked B&B to look into it.

All I knew at the time, though, was that a fish had finally nibbled—a very big fish, a whale. Texaco was one of the largest corporations in the world, with racing involvements in Europe though not in the United States. A full-blown, formal, documented proposal was in order. It must show the reality of what I could accomplish, with whom and for how much money. This must be cast in concrete and decorated with the fancy feathers of PR, the lure of mass media exposure, the pizzazz, the sizzle. And it all had to be done right now. I needed help.

Not that I didn't have plenty of experience with business proposals, from my days at Sperry. But oh, for another brain, a cool perspective, another pair of hands and eyes; someone who knew racing, and who cared.

I called Alex, who caught an overnight flight from the West Coast, and was there in the morning.

Friday March 24. Alex and I sat at the table in my apartment and put the proposal together. He detailed the crew expenses—salary, housing, transportation. Together, we listed the spares and equipment I would need. Radios? I couldn't borrow Lynda's; the unit was too big for an Indy car. Skip the radios, we'll wing it. Crew uniforms, decked out in sponsor ID. Golf-cart rental (to ferry tools and parts); mini-tractor rental—the means of towing the car out to its spot on pit road from the garage area. Dick Oeffinger's estimate for pre-race preparation costs. A new Hewland transaxle. Phone and heat for the garage. A starter motor. What special tools might I need that Oeffinger didn't have? Entry fee, a thousand dollars. Liability insurance, how much? I was on the phone. What about insurance for the car itself? Frightfully expensive, twelve percent of the value of the car. But if we were to end up with a modest bottom-line figure for the proposal, we had to subtract from the gross cost a probable resale value for the car and engines. If the car was scrap metal, the resale value would be zip. We needed insurance.

And on and on.

I wrote the pizzazz about the Indianapolis 500. Media and spectator exposure. Race attendance, TV, worldwide live radio, newspapers, magazines. Tie-ins: corporate entertainment, trade-show display of race car, employee excitement and motivation. Chances of winning. Audience demographics, a full page of age groups, salaries, dwellings, drawn from a USAC study.

Backup materials. The president of my fan club, Irene Nagy, had drawn up a one-page summary of 1977 race highlights, and I bound it right in with the rest. Bio. Glossy black and white photos. The most impressive clippings I had: newspaper front pages from last May, with the sponsor name large and clear—the Los Angeles *Times*, New York *Post*, Chicago *Sun-Times*, Detroit *Free Press*, Indianapolis *Star*. Magazine covers. Where can I get color photocopying done on a Saturday? Back on the phone. What about printing? Binding? Saturday? Sunday? No, it would all have to be done on Saturday. Color copies of the covers of *Parade*, *WomenSports*, *Auto Racing Digest*. Sponsor name everywhere. Clippings from Japan, Australia, Greece.

We finished the proposal on Saturday evening. The subtotal was $117,600, and with a projected resale value for the car and engines of about fifty-five per cent of cost, the net bottom line was $72,600. The New York agency would pick up Texaco's copy at 8 a.m. Monday. Alex caught a plane out of LaGuardia on Sunday, the day of the Indy-car race at Ontario, California. Danny Ongais won. Open testing for the 500 would begin at Indianapolis Motor Speedway the next day.

Monday March 27. Eight a.m. Nine a.m. Nine-thirty. No courier. Called the agency, where was he? I couldn't send it direct to B&B myself; I didn't have the names, plus my contract was with the agency. Ten a.m. Eleven a.m. Called the agency again. Didn't they understand that every hour counted? I was bouncing off the walls and ceiling. When their courier finally appeared at noon, the agency said the proposal could go directly to B&B, and gave me the vital names.

Meanwhile, I had kept Jerry Pillersdorf abreast of all this. He swung into action, and set up lunch the next day at Le Chanteclair, the elegant motor-racing hangout, with the B&B people whose names I had obtained. How he managed this I don't know, but he had a great presence. He was even better in person than on the phone.

Tuesday March 28. Jerry and I arrived early at Le Chanteclair, which was my home away from home. "We have a fish on the line!" I said to owner René Dreyfus, the former French racing champion. When our guests appeared, René was magical. It seemed we were the most illustrious group ever to grace his premises. He sent a bottle of fine French wine to our table, and fussed over us in his most dignified, elegant Gallic fashion. He knew exactly what he was doing, and he was wonderful.

I let Jerry do most of the talking. Peter Rockwell and Lee Revere of B&B listened politely. Jerry was splendid, kindling quite a fire. Meanwhile, I felt their scrutiny. They needed to see that I had a vocabulary extending beyond four-letter words. Suspicions concerning a female race driver tended to run high.

They also needed to be convinced that I was real. On Madison Avenue, reality comes in around tenth place, and probably that high up the list only because of consumer-protection laws. These people would expect hype. But it wasn't an advertisement we were talking about, it was a real race with real participants, where hype wouldn't even get you in the pit gate. So I didn't hide behind my eyes, as I usually did. When we talked about my proposal, I let them see in. With all my strength, I conveyed that I could do what I proposed.

After they left, Jerry and I took a deep breath. He had pulled out all the stops. René joined us for a glass of wine, we unwound a bit, and I went back to my apartment to tend the phone. The first call was a bombshell.

Dick Oeffinger said, "It looks like I won't be able to prepare the car for you." He was going into the hospital. They might have to operate. My hair practically stood on end.

"I'm very sorry to hear that, Dick. If you happen to think of anyone who might take your place, could you let me know?" I sounded like a rational person encountering an obstacle that had to be dealt with in a rational way. That wasn't how I felt.

My sponsor-seeker in San Francisco called with eighteen more rejections. I wished he hadn't told me about Trader Vic's. "They put me on a speaker phone, and I laid it out to a big group of them, and then they all started laughing like hell, and hung up on me."

Wednesday March 29. Jerry called. "Peter Rockwell's boss at B&B turned thumbs down. He says if you don't perform well, it'll reflect badly on Texaco."

Well, there it was, right in line with all the rest.

"Wait, there's more," Jerry said. "I almost can't believe this myself. Peter is going to go over his boss' head. He's taking the proposal directly to Texaco tomorrow morning, without the agency endorsement.

"We need to drum up support," Jerry went on. He paused. "I know some people at *Good Morning America*. I'll get you on the show and you can tell the world why you ought to be sponsored." And indeed, by afternoon I was scheduled for Friday. Years later, Roberta Doherty, who booked *GMA*'s guests, told me that the call came to her completely cold. She had never heard of Jerry Pillersdorf.

Thursday March 30. Peter Rockwell called to say the meeting with Texaco had been inconclusive.

Friday March 31. *Good Morning America* with David Hartman. He was wonderful. He gave me perfect leads. I was able to say everything that I needed to say. David was warm and real as always, exactly the same when the cameras went off as when they were on. Afterwards, he had a suggestion or two. Jerry Pillersdorf made sure that the powers at Texaco were watching the show.

Meanwhile, I was due in San Francisco by Monday afternoon for two days of media stuff for my NASCAR sponsor, Kelly Girl. Alex and I hoped to spend the weekend along the Pacific Coast, a desperately needed respite. I was juggling reservations when Jerry called.

"Texaco has gone for the whole thing," he said. "We're meeting them in the Chrysler Building at 4:30. They're drawing up contracts right now."

Had I been the fainting kind, this surely would have been the moment for it.

I spent the next couple of hours on the phone, grappling with the crisis presented by Oeffinger's illness. Under the circumstances, it made my blood run cold.

As my taxi headed for the Chrysler Building, I glimpsed its spire. Its gleaming Art Deco arches and gargoyle-like eagles had always been my favorite sight in the Manhattan skyline. It seemed a good omen to be meeting there.

Jerry was pacing the marble lobby. I thought he resembled a

pressure cooker: contained, with little puffs of steam. We found our way to Texaco's old offices on the fifteenth floor, recently vacated for White Plains. I noted, in the lobby and above, men with hard dispassionate eyes who looked and acted as if they were Secret Service, and who noted us in return.

Texaco's floors felt spooky and abandoned. We were the first to arrive. A secretary ushered us into what had lately been Texaco's boardroom. With its wealth of baronial detail, it spoke eloquently of long-established power. Dark walnut wainscoting lined a long, narrow room, punctuated on one side by a huge stone fireplace. Massive armchairs flanked the table, which stretched deep into indefinite gloom. Presently, the delegation from Texaco's new world headquarters filed in.

Kerryn King, one of Texaco's top executives, sat at the head of the table. He was a large, dark, fleshy man, perhaps six feet two and some sixty years old, a heavy mantle of power draped over his shoulders. The bowing and scraping in his direction by the rest of the delegation was conspicuous. I was placed one chair down on the right, Jerry across the table and farther down. Peter Rockwell stood behind Jerry, not daring to sit at all.

King got straight to business, firing questions at me that were hostile to the point of insult, an unexpected assault. Had I been prepared for it, I might have been more diplomatic; but his steely questions took me by surprise and drew steel in response. Jerry, socially deft and diplomatic, intervened in the deadly fencing. The crisis passed, and the discussion turned to how, not whether, the association would proceed.

"You will use Texaco products only—lubricants, gasoline..."

Uh-oh.

"Indy cars run on methanol, wood alcohol," I said.

"Texaco doesn't produce methanol. What will it take to modify the engine to run on gasoline?" A mandate that this *would* be done lay heavily on the inflection of the words.

"The fuel is prescribed by the rules of competition."

It was a shaky moment. Jerry's eyebrows had gone up, and he wasn't moving a muscle. The room was utterly still.

Finally someone said, "Well, we really wanted to emphasize the lubricants anyway."

The collective exhalation of breath came like a gust in the heavy atmosphere, punctuated by stirring and shuffling of papers.

Indy's alcohol fuel was made by Ashland Oil, and supplied free to all participants—together with decals, driver's suit patches, and an advertising release. Impossible. "Roger Penske's team is in the same position," I said, "sponsored by Sunoco." They would look into it.

Now for the lubricants, especially the oil. Oil for these highly specialized engines was critical. It was primarily a matter of additives—or lack of same. Antioxidants were neither necessary nor desirable, I told them, and very little detergent, but an anti-foaming agent was essential. The formula for a successful oil for Indy cars, originally written up for Ford, had been published in the technical literature. Surely this matter deserved their laboratory's immediate attention.

They moved on to the commercials I was to make for them—TV, radio, print—and the meeting ended with smiles and handshakes all around.

Too elated to take a cab, Jerry and I walked up Madison Avenue toward Le Chanteclair in the spring dusk. Champagne was in order, and gratitude. Jerry had invited Peter Rockwell and his wife to join us for dinner there. High-energy mid-Manhattan swirled around us, electric and exhilarating, as we hashed over the next steps.

At Le Chanteclair, René was preparing for the evening rush. He was delighted with the turn of events. My answering service had a call from Murph. Struggling with my notebook in the minuscule phone booth, I returned it.

Murph had been as good as his word.

He had indeed negotiated a comprehensive deal with George Bignotti. Bignotti would rebuild the race car in question, install a used engine, and provide it to me ready to run when practice opened. He would have one of his team drivers shake the car down if need be. Bignotti or one of his men would be available for consultation and assistance. After qualifying, Bignotti would tear down the car as necessary, install a rebuilt engine, and make the car race-ready.

It sounded too good to be true.

"What car is it, Murph?"

"George designed it for road-racing circuits. Wally Dallenbach tested it at the Speedway last year, but switched to the car he drove the year before. Wally qualified eighth at Mosport [a road-racing circuit in Canada] and finished sixteenth. Then he qualified eleventh at the last race at Phoenix, and finished sixth. Those were its only two races. George says it should qualify at the Speedway at a hundred ninety."

A hundred and ninety was at least ten mph slower than what pole position was likely to be. A car that was ten mph slower than the leader would be some ten laps down at the end of 500 miles; but in the late 1970s that kind of spread was the rule rather than the exception, both in Indy cars and Winston Cup. Often enough, a race ended with only the winner on the lead lap. The trouble was, I had a vague recollection of some conflict between Dallenbach and Bignotti over this very car. Nevertheless, a hundred and ninety was a shade faster than the difficult, tricky Lightning. One thing I knew for certain: as of this date, these were our best options.

"How much does Bignotti want?"

"He wanted a lot, but we go back a long way. I jawboned him down to seventy-five thousand dollars. The trouble is, he won't hold the car for me, not even for fifty grand."

"Murph," I said, "*I've got the money.*"

I filled him in, and told him also that I had a deal pending for the Lightning.

"I'd walk around that bear trap once or twice before I stepped in it," Murph said.

"Sometimes the devil you know is better than the devil you don't. We can't do anything over the weekend anyway. I'll call you on Monday."

Then I called Rolla, and told him what was up.

"You know, Jan, I think that's the car that caused Wally Dallenbach to leave the Speedway last year. He didn't come back until Bignotti agreed to let him drive the previous year's car."

It clicked into place. Everyone had been astonished when Dallenbach went home. If I recalled correctly, he said the volunteer fire department in Basalt, Colorado, needed him. A more preposterous excuse for leaving the Indianapolis 500 could hardly be imagined.

No hint of this turmoil, of course, could be revealed to Peter Rockwell. We had a merry and convivial dinner of which I haven't the slightest recollection.

And that was Friday the 31st of March. What a day.

DUCKS IN A ROW

At eight in the morning on April 1, 1978, the sky over Kennedy Airport was a strained pale blue, the misty shade of early spring. Across the wetlands, salt haze off the Atlantic blended into yellowish air pollution over Brooklyn and Queens. This was the time of year when boats went into the water, and I had driven Ralph Farnham's truck all through these marshes, hauling thirty-five foot cabin cruisers and deep-keel sailboats along the patched, rough asphalt trails. You can never step twice into the same river, I thought, and the river of my life had changed beyond recognition in the three years since then.

Just before boarding my flight to Seattle, I returned a call from Dick Oeffinger. He had thought of a possible replacement as crew chief. "His name is Kenny Ozawa," Dick said. "He helped me at the Speedway four years ago, and he chiefed Tom Bigelow's car at the Ontario Indy-car race. I talked with him yesterday, and he's definitely interested in working for you. He lives in Quincy, Washington."

Unreal. How could things be falling into place like this?

"Dick," I said, "I'm going to be on a plane for Seattle in half an hour."

I told him of the previous day's events—my deal with Texaco; Murph's deal with Bignotti. I laid it out slowly and carefully, and held my breath while I waited for his opinion.

"That'd be doing it the easy way," Dick said. Bignotti's comprehensive facilities were right in Indianapolis. But, Dick wondered, *was* this car the controversial chassis assigned to Dallenbach last year?

I scrambled on board the plane just as they shut the doors.

I was *so* glad to see Alex. My good adviser, my lover. Body, soul and mind, I was glad to see him.

We followed a two-lane road to the ocean, and stayed the night at the edge of the Pacific. The rooms had no phones. The wind blew off the sea, and the surf roared.

In the morning I called Bignotti, bracing my notebook against a chill wind at a pay phone set on a roadside pole. "It's a good sound car," Bignotti said. Yes, it was built as a road-racing car; but Gordon Johncock had gotten 192 out of it in a test session at Ontario. At Indianapolis, it should qualify at 190. Yes, another chassis would be available if I should destroy this one; it was a second car of the same design, though it was presently in pieces.

I said I would have a decision for him by tomorrow. Next, I tried to call Tom Bigelow; I wanted to ask him about Kenny Ozawa. No one was home. Most urgently of all, I wanted to talk with Wally Dallenbach. I hoped he would give me his honest view of this machine. But no one I knew had his phone number, and the USAC offices, which could supply it, were closed for the weekend.

It was dark when we reached Seattle again. Alex had called Kenny Ozawa while I was on the plane west, setting a meeting for eight that night at the crest of Snoqualmie Pass. Kenny's home in Quincy lay amid the apple-growing plains east of the Cascade Mountains, and Snoqualmie Pass was the highest point of the road between. As Alex and I climbed up into the dark and snow-swept mountains to meet, query and judge a stranger in whose hands I might be placing my life, the decisions on car and crew filled my mind. A massive accident held us up. By the time we reached the pass, I was fatigued to the point of nausea.

At our rendezvous, a ski lodge, we found Ozawa in the upstairs lounge—a bleak red-carpeted room nearly empty at 10 p.m., tainted with smoke and stale popcorn. He was in his mid-thirties, with a slightly reticent manner; amiable, with a clear strain of seriousness under that. His full-time job was in charge of agricultural machinery for the orchards, but racing was his passion. His family had been property owners here, but lost their land when they were interned during World War II.

The questions I put were practical, but it was the manner of his response that I was looking for. What equipment and spares would we need; did he have the full supply of specialized tools that an Indy car would require. Alex didn't ask much of anything—I wished that he would—but I knew he was carefully taking it in.

"What about tactics during the race?" Matters such as the timing of pit stops were a tricky business.

"I don't have a great deal of experience at that. Will Dick Oeffinger be there for the race?"

Oeffinger had said yesterday that he should be able to come up to Indianapolis on weekends.

"That would be a big help."

I sketched out the issue of the cars. Like Oeffinger, Ozawa thought it might be better to go with the Bignotti deal.

It was midnight when we left.

"What do you think?" I asked Alex.

His impression was favorable, as was mine. Clearly, Ozawa was deeply conscientious, and realistic about what he could and could not do. I felt comfortable with this man, and pending what Tom Bigelow might have to say, I reckoned I probably had my chief mechanic at hand.

On Monday April 3, I was back on the phone at 6:30 in the morning. I felt sure that Tom Bigelow would give me the straight scoop. "Kenny's a super guy," Tom said. "He's a really hard worker, and you can absolutely rely on whatever he screws together."

So that was that.

Now came the big one. Wally Dallenbach was a reserved man; we hadn't exchanged more than a few words. He was one of the top drivers in the country; if he had felt this Wildcat was bad enough to leave the Speedway over, I ought not touch it with a ten-foot pole.

Would he tell me the truth, the whole truth? He was no longer driving for George Bignotti, so no loyalty issue should be involved.

"When I first took it out, it was undriveable," Wally said.

"Is it true that you left the Speedway over it?"

He ignored the question. "The problem was in the front end geometry. George re-designed it three times, and by the end of the year it was pretty close. It ended up a hundred percent better than when I first drove it. It doesn't seem to have any evil habits. On a scale of one to ten, I would say this car is a six."

"Do you think it can make the field at Indianapolis?"

"Oh, certainly."

The conversation with Wally was invaluable. But it wouldn't hurt to let the facts settle for a few more hours. I caught a plane to San Francisco while Jerry Pillersdorf organized a press conference in New York for Thursday, at Le Chanteclair.

By morning, my choice was clear. I called Murph in Indianapolis. "I'll take a $75,000 check to George Bignotti," Murph said. I would reimburse him when I got the money from Texaco, in a week's time.

On Wednesday April 5, my Kelly Girl obligations completed, I headed back to New York. In spite of all the stresses, I felt uncaged, alive, free. My hat was back in the ring.

At the airport ticket counter, the blonde agent asked, "Are

you *the* ...?" As she wrote the ticket out she said, "I saw the *Good Morning America* show, about how you didn't have a sponsor, and I thought, if every woman watching this program sent in a dollar, she'd have it."

I told her what had happened, and she broke into a smile.

"Good luck!" she said.

On the plane, I mulled over the next day's press conference. The recent oil crises were sure to raise questions about auto racing as a frivolous use of fuel. The best answer would be the football-team analogy. It took more fuel to fly a team from one coast to the other for a game than it did to run all the cars in the Indianapolis 500. I knew that, but I wanted numbers. Writing out the question on the back of my card, which had nothing but my name and address, I asked a bored steward to take it up to the cockpit. He came back with the answers and a change of attitude. "Are you...? They'd like to invite you up front if it weren't against the law."

I wrote in my journal, "A month ago, when I had no ride, recognition made me sick, like a fist squeezing my stomach. Now, it's more like the spring sun."

Eight in the morning was an ungodly hour for the staff of Le Chanteclair. The upcoming press conference had wreaked havoc. Chairs and tables were in disarray, TV cameras and cables everywhere. René Dreyfus carried on with his customary aplomb. Murph had flown in from Indianapolis, and my folks came up from Miami the night before, staying with my brother Stewart and his wife. Dad was full of enthusiasm, telling everyone who would listen how one of my first childish sentences was "We put Marfax on the rocker arms" (of airplane engines)—Marfax having been a Texaco lubricant back then.

Walter Cronkite walked in the door, to my surprise and delight. The legendary CBS anchor was a former sports car racer, and René had invited him. By the appointed hour of nine, the restaurant was jammed.

Cameras, microphones, questions.

"What will be your goal at Indianapolis this year?"

"I think we have an excellent chance of finishing in the top five." Actually, I figured that if all went well, fifth was the best we could reasonably expect with this machine. And with Bignotti's assistance, fifth could be realistic.

Afterwards, when the commotion subsided, René Dreyfus took

from his pocket a small suede pouch. He had brought me a talisman, so special that I shivered. René's racing exploits before World War II were the stuff of legend. Inside the pouch was the medal he won in his first race, in 1924, fifty-four years before.

Every moment of April counted toward preparation for the race. My phone bills were astronomical. Jerry Pillersdorf stayed involved, and his assistance and advice were invaluable.

Benton & Bowles held a meeting on the color scheme of the car and uniforms. Their big Madison Avenue conference room was expensively decorated and full of men in expensive clothes. "We want to paint the car pink," they said, "and we want your driver's suit to match."

Pink.

I pulled out all the stops, every ounce of persuasion I could muster, and just barely carried the day. They settled on white with a shocking-pink stripe bordered by Texaco red, a good-looking design. We agreed to refer to the pink part as fuchsia. Thank God, Nomex fabric didn't come in any kind of pink at all.

I asked Jim Lindholm to come to work for me. Unfamiliar though he was with Indy cars, he had proved last year how valuable he could be. Jim settled in at Indianapolis, and took over a lot of the ground-laying there.

Kenny Ozawa had a friend, Jim Nakamura, with whom he had worked before; and Jim Lindholm had a friend, Don Hume, a former stock car racer who took early retirement from the police force after a crash made splinters out of one knee. I hired them both for the month, giving each of my main men an ally. Carl Holtman, the Eastern Air Lines captain who was one of Rolla's volunteers, would join my group. Dick Oeffinger would also be there part-time. With my NASCAR guys—Jack Bryant, Toby Varner, Darrell Bryant, and Jim Clodfelter—for the long race weekend, my crew was complete.

By mid-April, I was desperate for a break. The upcoming weekend was miraculously free of obligations, the last such moments for as far as I could foresee. I pulled out a map of the Eastern United States, and ran my finger down the coastline.

Springtime should be ... *here.* In Charleston.

Alex would meet me there.

At the seventeenth-century plantation known as Middleton Place, golden green salt marshes bordered the banks of the Ashley River. Beneath giant oaks, masses of azaleas glowed in every hue, shape and shade. We talked quietly, walked among the head-high mazes of bloom—crimson, peach, lavender, white, magenta, scarlet, yellow, orange. We stored up the images and the scent of spring and the sound of birdsong, against the unforgiving asphalt and concrete of the Speedway, its non-negotiable demands, the howls of competitors' cars, among them my own. Which I so much desired to hear. Three weeks from now.

The longtime head of the USAC Technical Committee, Frankie Del Roy, was wonderfully helpful with licenses and a myriad of such issues. "Now, what do you want for a car number?" he asked.

I named a few favorites. All were taken. "What's available, then?"

The third one he gave was 51, and I stopped him. It was the number that A. J. Foyt carried when he ran NASCAR stock car races ... the red 51 that I had drafted so closely in the final laps at Charlotte last October. What could be better luck?

When A. J. saw my Wildcat for the first time, in May, his double take was most gratifying.

On Sunday April 23, Murph gave a dinner party at the Woodstock Country Club. It was Indianapolis' premier club, and Murph was a genial host to dozens of distinguished guests. Among them was Mari Hulman George, whose son Tony was heir apparent to Indianapolis Motor Speedway. Late in the evening, when flashes of lightning illuminated the tables and rain-lashed branches beat against the roof, she shifted nervously in her chair. Perhaps it was her intuition that made her so ill at ease.

In that storm, in a cornfield not far away, the USAC charter plane returning from the Trenton race crashed, killing Frankie Del Roy, Stan Worley, Shim Malone, Ray Marquette, Dr. Bruce White, and everyone else on board.

Not until morning was the extent of the disaster clear. These people were at the heart of the USAC structure, essential members of its functioning core. Their absence left a gaping chasm. The shocking loss reverberated for a long, long time.

Next morning, our scheduled meeting with George Bignotti went on as planned, though its tone was subdued. Murph and I were joined by Kenny Ozawa, Dick Oeffinger and Jim Lindholm. It was our first assembly at full strength.

Each of these men had to mesh smoothly with the others. I wasn't exactly easy in my mind. The ability to interpret and integrate a group of divergent personalities was not a known strength in my roster of skills.

The group dynamics needed careful tending. Jim Lindholm, for example, had insufficient respect for Murph, privately mocking him. I could deal with that, but I didn't like it.

George Bignotti was the 800-pound gorilla in this cage. We were clearly and definitively *not* part of Bignotti's team, but we were dependent on his good will. If for any reason he became unwilling to share his knowledge or to provide the backup services of his shop, our effort would be hamstrung. Although alternatives existed, this was Bignotti's car and his setup, and he had fielded winning cars here for years.

In any case, the meeting went well. We covered a lot of territory before adjourning to Bignotti's shop. It was our first look at his premises. All four of us were goggle-eyed at what we saw. The dynamometer installation alone was larger than my Manhattan apartment.

My car, my Wildcat, sat naked on a knee-high stand. It lacked engine and wheels. Its cowling and bodywork leaned on the wall. It awaited a fit to its driver. I shed my ladylike high heels and stepped into the seat.

I wriggled down into the chassis. It was too short, terribly short. Gordon Johncock had driven it last. He was shorter than I, and the difference was all in our legs. My knees collided with the dashboard. It was impossible to operate the pedals. The pedal assembly would have to go as deep as possible into the nose. Even so, there could still be a problem.

I moved my hands around, from wheel to gearshift and back, imprinting into my senses the location of the gauges and controls. I smelled it and felt it, in my hands and my seat and my toes ... this wild machine in which I would lap the Speedway faster than a jet on takeoff. My pulse rate had doubled.

Bignotti gave us a great deal of his time this day (Murph had arranged it, of course). Kenny, Jim, Dick and I thanked him, and the tour ended with handshakes all around. The four of us drove back to the rented apartments, sat at the rented table, and brainstormed. We made lists of everything we could think of that needed to be done or acquired. Dick Oeffinger's input was strong here; he had done this before. It was a long list. Lynda Ferreri would lend me her impact hammers for changing wheels, for example, but did the regulators operate up to a high enough pressure to torque the huge single nut on Indy-car wheels to spec? Where could we buy the sockets to fit those nuts?

"Maybe we could borrow them from Bignotti," someone said.

"We need to be careful about that," I cautioned. "We mustn't go to him for anything unless we've exhausted every other possible source, because there will be more than enough times when he'll be the *only* source." Jerry had already mentioned to me that Texaco people seemed to be acting as if Bignotti were employed by them, and I was worried about it. It was clear to me that whatever Texaco wanted, they expected to get. That needed to be my problem, not Bignotti's.

We listed the products to get from Texaco, since other brands were forbidden: wheel-bearing grease, water pump lube, hand cleaner, brake cleaner, other cleaners and polishes, molybdenum grease, anti-seize compound, ninety-weight gear oil. And on and on. Each man had important contributions to make to the discussion, and so did I. By the time it was over, we had wrestled the situation to the ground, and we were tired as hell.

All day I kept telling myself, calm down, you've done this before, you've run your own show for thirteen years.

But this was different, and I knew it.

Kenny left for Seattle, Dick drove back to New Albany, and I caught a plane for New York, where I was to make a Texaco TV commercial the next day.

The commercial had a long, intricate script to be recited nonstop while looking at the camera, simultaneously positioning oil cans with their labels in precise alignment, keeping my fingers off the critical parts.

"Take forty-six..."

What a day. And I wishing I were in Indianapolis. But this was part of the price of my ride. The commercial came out well. Peter Rockwell told me that when it was tested, the ratings were so high that Texaco demanded it be tested again. Specifically, the audience question that indicated how many more people would buy the oil after seeing the commercial than before seeing it achieved the highest score that the testing agency had ever recorded for a petroleum-related product

Next morning, I was back in Indianapolis—and found a catastrophe in the making. With just ten days left until the opening of practice, Texaco was pressing me hard for publicity pictures of me with the car, and Bignotti had agreed to a photo session in his shop today. By the time my plane landed, a battalion of Texaco people had walked into Bignotti's place as if they owned it. Apparently, they had ordered his men around. Whatever it was that actually occurred, our 800-pound gorilla was ready to squash everything in sight.

We were interfering with his own team's preparations for the Indianapolis 500, he said.

It was my worst nightmare. I called the key figure at Texaco and told him to call off the shoot. As a result, they cancelled a projected PR tour. Then I called Bignotti and apologized. Bignotti let off steam at some length.

From this frying pan, I turned directly to the fire: the garage situation was desperate. The lack of a garage, that is. As one of the last entries to be received before the April 15 deadline, in a year that saw a record ninety-two entries filed,[1] my team was among several that were denied garage space on the Speedway grounds.

It was a handicap of enormous proportions. All month, a team was back and forth between the track and its garage, dozens of times a day. Your garage was where you worked on the car to make the changes that each set of practice laps dictated, where you kept the car when it rained, where you had a chair that you could sit on, where you could close the doors and let no one in while you thought about what the car told you last time out. The garage was where you kept your equipment, tools and spares; where your phone was; where you changed into and out of your driver's suit. The garage area was a driver's only refuge from the onslaught of spectators.

Oh, the joys of being a team owner/manager/driver! I thought wistfully of last year, when Rolla Vollstedt handled the sponsor interfaces and the rest of the hassles, and all I had to do was show up when and where he told me to, and drive the car.

In reality, there were enough garages for all the teams. But some of them had been rented for years by companies or individuals who entered a fictitious car, in order to have a place to party for the month. I contacted Joe Cloutier, the Hulman family retainer who became president of the Speedway after Tony Hulman's death. The Speedway entry form specified, in the same paragraph under which I was denied a garage, that a "garage assigned in Gasoline Alley will be relinquished upon request by the Speedway ... whenever it becomes obvious that no bona-fide attempt will be made to earn a starting position." I raised the subject of the party garages.

Cloutier evaded me. He really didn't know, he said, any way to tell

---

[1] UPI in e.g. Columbus (Ind.) *Republic*, May 5, 1978

who was a bona-fide entry until qualifying was completed and the field for the race was set.

Bullshit, I wrote in my phone log when I hung up.

On May 4, still garageless, I settled in at my little apartment, which faced west across a lake, with a terrace outside the sliding glass doors. Most evenings, Alex and I had supper quietly there. It was like a honeymoon under pressure. Fierce pressure. But so much the better, for Type-A's like us. I felt happy and secure.

The Wildcat was now painted in its Texaco colors, and had been christened "The Texaco Star." (Indy cars always had names of that sort.) George Bignotti invited us back to his shop, and I went for a second fitting while the Texaco photographers set up their equipment. The pedal assembly was now as far forward as it could go, but the instrument panel still interfered with my knees. We pulled all the padding from the seat back, leaving only a thin layer of vinyl; my vertebrae were to be sore all month where they vibrated against the aluminum fuel enclosure. It still wasn't enough. The only other thing he could do, Bignotti said, was cut arcs out of the dashboard where my bent knees hit it.

The photographers were ready, and I grinned merrily into the cameras. The Texaco pictures went out on the wire services that afternoon.

As a substitute garage, Jim Lindholm lined up both a tractor-trailer body and a tent to shelter our car. Each had appalling disadvantages. Our dilemma was in newspapers across the country by now. Late in the afternoon, as I walked down Gasoline Alley under the great winged wheel that was the emblem of Indianapolis Motor Speedway, George Bignotti came out of his garage

"Say," he said, "I think I might be able to let you have my fourth garage, the one we use for welding."

I stared at him.

"The only thing is, if we get our two cars into the show on the first weekend, we might decide to field a third. In that case, I'd need to have it back. All I want for it is the thousand dollars that it cost me."

I had the check written out so fast it was still smoking when I handed it to him.

On Friday morning at eleven, the garage was ours. We were as glad of this treasure as of a palace, even though it looked more like the gates of hell. The former welding shop had not been painted in years. It was gray with smoke and heavily mottled with bats—the jet-black wisps of carbon that flew up from the torch when the acetylene mixture was rich, stickily besmirching everything they touched. Trash covered a floor caked with dirt. Two naked light bulbs dangled over a filthy bench.

I fought back a sinking sensation as I stood in the open doors. Texaco's Vice President of Public Relations would be in town tomorrow. An advance contingent was to arrive this very afternoon. The contrast between these premises and the spotless garages of established teams like Foyt's, two doorways away, or Bignotti's, facing us, could not have been greater.

The crew flew into action. Kenny Ozawa and Jim Nakamura tackled the initial cleanup. Jim Lindholm and Don Hume gathered supplies, and tore into the work of renovation without missing a beat. Within hours, they transformed the dark and grimy cavern into a space that matched, in professional appearance, any garage on the grounds.

While the guys painted and hammered, I perched near the doors, working out of my briefcase. That briefcase, my travelling office, was a semi-permanent appendage in those days, on my knees or under my feet in airplanes, next to the phone in hotel rooms. Sometime that afternoon, a drop of white paint fell on the fine brown leather. I didn't wipe it off. The little white spot stayed there forever after, a mark of how we all did the impossible, in those days.

My list of stuff that had to be done on Friday was humungous, complex, and urgent, but somehow it all got handled. In mid-afternoon, the car arrived. Kenny Ozawa took over immediately. The first order of business was to get it through tech inspection.

Tomorrow, the curtain would rise on the sixty-second running of the Indianapolis 500, the greatest race in the world. Against all odds, we were about to contend for a spot in the field.

PART III

QUALIFIED FOR THE INDIANAPOLIS 500, 1978 ... From left: Jim Nakamura, Dick Oeffinger, Ken Ozawa, Jim Lindholm. Don Hume unfortunately had to leave for the day.

INDIANAPOLIS, MAY 1978

You could live a whole lifetime at Indianapolis Motor Speedway in the single month of May. Enough passion, melodrama, adrenaline, suspense, and superhuman effort flood the premises to fuel a medium-size war. But unlike war, the fuel isn't tainted with hatred, and if there is violence, it is inadvertent. No one is there because they have to be.

On the morning of the first day of practice, May 6, I woke with an emotional hangover from the turbulence of the previous days. The first thought that swam into focus was, *today's the day. Today I will take the car into my hands, we will hurtle down the straights and I will begin to find out what kind of an animal it is in the turns.*

It was eight months since I had last driven one of these machines. Had I forgotten how?

Steam billowing through the shower infused its magic, like cleansing rituals since time immemorial. After an anointment of Norell perfume, I was in considerably better shape.

At the track, the Wildcat was taking on fuel under the eye of a tech inspector—the last step before we could be certified to run. Sounds of the track-opening ceremonies drifted faintly into the garage area: bagpipers, speeches, marching bands.

Garage 36, Bignotti's former welding shop, sparkled in the morning sun. Texaco-red stripes at floor level and at waist height set off its fresh white paint. My "dressing room," the size of a phone booth, matched all the rest. The golf cart had been delivered, the little tractor for towing the race car was there, and everything was falling into place.

I walked out the garage-area gate toward the pits, and was swarmed: the autograph-mobbing had started. Ducking into the Goodyear shop, I ran into Wally Dallenbach. We hadn't spoken since he gave me his opinion of the Wildcat, just a month ago. We hugged. Wally was lean and tan, never without the black Western hat of his adopted Colorado. His face had fine bone structure and the remote, detached look of a pilot or outdoorsman.

"How's it going?" he asked.

"Good, we should be ready to run pretty soon. I want to thank you again for your comments, you were a tremendous help. How're things with you?"

"Looking good. We have a Cosworth engine so you know it should be fast."

That was true. Cosworth engines had established their superior speed (if not reliability) the previous year. George Bignotti was the only top mechanic who had stuck with the four-cylinder Offenhauser.

We parted. I left Goodyear with the precious spare key to Leo Mehl's private office, the tiny, ancient dark labyrinth that concealed the only private restroom in the garage area. Back in our garage, mirrors were being mounted on the sides of the Wildcat's cowling, the oil heater was plugged in. I hid in the back, pulling a shell around myself; saving everything for what came next, on the track.

George Bignotti came to start our engine for the first time. Kenny, Dick and Jim followed his procedure intently. As they pushed the car back out of the garage, I slipped behind the little partition to change.

On my first warm-up lap, a tall, dignified figure stepped out from behind the fire trucks in Turn 1 to wave. It was Murph, watching the first lap of the car that he had done so much to put on the track. I threw him a salute, then turned my attention to the gauges.

There were bound to be rough edges when you were shaking down a car for the first time. When I brought it up to speed, the car wandered, almost wobbled, and the tires seemed out of balance. George Bignotti was in the pits when I pulled in.

"It's hard to keep it straight, and it's super sensitive to the wheel," I said. "What kind of caster do you have in it?"

"About four degrees." With that much, it ought to be stable. Consultation and discussion. Then, with an air of suppressed alarm, they took it back to the garage. It seemed that the tires were intended only to hold the car up while it was en route, weren't race tires and hadn't been balanced. The front dive planes were in the position the painter had left them, a position of no particular utility. No wonder it wobbled!

Back to the track. We were close to the end of the day. Kenny's stopwatch showed my speeds to be in the 180s, which was fabulous. Too fabulous.

"Are you sure about that?"

"*Yes*," Jim said, excitedly, "I double-checked it."

"If I'd been guessing," I said, "I would have guessed one sixty-eight." Was the car really that good, that so fast a lap could feel so slow? "Let's get another watch."

Out again. The second watch read six seconds a lap slower. At that moment, the loudspeaker announced my speed at 181. Where did they get that from? Was it official? An emotional roller-coaster. I took off my wristwatch, which had all the stopwatch functions, and gave it to Don. Time for just one more lap, and the track closed for the day. My guess on the speed had been precisely correct, 168 mph. The PA system's 181 was a mystery.

For all the elation of being really fast in a race car, being really slow is the utter pits.

Earlier, while we still thought the speeds to be in the 180s, I had spotted Bignotti in Gasoline Alley, and exuberantly greeted him with a kiss. "It was so easy," I said. Now, I had to tell him the bad news. He was visibly disappointed.

"Well, we'll just have to see how it goes tomorrow," he said. His promise to Murph that Gordon Johncock would shake down the car if necessary was at the back of both our minds.

Johncock and Pat Patrick, who owned Bignotti's team, came up to us just then. I hadn't spoken with the petroleum-company multimillionaire since our brutal meeting two years before. Patrick said to Johncock, "Janet gave George a big kiss earlier this afternoon and I want you to kiss him too."

It might almost have been taken as an order rather than a joke, and Johncock squirmed. Pat Patrick constituted another of my worries. It wasn't inconceivable that he might order Bignotti to cease and desist his assistance. I smiled—made the corners of my mouth go up, that is—and retreated, seeking sanctuary in Jim Hurtubise's garage. We shared a day's-end beer, leaning on the rear wing of his elderly race car. Herk's friendly haven was marvelously restorative, and I went back to Garage 36.

I found Kenny Ozawa upset about the misleading lap times, for which he felt responsible. I brushed it off as insignificant; what mattered was that we were damned slow and I didn't know why. Was it me? Had I really forgotten how to drive one of these things?

Kenny said, "Look, we think you're doing fine."

Jim chimed in, "What do you expect, that after eight months you're going to get a strange car all figured out in ten laps?"

Maybe not quite, but I certainly had expected to be faster than this, at least in a car prepared by George Bignotti.

New problem areas had cropped up, of course, and we went over our list. Padding, for example, on the arcs cut into the dashboard for my knees. The arcs were as high as possible, right up against the instrument bodies that protruded behind the dash, but their sharp edges dug painfully through my double-layer driver's suit and Nomex long johns.

They made a heel stop for my accelerator foot, a flange on the floor of the car so I could brace my leg. Since my knees were bent up so far, I had been carrying most of the weight of my right leg with the muscle on the front of my thigh. That made it tough to sustain throttle sensitivity at the ball of the foot. For stability and accuracy, a fix was essential.[1]

On Sunday May 7, it rained. Not a wheel turned. On Monday, rain continued to pelt the Speedway, flooding the middle of Gasoline Alley four inches deep, with a forecast of rain through Tuesday. I took the guys for a relaxed lunch at the Speedway Motel, but by the time lunch was over, the sky had cleared and the sun was out. We were on the track a little after four. I couldn't make sense out of anything the car did, and felt sure the problem was in my head. I reported a few minor problems, but nothing that accounted for such slow speeds. The only thing I could put my finger on was that the car seemed to jump around a lot in the gusty wind. The wind blew through a gap in the grandstands on the front straight, and there the car wanted to veer sideways by two or three feet. Steve Krisiloff passed me once at exactly that point, and it gave me a bad moment: between the wind's effect and that of the turbulent, "dirty" air from his car, we got too close for comfort.

The only cheerful development was that by the end of the day I had finally begun to relax physically; to allow myself to be pressed into the side of the car, to wipe against it in the turns as you'd smear soft butter into bread. This was an absolute necessity, a prerequisite to going fast, but easier said than done.

It was a lovely, mild, clear evening. Pink and lavender clouds filled the eastern sky, reflecting sunset, in serendipitous harmony with the redbud trees and pink flowering cherries. Alex was downcast this evening, fretting over his small son who had been ill. He feared his ex-wife wasn't taking good care of the boy. We talked

---

[1] The question of a car's fit isn't frivolous. At the beginning of 1995, superstar Nigel Mansell opted to miss the first two races of the Formula 1 Grand Prix season, an unthinkable handicap in his quest for another World Championship, because Team McLaren's chassis was too short for him. The official McLaren statement read, "he and the team realized he could not achieve a comfortable driving position in the car and that this would compromise his performance." (*National Speed Sport News*, March 22, 1995)

until the stars appeared, then slipped out for pizza and made an early night of it.

Tuesday morning, May 9, I was ready, loaded for bear, set to wrestle the car into submission. I was still apprehensive about finding the speed, but confident that I had started to get the feel of it back again. The guys were ready too, and had the car on the line for the opening of the track.

When I brought the car in for a spark-plug check, Kenny said, "George wants Gordon Johncock to take the car out next."

Nuts. Just when I thought I might get a grip on this...

I climbed out as Gordon walked toward us along pit road. While they fitted the seat with its padding, he queried me. The day was dark, gloomy, the wind strong and gusting.

"I don't have any specific complaints," I said, "except that it jumps around in the wind. Frankly, I think I'm just having a hard time remembering how to drive one of these things."

Gordon looked at the Wildcat. "We'll see," he said.

Two dozen other cars were on the track that day, but they were invisible to Kenny, Jim, and me. We followed our Wildcat with eyes, ears, and stopwatches. And what we saw was this: that Gordon backed off the throttle early, very early, in the turns. He shied away from the wall, scribing a line much like the one I had used. When he brought the car back to our pit, Bignotti was there.

"It's wandering," Gordon said, "and in the turns, all the weight is going to the right front. Something's wrong." He made snaking motions with his hands, like the movement of a water moccasin through a swamp.

On and off through a day of frequent track closures due to rain, they made numerous chassis changes. I hung on every word. Johncock never named a component of the car; instead, he characterized its behaviour. Bignotti then specified the changes to be made. They had worked together for a long time.

Meanwhile, hecklers gathered. "Hey Janet, you gonna let Gordie show you how to drive?" The coarse voices went on and on.

My guys were really good about it; but when I finally remarked, "I'd like to turn right around and give those creeps the finger," they cracked up as if I had said something genuinely hilarious. It loosed a flood of imaginative proposals for the disposition of the hecklers, and the tension eased.

When the track closed at six, Gordon said, "It's better, but it's not fixed."

George Bignotti turned to me and said, "I'm going to put it in the van and take it back to my shop. We'll go through it tonight and see what we can find."

I was profoundly grateful for the opportunity to learn from the experience of Gordon and George. When the track closed, I formed a little delegation—Kenny, Jim, Don—and crossed Gasoline Alley to Bignotti's garages to express our thanks for their help. "So do I get a free Texaco credit card for this?" Gordon asked.

"We'll see what we can do," I laughed.

While we waited for Bignotti's van, we tossed the credit card thing around. We didn't have a free Texaco card ourselves, much less the ability to get one for Gordon. It was Don who had a bright idea, and promptly went off to put it into execution.

Meanwhile, Jim and Kenny discovered that two of the Heim joints in the right rear suspension had excessive play, allowing the massive rear wheel and tire to wobble slightly. They showed this to Gordon and George, who were most intently interested. It might logically account for at least part of the wandering.

Bignotti never told me what he did that night, though I heard that some of his men worked the whole night through. His wife Kay, who had started my engine for the race last year, told me later that Johncock said it had scared him just going down pit road.

The next day, in perfect weather, we waited for our Wildcat to return. The uncertainty was excruciating. How *long* would it be until I learned how, or whether, it had changed?

I perched on the golf cart in front of our garage, where I could see the full length of Gasoline Alley—where Bignotti's huge truck would first show its nose. Practice was under way, and Gasoline Alley bustled with crew. Tractors towed race cars slowly out to the track and back again, golf carts sped to and from pit road laden with tools and parts.

In the garage next door, rookie driver Phil Threshie's crew hovered over my old Lightning, which he had bought from Rolla Vollstedt. Phil came to sit with me, and I shared more of my experience with the car. "If you lose it," I said, "if you spin, be sure to look at your hands on the wheel. That's the only way you'll know whether you've actually got the wheel cranked left."

One of Phil's crew walked over to show him a broken bolt they found in the rear wing support. A rear wing that came askew at full speed could spoil your whole day. It wasn't the first broken thing they had found.

The Wildcat arrived at noon. An hour and a half later, I was out on the track. Yesterday's neurotic Wildcat had undergone a personality transplant. It was a different animal, sure-footed and secure. My very first timed lap was six miles an hour faster than any previous one.

With deliberate haste, and copious sweat, I started working it up to proper speed. The first step was to get a grip on its idiosyncrasies. Thirty-five drivers came out to practice, causing frequent yellow lights. But before too long, I homed in on something.

"When I lift," I said to Kenny Ozawa (meaning, when I backed off the gas at the end of the straights) "the back end feels like it's coming off the ground. It feels as if, when I start to turn in, the back end won't stick." I paused an instant. "As if the rebound on the shock absorbers isn't stiff enough."

Kenny wasn't sure. Bignotti, nearby on pit road, was busy. When we saw him pause, Kenny put the question. Yes, Bignotti said, try it. Kenny stiffened the rebound by three turns, and I roared back out onto the track. Sure enough, that fixed it. My valid analysis helped relieve my embarrassment at not having figured out how far off the mark the car was when I first got into it.

A few more laps and a couple of changes later, we were at 182 mph. The territory between here and 190 mph, what Bignotti had said the car could qualify at, was all honorable ground.

The next time out, in two laps I was at 184 mph. When practice came to an end, I was content with the day's progress, looking forward to more.

Back in the garage, crewman Don Hume was bursting with news. "George Bignotti wanted to know how fast you were going," he said, "and when I told him, he got a big smile on his face, and said they had twiddled the jets [the apertures in the fuel-injection system] to slow you down until they knew it was safe."

Aha! That explained the day's top mystery: the tachometer showed that the car gained little speed down the long straights.

Don continued, "George said, 'Tell Kenny to come see me when practice is over and we'll fix her up with a bit more speed.'"

Indeed, what great good cheer! We formed another procession to Bignotti's garage, bearing with us Gordon Johncock's credit card. Delivered to Don Hume's specifications, it was a cake almost three feet across, shaped and frosted in white, red and green like a Texaco card, with Gordon's name. We made a ceremonious presentation, and the cake was no sweeter than the outcome of the day.

There was even more good news. Leo Mehl, who ran Goodyear's racing program, related a conversation with Pat Patrick, the owner of Bignotti's team. Contrary to my fears, Leo said, Patrick was very much committed to having "his" car go fast in my hands. It was a great relief to know that we weren't in imminent danger of having Patrick order George to keep his hands off.

After Wednesday's elation, Thursday was a day of setbacks, with intervals of rain. I expected to add speed, not lose it, and felt bewildered and distressed.

During one of the rain delays, Kenny snooped through the suspension with a dial indicator. He found excessive play in the Heim joints of the steering assembly, and replaced them. This meant that the bump steer—ensuring that the wheels didn't change direction as the suspension travelled—should be done over, a tedious business requiring the use of Bear's suspension rack. We didn't have time for it.

The next day would be the last day of practice before qualifying. Texaco executives would be back at the track, in full force. Where was I going to find the speed—the speed that yesterday seemed to be within our grasp? I holed up in my apartment, consoled myself with junk food, and escaped into the realm of print. Almost anything in print would do, as long as it evened out the brain waves.

Friday morning was overcast and gloomy, giving every indication of rain. All day long I could smell it, especially at the exit of Turn 2 where the wind bore down the back straight. But while it rained all around, the little black clouds stayed away from our heads and the raindrops stayed off the track.

We ran sixty-eight laps, making changes every four laps or so. With an hour and eighteen minutes of track time left, I reached 187 mph, and felt like a surfer who has just caught a wave.

Yellow light.

What Jim's laconic notes don't say, never say, is what these yellows were for. Maybe random debris on the track—or maybe a crash. A driver in the pits waits with detached curiosity for the PA system to announce the cause of the yellow. If it's a crash, the emotional reaction is held in suspense. Now is not the time to allow yourself the vicarious experience of someone else's misfortune. You will do that later. What you are not detached from is the question of how long the yellow will be. A crash causes a long yellow.

The stress of a yellow light of uncertain duration is like a pervasive sound at ultra-high frequency, almost beyond hearing, yet it is the only sound in the world. All else is silence. The casual chat with your crew is like the buzzing of a gnat in this vast silence, against that sound.

As you wait, you watch. There are only two sights that you allow yourself to care about. One is the moving about of the guys on your crew, the guys who work on this car, who put their hands on it and change it and make it better or, occasionally, worse, who care tremendously about what it does, and who are there with you.

The other sight that will not escape you is the movement of the pace car. When the crash trucks have done their job—when the engine or chassis bits have been picked up, when the spilled fluids have been Speedi-Dried and the saturated particles swept off, when a dozen guys in orange suits have scanned every foot of the surface for hazard—the pace car will leave its position at the head of the pits. It will pull out onto the track, and official track inspection will begin.

Then the pace car will return. You watch the attitude of the distant figures in it and near it. Will the track remain yellow or will it go green? Based on what the figures do, you prepare. You pull on your helmet and climb back into your car.

Sometimes the yellow is simply for track inspection: a few raindrops have been spattering on the back straight, or an observer has spotted debris. You stay strapped into the car, helmet on, pulling a sort of turtle shell down over yourself. You don't even look toward the head of the track. One of your crew will be fixated on that signal light in Turn 1; one of these men so close to all that you do will say, "Green." And at that moment the starter will whine at the back of the car. You will already have checked the gearbox for neutral position and put your foot down hard on the brake, your hand will have moved to the ignition switch. Up and down the line, a dozen other drivers will have done the same thing. The turbocharged engines will catch and fire with that peculiar throaty whining scream and the quickest of us will leap onto pit road, rushing to be first on the track, ahead of the next set of problems.

With thirty minutes of the last day of practice left, "happy hour" was going full blast. The fastest cars were turning their most earnest laps. Our problem of the moment was a substantial twitch as I entered each turn, a brief oversteer condition. The result of the twitch was that I didn't have more than two and a half feet of control over my line on entrance. The exit, fortunately, was okay. But no matter what I tried, the entrance remained sloppy because of the transient oversteer.

We tried a new set of rear tires. When the tires were scuffed and the stagger adjusted, I turned three consecutive laps over 188 mph.

At the eleventh hour, I had brushed the ceiling of the Wildcat's potential. The rest of it would be pulled out of that existential space in which a qualifying run is made. George Bignotti and Wally Dallenbach had both said this car should qualify at 190 mph. We were at the threshold, and needed only to step through the door.

We didn't qualify that weekend. Nobody qualified that weekend. The rain came down for three and a half days.

The uncertainty posed by rain on a qualifying weekend is at least ten times as nerve-wracking as rain on a practice day. Drivers get edgy and snappish, and lurk in the backs of their garages (or motor homes, if they have that luxury). A jillion reporters play hide-and-seek with the drivers, looking for a story. Almost any story will do.

Kenny found an error in the front suspension setting: toe out instead of toe in, by an eighth of an inch. That was a lot. It might account for the car's twitch on entry. We signed up to get onto the Bear suspension rack ASAP.

At dawn on Sunday, it was still raining. Grouchy and irritable, I was all tweaked up to qualify with nowhere to go. Alex jollied me out of it. When I reached our garage, Kenny bounced in the door, full of enthusiasm. "Come take a look at this," he said.

The rack area at Bear was curtained off like an operating room; teams kept their suspension settings to themselves. Behind the curtains, the Wildcat was up on lifts, a patient prepped for surgery. It was rigged with mirrors and hairlines and electronic readout equipment. George Bignotti had come with me. He saw something to be concerned about, and fetched a gauge of his own.

"I'd like to put some more caster in it," he said after confirming the numbers.

"A lot of caster suits my style very well, but that means we'd have to do the bump steer again, and the toe," I said.

"Well, yes."

I mulled it over. If the rain stopped, we would have just half an hour of track time before qualifying. These adjustments to the front suspension were a leap into the unknown. As the car was now, I felt confident of running 190 mph. In principle, the changes would improve our speed; but in practice, we were awfully short of time to check them out.

We hashed it over, and agreed: we would wait.

It kept on raining. The Texaco contingent and Jerry Pillersdorf left. Not long after, George Bignotti came to our garage. He looked vaguely upset.

"Have you heard anything about Texaco buying another car for you?" he asked.

"No, that's news to me." It was no joking matter.

George was silent for a few moments. "Well, if there were anything to it, you probably would have heard something. Most likely it was just one of those rumors."

There's nothing like a rainy day at the Speedway for rumors. But by morning, I would know a lot more about this one. Jerry Pillersdorf's call came before dawn. "You won't believe what's been going on," he said. "Pat Patrick has been on the phone with Granville, the chairman of the board of Texaco, and McKinley, the president. He told them you won't be able to qualify the Wildcat. He said that Gordon Johncock could qualify it at one ninety-five but that you won't get out of the one-eighties. He wants to sell them Penske's fourth car [Bignotti had told me that Patrick owned part of Penske's team] for a couple of hundred thousand dollars. He says it won't finish but that at least you'll qualify. You can imagine the ruckus this has caused at Texaco, when word comes down from the chairman of the board and from the president, wanting to know what's going on."

How utterly foul.

No wonder Roger Penske had looked at me so intently yesterday, when our paths crossed near the cafeteria. I must have looked just like a big bundle of thousand dollar bills.

Jerry and I hashed it over. It wasn't clear when Patrick had placed those calls, but surely the speeds we reached on Friday should have cast a different light on the matter. We were as certain of qualifying as one could be in this chancy game.

The Penske-Cosworth was inherently a much faster car, but we would be starting all over again with something completely new and different. We would be losing Bignotti's advice, with God knew whom or what in his place. I wasn't eager to spend another five days like the week just past, with a single do-or-die qualifying weekend at the end.

Jerry said he would handle the situation, and there wasn't a doubt in my mind that he could and he would. And he did. We heard no more about it.

On Tuesday May 16, the rain ended, at last. We were on the track by early afternoon. Try as I might, I could barely graze 186 mph. I was frustrated and mystified. It took Johnny Rutherford to point out that track conditions were dramatically different after three days of rain.

Second-year driver Danny Ongais was shaking down a car for eighteen-year veteran Lloyd Ruby, in an arrangement similar to Murph's deal with Bignotti and Johncock for me. Ongais was running fast when he spun at the exit of Turn 4. The left rear of his car smashed into the wall, and flames traced its path almost five hundred feet down the track.

An accident in Turn 4 is visible from the pits. You don't have to wonder how bad it is, you can see it. This one was bad. Bad enough to die of. Up and down pit road, team members held their breath, not saying much, waiting for word. The loudspeaker broke the silence: Ongais was conscious and out of the car. A sigh of relief swept through the pits like the wave of a breeze across a wheat field, as crewmen turned back to their business.

Presently, the wreckage came by. The main part of the car dangled from the wrecker's hook; the rest of it, in small pieces, littered the truck bed. Rarely have I seen a car so badly trashed. Ongais had bruises and a cut tongue. He was running again, just as fast, the next day.

I took the crew out for pizza that night, feeling dejected over the loss of two miles an hour. Carl Holtman, however, reported that his evening garage tour garnered a near-unanimous opinion that the track was just too terribly clean after the rains. Most cars were loose, oversteering, and speeds were down by as much as 10 mph. It should have made me feel better, but it didn't. Speed is like a barometer: the higher it is, the sunnier the driver's weather.

On Wednesday May 17, before the track opened, I talked with George Bignotti about the caster change he had suggested. "It will be more stable going into the turns," George said, "if you have more caster on the left than on the right."

I was puzzled. This was the exact opposite of a stock-car racing setup, and would make the car pull toward the right. "Why would you want reverse lead?"

George explained, and it was crystal clear.

An Indy car required precision and the most delicate balance, not brute force. (Need I mention again the mythology that said women don't have the strength?) With reverse lead, you would go down the straightaway holding a little force on the steering wheel toward the *left* in order to keep the car going straight. The result was that as you entered the turn, you didn't make a transition from holding force to the right, to neutral, to holding force to the left, with that minuscule inherent sloppiness at the neutral point. Instead, you continuously increased the left-hand force, smoothly, seamlessly.

One more little secret. How many thousands were there to learn?

"On the left side," George said, "take one thick washer, that's sixty thousandths, from the back side of the upper wishbone and..." I watched carefully as Kenny and Jim got it done, and took the car to Bear for the bump steer and toe.

The day's running began. We trimmed the car with ever more delicate refinements, and one major change: I wanted to try a stiffer right front spring. The change was successful. Without crowding the car's capabilities too close to the limit, I had solid 186s and a 187.

Not quite at the limit ... but even that required something, a state of being, beyond reason or understanding. A minor change, careful now, and the lap is faster by half a second. Half a second: an eternity on the track, the mere flicker of an eyelash in ordinary life. God, what those tenths of a second require.

Is that part of the compelling nature of racing, its addictive quality? This relativistic expansion of time? It is immortality of a sort, when half a second can be an eternity.

The next problem was a mid-turn push. I drew a diagram, and went to see Bignotti again.

"Raise the front wings an eighth of an inch," he said.

The fix turned out to be perfect. The car was well-balanced, the faint tire squeal disappeared, and the electric eye had me at 189.474 mph.

I sat there thinking for a minute or two; went out to get 190, and got it: 190.294 mph. If I found my typical extra speed on the qualifying attempt, we'd be in deep clover.

On Thursday May 18, the weather was sunny, hot, and hotter. Everyone's lap times were down. My big objective for the day was a simulated qualifying attempt: four consecutive fast laps to test whether, as looseness developed, I could control it from my seat with the sway bar adjuster. Track temperatures would fall in late afternoon. Kenny and I decided to wait.

The previous morning we had put Texaco oil into the car for the first time, and over the course of the day the engine oil pressure declined by twenty pounds, from 150 to 130 psi. It was alarming in the extreme. Texaco had never acted on my suggestion at the March meeting that they look into the published formulation of oil for these specialized engines, and we were using one of their off-the-shelf oils.

When I warmed up the car at 4 p.m. and set out to get my hot laps, my first one was 188.7—but the oil pressure dropped another ten pounds. I stopped to confer with Bignotti about it. He sent me out again. I stood on it, eased into the first turn, stood on it again in the short chute between Turns 1 and 2.

Chnk-chnk.

It was the faintest noise, a two-part noise. It was such a little thing ... but it wasn't right. I backed off immediately, pulled to the inside of the back straight, checked the gauges. Everything looked normal. There was still some room left before the entrance to Turn 3. Just to be sure, I planted my foot again.

Chnk-chnk.

I killed the engine and coasted the rest of the way around, into pit road. Don Hume and Jim Nakamura pushed me down to our pit. Bignotti was already there. "It's not in the engine," I said, describing it to him. "It's in the drive line somewhere."

"Take it back to the garage and take it apart," Bignotti said. We did. Bignotti sent one of his mechanics over to us, a chunky blond fellow who made no effort to disguise his skepticism.

A mechanic who didn't believe what you told him could miss something important. "I have a good ear," I said to him quietly. "This noise is in the drive train." The man remained skeptical and impatient. I didn't need the aggravation, and wandered off, leaving Kenny and Jim to deal with him. Jim had worked with me long enough to be persuasive. Practice came to an end.

An hour or so later, I found the blond fellow dismantling the Wildcat's transaxle. "Did you find out what the trouble was?"

Kenny gave me a funny look. "These big nuts, here on the bench— they secure the ring and pinion," he said. "They were loose, they'd backed off. What you heard was the excess backlash." Kenny's voice carried a slight note of incredulity. "You do have a good ear."

Another of Bignotti's men walked up, took a look, and whistled softly. "You know," he said, "the same thing happened to Johncock's car at Trenton, but he drove it until it came apart. The pieces took the entire back end of the transaxle off, destroyed the whole thing."

"The only thing I know of that might cause those nuts to back off," Bignotti's man went on, "is detonation. Check the spark plugs first thing, when you run again."

Friday May 19, was the last day of practice before our single qualifying weekend. I warmed up, caught fourth gear on the front straight, and exited Turn 2 at full speed. I intended to pit the second time around for the plug check.

I never made it. Deep inside the engine, something broke.

It was sudden and it was bad. I hit the clutch and killed the switches, coasting nearly two miles to our pit. Kenny pulled the spark plugs. The third one was coated with oil and bits of aluminum. Disaster.

George Bignotti was dismayed. This was to have been my qualifying engine, and the pieces for my race engine had been late in arriving. It wasn't yet assembled. Qualifying began tomorrow. Assuming the weather held—and assuming also that the car was ready—we would have just one hour and fifteen minutes of track time tomorrow in which to check everything out.

On Saturday May 20, I reached the track with a careful plan for our brief hour and a quarter of practice. Bignotti and his shop had somehow delivered the goods. The Wildcat was back, its new engine installed. And they had found the cause of our engine failure: a clogged fuel filter, presumably from our non-standard fuel supply. Detonation indeed! George's man had been right on target. We must be sure to strain the fuel through a chamois from now on. When the track opened, we were ready to go.

Raindrops spattered my windshield, and the yellow light summoned us to the pits. We looked at our watches every ten seconds. The track reopened. I finished the engine break-in and tried out the first set of new tires. Yikes! The utmost I could get out of them was a mid-187. The car needed fuel, and they took it away. Time was rocketing toward the close of practice. The car reappeared. Quick, I said, the next set of tires. On the first lap with these, a great force on the steering wheel: the front was sticking well, but the net chassis effect was a push. On the second lap, the balance shifted toward neutral.

Enough! Pickle it! I wanted these tires just as they were. My experience in stock cars had been that a two-lap scuff revealed the inherent characteristics of a given set of tires. I wanted two additional laps—but not enough to risk using up the best part of the tire life. I pitted. They had me at 189.47 mph. We were fat by almost ten minutes of practice time when we chose to stop.

I stayed with the guys as the line formed for qualifying. Our number should be up in less than an hour. As we crept forward, I listened with half an ear to the speeds. There were no surprises. Gordon Johncock, in the fastest Offenhauser-powered car this year, posted 195.883. His teammate Steve Krisiloff clocked 191.255. Tom Sneva set the crowd on its ear with a run at 202.156, a new record that put him on the pole for the second year in a row. Rick Mears, who failed to make the field the previous year, notched 200.078. Mears had made the acquaintance of Roger Penske during Wally Dallenbach's famous off-road motorcycle gathering in the mountains of Colorado (men only, of course) and got himself a seat with the most competitive team in Indy-car racing, teammate to Mario Andretti.

A young clod plunked himself aggressively down on the pit wall close beside me and said in a coarse, brash voice: "Ya gonna qualify this year?"

How did these creeps all get pit passes, anyway? There was no possible response to the question. I ignored him. Perceiving me to be deaf, he punched my thigh and repeated, "Hey, you gonna qualify this year?"

I skewered him with a look that could have charred asbestos, and without speaking transmitted: keep your #@&* hands off me. It was enough. He left, projecting the self-importance of a ruffled hen. *Steady, steady,* I told myself, *you have no energy to waste on this.*

When we looked to be half an hour away from the front, I walked back to those precious facilities at Leo Mehl's private Goodyear office. The continued lack of a women's room in the garage area had been a running joke all month, very funny to some members of the media. But if you happened to remember that one of the things that nearly killed Pancho Carter at Phoenix last year had been that the crash ruptured his bladder, the women's-room issue didn't seem quite so funny any more.

When I got back, the Wildcat was nearly at the head of the line.

I wasn't perfectly sure I was psyched to the right level. Overconfidence could be deadly. You needed to put a fairly fine regulator on your adrenaline-generating mechanisms in order to reach the proper space for a qualifying attempt at the Indianapolis 500.

Then I was in the car. All was in order, there were no loose ends. Jim Lindholm fastened the belts, "tucked me in." Tom Binford recited the formal instructions.

Jim and Kenny in turn touched my shoulder, passing to me what power they could. In the moments when you wait for the signal to start your engine, I think you don't breathe at all.

Green light.

Along pit road, thumbs-up and waves from friends, officials, other crew. At the pit exit I was briefly aware of the grandstands jammed with tens of thousands of tiny pointillist dots, each dot a person. Then I shut that off—shut off the awareness of anything at all except the matter at hand.

How does the track look? I watched it, and the gauges, on the first warm-up lap. Considered the blowing trash, tossed by the day's gusty winds. *Not too bad, not enough to make slipping on it a major concern.* On the back straight I caught third gear, then fourth, and full throttle down the front straight. Top speed into the north turns, for the fastest possible start.

High up on the starter's stand, Pat Vidan waved the green flag.

Will those four fast turns this morning really have heated the tires up enough to stabilize their behavior? Too much? Will they continue to change? Our Goodyear man had let quite a bit of air out just before the run; I was wary of that.

So far so good. Into Turn 1, hard. This would be the third of the turns I took as fast as the car would go.

The right front screamed, the squeal of punished rubber rising over the engine's howl.

A push, a push, far too much push.

Perhaps as the tires heated up it would neutralize.

It got worse. It didn't respond to sway bar adjustment.

On the first lap they didn't show me a time. On the second, a 191. I didn't know whether that was for the first lap or the second, but I did know the laps were becoming slower as the tire temperatures rose. The right front continued to scream in the turns.

Get that thing hot enough and it will go away completely. Lose all semblance of adhesion to the track.

They showed me two 190s in a row. The checkered flag fell.

It wasn't what I had hoped for; but I knew that once again, I was in the field for the Indianapolis 500. The warmth of that simple, unalterable fact would be part of my life forever.

Damn that push. I had hoped for, expected really, a 192. I could almost always count on pulling a couple of miles an hour out of a qualifying run. But there was no doubt in my mind that I had driven the car as fast as it would go under the circumstances, and there was satisfaction in that.

Around and into pit road, people waving and smiling, track officials gesturing toward the ceremonial post-qualifying spot. Hugging my guys while I was still standing in the seat. The photographs, the folderol. The four-lap average was 190.325 mph, with a fastest lap—the first—of 191.002. It would put me on the fifth row for the start of the race. The elapsed time was 3:09.15. Those are the longest three minutes in the world.

Finally, we were back at our garage. Once again we formed a delegation to go thank George Bignotti. George was all smiles.

"You almost outqualified my driver," he said, meaning Krisiloff. Pat Patrick was nearby, and Jim Lindholm was watching his face as George spoke. Jim reported afterward that Patrick's look was priceless.

I'm glad, I thought. *The bastard.*

Gordon Johncock said, "I went over to the back straight with a radar gun after I ran. Tom Sneva was doing two-twenty-four miles an hour, two-twenty-three. Danny Ongais was at two-twenty-two. I got you at two-twelve. The Offies are going to be history after this race. The Cosworths are just too fast, and I think they have figured out how to make them reliable."[2]

A ten or twelve mph speed differential on the straights, which was a relatively pure measure of engine strength—there was no way to overcome it, even if I got through the turns as fast as anyone. My Wildcat, designed for road racing, was taller and less aerodynamically slick than those of Johncock and Krisiloff.[3] But a lot could happen in 500 miles. My opinion remained what it had been after those first conversations with Bignotti and Dallenbach about this car: if all went well for us, we might finish as high as fifth.

But my mindset had changed in a year's time. Putting a car in the field at the Indianapolis 500 for the first time last year had seemed like climbing Mt. Everest. It was the challenge of a lifetime, one that many great drivers had failed to achieve. But now, a year later, what had looked like Everest was rather more like K2. My head was out of the clouds, and what I wanted was to win the thing.

It wasn't going to happen this year, not with this car and engine, except by some great and unjust fluke. With Texaco, though, the possibilities were clear. If they shifted just a fraction of their resources from European to American motor sport, I could have what I needed: competitive equipment, a hand-picked team, and a program that included enough races to reach Indianapolis as well-prepared as anyone. The thought set my heart on fire.

The Texaco people hosted a dinner for all of us that night, at a nearby Holiday Inn. Kenny Ozawa, Jim Lindholm, Don Hume, Jim

[2] Chicago *Tribune*, May 28, 1978
[3] *Hi-Performance Cars Magazine*, Sept. 1978

Nakamura and Brenda and Dick Oeffinger came with me. Carl Holtman, the airline captain, was off flying a trip. Jerry Pillersdorf had extended Texaco's invitation to Kay and George Bignotti. Pat Patrick was standing with them when they accepted. Jerry then turned to Patrick and said, "You're not invited."

On Sunday May 21, I watched the drama of the last day of qualifying from the Champion Spark Plug suite. Its TV reported that in Belgium, Mario Andretti had won the Formula 1 Grand Prix. The rainout of qualifying here had forced him to let another driver put his car in the field, and Mario would start the 500 in last place as a result. Phil Threshie did a fine smooth job in my old Lightning, putting it on the tenth row at 187.520 mph. Phil was as happy a man as I've ever seen.

The day ended in the usual welter of superhuman efforts in marginal machines. Drivers made the field only to be bumped out of it by a faster attempt. Cliff Hucul was the last driver in, bumping Graham McRae. Jerry Sneva, the prior year's Rookie of the Year, was left with the slowest run at 187.266 mph.

By then I was back at the apartment, cooking up a storm. This was the night for celebrating with all the guys on my crew. We had champagne and steaks and salad, but the apple tart was best of all. Before he left Washington, Kenny Ozawa had chosen a box of the best big red crunchy apples his orchards produced. The apples travelled east with Don Hume, nestled against Kenny's huge tool chest in the back of Don's pickup truck. Julia Child's *Volume I* provided the recipe, and the apple tart came out steaming, golden and fragrant. It was a fine evening, the best. We were in the field. We would take only one deep breath before the next preparations began.

In the week between the end of qualifying and race day, the track would open only briefly, on Thursday. Thursday was still called Carburetion Day, though carburetors had long since been superseded by fuel injection. Reporters came to Garage 36 in huge bunches and batches. When the size of a group became too unwieldy, I took them off to the noisy cafeteria, to get them out of the crew's way. Each wanted an exclusive, but there weren't hours enough in the day. Each time another someone walked up and said, "Miss Guthrie? I'm with the (newspaper, radio, TV station, wire service, magazine...)" I added it to the lists I kept for Texaco. And in each interview I made sure to say, "I hope every woman in the country remembers that Texaco was the only company that would sponsor my car." I already knew that, mixed in with enthusiastic letters to Texaco about their sponsorship, angry customers had sent cut-up Texaco credit cards, in protest.

My stock-car crew arrived from North Carolina on Wednesday: Darrell Bryant, Jack Bryant, Toby Varner, and Jim Clodfelter. Toby took one look at the Wildcat—he had never seen a real Indy car before—and said, "You gotta be crazy!" But they took to it all like ducks to water, easily transferring their skills and teamwork to this new machine. We shook the glitches out of the operation on Carburetion Day: practiced pit stops, improved (but didn't get rid of) the push that slowed my qualifying run, and completed a ten-lap fuel consumption check. It was a good idea to start the race with a bit of push anyway.

My family trickled in to town over the last few days of the week. I had an apartment for them in the same complex as ours. My folks came out of loyalty; they were deathly afraid of this game. At the start of my first Indianapolis 500 the previous year, my brother Stewart's wife, the photographer Martha Cooper, had snapped a picture of my parents as they looked up the track toward the onrushing field of cars when the green flag fell. In that picture, my parents both looked as if the gates of hell had opened before them. Fortunately, my siblings could and did induce a lighter mood. My parents' oldest friends, Grace and Henry Linder of Iowa City, helped leaven the mix.

Most of my family had met most of my crew at one race or another, and when time and circumstance permitted, they mingled comfortably and enthusiastically. My family would bend over backward to avoid interfering; it was characteristic of them that they thought they ought not attend the team dinner that I planned to host in my apartment on Friday night, prior to our pre-race team meeting. But I very much wanted them there—my own natural family with my racing "family"—and my wishes prevailed.

On Friday May 26, just after dawn, the guys pulled the Wildcat out onto pit road and I did a live remote with David Hartman on *Good Morning America*. I was delighted to confirm the part he had played in my being there, with his wonderful interview back in March.

The day turned warm, the sky yellowish with irritating pollutants. But my mellow mood was far too profound to be affected. Two days and counting.

As the minutes and hours tick away toward that instant when the green flag will fall for the start of the Indianapolis 500, anticipation inhabits the back of your skull and the pit of your stomach. It tingles in your fingertips and weakens the calves of your legs. Suspense, suspended animation, two days. You keep it reined in, you go through the motions of ordinary life, holding your strength in abeyance. You don't spend any of your self, you will need it all in two days.

The butterflies shouldn't be let out of their box yet. It's far too early for them to be useful. But the box keeps popping ajar, you push down the lid in one place and a seam splits somewhere else. You are replete with the coming event, the moment that will inevitably come.

With all this, you feel glad. Your car is in the field, you have made the show. You can savor that, although the game is far from over. In the time between qualifying and race day at Indianapolis, you feel most intensely, utterly alive.

I quit writing in my journal; I filled it in later. That was part of saving my strength.

On that warm Friday morning after *Good Morning America*, I ran into Larry McCoy. Larry had driven Indy cars since 1972, twice putting a car in the field for the 500, though not in the last two years. We were friendly, and he had long ago told me his deep, dark secret: he held a master's degree in psychology. He figured if word of that got out, it could utterly destroy his standing among the other drivers.

"Are you going to play in the celebrity tennis tournament?" Larry asked.

I was in fact going, but not to play. What I knew about tennis would fit on the head of perhaps a thumbtack. Lynda Johncock had asked me to make an appearance anyway, since the tournament was a benefit for the USAC Benevolent Foundation. "Just be there to sign autographs, won't you?" So I tucked a box of Texaco's photos under my arm, and was on my way.

Larry said, "I don't play tennis either—why don't we play together? We'll both look like fools, but it's for a good cause. Come on, join me."

And I said yes.

We reached the club early, hoping that our rousing defeat would take place while the stands were relatively empty. To my surprise, we were holding up our end of a doubles match moderately well—partly because my shots were so bizarre and unpredictable that they were difficult to return. Then, reaching awkwardly for a low ball at the back of the court, I tripped over my own toes and fell. Hard. On my right hand, holding the racquet.

I picked myself up and continued to play.

Except the wrist was swelling.

I had no interest in having an injured wrist two days before the Indianapolis 500, therefore this hadn't happened. I kept on playing. The wrist kept on getting bigger.

Ten minutes later I packed it in, conceding the match between sets. God knows, I didn't want anyone watching to become aware of cause and effect. A cold feeling was growing in the pit of my stomach, and the hairs were prickling on my neck.

I walked inside the club amid a burgeoning crowd of spectators and players and signed a few autographs, feeling scared half out of my wits. If USAC or Speedway authorities found out about an injury, I might easily be ousted from the field. That fear vied neck-and-neck with fear of damage to the wrist with which I shifted gears. And though the pain wasn't great—probably because pain was the least of my concerns—somehow I knew that whatever was lurking under the big lump near my wristbone wasn't trivial.

What to do?

Driver Wally Dallenbach was somewhere outside. Wally was, among other things, an Emergency Medical Technician who might offer a clue as to what was under the lump. And surely, he wouldn't tell. Larry McCoy went to look for him, while I fought back a growing sense of panic.

Hordes of people were milling about the club by the time Wally Dallenbach found me. Too many people. Where to hide? How in the world did we conclude that a good place to hide was in the ladies' room? Anyway, in we went. Wally wiggled the wrist and felt it; but it wasn't a minute before there were some other ladies in there too, looking at us *most* peculiarly. Back out in the lobby, Wally gave his opinion. "Where that lump is—that's just what happens when your wrist is broken. I think you had better get it X-rayed."

If I went to the main hospital, word would spread like wildfire. Doc Hanna, Dr. Thomas Hanna, had served as Medical Director of the Indianapolis 500 since 1932. It was he who conducted my first official Speedway medical exam two years before. A woman driver? His hands shook throughout. I felt absolutely certain that, even if this injury was slight, he'd throw me out of the race. Not that he was hostile or malicious; but he was steeped to the gills in tradition. Since 1911, tradition had declared that no woman could handle the competition here. Never mind a woman with an injured wrist.

Wally suggested I ask the club manager for advice. That made sense; there were bound to be occasional injuries here. Sure enough, the club manager knew just what to do, and was entirely sympathetic with the urgency of keeping this quiet.

Just down the road, he said, was a small osteopathic hospital, out of the main line of civic life. I could get an X-ray made there, he knew the head technician. Then I should bring the films back to the club. A doctor whom he knew would soon be arriving to play, a man whose discretion could be relied upon and whose specialty was emergency medicine.

Back at the club with the X-rays, I squeezed into the director's tiny private inner office with the doctor. He was tall, lean, gray-haired, good-looking, about my age. I offered him the envelope.

The doctor said, "I am the Assistant Medical Director of USAC, Hank Bock."

My hair stood on end. Speechless, I must have done something like grab the envelope and prepare to flee, because the next words were still Bock's.

"No, no, it's all right, here, give it to me."

Staring at him in horror, I saw that I was trapped. I handed it over.

I had already studied the X-ray, and saw nothing. "It seems fine," I said, "I'm sure there isn't any real problem..."

"No, look here," he said cheerfully, "see this, that's a fracture." It was a little dark line running across the knob of the big arm bone.

The cold feeling in the pit of my stomach turned to ice. How could he not let USAC know? What a dumb, appalling, inconceivable, stupid end to the months of effort, the hard work and hair's-breadth saves on the part of everyone from Pillersdorf to Ozawa—all to end with a little dark line on an X-ray and a wrist that was becoming stiffer by the minute. I think I was turning pale.

Then: "It doesn't look too bad," he said. "Tell you what, come by my place later this afternoon and I'll see if I can't fix you up with something that'll get you through the weekend."

I went weak in the knees and sat on the edge of the desk, falling instantly, madly in love. Relief and gratitude made me light-headed.

Bock went off to play tennis, and I called our garage. Jim Lindholm answered the phone.

"Come and get me," I said, "I've fractured my wrist." Jim evinced no reaction, which disappointed me. I wanted him to be as shocked as I was. Actually, he told me later, he was shocked to the point of not being able to say a word.

We still had work to do at the garage, checking out the radios and so on. I told my crew what had happened, and cautioned them against letting anyone else know. Later, I found my way to Hank Bock's condominium in the north end of town.

He was breezy and cheerful as he fashioned a splint in his stylish kitchen. I perched on one of the bar chairs at the counter, and gratefully sipped the Chardonnay he poured. Made of plaster and gauze on an improvised base, cured in his microwave, the splint extended from elbow to mid-fingers. We chatted while the plaster set.

"Ah, what a work of art," he said, admiring his handicraft. "Don't you dare throw it out. But on Monday you ought to see Dr. _____. He'll make a splint out of heat-deformable plastic, that won't be as clumsy as this."

Weeks later, I sent the plaster splint back to Bock in a florist's box, with a dozen red roses tied into it.

He wrapped the splint on to my arm with an elastic bandage. "Wear it whenever you're not in public. Come and see me at the track hospital tomorrow."

Hank Bock knew and cared about racing, and understood the mindset of a racing driver. He also understood the threat posed, in my case, by the old school. Bock was able to evaluate the injury objectively; it wasn't as if my wrist was shattered, after all. Meeting him was my incredible good fortune. But then, so many things were, that month. I could only marvel at it.

I had long since set the final pre-race crew meeting for this Friday night, inviting everyone to dinner at my place. Fortunately, there were good cooks among my crew as well as in my family, and they all took over my kitchen to excellent effect. (It was typical of my family that they kept their concerns over my wrist to themselves.) Afterwards, Kenny Ozawa conducted the crew meeting with initiative and authority. We had a lot of territory to cover.

We finalized the pit assignments: Jim Lindholm to change the front tires, Darrell Bryant the rears, Jack Bryant to handle the jack, Toby Varner to do the fueling, Jim Clodfelter on the overflow. Kenny Ozawa and Dick Oeffinger were in charge of tactics to suit the race's developments. Carl Holtman, the airline captain, would handle the radios and keep the lap count and times, which would tell us when to pit for fuel. Don Hume, the former stock car racer and police officer, would work the wall that separated the race track from pit road, with a chalkboard as backup for the radios. We covered my hand signals in case the radios failed: for chassis adjustments, for overheating, and for a relief driver.

Relief. Indeed. The wrist. After everyone else left, Kenny and I discussed our choice for relief, if it came to that. We settled on Graham McRae, who was first alternate, unless someone really good had fallen out of the race by the time we needed him. If we needed him.

The situation was this: I had never yet finished any 500-mile race in an Indy car, although I had finished nine 500-mile Winston Cup races. This car was new to me. The most consecutive laps I had driven it were on Carburetion Day, in the ten-lap fuel consumption check that lasted less than eight minutes. I didn't know how the Wildcat's handling might change as the track changed, or how it was in heavy traffic, when turbulent air from other cars altered its aerodynamics. After searching through all my experience, and factoring in the use I had of my right hand, I felt confident of going at least an hour or so, around seventy laps. Beyond that lay the unknown.

Never in my racing career had I chosen to endanger another competitor. If I were to lose the precision of placement that this car and track and race required, if I had to have relief, I would bite the bullet and take it. But I would hate that like hell.

Late that night, the phone rang. It was a Texaco executive. Their PR man at the track had somehow found out about my fractured wrist, and called headquarters. The executive threatened to make it public, and prevent me from starting the race.

"Don't be silly," I said, feeling my face go white, "this is trivial. It's just a minor fracture. Gary Bettenhausen drives with one arm all the time." Somehow, we got them calmed down. Jerry Pillersdorf must have helped. Next day, Jim Lindholm and Don Hume caught up with the PR man. Jim promised that one more peep out of him would get him stuffed upside down into a trash barrel.

Meanwhile, Kenny told McRae he was our choice for relief, but didn't tell him why. McRae would be suited up and in or near our pits, come race time.

On Saturday morning, May 27, we locked the garage doors and took a close look at the trouble my little problem was likely to cause. I asked the two heaviest guys to sit on the front tires while more guys gripped the tires fore and aft, resisting while I turned the steering wheel. It appeared there'd be no difficulty with steering. The gearshift was another matter.

In an Indy car, your shifting wrist had to bend. You couldn't change gears by using your whole arm, with elbow motion; there wasn't room. You picked off the gears with a flick of the wrist, flash-quick. And my wrist wouldn't flick. It was stiff and painful, clumsy, jerky and slow. Also, no slots or spring loading guided the shift lever from one gear to the next. Your right hand had to learn where each gear was located. In neutral, the stubby little lever simply flopped about. I tried reaching across to shift with my left hand, and thought it hopeless.

I walked out into Gasoline Alley with plenty to think about. By this time, I had the name of a doctor who shall remain anonymous. He had said, "Come and see me this evening. We'll try something out." But a systemic painkiller—a pill—was out of the question. It might affect reactions, perceptions, sharpness. No way would I risk that.

In between times, I berated myself for whatever psychological quirk had made it necessary for me to do this, to fracture my goddamn wrist two days before the race, so that this whole impossible undertaking would be just that much tougher.

An hour or so later, at the public drivers' meeting preceding the traditional parade through downtown Indianapolis, we drivers formed the rows and columns of qualifying order on a special grandstand at the start-finish line. Chief Steward Tom Binford spoke, we stood and waved, dignitaries and celebrities had their moment. Then we and our families piled into a pair of huge buses for the ride downtown to where the parade began. Before we were even out of the Speedway, the bus driver, muttering to himself, scraped the side of the bus against a concrete bridge embankment. The collision made a heck of a noise, and a shorts-clad spectator who was sunning himself on the wall escaped amputation only by a backwards somersault into the ditch below. Apparently oblivious, the bus driver pressed on like a madman. Perhaps that was what precipitated the black humor.

"This is worse than the race," someone said. I think it was Billy Vukovich, whose father was killed while leading the Indianapolis 500 in 1955.

"That's the problem, the race is too safe nowadays. We need something like this to keep us on our toes." That might have been Johnny Rutherford, who once broke *both* arms in a sprint-car crash—one of them so badly that he could never again fully straighten it out.

"It isn't fair. These cars are so safe that none of you old guys get knocked off like you used to. Us young drivers don't have a chance!"

Maybe it was Gary Bettenhausen who said that, whose father was also killed here. Gary had lost the use of his left arm in a racing crash.

This sort of backchat continued as the bus swerved through heavy traffic at high speed. What I didn't know was that Gordon Johncock was watching me. Wally Dallenbach must have said something to his former teammate. Several days later, Gordon told me, "I was watching the way you held your arm on the bus, and I didn't think there was a chance in the world that you'd be able to finish the race."

On the trip back after the parade, I made certain that my family got into a different bus.

That evening, Jim Lindholm drove me to the office of Dr. Anonymous. Soon we were looking at a needle full of fluid—I don't think it was novocaine, but something similar. The barrel seemed huge.

"All that?" I asked as the doctor ran it into my wrist.

"All that. Does it hurt?"

"No."

"Liar," he said.

Jim and I studied intently the location and angle and depth of the needle, for if this seemed to work, Jim would have to help me with it the next day. We chatted while it took effect.

"I think that's going to do it," I said after a while. With this mild anesthetic, I could snap my wrist through the H-shaped shifting motions quickly enough, and with enough precision.

What a relief. I thanked the doctor profusely, and went home to a sound and peaceful night's sleep.

Sunday May 28. Race day, dawn. The sky beyond the lake was tinged with red. Light breezes bore the late-spring scent of moist earth, of freshly uncurled leaves. From all points of the compass, race workers, crews, and drivers were following their carefully plotted back-door routes to the two Speedway gates that opened prior to public access. Hundreds of thousands of spectators clogged the highways, backing up for miles along 16th Street and Georgetown Road, and the threat of getting stuck in traffic was quite real.

By 5 a.m., all of us were safely assembled in Garage 36—all but one. Jack Bryant had been out carousing, and cut it too close. Half an hour before the start, he abandoned his car, sprinted to the Speedway, climbed over the towering chain-link fence, and made it by the skin of his teeth.

About the time Jack was climbing the fence, Jim Lindholm and I sequestered ourselves in the garage. The anesthetic was injected. Jim wrapped my wrist with elastic bandage, then helped pull my glove over it. My largest crew members, Don Hume and Toby Varner, stood guard outside, stalwart against invaders.

Foremost among the would-be invaders, with perfect timing, came our sponsors, a heavy-duty delegation from Texaco's world headquarters.

"You can't go in," said Don.

"Oh yes we can, this is the president of Texaco." Their chief factotum, a bald giant who'd been a heavy presence at the Speedway all month, tried to push past. A minor scuffle ensued. He was bound to lose. It would have taken a lot more than that fellow to get by Toby and Don.

"She's, uh, she's dressing," Don said.

At that precise moment, mission accomplished, Jim and I emerged together. Blissfully unaware of the preceding scene, and of the reason offered for my seclusion (with Jim!), I greeted them with an effusive display of good cheer. The executives and their wives were thanked for their support and wishes for success, and they walked on.

Flanked protectively by Toby and Jim, I strode up pit road toward the car while Don, rocking with laughter, filled me in. Toby and Jim were a lot more amused than I was, but now wasn't the time to fret about the ruffled feathers of power.

Kenny and the others were waiting on the starting grid, buffering the Wildcat against inadvertent harm. Crews, sponsors, owners, and others who'd managed to secure the coveted silver badges crowded in among the rows of cars. The day was hot and humid, the air milky with pollution. Ninety degrees was forecast for the afternoon. Helicopters thwopped past the Goodyear blimp overhead. I stood next to the car, embedded among my guys, reassured by their nearness, ready. The butterflies had done their job, and the proper state of mind was on imperceptible hold. Reaching into my pocket, I touched the talisman that René Dreyfus had given me, the medal from his first race in 1924.

"Back home again ... in Indiana..." Even now, the sound of it sends little riffles of remembered sensation through the network of my nerves. Clumsily, I pulled on my head sock—a new version that covered the nose, with two separate eyeholes. This style, which offered improved fire protection, was newly introduced from Europe and much in demand. I had only managed to acquire one a few days before, and hadn't worn it on the track.

Mistake. Bad, bad mistake.

I fastened the helmet, then stepped into the seat and wriggled clumsily into position. Jim and Kenny buckled me in, hooked up the radio connections that dangled from my helmet, and taped its cables to the shoulder harness. I pulled on my left-hand glove and Jim tucked it in at the wrist, then buckled my watch on top.

Unquestionably, the hardest part of a race is the time just before the start, when all that force you have mustered is ready, with nothing for it to do yet and nowhere for it to go.

Rolla Vollstedt rushed up at the last moment to wish us luck, and I squeezed his hand with my left and wished him luck in return.

"Ohh, say can you see..."

At the starter's stand high over the yard-wide strip of original paving bricks that mark the start-finish line, Mary Hulman stepped to the microphone.

"... and the land ... of the ... brave!" Thousands of red, white and blue balloons soared free of their net, into the milky sky. It was a particularly poignant moment: Mary's late husband Tony had called the start for the previous twenty-three years.

"Lady and gentlemen, start your engines." The PA system, I later learned, mysteriously clipped off the first two words of her command.

Amid the uproar, the fact that the Offenhauser sprang to life was detectable only by a sudden leap of the tachometer needle. Methanol fumes obliterated the rank scent of hot asphalt. My guys wiped their watering eyes.

Jim Lindholm raised his arm, signalling the starter that we were running and ready. The starter scanned the field. Satisfied that all was in order, he raised the green flag. The pace car pulled away, and row by row, we followed. The gearshift gave me no great trouble. The last of the crew sprinted for the edge of the track.

My folks were in the upper grandstands of Turn 1. I waved in their direction; and from then on, nothing existed but the track and the cars and the signals from my crew.

Part of my mind was given over to the warmup, the gears and the gauges. And partly, I reviewed the field. Barring some sort of screwup at the front, I'd be most concerned with my immediate neighbors; and also with the fast cars coming up from the back—Foyt and Andretti.

Directly ahead of me on the outside of the fourth row was Sheldon Kinser. Making his fourth start here, the phlegmatic sprint-car driver was unlikely to do anything stupid. To his left, Roger McCluskey was starting his seventeenth Indianapolis 500. He would be cool as ice and solid as a rock. On my left, Tom Bagley offered no cause for concern. He was calm and smart and I expected his intelligence to overcome the multiple sensory inputs of his first Indianapolis 500 start.

Immediately behind me, Tom Bigelow would be aggressive but scrupulously clean. On Tom's left, John Mahler was a question mark. I thought him flaky. He could certainly wring the most out of an uncompetitive car on a qualifying attempt, and had done so. Would he stay sensibly within his car's limitations at the start of this race, or would he try to make a splash? And on Mahler's left, Spike Gehlhausen was very young and had behaved rashly in the past. I hoped that by now, in his third year at the Speedway, he had been around long enough to calm down.

The row behind them contained fast cars that had qualified on the second day: A. J. Foyt, Bobby Unser. Whenever they arrived on my heels, they would get whatever room I could give them. The sooner they were out of the way, the better off I'd be: free to scrap with the cars that were actually competitive with mine. But when would they reach me? There was no way to tell, though I rather expected that Foyt would jump the start. He might be upon our row as early as the first turn. I would have to watch out for that. And if Foyt jumped, Bobby Unser would too. I was more concerned about Unser than about Foyt, whom I had run with in stock cars enough to understand his style.

The nose aspects of these fast cars, what I could see in my mirrors, were almost as familiar to me as my own: Foyt's orange-red, with a broad nosepiece that almost hid the wheels; Unser's narrow black, with white dive planes sprouting to the sides and a red and yellow V that stretched up to the windshield.

Directly behind Foyt, George Snider had Foyt's second car. The colors and nose aspects of the two cars were identical, and the numbers—hard to read in the mirrors—were similar, Foyt's 14 and Snider's 84. Both had the powerful Foyt/Ford V8 engines, nearly as fast as the Cosworths. Snider had qualified at 192.627 mph, but now that my Wildcat's excessive push had been cured, I expected that I would be competitive with him in the race.

And back at the very back, of course, starting in thirty-third position, was Mario Andretti, at the wheel of what was arguably the fastest car in the field. Mario wouldn't be along for a while. With all his experience, he wouldn't make a fatal mistake or take foolish chances while picking his way through the back of the field. I didn't expect to see his narrow white nose and red fuselage in my mirrors until several laps had gone by.

The primary thing was this: whatever foul-ups might happen at the start of the race, I didn't intend to be part of them. This meant developing a little extra space all around my car, ready to thread my way through anyone else's mishap.

On the second parade lap we started to scrub our tires, and our neat rows and columns came apart. A car properly set up for Indianapolis doesn't take well to the abrupt snaking that heats its rubber, so each of us wanted extra room. Then, on the pace lap before the start, we formed ourselves back into the proper order again.

At 80 mph, we were still in second gear. Tom Binford's instructions, as always, were to keep our rows orderly and maintain the hundred-foot spacing between them until the start.

When the pace car dived into pit road, the speed of the field would be in Tom Sneva's hands. I expected him to make a proper start of it: smooth, and not so slow as to create problems when he chose to put his foot on the floor. Sneva was twenty-nine years old going on forty-five, deceptively mild-mannered, a ferocious competitor but responsible and mature. Excessively slow starts had precipitated several of the worst incidents at the beginning of Indianapolis races past (and would in the future as well) when drivers back in the field put their cars sideways by standing on the gas in second gear. Second gear was okay in stock cars, but not in those machines. Tom Sneva was not a man who would jeopardize the field in order to give himself some minuscule advantage on the start. He brought us out of Turn 4 in third gear.

Green light.

Three days' accumulation of dust and grit and hot-dog wrappers churned into a sandstorm as 25,000 horsepower propelled 53,000 pounds of race cars toward Turn 1.

The Wildcat trembled in the turbulent wake of the first four rows' passage down the front straight. Fourth gear, no problems.

On the front row, Danny Ongais reached Turn 1 slightly ahead of Sneva, while Rick Mears missed his shift into fourth and was passed by most of Row 2—fortunately, without incident. (Mears had also forgotten to buckle his helmet, which must have been distracting.) By the time my row crossed start-finish under the waving green flag, the field around me had turned ragged. Steve Krisiloff, who dropped back almost to Row 6 before the green, had jumped the start and was well ahead of Tom Bagley and me. I blasted down into Turn 1 on the outside of Bagley, only too well aware that Foyt was coming up through the row behind us like a hot knife through butter. Directly ahead of me, Sheldon Kinser abruptly and unexpectedly slowed, but he eased out into the gray to give the rest of us safe passage.

Turn 1 could be ticklish in the extreme: the junk on the track, the turbulence. But the Wildcat displayed no faults, no unexpected aerodynamic quirks. It remained well-balanced, just not stuck quite as well to the pavement as it would have been on a clean track in undisturbed air.

Tiptoe through this stuff, now. The start and the first turn at Indianapolis were the most dangerous by far.

The red-orange nose of Foyt's Coyote was just a few feet behind Bagley's Watson/Offy through most of Turn 1, and I held my position on Bagley's outside. In the short chute I eased off a bit, expecting that Bagley would yield the line in Turn 2 and let Foyt past. But he didn't, and Foyt had to wait. Bobby Unser came by on the back straight. So those two were taken care of. The first lap was entirely clean. Ongais set a new record for it at 185 mph.

Yellow light. That was quick! After just one lap. Sheldon Kinser had coasted to a stop on the back straight.

As we circulated under the yellow, I considered my wrist. It had done what was required; had cost me no time, not a fraction of a second, on the upshifts at the start. (On a normal lap at full speed, of course, you stayed in fourth gear.) After we slowed for the yellow, I had engaged second gear without difficulty. Steering was no problem. Steering could be done with a straight wrist, and my right was carrying about a quarter of the load. But the numbness was wearing off—already! We were less than six minutes into a three-hour race.

Meanwhile, I was puzzled that I'd heard nothing on the radio. Under a yellow, I would have expected to hear some remarks. I pressed the transmit button and said something inconsequential. There was no acknowledgement.

One lap to the green.

When the leader exited Turn 4, the starter would throw the green at his discretion. The new pacer-light stations had done their job of keeping the field strung out. I focused on the double light that still showed yellow.

Green light.

The Wildcat leaped forward. I went for third gear at the entrance to Turn 3, just as I peeled away from the outside wall.

I missed it. My wrist hadn't done what it should have.

The skin prickled on the back of my neck. Surely, I was going to be run over. An eternity passed while I resynchronized the engine and caught the gear. Clock time would have been less than a second. Tom Bigelow was the only driver who got by me.

This must not happen again.

Emotional detachment was key here. The situation would be dealt with. As the engine revved toward its limit in third gear, I reached across the cockpit and caught fourth with my left hand. It worked. I had thought it impossible; but under the pressure of necessity, the left hand learned.

Up ahead of me, Danny Ongais continued to lead. He seemed to be using full boost, the most powerful setting of the turbocharger, from time to time. He would have to be careful about that, so as not to use up his allotment of fuel before the end of the race. Our choice had been to go with low boost at the start. We would increase the power only when we had fuel enough to go the rest of the distance. This tactic suited my strategy: conservative in the early going. Unless you were starting at the front of the pack, heroics in the first few laps were inappropriate: a lot of risk for little or no gain.

I was staving off George Snider, in Foyt's second car. As the pack got strung out, I gave myself freer rein, and passed Roger McCluskey before the yellow flashed on at Lap 9. It was Kinser, stalled on the back straight again. We circulated under the yellow for three laps. The restart would be a major test of my left-handed shift.

Green light. The Wildcat surged forward. Third gear, neat and clean. Foot to the floor. Fourth gear, clean. Whew!

Four laps later, my speed dropped by a couple of miles an hour. My focus had been diverted, but not by my wrist. I vainly squeezed and prodded the radio connections, anticipating my first stop for fuel; but the real difficulty was the result of something I did myself—and I should have known better.

Never, never start a race with a new, untried piece of gear.

My new head sock hadn't been reinforced around the eyeholes. The cut edges of the knitting were loosely stitched. As 200-mph turbulence buffeted the cockpit, the fabric sagged into my field of vision. In order to see all the way down the track, I had to tilt my head far back. In addition, the edges had frayed, and long threads whipped in front of my eyes.

My vocabulary deteriorated.

Of all the things to have affected, vision was surely the worst. I fished around the back of my neck with my left hand, trying to pull on the head sock, without results. The helmet was too tight.

The radio was still silent. My first fuel stop ought to be fairly soon. Don Hume, stationed at the wall between pit road and the track, hadn't shown me a board. Did they know that I couldn't hear? Time to get his attention. On the front straight, I checked my mirrors and pulled far left, dusting off the wall where Don stood. Grit flew. Don had never before stood so close to such machines; he later said that at the start of the race he nearly—well, you can imagine. Next time around, he held up the board with a question mark chalked on it. I gestured toward my ear.

I had also been watching Danny Ongais' approach in my quivering mirrors for the last several laps. Still leading, he overtook me about fifty miles into the race, as we entered Turn 1. I stayed toward the outside and gave him a clean shot. We knew each other's habits reasonably well. He wasn't getting through the turns an awful lot faster than I, but with that fabulous new Cosworth at his command, he squirted away even on the short chute. Danny was always fascinating to watch in the turns. Most of us normally tried to keep our cars on the ragged edge, but Danny bounced along somewhere out there in blue space, touching the crests of the ragged edge every now and then. It was spectacular, even if he did crash a lot. He never made his moves at the expense of another driver.

Don Hume had given me "Pit 3" on the chalkboard at the nineteenth lap, just as Ongais was approaching. Three laps, two and a half minutes, until my first fuel stop. Could I possibly fix the obnoxious head sock that sagged and flittered in my line of sight? I diverted a fraction of my mind, a bit of that crystalline focus, to consider the necessary steps. Gloves off ... my watch was fastened over the left one, which my right would be unable to unbuckle. Undo the radio connections, wired into the helmet and taped to the shoulder harness. Helmet off, adjust head sock. Then, reverse the process. The crew couldn't expedite any of this, because without a functioning radio, I couldn't alert them; they would have no idea what was wrong. It would take three laps at least. And the fraying edges of the eye openings were irremediable. The conclusion was clear: I'd have to live with it.

"Pit," read the chalkboard. At Lap 22, under green, I swept down pit road at the 80 mph limit and stopped on my marks. They slammed in the refuelling nozzle and checked for tire wear while I tugged desperately and ineffectively at the head sock. Fuel only; and I was out in nineteen seconds—slower than I might have liked. My guys were easily capable of fourteen-second pit stops; they did it for my stock car all the time. What I didn't know yet, nor did they, was that the vent in our pitside fuel tank was somehow plugged. Air couldn't rush in to replace the outgoing fuel, and the flow was impeded.

On Lap 25, Spike Gelhausen crashed in Turn 2. The yellow light flashed on just as I committed the Wildcat to Turn 1. All the adhesion my tires could generate was being used up by the turn. Nothing would be available for braking until the exit. My left foot leaped to hover over the brake pedal, then fed in as much brakes as the car would bear as I straightened out the wheel for the short chute, next to the wall. Errant chunks of race car were still bounding about when I reached them. Avoiding the bits and pieces at close to full speed was ticklish business. Gelhausen was unharmed, but debris was scattered everywhere. Had I run over some small sharp thing? Might a tire have a slow leak? If only my pit stop could have been postponed!

We ran under the yellow for five laps, almost ten minutes. Danny Ongais refueled under the yellow. Cosworths got about 1.8 miles per gallon, the Offys about 1.5. Meanwhile, snaking the Wildcat back and forth, I sought signs of a softening tire. I felt nothing. The handling seemed unchanged. Green light, and away we went. The left-handed upshifts were smooth.

The sequence of pit stops put Steve Krisiloff in the lead, while Tom Sneva edged out Danny Ongais for second place. Sneva was soon balked in a turn by Salt Walther, enabling Ongais to repass. Meanwhile, Krisiloff was penalized a lap for violating the pacer lights.

Tom Bagley, Sheldon Kinser, and Phil Threshie in my old Lightning were already out of the race. Dick Simon, in Rolla's black Vollstedt-Offy, was held in the pits for half an hour while a wheel bearing was replaced.

Ambient temperature had risen to 91°C. (Three members of the drum and bugle corps suffered heat prostration before the race even began, one spitting blood.) I suppose I was saturated with sweat, but I didn't notice. Since my heat tolerance was good, heat wasn't among the data I processed. Winston Cup stock car races had been much more physically taxing, in higher ambient temperatures. Indy cars demanded precision, finesse, balance, and focus—a level of concentration unparalleled in sport.

So it went. My next fuel stop was at Lap 46. It was even slower than the first, thirty seconds. Damn! Then, two laps later, the track went yellow (for debris). My guys were being conservative, not yet quite sure what the fuel consumption was; but to see the yellow come out so soon after our pit stop under green was excruciating. George Snider, whose timing was luckier, pitted under yellow and came out in eleventh place. When the green flashed on, we were just over a quarter of the way into the race.

Ongais continued to lead. Mostly he ran 186 mph, sometimes 184, sometimes over 190. The fastest lap of the race was turned by Mario Andretti at 193.924, in the car he had practiced at 203.482. Al Unser seized the lead on Lap 76, in the wake of pit stops. Tom Sneva, who had led occasionally, was third.

I had finally figured out what was wrong with our radio: the volume control knob vibrated all the way closed within a few seconds, unless held firmly in place. It took one hand to steer and one hand to press the "transmit" button. All I needed, I thought, was a long prehensile tail to wrap around the volume knob, and I'd be set. Carl Holtman was still listening on the other end. As we circulated under a yellow, in second gear, I asked my most pressing question.

"Can I turn up the boost?" Then I let go of the transmit button, and reached for the volume control. Fuel-consumption calculations weren't simple, and Carl asked me to wait.

The yellow lasted just two laps. We were off and running before I had my answer. I needed two hands on the wheel in the turns. Then, finally: "That's affirmative," Carl said. "You can turn up the boost."

"Hot dog!" I yelled back, and let go of the knob. I was then in eighteenth place; but our fuel supply was secure. It was time to have at it. I felt as if a dead weight had been lifted as I reached for the boost switch.

With more power at the rear wheels, the car was better balanced. Its tendency to push or understeer was neutralized. So not only was I getting 300 more rpm, I could get through the turns better than before.

Up to this point, I had been running mostly 180 to 183 mph—a bit faster than the typical 10 mph drop from qualifying speed. Suddenly, I could run 186 or better. It would be a different race from now on.

By the halfway mark, I had gained three spots. Ten laps later, I was eleventh. A. J. Foyt was tenth. This was more like it. Like a dragon in a medieval tapestry, flames seemed to come out my nostrils with every breath. My 114th lap, according to the official scorer's sheet, was forty-eight seconds. It was the first such lap, though not the last. That was 187.500 mph, just 2.8 mph slower than my qualifying speed.

Dick Simon lay ahead (though several laps down). I reeled him in. Simultaneously, I watched Al Unser, leading the race in his Lola Cosworth, approach from behind. I saw that I would overtake Simon just a heartbeat or two before Unser overtook me, and that this would occur on the front straight. Earlier in the race, I'd have tucked meekly in behind Simon while Unser went by. Not now. The width of the front straight could accommodate three cars abreast. I wouldn't hold a lapping car up in the turns; but I wasn't going to surrender this hard-earned pass. And so it went. Simon stayed near the outside wall, I popped out from behind him at the last minute, and the three of us crossed the start-finish line neck and neck. When we reached Turn 1, we were back in line again, Simon last.

Our most devastating pit stop came on Lap 129. I zoomed into the pit, stopped on my marks, and they changed the right rear tire, slick as a whistle. Jim Lindholm, at the front of the car, held up his palm to me: refueling wasn't yet complete.

I waited. And waited.

Fuel and air rolled lazily back and forth in the transparent refueling line. Jim looked ready to burst. Kenny jounced the line up and down, desperate to extract the fuel.

It was a minute and eighteen seconds before I charged away from the pit. Even then, they weren't sure I had gotten a full tank. There was nothing to do but grit my teeth and forget it.

Mario Andretti, who had suffered a long pit stop with ignition problems, came by me not long after. He reached me in Turn 2, and I gave him the room to go underneath. He swept down into the lane that led out of the pits (which was technically illegal), all four wheels below the yellow line—right down next to the grass. His Penske-Cosworth wriggled as it touched the slippery yellow paint, using up every inch of pavement. Since the difference between our speeds in the turns wasn't enormous, I could admire his technique at leisure and close up.

Even Mario wasn't perfect, though. On his first pit stop in this race, he actually entered the wrong pit, causing no end of confusion and lost time.

Meanwhile, the last of my significant problems was making itself felt. The chassis of the Wildcat was at least three inches too short. With my knees bent up into the scallops we had cut into the dashboard, pressed against the bottoms of the gauge housings, my feet had minimal mobility. My toes stuck up over the top of the accelerator pedal, which I operated with the ball of my foot.

By the halfway point, it felt as if I were standing on a red-hot poker. In the context of the race, this was merely an annoyance; but after a while, the ball of my foot started to go numb. Now, *that* was a problem. It was necessary, with this year's rules and technology, to feather just a little approaching Turns 1 and 3—to back off the throttle ever so slightly. Feathering required delicacy and precision.

Things were starting to stack up a little.

My left foot was okay. I had kept it stretched out underneath the clutch pedal assembly, deep in the nose of the car. Maybe I could use my left foot on the brakes, while keeping the throttle all the way down? I tried it. Unsettled, the chassis didn't respond well. Besides, this would waste fuel.

So for the rest of the race, I held the throttle down with my instep on the long straights, sliding my foot forward into the nose and wiggling my toes like crazy so that some modicum of feeling returned. Then, just before diving into Turns 1 or 3, I'd slide the ball of my foot back down onto the pedal, ready for that minuscule lift.

Regardless of the various discomfits of the driver, the Wildcat was running like a train. As I had expected, I found it relatively easy to stay close to the edge. The Wildcat was by far the most solid-feeling, most obedient, most communicative Indy car I ever drove in a race. Its behavior was predictable and consistent. It told you exactly what it was going to do, and it had no nasty tricks up its sleeve. You could even put it sideways a bit and still get it back again. I couldn't have asked for more.

All this meant that I could get through the turns better than a lot of the other cars on the track. My tape of the race-day TV broadcast shows a moment somewhere around Lap 150 when I dove to the inside to take two cars at once at the entrance to Turn 1. I don't really remember that moment, or who they were; but I do remember how I felt.

Ferocious.

Jim Hall, the Texas oil millionaire who owned Al Unser's car, had said he figured there were just eight cars in the field capable of winning.[4] Mine sure wasn't among the fastest; but I was driving it as if Victory Circle lay just ahead.

Danny Ongais' charge came to an end on Lap 145. A huge plume

---

[4] Coatesville (Penn.) *Record*, May 27, 1978

of smoke trailed his car to the pits. Sometime before the 160th lap, Mario Andretti dropped a cylinder (though he continued at an amazing pace, considering the handicap) and I passed him to take over ninth spot. The order was now Al Unser, Tom Sneva, Gordon Johncock, Steve Krisiloff, Bobby Unser, George Snider, A. J. Foyt, and myself.

So it remained for the next twenty laps, a distance of fifty miles. Running as fast as Foyt, I lay about seven seconds behind him (though a lap down). I continued to turn laps at 185 to 186, two or three miles an hour slower than the race leaders.

I took on my last load of fuel at Lap 174, in twenty-five seconds. Al Unser pitted around the same time. He overshot by twelve feet, scattering his crew in all directions. In the process, he struck a waiting fresh tire with his right front dive plane, bending it out of shape. Tom Sneva slowly reeled him in, running 186 to 187 mph as Unser's speed dropped into the 170s.

Meanwhile, I was hauling in George Snider, whose last pit stop enabled Foyt to take over seventh place. I could see from the pillar that Snider was eighth and I ninth. Were we on the same lap? I had no way to tell.

I caught him in the south chute, gaining the last fifty feet in Turn 1. His huge rear tires loomed up, a charcoal blur. His high-pitched Ford V-8 beat against the throatier voice of my four-cylinder Offy. He bent down toward the apex of Turn 2. I paused a heartbeat to increase our distance, then started feeding in the fuel. At the apex I was on his heels, and eased left as we straightened out for the exit. When our wheels were centered again, aimed down the back straight, George was next to the white concrete wall and I was a nose ahead of him, on the inside. Coyote orange-red saturated my peripheral vision. We were both at full throttle, I with slightly more exit speed.

George just motored off into the distance.

This wasn't going to be easy.

We hurtled toward Turn 3. Dispassionately, I ran the elements of the situation through my mind. We were over three hours into the race; the end was near. Body and mind had been operating in the metaphysical territory over one hundred per cent for all of that time. Quite possibly, a pass wouldn't even improve my position, but simply put him one less lap ahead. He was holding me up in the turns; and at Indianapolis, you couldn't put two cars next to each other through the turns without both giving up some speed. George knew that as well as I; it was he who had told me so, two years before. He wouldn't be about to give me the room.

Once again, I got my nose ahead of him coming out of the north chute; and once again, when he planted his foot on the straight he just motored away.

I thought, *this will be the most difficult pass you've attempted all day. There's a fair amount of risk to it. You're in the top ten. Why not let it go at that?*

I couldn't. I just couldn't. Eight hundred million Chinese might not care whether I finished eighth or ninth, but the pass could be for position. And whether it was or wasn't, I had to go for the internal reward, the certain knowledge that no one, *no one*, could have driven my car harder than I.

The only way to do it would be to rush him. We howled over the yard of bricks at the start-finish line. Two laps to go. I backed off the throttle. Exactly how much ground would I gain, if he wasn't holding me up? Exactly how much faster was I through the turns?

When I thought I had created enough space, I got back on the throttle. I caught him too soon. The Wildcat's nose rushed up toward his transaxle, and I had to back off as we exited Turn 2, in order not to hit him. It ruined my speed for the straight.

One and one half laps to go. This time, I had to get it right. I would have to begin it a mile and a half away from the point of passing, the moment of truth.

At the end of the back straight I got off the gas early, watching the distance between us increase. It seemed huge. If I had to guess, I'd say a hundred feet.

If I started my move too close to him, I'd have to get off the throttle at the exit of Turn 2 again, in order not to hit him, and the game would be lost. If I let him get too far away before planting my foot, even the extra speed that I carried through the turns would be insufficient to overtake him. I had to arrive on his heels just after the exit of Turn 2, running with every iota of speed I could muster.

At the exit of Turn 3, I began. I ran Turn 4 as fast as I could. The die was now cast. I gained a little, and then he pulled farther away. The white flag waved overhead as we crossed the yard of bricks. One lap to go.

I bore down into Turn 1 with everything I had. As I reached the outside wall in the short chute, the red-orange Coyote was almost at the apex of Turn 2.

The Wildcat squirmed as I grazed the yellow line at the inside of Turn 2. And in that last instant, I saw that the calculation would succeed. The thick hot methanol exhaust of George's Coyote enveloped me as we reached the outside wall, and then I pulled left and around. Down the back straight my speed advantage dwindled to nothing as his power came on, but even the strong Foyt engine couldn't make up the difference before we reached Turn 3. Those last two turns belonged to me, and I took the checkered flag with George Snider a comfortable distance behind.

Off the gas. It is done. The pressure comes off, the muscles unwind. The trees and grass come back into view; and the sky, the clouds, the grandstands, the hundreds of thousands of brilliant people-dots. I smell the warm summer Indiana air. I notice, for the first time in hours, that my wrist hurts. But it's trivial.

I reach for the radio knob. "Good going, guys," I say. Carl Holtman's voice, that calm airline-pilot voice, has gone up half an octave, and I can't make out what he is trying to say.

Pit entrance. Pit road, cream-colored concrete garnished with seams of black tar, whoppity whoppity under my tires. Crews in their sparkling colors are clapping and cheering those who have finished the race.

I look toward the pylon that shows the order of the finish. My number, at that moment, moves to eighth.

MY FIRST CAR ... *I am waiting in line to compete in a gymkhana (now called Solo competition) at Roosevelt Field on Long Island in 1961 in my beautiful 1953 Jaguar XK 120M coupe.*

EPILOGUE

In May of 2003, I gathered my 1978 crew in Indianapolis for a twenty-fifth-anniversary reunion. There were hugs and tears, laughter, and reminiscences of the time when we few overcame large obstacles to post a top-ten finish in the greatest race in the world. (Our official finish had dropped to ninth the day after the race, when scorers added another lap to George Snider's count; but through 2004 it remained the only top-ten finish by a woman in the Indianapolis 500.) At the legendary Indianapolis Hall of Fame dinner that month, emcee Tom Carnegie, the resonant voice of Indianapolis Motor Speedway, did us the unusual honor of asking me to name each man in my crew from the podium, and then asked them all to stand as the spotlight swept around.

What a long way we had come since Rolla Vollstedt gave a woman a shot at Indianapolis and set the oval-track racing world on its ear! Rolla turned eighty-five in 2003, and at that dinner he received the prestigious Louis Meyer Award for lifetime achievement.

Some things have changed for women in auto racing; some things haven't. Women are no longer barred from the pits and the track at the hundreds of short ovals across the country, as they were in 1976. Women are no longer required to present, each day of an event, a certificate signed by a doctor on that same date stating that they are not pregnant. NASCAR has begun a diversity program that stands a chance of bringing women and minorities into the fold. Jim Hunter of NASCAR, eminently fair-minded then and now, has risen to the position of vice president. In the lower ranks of oval-track racing, where expenses don't run into the tens of millions of dollars a year, there are plenty of talented young women who are making the most of their opportunities. Drivers like Erin Crocker in the ferocious World of Outlaws Sprint car series, Sarah McCune in midgets, Christi Passmore in ARCA stock cars, and many more are making their mark.

As of 2004, driver Sarah Fisher is the only woman with a chance at the top levels of the sport. She has qualified for the Indianapolis 500 each year since 2000. (Lyn St. James, who retired in 2001, is the only other woman to qualify for the race.) Sarah is young, talented and experienced. What she doesn't have at present is the sponsorship money needed to get the job done. In fact, that has remained the one constant for women drivers: lack of money. I have said for years that what this sport needs is a woman with all the stuff that it takes, plus her own fortune. That's what Elsa Junek had in 1928, when she nearly won the Targa Florio, and that's what we need now.

After the Indianapolis 500 of 1978, I found sponsorship for only a handful of top-level races. Among the high points: qualifying fourth to A. J. Foyt, Danny Ongais and Johnny Parsons Jr. (by 0.004 mph) for the Pocono 500 Indy-car race in 1979; and finishing fifth at Milwaukee later that year. The woman who would qualify and finish as high as that in any Indy-car race, Sarah Fisher, hadn't yet been born.

Altogether, I drove so few Indy-car races—only eleven, spread over four years—that I had little time to relish the fullest, passionate enjoyment of those incredible machines. In 1980, when I was turning some of the fastest corner times of anyone at the Speedway, I wrote in my journal of "warming the car ... at last, stand on the gas. All is prepared, the engine unleashed, the great machine leaps forward, springs from a crawl into full flight, and the song begins ... the power rushes to respond, and I have it in my hands." It was a pleasure that came with experience, and it saturated my soul.

I kept on seeking sponsorship through the beginning of 1983, then realized that if I kept it up, I was likely to jump out of a high window. It was time to let go; to acknowledge with unspeakable regret that my chance at winning top-level races had been cut short, chopped off. It was time to start writing this book, and I moved to the mountains of Colorado for that purpose. Among accessible experiences, skiing is perhaps the most similar to motorsports—the same balancing on the edge of adhesion, the same joyful acceptance of risk—and skiing proved to be at least a counterbalance to the typewriter and then the computer screen.

Life is what happens while you're busy making other plans, they say, and the ordinary things of life interfered with writing: illness and death in my family; my marriage and a house of our own; Hurricane Andrew, which ravaged my parents' home. But as the reader may have noticed, I have a stubborn streak (tenacious? pigheaded?) and the book was finally done.

As I often said at the time, it was the women's movement of the late 1960s and early 1970s that made it possible for a woman to drive at Indianapolis and Daytona. I was simply the woman at the right place at the right time with the right background, and an overwhelming passion for the sport. Some observers seemed to think that what I did, indeed, made a difference:

> *Guthrie drove superbly, intelligently ... What she did, of course, was demonstrate for all who required further demonstration that a woman can run 500 miles at Indianapolis with the best male drivers in the game.*
>
> —Bill Nack, *Newsday*, May 29, 1978

> *Perhaps to put Guthrie's accomplishment in the proper perspective, the following drivers did not finish as high as eighth [sic] in their second Indy 500: Al Unser, Bobby Unser, Foyt, Sneva, Ongais and Johnny Rutherford.*
>
> —Shav Glick, Los Angeles *Times*, May 29, 1978

> *Janet Guthrie has erased all doubts about whether women can compete in the Indy 500.*
>
> —John Wallace, Reuters, May 31, 1978

I believe that physically, emotionally, and mentally, women are as well-equipped as men for this most challenging of sports. Not every woman would aspire to be a racing driver; not every man would. Or could. But many, many women have been drawn to adventure in the past—from the women hot-air balloonists of the eighteenth and nineteenth centuries, to the women pilots of the very early twentieth century, to the women who raced cars in floor-length skirts when motorsports first began. And women are drawn to adventure now: the astronauts, the women who fly fighter planes from aircraft carrier decks. Women's nature has not changed; their opportunities have. Somewhat.

If I contributed some small bit to the changing perception of women's abilities, I am glad of that. It was not the reason that I did what I did. I drove race cars because I could not do otherwise; because it was an obsession and a passion. Not everyone wants to drive race cars, but for each person, the right challenge is out there, the challenge that is just the right size, the challenge that will evoke the best that a person can be.

For women, the Everests of racing remain to be climbed. Someday, a woman will win the Indianapolis 500; someday, a woman will win the Daytona 500. I wish I could have been that driver. I hope some reader of this book will be.

INDEX

A-1 Toyota (East Haven, Conn.), 119, 122
Adderley, Terry, 214, 276, 305
Advanced Orbiting Solar Observatory program, 99
Albritain, Gary, 153, 164
Allison, Bobby
  Daytona 500 ('78), 316
  Dover, Delaware Winston Cup race, 226
  Los Angeles Times 500, 311–12
  Michigan International Speedway race, 287–88
  Southern 500, 289, 296
  Talladega 500 Winston Cup race, 266, 284
  Times 500 (Ontario, Calif.), 313
Allison, Donnie, 306
  advice from, 203, 242, 284
  Atlanta 500-mile Winston Cup race, 254, 256, 257
  National 500 (later NAPA National 500), 228
  Talladega 500 Winston Cup race, 287
  World 600 Winston Cup ('76), 206
Anderson, M.C., 315
Andretti, Mario, 164, 190
  Daytona Continental 24-Hour, 100
  Formula 1 Grand Prix, 357
  on Guthrie as driver, 163, 187
  Indianapolis 500 ('77), 17, 47
  Indianapolis 500 ('78), 354, 367, 368–69, 374, 375, 377
  Ontario 500 USAC Championship race, 292
  Sebring 12-Hour International Manufacturers Championship race, 105, 114–15
ARCA stock cars, 381
Atlanta 500-mile Winston Cup race, 253–58, 318
Aymar, Bob, 79, 83, 85

Bagley, Tom, 368, 370, 373

Baker, Buck, 219
Baker, Buddy
  Daytona 500 ('77), 244
  Dover, Delaware Winston Cup race, 226
  Firecracker 400 Winston Cup, 219
  on Guthrie as driver, 265
  racing advice, 261, 303
  Talladega 500 Winston Cup race, 284
  World 600 Winston Cup ('76), 197, 205
Bandini, Lorenzo, 100
Baus, John, 105
Beckers, Christine, Firecracker 400 Winston Cup (NASCAR), 272–76
Bedard, Pat, 19
Benton & Bowles
  Texaco proposal for sponsorship, 319, 321–24, 330
Bernstein, Leonard, 72
Bettenhausen, Gary, 186, 221, 363
  Indianapolis 500 ('77), 16, 24
  Indianapolis 500 ('78), 365
  Ontario 500 USAC Championship race, 293
Bettenhausen, Merle, 221
Bettenhausen, Tony, 221
Bigelow, Tom, 130, 154, 186, 326, 327, 328
  Indianapolis 500 ('77), 22–23, 33
  Indianapolis 500 ('76), 193
  Indianapolis 500 ('78), 368, 371
  Michigan 200-mile Indy car race, 221
  Pocono 500 (USAC), 212
  Trenton USAC Championship race, 164
Bignotti, George, 28, 43, 210, 297, 315, 333–34, 357
  Bignotti Wildcat, 340, 341, 343–45, 348, 350, 356
  conflict with Wally Dallenbach, 325
  engine cost, 316

Indianapolis 500 ('77), 9
  meeting with Guthrie team,
    331–33
  negotiations with S.D. Murphy
    (Murph), 318, 324–25, 328
Bignotti, Kay, 297, 344, 357
  Indianapolis 500 ('77), 28, 43–44,
    48
Binford, Tom, 36, 45, 49, 176, 354,
  364, 369
Bivens, Terry, 300
Bochroch, Al, 112
Bock, Hank, 361, 362
Bogan, Louise, 70
Bonnett, Neil, 284, 285, 312
Bowman, C., 134–35
Bridgehampton 400, 115
Bristol 500-lap Winston Cup race,
  259–63
Brooks, Dick, 226
Bryant, Darrell, 315, 330
  Indianapolis 500 ('78), 358, 362
Bryant, Jack, 263, 275
  Indianapolis 500 ('78), 330, 358,
    362, 365
Bryant Heating and Cooling, 21, 26,
  193
  funding and sponsorship, 126–27,
    128, 130–31, 166, 213–14, 229,
    251, 272
  press conferences, 146–47, 235
Buglione, Tony, 119, 123
Burcham, Bob, 204
Burton, Richard, 89

Campbell, Kenneth, 246
Canadian-American Challenge race,
  101
Cannon, Larry, 212
Carnegie, Tom, 381
Carren, Tom, 117
Carter, Pancho, 162, 354
Casey, Phil, 8, 17, 21, 24, 29, 31, 44,
  50, 270
Cévert, François, 159
Charlotte Motor Speedway, 196, 199
  Curtis Turner Award, 210
Charlotte World 600 ('76), 196–209
Childress, Richard, 218, 280–81
Christian, Sara, 199

Clodfelter, Jim
  Indianapolis 500 ('78), 330, 358,
    362
Cloutier, Joe, 334–35
Coca-Cola, sponsorship offer, 178,
  180
Cooper, John, 280–81
Cooper, Martha, 358
Coral Gables High School, 64
Cosworth engines, 8, 20, 340, 356,
  368, 372, 373
Crocker, Erin, 381
Cronkite, Walter, 329
Cronkrite, Will, 201, 216, 217, 226,
  227, 237, 240, 244
Cunningham, Briggs, 91
Cunningham, Walt, 121–22
Cuomo, Ray, 115
Curtis Turner Award, 210

Dallenbach, Wally, 210, 354
  Bignotti Wildcat, 324–25, 327, 328,
    348, 356
  and Guthrie's wrist injury, 360,
    365
  Indianapolis 500 ('77), 9
  Indianapolis 500 ('78), 339–40
  Trenton USAC Championship race,
    164
Dangerfield, Rodney, 162
Datsun (later Nissan), 116
Daytona 24 Hour International
  Manufacturers Championship
  race, 101–3
Daytona 500 ('77), 235–45
Daytona 500 ('78), 315–16
Daytona Continental 24-Hour,
  99–101
Del Roy, Frankie, 146, 191, 331
De Palma, Marion, 43
De Palma, Ralph, 43
Devin, Mike, 127
Diatlovich, Paul, 21
Dickson, Larry, 221
Dietrich, Suzy, 100, 104, 105
Dixie 500 Winston Cup race, 307–8
Doherty, Roberta, 322
Donleavy, Junie, 274
Donohue, Mark, 44, 100, 117
Douze Heures du Reims, 105

Dreyfus, René, 105
  Le Chanteclair restaurant, 321,
    324–25
  talisman from, 329–30, 366
Drolet, Smokey, 100, 102, 104, 105

Earhart, Amelia, 308
Earnhardt, Dale
  Firecracker 400 Winston Cup, 218
  World 600 Winston Cup ('76), 202
East, Roy, 127
Economaki, Chris, 120, 156, 233, 313
Ellenville hill climb (N.Y.), 73–75,
  76–77
Elliott, Bill
  Daytona 500 ('77), 241
  Firecracker 400 Winston Cup, 218,
    219
  Michigan International Speedway
    race, 287–88
  National 500 (later NAPA National
    500), 304
  Talladega 500 Winston Cup race,
    284
  World 600 Winston Cup ('76), 202
Engeman, Liane, 104, 110–13, 114
engines, 316
  Cosworth, 8, 20, 340, 356, 368, 372
  Ford V8, 368
  fuel consumption, 373
  Matra, 103
  Offenhauser, 9, 11, 16, 20, 24, 43,
    136–37, 141, 180, 340, 356
  oil, 324, 351–53
Erlichman, John, 120
Experimental Safety Vehicle
  (Fairchild Hiller), 99

Fairchild Hiller, 99
Fangio, Juan, 156
Farley, Cory, 234
Farnham, Ralph J., Jr., 35, 88–92,
  101, 107, 117, 119, 228, 238
  500-mile SCCA National
    Championship race, 92–94
Fellows, Kent, 115
Fellows, Mary, 56
Ferrari North American Racing
  Team, 105
Ferreri, Lynda, 214–15, 288, 315, 332

Atlanta 500-mile Winston Cup
  race, 253–58
Bristol 500-lap race, 261, 262
Daytona 500 ('77), 241, 245
Daytona 500 ('78), 315–16
Dover, Delaware Winston Cup race,
  225–27
Firecracker 400 Winston Cup,
  272–76
funding and sponsorship, 214, 229,
  245, 308–9, 315
as Guthrie's NASCAR team owner,
  35, 197, 216, 257–58, 261, 307
Los Angeles Times 500, 231, 233,
  309–13
Michigan 200-mile stock car race,
  221, 222–23
Michigan 400 Winston Cup race,
  269–70
National 500 (later NAPA National
  500), 302–5
negotiations with Vollstedt, 214
Richmond, Virginia race, 246–50
Southern 500, 289, 293–97,
  299–301
team truck, 246
and women in NASCAR racing,
  200, 280–81
World 600 Winston Cup ('76), 202,
  208
Field, Ted, 11
Filippis, Maria-Teresa de, 91
Firecracker 400 Winston Cup, 214,
  215–20, 272–76
Fisher, Sarah, 381, 382
Forbes-Robinson, Elliot, 257
Ford V8 engines, 368
Foyt, A.J., 130, 156, 197, 225, 229,
  251, 284, 331, 382, 383
  Daytona 500 ('77), 10, 235, 242, 245
  Firecracker 400 Winston Cup
    (NASCAR), 216, 219, 273
  on Guthrie as driver, 166, 258
  Indianapolis 500 ('76), 26–27, 180,
    188, 189–94
  Indianapolis 500 ('77), 12, 17, 20,
    32, 40, 47, 49, 51, 267
  Indianapolis 500 ('78), 367, 368,
    370, 374, 377
  Los Angeles Times 500 (NASCAR

race), 311
Michigan International Speedway
 doubleheader, 221, 223
National 500 (later NAPA National
 500), 228, 304–5
Ontario 500 USAC Championship
 race, 291, 292
Sebring 12-Hour International
 Manufacturers Championship
 race, 105
Trenton USAC Championship race,
 164, 169, 173
France, Bill, 273
 television rights World 600, 203–4
Frasson, Joe, 241
Frenzel, Nick, 229
Fujimoto, Shun, 238

Gaffaney, Mary Tracy, 69
Galardi, Dom, 119, 122
Gale, Gary
 World 600 Winston Cup ('76), 198,
 201
Garner, Don, 176
Garner, James (*The Grand Prix*), 102
Gazaway, Bill, 282, 294, 295
Gazaway, Joe, 282
Gelhausen, Spike, 171, 183, 368, 373
Gilbert, Howard, 26–27
Gilmore, Jim, 194
Glick, Shav, 383
Good Morning America, 322, 329,
 358
Goodyear, 180, 181, 187, 193, 340, 354
Gordon, Cecil, 217, 219, 233, 254
Grand National series, 197n1
Grand Prix, The (film), 102
Grand Prix racing, 91, 276–77
Grant, Harry, 315
Grant, Jerry, 258–59
Granville (Texaco chairman of the
 board), 349
Gresl, Charlie, 117
Gross, Pete, 10, 21, 25, 26, 36, 40, 41,
 291
Grossman, Bob, 77
Grumman, Lunar Excursion
 Module, 98–99
Gurney, Dan, 91, 101
Guthrie, Anne (sister), 44, 58

Guthrie, Beryl (Babe, aunt), 61
Guthrie, Gerald (uncle), 61
Guthrie, Janet
 aerospace engineer Republic
 Aviation, 70, 71, 72, 84, 95,
 96–97, 98–99
 childhood and youth, 55–70
 family's concerns for, 7–8, 13, 35,
 358, 367
 family history, 55, 56
 fear of sailing, 64–65
 feminist consciousness of, 78, 139
 life after racing, 382
 love of flying, 65, 66, 70, 71, 72, 95
 love of racing, 116, 277
 and Nick (first romance), 68–69
 parachute jump, 66–68
 pilot's license, 68–69, 70, 153
 relationship with Alex, 15, 19, 23,
 25–26, 30, 33–34, 42, 254,
 263–64, 295, 307, 326–28, 342–43
 Scientist-Astronaut Program
 (NASA), 96–97, 104, 106, 121–22
 social life, 84–85, 89, 95–96, 98, 116
 technical editor (Sperry), 109,
 113–14, 119
 University of Miami teaching
 fellowship, 103, 106
 at University of Michigan, 70
Guthrie, Janet: amateur road racing
 Bridgehampton, 101
 Bridgehampton 400, 115
 Daytona 24-Hour International
 Manufacturers Championship
 race, 101–3
 Daytona Continental 24-Hour,
 99–101
 funding and sponsorship, 119, 123
 introduction to competitve racing,
 71–78
 Lime Rock, Connecticut, 77, 85,
 118, 122–23
 mechanical experience, 76, 79, 81,
 84, 86, 87–89, 90, 97–98, 117
 North Atlantic Road Racing
 Championship series, 119
 novice race driver license, 83
 Ring-Free Motor Maids, 110–13, 114
 SCCA competion drivers' school,
 79–83

SCCA Divisional Championship
race, 85–86
SCCA National Championship 500-
mile race (Watkins Glen), 91,
92–94
SCCA National Championships
(Daytona), 107–8
SCCA National competition
license, 86
SCCA Nationals (Watkins Glen),
106
SCCA October Nationals (West
Palm Beach), 107
Sebring 12-Hour International
Manufacturers Championship
race, 103–5, 114–15
sports car racers *vs.*stock car
racers, 80
Toyota Celica, 117–18, 120, 122–23,
124–25
Toyota national media tour, 124,
125, 127
Trans Am professional racing
series, 97
Vanderbilt Cup races, 124–25
Vineland, New Jersey, 83–84, 86
Watkins Glen, New York, 84
Guthrie, Janet: NASCAR racing
Atlanta 500-mile Winston Cup
race, 253–58, 318
Bristol 500-lap race, 259–63
Bristol race, 288
commitment to, 281
conflict between NASCAR and
USAC, 276
Curtis Turner Award, 210
Daytona 500 ('77), 235–45
Daytona 500 ('78), 315–16
Dixie 500, 307–8
Dover, Delaware Winston Cup race,
225–27, 302
fan reaction to, 220
Firecracker 400 Winston Cup, 214,
215–20
funding and sponsorship, 214, 229,
306, 308–9
Los Angeles Times 500, 230–34,
309–13
Lynda Ferreri as team owner, 35,
197, 214, 257–58, 261, 307

media attention, 198, 203–4,
208–9, 210, 233–34, 250, 259–60
Michigan 400 Winston Cup race,
267–70
Michigan International Speedway
race, 287–88
Nashville Winston Cup race,
279–81
National 500 (later NAPA National
500), 302–5
Pocono 500-mile Winston Cup
race, 281–82
pressures on crew, 274–75
Richmond, Virginia race, 245–50
Rookie of the Year competition,
247, 249, 255, 257, 264, 268, 276,
287, 302, 305, 306, 308, 313
Southern 500, 289, 293–97,
299–301
Talladega 500 Winston Cup race,
282–87
Top Rookie Daytona 500 ('77),
9–10, 245
Winston Cup series, 9–10, 188
World 600 Winston Cup ('76),
196–209
Guthrie, Janet: professional life
A.J. Foyt and, 188, 189–94
broken foot, 131–35, 137
fan reaction to, 179, 183–84
funding and sponsorship, 224,
229, 315, 329–30
Good Morning America, 322, 329,
358
International Award for Valor in
Sports, 237–39
loyalty to Vollstedt, 211, 214
mechanical experience, 262
media attention, 52, 146–47, 154,
158–60, 162–64, 166–67, 174–75,
267
mental rehearsal, 12, 36, 93, 169,
290
movie option, 272, 306
North Atlantic Road Racing
Championship, 9
proposal for Texaco sponsorship,
319–25
Purdue University speaking
engagement, 308

racing history, 153
search for funding and
   sponsorship, 314–25
Sebring 12-Hour, 9
Six-Hour World Championship of
   Makes race, 276–77
Sportswomen of the Year
   nomination, 315
as symbol of women's abilities, 27,
   42–43
team unity, 164
Trans Am professional racing
   series, 97
women's closed-circuit speed
   record, 222
Guthrie, Janet: USAC Championship
racing
Bignotti Wildcat, 318, 324–25, 327,
   328, 332, 335
celebrity tennis tournament,
   359–61
conditional Championship license,
   155
contract with Rolla Vollstedt,
   130–31, 134–35, 145, 276
as driver for Rolla Vollstedt, 9–10,
   120–21, 125
driving ability, 383
eligibility for licensing and
   competition, 147
FIA license, 276
first test drive in Indy car, 127,
   130–32, 135–45
Gasoline Alley garage, 335–36
Hinchman driver's suit, 167
Indianapolis 500 ('76), 9, 26–27,
   126, 178–95
Indianapolis 500 ('76) rookie test,
   181–82, 184–87
Indianapolis 500 ('77), 267
Indianapolis 500 ('77) qualifying
   run, 36–42
Indianapolis 500 ('77) race
   preparations, 3–18
Indianapolis 500 ('78) funding and
   sponsorship, 316–25, 329–30
Indianapolis 500 ('78) preparation,
   330–36, 339–55
Indianapolis 500 ('78) pre-race
   crew meeting, 362–63

Indianapolis 500 ('78) qualifying
   run, 355–56
Indianapolis 500 ('78) race day,
   365–79
Indianapolis 500 ('78) 25th-
   anniversary reunion, 381
Lightning prototype, 251–52, 316
mechanical experience, 352
media attention, 178, 180, 195,
   329, 357
meeting with George Bignotti,
   331–33
Michigan International Speedway
   doubleheader, 221–23
Murphy/Bignotti car deal, 318,
   324–25, 326–27
Ontario 200-miler, 251–52
Ontario 500, 224–25, 289–93,
   297–99
Phoenix Championship race,
   228–29
Pocono 500, 211–13, 270–71, 382
pressures on crew, 178–79
resignation from USAC, 281
team dynamics, 332–33
Trenton Championship race, 147,
   154, 158–77, 302
wrist injury, 359–62, 363–64, 365,
   366, 370
Guthrie, Jean Ruth (née Midkiff,
   mother), 56–59, 61–62, 63, 132, 329
letters to family, 57, 58, 61
Guthrie, Margaret (sister), 58
Guthrie, Marty (wife of Stewart), 109
Guthrie, Stewart (brother), 56, 58,
   109, 165, 329, 358
Guthrie, Walter (brother), 8, 12,
   13–14, 61, 132
Guthrie, William Lain (father),
   55–58, 61–63, 132, 329
flying lessons, 65
on Janet's success, 215
parachute jump, 66–68
gymkhanas, 72–73, 76, 81

Haas, Len, 163
Haldeman, Bob, 120
Hall, Bill, 194
Hall, Jim, 101, 102, 376
Halliburton, Richard, 59

Hamid, George, 175
Hanna, Thomas, 360
Hansgen, Walt, 91, 100
Hanstein, Huschke von, 100
Harris, Julia Fillmore, 59–60
Hartman, David, 322, 358
Hawkins, Paul, 112–13
Healey, Donald, 114
Hermann, Hans, 113
Higgins, Tom, 289
Hill, Phil, 100
hill climbs, 73–75, 76–77, 81
Hillin, Bobby, 20
Hiss, Arlene (née Lanzieri), 127, 128, 156–57, 160
  fan reaction to, 134–35
  Phoenix Indy-car race, 133, 149–53, 161, 162
Hiss, Mike, 127, 194
Hodgdon, Warner, 289, 297–98
Holman-Moody team, 198, 203, 285
Holtman, Carl, 330, 350, 357, 362, 374, 379
Holum, Diane, 121
Hucul, Cliff, 32, 45, 357
Hulman, Mary, 367
Hulman, Tony, 27, 49, 331, 334, 367
  and Indianapolis Motor Speedway, 147
  on women in racing, 186–87
Hulman George, Mari, 331
Hume, Don, 330, 336, 357, 362, 363
Indianapolis 500 ('78), 366, 372
Indianapolis 500 ('78) car preparation, 345, 352, 356–57
Hunter, Barbara, 252
Hurtubise, Jim "Herk", 155, 190, 191, 240, 341
Hutcherson, Dick, 275
Hutcherson-Pagan, 273, 275, 276
Hutton, Rex, 14, 159, 165, 177, 178, 183, 185
Hylton, James, 239, 240
  Los Angeles Times 500, 310–11, 313

IMSA (International Motor Sports Association), 122–23
Indianapolis 500
  Gasoline Alley, 334–36
  qualifying rules, 19–20, 36

rookie test, 181–82
starts at, 27, 45–46, 136
volunteers at, 15
Indianapolis 500 ('76), 9, 178–95
Indianapolis 500 ('77), 3–52, 267
  drivers' meeting, 45–46, 47
  parade, 47
  Pole Day, 18
  qualifying, 18–42
  race day, 48–52
  race preparations, 3–18
Indianapolis 500 ('78), 339–79
  Carburetion Day, 357–58
  car preparation, 339–42, 343–45, 347–53
  funding and sponsorship, 316–25
  open testing for, 320
  pre-race ceremonies, 364–65
  pre-race crew meeting, 362–63
  qualifying runs, 353–56, 357
  race day, 365–79
  team Guthrie, 316–18
Indianapolis Hall of Fame dinner, 381
Indianapolis Motor Speedway, 3, 129–30, 147, 251
Indy cars, 126
  alcohol fuel, 323–24
  car design, 136–37, 139–41, 152, 223–24, 258–59
  costs involved, 316–17, 318, 319–20
  fuel consumption, 373
  head support, 152
  oil, 324, 351–53
Indy cars compared to stock cars, 199–200, 201–2, 207, 373
International Award for Valor in Sports, 237–39
International Manufacturers Championship races
  Daytona 24-Hour, 101–3
  Sebring 12-Hour, 103–5, 110–13, 114–15
International Motor Sports Association (IMSA), 122–23

Jennings, Bruce, 82
Johncock, Gordon, 130, 327
  Bignotti Wildcat, 341, 343–44, 349, 350

and Guthrie's wrist injury, 365
on Guthrie as driver, 222
Indianapolis 500 ('77), 11
Indianapolis 500 ('78), 353, 356, 377
and Patrick Racing, 210
Texaco "credit card", 345
Trenton USAC Championship race,
    164, 171, 175, 352
Johnsgard, Keith, 167
Johnson, Junior, 201–2, 287
Joiner, Carl, 231, 233–34
Jones, Bubby, 45
Jopes, John, 231
Junek, Elsa, 382

Kaplan, Ronnie, 110
Karl, Jerry, 15
Kaser, Jim, 113
Kelly Girl
    doll promotion controversy, 306–7
    funding and sponsorship, 214, 215,
        229, 245, 274, 276, 277, 308–9
    Kelly Girl Chevrolet, 216, 221,
        222–23, 253–54
    sponsor functions, 234, 235–36,
        322, 328
Kenyon, Mel, 151
King, Billie Jean, 43, 119, 121
King, Dick
    conditional Championship license,
        155
    as USAC Director of Competition,
        147, 153, 164, 176
King, Grant, 16, 20, 24, 212
King, Kerryn, 323
Kinser, Sheldon, 155
    Indianapolis 500 ('77), 16, 20
    Indianapolis 500 ('78), 367, 370,
        371, 373
    Pocono 500 (USAC), 212
Kissler, Al, 134–35, 145
Kondratieff, Judy, 114
Krisiloff, Steve, 151, 180, 342
    Indianapolis 500 ('78), 354, 356,
        369–70, 373, 377
Kunzman, Lee, 212

Langley, Elmo, 233, 282
Lanzieri, Arlene. *see* Hiss, Arlene
    (née Lanzieri)

Lauda, Niki, 238
Le Mans (film), 102
Le Mans 24-Hour race, 105
Levy, Ruth, 104
Lime Rock, Connecticut, 77, 85, 118,
    122–23
Lindbergh, Charles, 66
Linder, Grace, 358
Linder, Henry, 358
Lindholm, Jim, 21, 26, 331, 332, 336,
    363
    Bristol 500-lap race, 262
    Daytona 500 ('77), 235–36, 237,
        240, 242, 245
    Firecracker 400 Winston Cup,
        273–76
    as Guthrie's NASCAR crew chief,
        235–36, 270, 276, 279–81, 307,
        315
    and Guthrie's wrist injury, 365,
        365–66
    on Guthrie as driver, 246–47
    Indianapolis 500 ('77), 12, 16, 31,
        36, 48
    Indianapolis 500 ('78), 317, 330,
        335, 354, 356, 361, 362
    Indianapolis 500 ('78) car
        preparation, 339–42, 356–57
    Indianapolis 500 ('78) race day,
        367, 375
    Michigan 400 Winston Cup race,
        268
    National 500 (later NAPA National
        500) (NASCAR), 302–5
    Pocono 500-mile Winston Cup
        race, 281–82
    Richmond, Virginia race, 249
    Southern 500 NASCAR race, 300
    Talladega 500 Winston Cup race,
        282–87
Lippman, Susan, 84–85
Lisberg, George, 115
Lombardi, Lella, 130–31, 146
    Firecracker 400 Winston Cup
        (NASCAR), 272–76
Long Island Sports Car Association,
    85
Loquasto, Al, 186, 213
Los Angeles Times 500 (NASCAR),
    230–34, 309–13

Louis Meyer Award, 381
Lowe's Motor Speedway. *see*
  Charlotte Motor Speedway
Lund, Tiny, 264

MacIntire, Dave, 27
Macmillan Ring-Free Oil
  Ring-Free Motor Maids, 99–101,
    102–3, 103–5, 110–13
Madison Avenue Sports Car Driving
  and Chowder Society, 109, 318
Magocsi, Marianne, 124
Mahler, John, 49–50, 368
Malone, Shim, 331
  USAC rookie tests, 182, 185–86
Mandel, Leon, 113
Manning, Skip, 282
Mansell, Nigel, 342n1
Marcis, David, 205, 226, 244
Marlin, Coo Coo, 286
Marquette, Ray, 331
Marx, Groucho, 70
Matra engine, 103
Matthews, Anita Taylor, 102, 104, 105
McCluggage, Denise, 77, 104, 105
McCluskey, Roger, 251
  Indianapolis 500 ('77), 24, 45
  Indianapolis 500 ('78), 368, 371
  Michigan International Speedway
    doubleheader, 221
  Trenton USAC Championship race,
    164
McCoy, Larry, 15
  celebrity tennis tournament,
    359–61
McCune, Sarah, 381
McElreath, Jim, 24, 185
McGee, Mary, 133, 134
McKay, Jim, 166
McKinley (Texaco president), 349
McLaren, Bruce, 105
McQueen, Steve, 102, 114
McRae, Graham, 186, 357, 363
Mears, Rick, 354, 369
media
  and women in racing, 17
Mehl, Leo, 187, 188, 193, 340, 346, 354
Merchant Bank
  funding and sponsorship, 229, 251
Meyer, Louis, 28, 43, 297

Meyers, Art, 176
Michigan 400 Winston Cup race,
  267–70
Michigan International Speedway,
  221, 287–88
Midget racing, 151, 381
Midkiff, Carl (uncle), 61–62
Midkiff, Florence (aunt), 61–62
Midkiff, Jean Ruth. *see* Guthrie, Jean
  Ruth (née Midkiff, mother)
Miles, Ken, 100
Miller, Eddie, 181
Mims, Donna Mae, 100, 104, 105, 114
Miss Harris' Florida School for Girls,
  59–60, 64, 68
Moise, Patty, 276
Monroe Shock Absorber
  Indianapolis 500 banquet, 26–28
Moody, Mitzi, 236
Moody, Ralph (team manager,
  NASCAR), 227, 285
  Atlanta 500-mile Winston Cup
    race, 253–58
  Bristol 500-lap race, 260–61, 262
  Daytona 500 ('77), 237, 239, 243,
    245
  Dover, Delaware Winston Cup race,
    226–27
  Firecracker 400 Winston Cup,
    215–20, 273–76
  on Guthrie as driver, 202, 217, 250
  Holman-Moody team, 198, 203,
    285
  and Jim Lindholm, 235–36
  Los Angeles Times 500, 233, 234
  Michigan 400 Winston Cup race,
    268, 269, 270
  National 500 (later NAPA National
    500), 228
  problems communicating with,
    240, 241, 241–42, 268
  Richmond, Virginia race, 246–47
  Talladega 500 Winston Cup race,
    264–66
  World 600 Winston Cup ('76), 196,
    200–202, 204–5, 206
Mooney, Dick, 79, 83, 84, 85, 96, 176
  co-driver, 92–94
Mooney, Pam, 92–94, 96
Moore, Bud, 316

Mosley, Mike
  Trenton USAC Championship race,
  164
Mosport, 324
Mull, Evelyn, 77
Murphy, S.D. (Murph), 331, 340, 350
  funding and sponsorship, 229
  negotiations with George Bignotti,
  318, 324–25, 328, 331, 341
Murray, Jim, 182

Nabors, Jim, 48
Nack, Bill, 383
Nagy, Irene, 320
Nakamura, Jim, 330, 336, 352,
  356–57
Nall, Parky, 275, 283, 297
Nap, Herb, 222
NAPA/Regal Ride, 214
NASCAR Winston Cup racing
  Atlanta 500-mile race, 253–58, 318
  attitude towards women in
    NASCAR racing, 198–99, 220,
    258, 280–81
  Bristol 500-lap race, 259–63
  Bristol race, 288
  Daytona 500 ('77), 9–10, 235–45
  Daytona 500 ('78), 315–16
  Dixie 500, 307–8
  Dover, Delaware Winston Cup race,
    225–27, 302
  driver-introduction ceremonies,
    304, 255
  fan reaction to women in racing,
    21–22, 42–43
  Firecracker 400 Winston Cup, 214,
    215–20, 272–76
  Grand National series, 197n1
  Los Angeles Times 500, 230–34,
    309–13
  Michigan 400 Winston Cup race,
    267–70
  Michigan International Speedway,
    287–88
  Nashville Winston Cup race,
    279–81
  National 500 (later NAPA National
    500), 228, 302–5, 302–5
  Nextel Cup, 197n1
  1978 rules, 307, 315

oversize fuel tanks, 284, 288
Pocono 500-mile Winston Cup
  race, 281–82
Richmond, Virginia race, 245–50
Rockingham Winston Cup race,
  305–6
rookie points rules, 302
sexism in, 198–99, 220, 258,
  260–61, 280–81
short-track racing, 233, 245–46
"slingshot" move, 207, 305, 311, 312
Southern 500, 289, 293–97
starts in, 46
stock cars compared to Indy cars,
  199–200, 201–2, 207, 373
Talladega 500 Winston Cup race,
  21, 264–66, 282–87
tech inspection, 260–61, 273,
  281–82, 283, 284
women in, 9–10, 272–76
World 600 Winston Cup ('76), 188,
  196–209
Nashville Winston Cup race, 279–81
National 500 (later NAPA National
  500), 228, 302–5
Negre, Ed, 232, 248, 312
Nehl, Tom
  World 600 Winston Cup ('76), 198,
  201
Newman, Paul, 119–20, 230, 234,
  267
Newsome, Rick, 263
Nextel Cup, 197n1
Nick (Janet's first romance), 68–69
Nixon, Richard, 119
Nomex racing gear, 138, 248
North Atlantic Road Racing
  Championship series, 9, 119

Oeffinger, Brenda, 357
Oeffinger, Dick, 316–17, 318, 320,
  331, 332, 357
  illness, 321, 322, 326
  Indianapolis 500 ('78), 327, 330,
  340
  pre-race crew meeting
    Indianapolis 500 ('78), 362–63
Offenhauser engines, 9, 20, 24, 43,
  136–37, 141, 180, 340, 356
Olivero, Bobby, 15, 45, 153

Ongais, Danny, 320, 382, 383
  Indianapolis 500 ('77), 4, 8, 11, 23, 45, 51
  Indianapolis 500 ('78), 350, 356, 369, 370, 371, 372, 373, 374, 376–77
Ontario Motor Speedway (Calif.), 137–38
  first test drive in Indy car, 127, 130–32, 135–45
  Los Angeles Times 500 (NASCAR), 230–34, 309–13
Opperman, Jan, 212, 222
Orff, Carl, 123
Oscar (Indianapolis track guard), 44–45
Osterlund, Rod, 268
Ozawa, Kenny, 331, 336, 357
  Indianapolis 500 ('78) car preparation, 339–42, 343–45, 347–53, 356–57
  Indianapolis 500 ('78) crew chief, 326, 327–28, 330, 354
  Indianapolis 500 ('78) pre-race crew meeting, 362–63
  Indianapolis 500 ('78) race day, 366, 367, 375

Parrott, Buddy, 227
Parsons, Benny
  Daytona 500 ('77), 10, 245
  Dover, Delaware Winston Cup race, 226
  on Guthrie as driver, 211–12
  Los Angeles Times 500, 309
  National 500 (later NAPA National 500), 304, 305
  Pocono 500-mile Winston Cup race, 282
Parsons, Johnny, Jr., 10, 162–63, 382
Passmore, Christi, 381
Patrick, Pat, 210–11, 341, 346, 349, 356, 357
Patrick Racing, 210–11
Pauley, Jane, 42
Pearson, David, 234, 265, 301
  Atlanta 500-mile Winston Cup race, 256–57
  Daytona 500 ('77), 10, 235
  Dover, Delaware Winston Cup

race, 226
  Firecracker 400 Winston Cup, 219, 273
  on Guthrie as driver, 210, 211
  Talladega 500 Winston Cup race, 284
  World 600 Winston Cup ('76), 197, 198, 206, 207, 208
Pei, I.M., 124
Pei, T'ing, 124
Penske, Roger, 20, 160, 162, 297, 323–24, 349, 354
Petty, Richard, 249
  Dover, Delaware Winston Cup race, 226
  Firecracker 400 Winston Cup, 214, 276
  on Guthrie as driver, 265, 274, 284–85
  Los Angeles Times 500, 309
  Southern 500 NASCAR race, 296
  Talladega 500 Winston Cup race, 284
  World 600 Winston Cup ('76), 197, 199, 208
Phoenix USAC Championship race, 228–29
  Arlene Hiss, 149–53
Pillersdorf, Jerry, 330, 357, 363
  funding and sponsorship, 318–19, 321–24, 328–29, 333, 349
Pocono 500 (USAC), 211–13, 270–71, 382
Pocono 500-mile Winston Cup race, 281–82
Pocono International Raceway, SCCA races, 118
Pond, Lennie, 226, 264, 266
Porter, Herb, 16, 17, 31, 32, 39
President's Cup, 230
Price, Baxter, 282

Randolph, John, 113
Rasmussen, Eldon, 50, 212
Reggazzoni, Clay, 24, 45
Reilly, Dave, 117
Reims 12-Hour race, 105
Republic Aviation, 70, 71, 84
Revere, Lee, 321
Revson, Peter, 114

Richmond Fairgrounds Raceway,
245–50
Rigby, Cathy, 121
Riggs, Bobby, 43, 119, 156
Rindt, Jochen, 100
Ring-Free Motor Maids, 99–101,
102–3, 103–5, 110–13, 114
Robbins, Marty, 268–69
Rockingham Winston Cup race,
305–6
Rockwell, Peter, 321, 322, 323, 324,
325, 333
Rodriguez, Pedro, 100
Rollo, Marianne "Pinky", 104, 105
Rose, Mauri, 25
Ruby, Lloyd, 100, 127, 194
  Indianapolis 500 ('77), 24
  Indianapolis 500 ('78), 350
  Sebring 12-Hour International
    Manufacturers Championship
    race, 105
Rudd, Ricky
  on Guthrie as driver, 220
  Nashville Winston Cup race, 281
  Rookie of the Year competition,
    247, 264, 268, 269, 282, 287, 302,
    308, 313
  Talladega 500 Winston Cup race,
    284, 287
Rutherford, Johnny, 156, 160, 258,
383
  advice from, 48, 189, 190
  Atlanta 500 mile Winston Cup
    race, 254
  Daytona 500 ('77), 241, 244
  Firecracker 400 Winston Cup
    (NASCAR), 216, 217, 219
  on Guthrie as driver, 165, 175, 285
  Indianapolis 500 ('77), 11–12, 17,
    23, 24, 45–46, 47, 51
  Indianapolis 500 ('78), 349–50, 364
  Ontario 500 USAC Championship
    race, 292
  Talladega 500 Winston Cup race,
    284
  on team effort, 216
  Trenton USAC Championship race,
    159, 164, 169, 175
  on women in racing, 163
Ryan, Terry, 269, 288

Saint-Exupery, Antoine de, 59
Saint-Gaudens, Augustus, 57
Saint-Gaudens, Carlota, 57
Saint-Gaudens, Penelope, 57
Savage, Swede, 136
SCCA (Sports Car Club of America)
  500-mile SCCA National
    Championship race, 91, 92–94
  Bridgehampton 400, 115
  and Canadian-American Challenge
    race, 101
  competition drivers' school, 79–83
  D Production National
    Championship, 230
  glory days of sports car racing, 102
  Lime Rock, Connecticut, 77, 85, 118
  membership in, 77–78
  National Championships
    (Daytona), 107–8
  National competition license, 86
  Nationals (Watkins Glen), 106
  October Nationals (West Palm
    Beach), 107
  Pocono races, 118
  racing circuit, 83–84, 85–86
Schirra, Wally, 104, 106
Schirripa, Doug, 124, 134
Scientist-Astronaut Program (NASA),
  96–97, 104, 106, 121–22
Scott, Tighe, 255–56, 282
Scott, Walter, 59
Sebring 12-Hour International
  Manufacturers Championship
  race, 9, 103–5, 110–13, 114–15
Seitz, Seymour, 314
Sekman (parachutist), 66–67
Sharp, Bob, 116, 119, 124
Sharp, Hap, 102
short-track racing, 223, 245–46
Siffert, Jo, 113
signal flags, meanings of, 80
Simon, Dick, 251, 252, 259
  aggressive driving of, 49, 171
  contract with Rolla Vollstedt, 11,
    26, 130, 134–35
  Dover, Delaware Winston Cup race,
    226
  and Guthrie as driver, 146, 147
  on Guthrie as driver, 162
  and Guthrie as driver, 270

Indianapolis 500 ('76), 126, 178–84
Indianapolis 500 ('77), 12, 16, 19,
   30–33, 41–42, 51
Indianapolis 500 ('78), 373, 375
and Janet Guthrie, 178, 270
Lan Hairpieces for Men
   sponsorship, 159
Lightning prototype, 14, 18, 23–24
Michigan 200-mile Indy car race,
   221, 222
Ontario 500 USAC Championship
   race, 290, 298–99
Ontario Motor Speedway (Calif.)
   test drive, 127, 130–32, 135–45
Phoenix Indy-car race, 150, 152
Pocono 500 (USAC), 213, 271–72
racing advice, 137–38, 143, 160–61,
   173
Trenton USAC Championship race,
   158–75, 223–24
Simon, Melanie, 224, 259, 270, 272
Simpson, Bill, 212, 213
Sisco, David, 281
Slayton, Donald K., 97
Slimp, Sidney, 256, 257, 279, 281, 284
Smith, Bruton, 289, 295
Smith, Louise, 199
Smith, Robyn, 121
Smith, Rosemary, 100, 114
Sneva, Jerry, 45, 51, 357
Sneva, Tom, 271, 383
  on Guthrie as driver, 175
  Indianapolis 500 ('77), 20–21, 23,
     45–46, 49
  Indianapolis 500 ('78), 354, 356,
     369, 373, 374, 377
  Michigan International Speedway
     doubleheader, 221
  Trenton USAC Championship race,
     159, 160, 162, 164, 173, 174, 175
Snider, George, 182, 183
  Indianapolis 500 ('77), 20
  Indianapolis 500 ('78), 368, 371,
     374, 377–79, 381
  Pocono 500 (USAC), 212
Snodgrass, Donna, 22
Sommers, Sam, 257, 282, 284, 300,
   302, 313, 315
Southern 500 NASCAR race, 289,
   293–97, 299–301

South Shore Sports Car Club, 76,
   101
Sowle, Bob, 184
Spencer, G.C., 295
Sperb, Harold, 14, 16, 136, 139, 143,
   174, 290, 298
Sports Car Club of America. *see*
   SCCA (Sports Car Club of America)
sports car racers *vs.*stock car racers,
   80
St. James, Lyn, 381
Stewart, Jackie, 166, 194
stock car racers *vs.*sports car racers,
   80
stock cars compared to Indy cars,
   199–200, 201–2, 207, 373
Stolze, Craig, 315
STP, 214, 306

Talladega 500 Winston Cup race
   (NASCAR), 21, 264–66
Talladega 500 Winston Cup race,
   282–87
Targa Florio, 382
Tennyson, Alfred Lord, 59
Texaco
   funding and sponsorship, 349,
      357–58
   and Guthrie's wrist injury, 363
   oil formulation, 351–53
   proposal for sponsorship, 319
   sponsor functions, 333–34, 335,
      336, 356–57
   "Texaco Star", 335
Thompson Industries, 229
Thrall, Roger, 134–35, 159, 165, 166,
   168, 169, 174, 178, 184, 187
   World 600 Winston Cup ('76), 198,
      201, 205, 208
Threshie, Phil, 344, 357, 373
Toyota national media tour, 124,
   125, 127
Trenton International Speedway,
   158–59
Trenton USAC Championship race,
   147, 154, 158–77
   Guthrie's qualifying run, 168–69
   press conference, 156–57, 175–76
   race day, 170–76
Twain, Mark, 168

Two-Five Challenge series, 116, 118, 119

Ulmann, Alec, 117
Ulrich, D.K., 300
United States Auto Club. *see* USAC (United States Auto Club)
Unser, Al, 383
  Indianapolis 500 ('77), 11, 20
  Indianapolis 500 ('78), 374, 375, 376, 377
  Phoenix Indy-car race, 150
Unser, Bobby, 156, 157, 166, 271, 383
  Indianapolis 500 ('76), 180
  Indianapolis 500 ('77), 23
  Indianapolis 500 ('78), 368, 370, 377
  Phoenix Indy-car race, 152
  Pocono 500 (USAC), 212
  Trenton USAC Championship race, 164, 170, 176
  on women in racing, 162, 163, 190
USAC (United States Auto Club)
attitude towards women in racing, 9–10, 9–10, 134–35, 134–35, 147–49, 162–63
  Board of Directors, 14, 126
  Carburetion Day, 357–58
  Indianapolis 500 rookie test, 181–82
  Indy cars compared to stock cars, 199–200, 201–2, 207, 373
  licenses, 331
  Michigan 200-mile Indy car race, 221, 222
  Michigan 200-mile stock car race, 221, 222–23
  Midget racing, 151, 381
  Ontario 500, 289–93, 297–99
  Phoenix USAC Championship race, 149–53, 228–29
  Pocono 500, 211–13, 270–71, 382
  popoff valves and legal boost, 17
  rookie meeting, 147, 149
  rookie tests, 182, 185–86
  Trenton USAC Championship race, 158–77, 223–24, 302
  USAC Benevolent Foundation, 359
  USAC Championship racing, 9, 126, 147, 320

vocabulary, 7, 135, 139, 183, 188

Vanderbilt Cup races, 124–25
Varner, Toby, 270, 284
  Indianapolis 500 ('78), 330, 358, 362, 366
Vidan, Pat, 39, 40, 41, 355
Vollstedt, Irene, 142
Vollstedt, Rolla
  background, 126, 142
  Bryant Heating and Cooling sponsorship, 26, 126–27, 213–14, 251
  contract with Guthrie, 130–31, 134–35, 145
  funding and sponsorship, 4, 11, 12, 180, 198, 209, 224, 258, 290, 334
  Guthrie's loyalty to, 211, 214
  Guthrie as driver, 35, 120–21, 125, 167, 169, 187–88, 193–94, 264
  Indianapolis 500 ('76), 126, 178–94
  Indianapolis 500 ('77), 3–7, 10–11, 13–14, 16–17, 19–20, 23–24, 30, 34–35, 36–42, 48, 50–51, 267
  Indianapolis 500 ('78), 316–17, 325, 367
  Lightning prototype, 251–52, 258–59, 271–72, 315, 344
  Louis Meyer Award, 381
  Merchant Bank sponsorship, 229, 251
  Michigan 200-mile Indy car race, 221, 222
  negotiations with Ferreri, 214
  Ontario 500 USAC Championship race, 224–25, 289–93, 297–99
  Phoenix USAC Championship race, 228–29
  Pocono 500 (USAC), 211–13, 270–71
  team unity, 14, 148–49, 164, 178–79, 270–72, 291
  and Tom Bigelow, 130
  Trenton USAC Championship race, 133, 159–77, 223–24
  and women in racing, 9–10
  World 600 Winston Cup ('76), 196–98
Vukovich, Bill (father), 22
Vukovich, Billy (son)
  on Guthrie as driver, 22, 163, 178

Indianapolis 500 ('77), 49
Indianapolis 500 ('78), 364
Ontario 500 USAC Championship
  race, 293
Trenton USAC Championship race,
  164, 172, 176

Wall, Don, 280, 284, 296
Wallace, John, 383
Walther, Salt, 255, 291
  Daytona 500 ('77), 236–37, 244,
    260–61
  Indianapolis 500 ('78), 373
Waltrip, Darrell, 222, 287, 288
  Dover, Delaware Winston Cup race,
    226
  Los Angeles Times 500, 309
  Michigan 400 Winston Cup race,
    268
  Nashville Winston Cup race, 281
  racing advice, 227–28
  Richmond, Virginia race, 247
  Southern 500, 294–95, 296, 300
Warren, Frank, 231, 232, 282
Watkins Glen, New York, 84, 159
  500-mile SCCA National
    Championship race, 91, 92–94
  SCCA Nationals, 106
  Six-Hour World Championship of
    Makes race, 276–77
Watts, Andre, 10
Wawak, Bobby
  Daytona 500 ('77), 243, 244, 248
  Los Angeles Times 500 (NASCAR),
    230–31, 234
Wennerstrom, Bruce, 131, 318
Wenz, Ted, 28, 240, 271
West Texas Strutters, 204
Wheeler, Humpy, 215
  and Guthrie at Charlotte Motor
    Speedway, 197–98
  and Janet Guthrie at Charlotte
    Motor Speedway, 273
  television rights Charlotte World
    600, 203–4
White, Bruce, 331
White, Stanford, 57
Wilson, Woodrow, 56
Winston Cup racing. *see* NASCAR
  Winston Cup racing

Women's Airforce Service Pilots
  (WASPs), 95
Women's Superstars, 121–22
women and women's movement, 27,
  35–36, 44, 78, 154, 259
  cultural attitude towards, 56, 70,
    121–22, 156–57, 214–15, 308, 383
  and gender-based barriers, 70, 95,
    308, 381–83
  "girl" issue, 306–7
  and women in racing, 382–83
women in racing, 12, 17, 121, 212
  changes in attitude towards,
    186–87, 235, 381
  European racing, 9–10
  fan reaction to, 21–22, 42–43
  funding and sponsorship, 381–82
  hostility towards, 147–49, 153–54,
    178–79, 183–84, 220
  Indy-car drivers, 127, 134, 149–53
  NASCAR racing, 199, 200, 272–76
  race drivers, 381–83
  road racing, 77, 91, 100, 102, 104
  and women's movement, 382–83
  see also drivers by name
World 600 Winston Cup ('76), 188,
  196–209
World of Outlaws Sprint car series,
  381
Worley, Stan, 331

Yarborough, Cale, 262, 287
  Bristol race, 288
  Daytona 500 ('77), 10, 235, 245
  Dover, Delaware Winston Cup race,
    226
  Firecracker 400 Winston Cup,
    219–20
  on Guthrie as driver, 250, 315
  Michigan 400 Winston Cup race,
    268, 269
  National 500 (later NAPA National
    500), 303, 304
  racing advice, 261
  Richmond, Virginia race, 248
  Southern 500, 300
  on women in racing, 220
  World 600 Winston Cup ('76), 197,
    198, 199, 201
yellow lights, stress of, 346–47